D1231750

The Origins of Modern Europe, 1660–1789

The Origins of Modern Europe 1660-1789

JAMES L. WHITE

JOHN MURRAY · *LONDON*

942.066
W58

PARKER & Son

$3.00

2 Feb 91

Contents

38135

Maps

Plates

(between pages 184 and 185)

Acknowledgments

Plate 3 is reproduced by gracious permission of Her Majesty the Queen.

Grateful acknowledgment is also made for permission granted by the following owners of copyright material:

Radio Times Hulton Picture Library (Plates 1, 11, 12, 17); The Mansell Collection (Plates 2, 4, 7, 8, 9, 10, 19); National Portrait Gallery (Plates 5, 6); Paul Popper (Plate 13); British Museum (Plate 14); The Wallace Collection (Plate 15—Crown copyright); The Metropolitan Museum of Art, Gift of John Bard, 1872 (Plate 16); La Maison Bulloz (Plate 18).

The author also wishes to offer his grateful thanks to Mrs. Margaret Whittle for typing the manuscript and to Mr. Peter Cobb for drawing the maps.

1 · Europe in 1660
(1) Political and Economic Aspects

(a) POLITICAL ASPECTS

Men often cling to cherished theories long after those theories cease to correspond to anything like reality. In about the middle of the seventeenth century, one such cherished theory, which had not fitted the facts for a very long time, was abandoned—the theory that Europe was a single entity. This open acknowledgement of a basic lack of unity was an important pointer to the climate of the time.

The idea grew up in the Middle Ages (by which is meant the thousand years or so after the collapse of the Roman Empire in the West), and undoubtedly had some justification in fact. The Middle Ages really were marked more by international ideas and institutions than by national ones. Scholars shared the same language, and went impartially from one university to another. The Crusades were regarded as a common effort against the heathen. Class distinctions mattered more than national ones. All Europe shared many more such things, the most important being the Catholic religion. Europe was one Christendom, although admittedly some people in Europe, such as the Turks, were not Christians at all; they were regarded as interlopers. The very word 'Europe', though it was known, was little used in the Middle Ages; the nearest equivalent was 'Christendom' ('Christianitas').

Christendom had a temporal as well as a spiritual aspect; men thought of one Christian Regnum, or Empire, whose temporal head was the Emperor, and whose spiritual head was the Pope.

An Empire, of sorts, existed. This was the Holy Roman Empire, founded in the year 800 by Charlemagne. It had been very extensive, but by 1660 it consisted very nearly of what in 1936 was called Germany, together with some neighbouring territories, of which the most important were most of Austria, Bohemia, Alsace, Lorraine, and the Spanish Netherlands. Thus it was predominantly German, and is often referred to as the German Empire, or simply the Empire. The Emperors were elected by the rulers of five great States within the Empire, viz. Saxony, Brandenburg, Bohemia, the Palatinate, and Bavaria, and by three great ecclesiastical princes, the Archbishops of Mainz, Cologne, and Trier. Before election the candidates had to sign a sort of charter which guaranteed the 'liberties', that is, the virtual independence, of the three or four hundred parts which made up the Empire. So the result was that the Emperor retained the prestige which in many people's eyes continued to be attached to his title, but of real political power he had little. The *Reich* (Empire) had long been a political phantom, a target for the wits of Europe. Most of its institutions, for instance the Imperial Chamber, met rarely and decided nothing much when they did. Of Imperial taxation there was virtually nothing but rare, small, and grudging voluntary contributions. The army existed only on paper.

Political reality lay with the *Länder* (independent territories) and the swarm of Imperial cities and Imperial knights. These separate entities were represented in a German Diet which itself gave some appearance of a united Empire. However, the Diet was more like a diplomatic congress than anything resembling some sort of parliament, and it even contained, by old custom, a representative of the King of France.

All this was true long before 1660. But in the tremendous conflict known as the Thirty Years War, which had convulsed Germany and most of the States of Europe from 1618 to 1648, the Emperors had made one last attempt to make their rule effective. They failed, and at the Peace of Westphalia (1648) the German princes were formally allowed to have their own representatives at foreign courts. Even the pretence of a united Empire could no longer be maintained; still less, therefore, could anyone continue to indulge in the day-dream of a united Europe whose temporal head was the Emperor.

The spiritual supremacy of the Pope over a united Christendom was at the same time just as obviously in ruins. The Popes had in former centuries claimed, and occasionally seemed to possess, more power than kings. They sometimes tried to depose kings. All such pretensions had vanished before 1660. The Protestant Reformation of the early sixteenth century saw about half of Europe throw off the authority of the Pope. Even in countries remaining Catholic in doctrine the governments elbowed the Pope out of most of his authority; for example, in Spain, one of the most devoutly Catholic countries, Papal Bulls (decrees) could not be published without royal consent long before the Protestant Reformation began in Germany. Various attempts were made to heal the split in Christendom, both by missionary work and by force of arms. Some success was obtained, especially by the most energetic of the missionaries, the Society of Jesus ('Jesuits'). If caught in countries having hostile governments, however, they were likely to be executed, and that meant that the Reformation could only be destroyed by military conquest. The necessary force could be furnished only by secular governments, and although governments talked about their religious zeal, in practice if they had to choose between religious and purely political aims it was the former which took second place. For instance, Cardinal Richelieu, who was head of the government in Catholic France, allied with Lutheran Sweden against the (Catholic) Emperor. Consequently the Thirty Years War was a disaster to the cause of a united Christendom. At the Peace of Westphalia three religions—Catholic, Lutheran, and Calvinist—were henceforth to be permitted, the choice between them resting with the rulers of the different States. The Peace was condemned by the Pope, but his thunders were ignored.

Clearly, the notion of a united Christendom had therefore vanished. Its place was taken by a very real fact, the fact that Europe was composed of a number of completely separate and wholly independent nation States. It is usual to date the emergence of the modern nation State at about the beginning of the sixteenth century, but it was in about the middle of the seventeenth century that it was seen that the nation State had really come to stay, and had replaced Christendom. Men were accordingly obliged to create ideas and institutions to replace the old idea of unity.

For instance, in international disputes, since the authority of the Pope could no longer usefully be appealed to, diplomacy and diplomatists flourished and multiplied as never before. There arose also a new importance attached to international law after about 1660. International law, naturally enough, had existed for a long time, for so, in fact, had independent nations. It is significant, however, that the first

EUROPE in 1660

0   3   600 mls.   Boundary of Empire..

P = Parma   M = Modena   L = Lucca

great book on internationl law to win a genuinely international reputation was Grotius's *De Jure Belli et Pacis*,[1] published in 1625.

Alongside these methods of arranging disputes between States there also grew into prominence a theory by which the rights and wrongs of disputes could be judged. This theory, important throughout our period of 1660–1789 and after it, was the Balance of Power. It partly meant that no one State should be allowed to become so powerful as to be able to threaten the independence of the others. If it did the others banded together to thwart it, as for example we shall see them do against the France of Louis XIV. Unhappily, it came to mean something more sinister as well. For statesmen tended to judge the strength of a State by reference to its size in land and population. Therefore, if one State acquired more land by conquest, those who thought themselves menaced by its increased strength held themselves perfectly entitled to 'compensation', which usually meant conquering land from someone else, or from the same victim. The most notorious example of this was to be the persistent partitioning of Poland in the late eighteenth century. This theory was by no means new in the middle of the seventeenth century, but it was then that it became very important. It appeared to have some advantages. At least it frankly admitted the sad truth that the States were ambitious and greedy, and it seemed to suggest a suitable way of keeping those qualities within reasonable limits. It was also a way of facilitating and recognizing inevitable changes in the growth and decay of States—a sort of safety-valve relieving the intolerable tensions that would be set up if the idea of the permanence of the State-system created at Westphalia had been interpreted too rigidly. (The Peace of Westphalia, made at the first big international congress, was regarded as providing the basic framework within which the States should and did exist. Subsequent treaty arrangements, no matter how important, were taken to be merely a matter of bringing Westphalia up to date.) Against these considerations it may be said that the Balance of Power was too inexact a notion if only because, in the almost total absence of reliable statistics of any sort, statesmen of the time could judge only very vaguely if a neighbour had become stronger or weaker. Thus, the notion of a Balance of Power often helped to cause wars.

The collapse of the idea of a united Christendom influenced wars in another way. The century and a half before 1660 had seen many ferocious wars take place, both civil and international, in which an important motive had been religious. That is to say that an important

---

[1] See Chapter 6.

element in many of them had been an attempt to bring back the Protestants into the Catholic fold. When wars are fought over differences of belief they are usually marked by savage fanaticism and cruelty. After Westphalia there were no more religious wars, and the attempt to impose a religion on other people by force of arms was largely abandoned. One reason for this was that after about 1660 the importance of religion declined quite sharply. (The point is discussed in Chapter 6.) Partly, no doubt, it was because the fanatics had had it proved to them by repeated failure that it was impossible to conquer or to convert their opponents, so they tended to regard it as no longer worth while to make the attempt. Other factors helped to eliminate religion as a cause, or excuse, for wars. One was the contact with the non-Christian world consequent on the expansion of Europe overseas— the gradual realization that the majority of mankind had been rubbing along more or less satisfactorily without even having heard of Christianity, and still less with any concern about doctrinal disputes within that religion. The strongest motive for European overseas expansion had been trade; the Dutch, in fact, so far from troubling their heads about the non-Christian beliefs of their customers, were even occasionally (as in Japan) prepared to renounce their own religious beliefs in order to obtain permission to trade. Another big reason for the cessation of religious wars is more subtle, and is discussed more fully in Chapter 6. It was that some men began to realize that religion led to wars precisely because agreement with religious opponents is unobtainable, for religious beliefs are not founded on demonstrable facts; if someone did not accept one's dogmas all one could do was kill him. So it began to occur to many men that religious dogma might itself be a piece of over-ambition on the part of the human intellect, on the grounds that we should never be able to reach provable certainty about God's purposes. Better by far to restrict the human intellect to those tasks which it can be sure of carrying out, to measuring what is physically measurable. In other words, it is better to stick to science. It is no coincidence, therefore, that the Scientific Revolution got into full swing in the second half of the seventeenth century, while religion decayed.

Unhappily, while religion as an excuse for wars faded away, the European States found plenty to fight about. Economic and territorial rivalry replaced religious hatred as the principal cause of national conflicts.

The governments of the nation States were by 1660 very evidently free from authority originating outside their boundaries. They had also been struggling for centuries against internal rivals to their power, and by 1660 they had in most countries achieved some degree of success.

Throughout most of Europe the central governments of the individual countries were in the hands of kings. Their power during the Middle Ages was very incomplete for it was limited by the powers of other bodies. Of these there were three sorts: the Church, the feudal baronage, and the towns. All three possessed rights which competed with those of the monarchs to such an extent that it has been said the authority of kings was 'driven into a corner'. The Church, for example, had the right to tax people, and was the only authority which could punish certain sorts of offenders. Barons and towns also had law courts over which the King had little or no control, and barons often had private armies. However, the Church in most places was brought fairly completely under royal control at the time of the Reformation. The nobles likewise, although generally retaining fiscal and social privileges, lost their military power before 1660—they could still be dangerous, nevertheless, as the *Fronde* of the Princes, a civil war in France from 1650 to 1652, showed. A further difficulty sometimes arose because of changing economic conditions. Royal officials in France, for instance, were often able to buy their posts. They therefore became a new, and virtually irremovable, nobility. Towns tended to give kings less trouble.

It must not be thought that clergy, nobles, and *bourgeois* offered invariably separate opposition to royal governments. In the later Middle Ages there had everywhere grown up institutions in which they also worked together. The English Houses of Parliament linked the different 'Estates' of the realm together, and other countries possessed similar institutions, though these varied widely in their power, in their procedure, and in their relationship with the monarch. They nearly all contained members of the clergy, aristocracy, and the *bourgeoisie*. Generalizations about the Estates are hard to make, but in most of them the most dangerous opposition to the monarch came from the aristocracy or gentry. Almost all of them were defeated in the period just before and after 1660—for example, in Spain, in France, in Naples, in Portugal, in Brandenburg, in Bohemia, in Denmark. It should be remembered, however, that the history of the relationship between monarchs and their Estates was not one of constant hostility. Kings often regarded their nobles as necessary to the maintenance of their own power, and of course were often good sons of the Church.

It should be remembered also that the triumph of monarchs was by no means complete: on the contrary, it was subject to serious limitations of two main sorts.

One was that the monarchs of the period of the Old Régime, as it is usual to call the period from 1660 to 1789, although having more control over their own subjects than had been usual during the Middle Ages, exercised nothing like the same degree of control as modern governments normally have over their subjects in the twentieth century. For instance, it was only about the year 1660 that they managed to get much control over their own armies. Before then it was common for governments to hire troops from mercenary captains such as Wallenstein, who had been almost as much of a terror to his nominal friends as to his avowed enemies during the Thirty Years War. The troops usually remained faithful to their generals rather than to the governments which hired them. Again, royal control over the machinery of government was imperfect; officials were often corrupt, inefficient, and idle. Any king attempting fundamental reforms which clashed with the privileges of any considerable body of people did so at his peril. For example, the King of France, the strongest king in Europe, could not reform the laws of his country; he could only codify the procedure by which they were administered. There were many customs-barriers within France; he could not remove them. The nobles paid very few taxes; he would not have dared to try to make them pay anything like their fair share. These were far from all the limitations of royal power. On the other hand, kings in those days were supported by religious and political theorists who taught a doctrine of the Divine Right of Kings (this point will be dealt with more fully in the next chapter). To sum up: while kings in our period did their utmost to control all aspects of national life, their success was great in comparison with that obtained in the centuries before 1660 but small by twentieth-century standards.

The other sort of limitation was simply that some countries had no monarchs while in others the kings were defeated by other elements in the State. Some small States, like Venice, Genoa, and Ragusa, had always been republics. Two others, Switzerland and the United Provinces (that is, Holland; for it is usual so to refer to the seven provinces of which Holland itself was the largest), gained their formal independence at the Peace of Westphalia and emerged as republics, although in the latter in times of danger the head of the House of Orange was usually given almost royal powers, but not a royal title. In Poland the king became completely subordinate to the gentry. In Germany the Emperors failed to impose their will on the princes, although one could describe this as a sort of monarchical victory also, inasmuch as the princes really emerged as heads of independent States, and within those States their control was reasonably effective. The most important exception to the triumph of kings was to be found in England, whose King was beheaded in 1649.

The period 1660 to 1789 was one of almost incessant warfare between the various States, so it will be appropriate here to indicate briefly something of the relative strengths of the most important of them and something of their relationship with each other in 1660. In these respects also the middle of the seventeenth century may be said to begin a new era.

It does so most clearly in the passing of preponderance in Europe from the Habsburgs to France. The great family of Habsburg seemed to come near to dominating the world in the sixteenth century. The Austrian branch ruled over enormous territories, the chief of which were Austria, Carinthia, Styria, the Tyrol, Bohemia, Moravia, Silesia, and parts of Hungary. In addition, during the whole of our period except for one brief occasion in 1741, the head of the Austrian Habsburgs was always elected Emperor of the Holy Roman Empire. So although the Emperors, *as such*, had little power, it should not be forgotten that in their capacity as head of the Austrian Habsburgs they disposed of very considerable strength. The dominions of the Spanish branch of the Habsburgs were even more extensive. They included Spain itself, the Southern Netherlands, Franche Comté, a great deal of Italy, including Milan and Naples, the Canary Islands, part of Morocco, the best of the West Indian islands except Jamaica, most of South America except Brazil, all of Central America, including California, the Philippines, and after 1668 the Marianas. Between 1580 and 1640 Spain had also ruled Portugal and its huge overseas empire. When it is added that for a short time this stupendous conglomeration of Austrian and Spanish territory had been united under one head, and that the two parts still co-operated, that the Spanish armies had been reckoned the best in Europe, and that large quantities of gold and silver came annually to Spain from the Americas, some idea of Habsburg strength may be obtained. For a century and a half before 1660 the Habsburgs appeared to dominate Europe.

By 1660 the Habsburgs, so far from being a menace to others, were hard put to it to defend themselves. During the Thirty Years War the Emperors had tried to make their authority in Germany a reality. At the end of it, with their victorious French and Swedish foes threatening Vienna, that ambition was abandoned. Their Spanish cousins fared much worse. Their richest provinces, the seven northern provinces of the Netherlands, obtained their formal independence on terms which for Spain were humiliating as well as disastrous, for among other terms the triumphant Dutch made them shut the River Scheldt to navigation, with the object of ruining the great port of Antwerp for the benefit of Amsterdam. Spain's war with France, which ended in 1659, was equally disastrous to her. After that, with an empty treasury, a declining population, armed forces incapable of defending even the Netherlands, and a shrunken trade largely in the hands of the French, Dutch, and English, Spain's future role was to be chiefly that of victim rather than that of aggressor. As we shall see, Spain, whose troops had once in the sixteenth century occupied Paris, asked at the end of the seventeenth to be taken over *en bloc* by the French monarchy in order to avoid the partition of its empire.

True, the Spaniards would hardly have been able to occupy Paris had they not been helped to do so by many Frenchmen, and the sudden rise of France to pre-eminence in Europe would almost certainly have occurred sooner had not the French been divided amongst themselves. France is a very large country in area. It was also easily the largest in population. There are no really reliable figures available for any country in Europe, for none of them at that time had a census, but France in 1660 probably had about eighteen million people. Spain had only six or perhaps eight million; in fact, no single united country in Europe had half as many people as did France, except perhaps Russia and Turkey, for which two countries no reliable estimates can be made. France is also a naturally rich country with a huge amount of good agricultural land. What perhaps needs explanation is not so much why France became preponderant in Europe by 1660 but why she had not reached that position long before.

The delay had been caused by many factors, chief of them being a crippling civil war. This had been fought during most of the second half of the sixteenth century between the Catholics and the Calvinists (called 'Huguenots' in France). The Huguenots, although a minority, finally won from King Henry IV a very generous measure of religious toleration in his famous Edict of Nantes (1598). However, they were not satisfied and remained such a nuisance to the authority of the government that, after further military action, most of their privileges were removed, though they retained freedom of worship (1629). The man responsible for curbing the Huguenot menace, Cardinal Richelieu, had also to struggle against countless other enemies of royal authority. He did this with considerable success, and after his death in 1642 his almost equally great successor, Cardinal Mazarin, completed the work. Mazarin had to combat two insurrections known as the *Fronde* of the

Parlements and the *Fronde* of the Princes (1648–52). The *parlements* were the great law courts of France. The struggle had been very severe, but at the end of it the opposition of the *parlements*, of the provincial Estates, of the military governors, and of the territorial nobility had been crushed. Better still, everyone had by then realized that the only possible alternative to complete and miserable anarchy was a royal despotism, so the way was cleared for the young King Louis XIV's strong personal government from 1661 onwards. In addition to grappling with the King's enemies within France the two great cardinals had managed also to organize the defeat of the Austrian and Spanish Habsburgs on the battlefield. Mazarin had also adroitly put France at the head of the League of the Rhine, an association of some of the German princes, so it is hardly too much to say that Louis XIV could exercise more influence in Germany than could the Emperor himself.

The real key to French supremacy was to be found in Germany. If all Germans had been united under one strong government they would have formed a State even bigger than France, for they outnumbered the French by three or four million people. Therein lies the significance of the victory of France in the Thirty Years War; the defeat of the Emperor meant exactly that Germany was not to be united under one government but that the various German States could do much as they pleased *vis-à-vis* the Emperor. The French had deliberately fought for the independence of the German princes, and after Westphalia were really the chief guarantors of that independence. They had done so because they knew perfectly well that their own premier position would be lost if Germany became united. That nightmare was never realized until nearly a hundred years after our period.

French influence extended a good deal farther than Germany. We have seen that Spain ruled great parts of Italy: her influence was also strong in some of the independent Italian States, notably Genoa. But many of them, such as Piedmont, Florence, and Parma, tended to try to escape from Spanish influence by turning to France. It will be observed that the political fragmentation of Italy was as bad as that of Germany, and that is why the Italians were politically insignificant throughout our period. France had also rather better relations than most other countries with the Ottoman Empire. To the scandal of Christendom, the French early in the sixteenth century entered into a sort of understanding with the Turks for the purpose of embarrassing their common enemy, the Habsburgs. The great military empire of the Ottoman Turks stretched from Morocco across North Africa, Asia Minor and the Balkans, and almost to the gates of Vienna. The Empire was in decline, but as we shall see the Turks were soon to make an attempt to capture Vienna. As friends of the French or of any other Christian people, however, the Turks were unreliable—they sometimes attacked French merchants, and the French retaliated by occasional expeditions against Turkish pirates and by helping the Venetians, who hated the Turks. Venice itself had been a very rich commercial Power, but its importance had declined after the discovery of the new oceanic routes to America and around the Cape of Good Hope.

Another enemy of the Turks was Poland, and in that country, too, French diplomacy was active. But Poland, though vast in area, was pathetically weak; indeed it is doubtful whether it should be described as a State at all. France had no influence in Poland's neighbour, Russia, but neither had any other country. Russia at that time had very few peaceful dealings with her neighbours, was very ignorant of Western ways, and gave small indication of her future importance.

A more powerful country than Russia was Sweden. Sweden was a tiny country as far as population was concerned, having probably about one million inhabitants. She had, however, considerable economic resources, chiefly in her forests and iron industry; she produced a most remarkable line of warrior-kings from the House of Vasa; and her army was among the best in Europe. With these assets she had in the fifty years before the beginning of our period made herself, in appearance at least, mistress of the Baltic. She played a major part in the defeat of the Habsburgs in the Thirty Years War. As a result of that she gained West Pomerania, Bremen, Verden, Wismar, Stettin, and the island of Wollin. As if that were not glory enough, she had found the resources during the war to fight another against Denmark. The Treaty of Bromsebro (1645), which ended that war, gave to Sweden a fresh confirmation of her immunity from the tolls which Denmark levied on ships passing through the Sound, the Danish province of Halland being given to Sweden for thirty years as a guarantee of this. In addition Sweden received the islands of Gotland and Oesel and the Norwegian provinces of Jemtland and Herjedalen. (Norway was ruled by the kings of Denmark.) After that, fresh fighting against Poland, a country with which Sweden had been intermittently at war since 1592, against Russia, against Brandenburg, and against Denmark gave Sweden virtual control of the Baltic (Treaties of Oliva and Copenhagen in 1660 and Treaty of Kardis in 1661).

Sweden was therefore the terror of the north, and she was the ally of France. At first sight it might appear that French predominance included northern and eastern Europe as well, but France's grip in these areas was most precarious, for many reasons. First, Swedish power, on which it was chiefly based, was itself rather a shaky and artificial affair. At home the King had to struggle against the power of the nobles and against his own lack of money, a double problem which persisted despite 'reductions'—resumptions of lands formerly alienated to members of the nobility. Second, Sweden's position was strategically weak, and would become desperate if one or more of her unanimously hostile neighbours ever grew significantly in strength. Third, Sweden was not really mistress of the Baltic at all. During recent hostilities the Dutch and English, to whom Baltic trade was so vital that they had not the slightest intention of allowing any one Baltic Power to acquire an unchallengeable supremacy, had intervened with their fleets to impose peace on all concerned. So if Sweden were mistress of the Baltic it was only on the sufferance of the two Maritime Powers. A further difficulty for the French was that they never managed to juggle with all the countries of North and East Europe at the same time, for they also tried to be friendly with Sweden's enemies, a policy incompatible with friendship with Sweden.

Holland and England, the two great Maritime Powers whose massive and decisive intervention in the Baltic has just been referred to, were none the less to some extent inside the French sphere of influence themselves.

Holland had just won her independence from the grip of Spain with help from France, and in 1660 was still her ally. Thanks to a wonderful fishing industry, to an unrivalled understanding and organization of finance and commerce, and to numerous other factors, the Dutch had become by far the richest trading nation in the world. They had virtually a monopoly of Europe's carrying trade, and had also an immensely rich colonial empire, chiefly in the East Indies. Nor were they merely the mean-souled 'cheese-merchants' that the jealous French called them. The Dutch highly prized education and the arts, having excellent universities and even more excellent artists. There was a greater measure of religious toleration in their land than in most of the rest of Europe. Even their staggeringly successful agriculture valued beauty as well as utility; tulip-growing was one of its glories.

Unhappily, all this dazzling wealth and this brilliant civilization were not matched by satisfactory political cohesion. The seven provinces (Holland, Zeeland, Gelderland, Friesland, Overyssel, Utrecht, and Groningen) are together called the United Provinces, but of unity there was little. Each province had its own States and was a virtually independent entity. Five of them even had their own admiralty. It is indeed doubtful if it is proper to speak of the United Provinces as one State or as seven. Worse, there was a serious divergence of interests between the wealthy *bourgeoisie* on the one hand and the nobles, soldiers, and common folk on the other. The last three tended to support the House of Orange, which had done so much to free the country from Spain; the *bourgeoisie* tended to be republican. In 1660 the latter held sway under the Grand Pensionary, John de Witt, a state of affairs bitterly resented by the adherents of the House of Orange. Still, so long as the country continued to swim in prosperity, and so long as the heir to the House of Orange was a minor, de Witt was safe. Yet, for a country which was shortly to incur the hostility of France, Holland had one frightening weakness. Although a great naval Power, she had a lamentably small army.

Another danger to the Dutch, and in certain respects a worse one, was the growing rivalry of the English. They had already fought a naval war against the Dutch in the time of Cromwell, and were soon to fight two more.

Anything like detailed treatment of the political history of England falls outside the scope of this book, but some references to it will be necessary because of the great and growing influence of events in England on those in the rest of Europe. In England the monarchy had grown weaker while the classes represented in Parliament grew stronger. Quarrels about religion, taxation, and other matters broke out between the first two Stuart kings and the Parliamentary majority. The result was a civil war (1642–6) which King Charles I lost. The victorious Parliament had no intention of abolishing the monarchy, but it fell foul of its own army (the famous 'New Model Army', whose most illustrious general was Oliver Cromwell). This quarrel, too, was partly about religion, for the Parliamentary majority wished to impose the Presbyterian religion on the country, a distasteful idea to the Army, most of whose members favoured the Independent sects. A second civil war followed in 1648 in which the Army totally defeated the supporters of Parliament, their Scottish allies, and the King's supporters. The Army contained many men of very radical views and was also enraged against the King, whom it blamed for the wars. So it executed the King and abolished the House of Lords in 1649. There followed eleven years of rule by the Army and its chiefs, a rule which the majority of Englishmen loathed. On the death of Cromwell in 1658 the other Army chiefs quarrelled amongst themselves, and that left the way clear for the return of the dead King's son, Charles II, in 1660. But if he was brought back from exile, so in effect was Parliament and, although the King had considerable powers left to him, in the last resort Parliament was the real master. Not least of the reasons for this was that Parliament, which controlled taxation, kept the King short of money.

That in turn helped to bring England under French influence to some extent. England had already helped Mazarin to defeat Spain. Now her King turned to France for financial help—his only possible expedient because he dared not raise money by irregular methods of taxation for they had helped to bring his father to the executioner's block. Charles had other reasons for being friendly with France. His sister had married Louis XIV's brother. More important, Charles also sympathized with his Roman Catholic subjects, who were harshly treated in England, and he needed French help in any serious attempt to ease their lot. He tried to give them toleration in 1662 by a Declaration of Indulgence, but had to withdraw it because of Parliamentary opposition. Accordingly, his next attempt was made behind the cover of a French alliance and a war against Holland (1672). The Test Act, which Parliament passed in 1673, made short work of the Second Declaration of Indulgence. The truth is that England could not really be regarded as a French satellite, because Charles could not pursue a pro-French policy against the wishes of Parliament as he was not master in his own house; indeed, during the Exclusion crisis of 1678–81, he ran some risk of losing his throne. Parliament was master in England, and Parliament was anti-French, although its members were not above accepting bribes from Louis XIV with the same eagerness as their King.

(b) ECONOMIC ASPECTS

The middle of the seventeenth century may also be taken as marking a turning-point in the economic history of Europe no less profound than in its political history. It is not in the least surprising that the two were in many ways intimately connected.

The foregoing sketch of the political situation of Europe in 1660 stressed the preponderance of France, and hinted at the importance of England and Holland. These countries owed this state of affairs very largely to economic factors. Of these the most dramatic had resulted from the great discoveries of Columbus, da Gama, and other illustrious explorers in the fifteenth and sixteenth centuries. Before their day European trade had followed two main paths. One was a great supply of timber, tar, naval stores of other sorts, hides, and other goods from the Baltic to the rest of Europe. A very different sort of commodity, chiefly pepper and spices, was fetched from Asia via the Middle East; this fantastically profitable trade had been mainly in the hands of Venice. Apart from these goods travelling great distances, there was also a considerable amount of trade in produce of the various European countries, such as wine and fruits from southern Europe, paid for by woollen goods from England, salted herrings from Holland, and so on. One big result of the great geographical discoveries was to shift the balance of economic power in Europe away from Italy, which had profited by the Asiatic trade especially, to the north and west of Europe, and in particular to France, Holland, and England, which turned out to be best able to exploit the new routes. This meant broadly that in our period the dynamic countries, speaking in terms of economics, were precisely those three. The other countries of Europe copied them, tried to catch up with them, or remained backwaters. Political influence accompanied economic power, since France, Holland, and England were the only three countries capable of financing a long war without monstrous sacrifices by their populations; Holland was the only country in Europe to remain solvent all through the seventeenth century.

Another great effect of the geographical discoveries was greatly to increase the total volume of trade. For not only could larger quantities be transported by ship than by pack-horse, but also the products of the continent of America—gold, silver, sugar, furs, and a host of other things—were added to the goods from Asia. This increase itself caused some vast changes.

Fairly obviously one of them was a growth in the wealth and power of those directly handling trade. The merchants of Holland dominated that country. In England there is still argument about the causes of the Civil War, argument about whether or not it was caused by a decline or an increase in the power of the gentry. Without venturing into the controversy, we may at least safely say that, whoever caused the Civil War, it certainly was not either paupers or feudal barons. It was caused by people with money, some of whom had made it in trade. We may say with more assurance that after 1660 the merchant class continued greatly to increase in influence, to the point, as we shall see, that they could even in 1739 force a reluctant government to declare war on Spain. As for France, the story is more complicated but in many ways not dissimilar. Some merchants made money, retired from trade, and then bought governmental posts. Where these posts became hereditary, their holders formed a new sort of aristocracy, the *noblesse de la robe*, a class which was to do more than most to bring down the French monarchy with a crash in 1788–9. This class became virtually a closed caste, and it was very difficult for other successful merchants to follow them up the social ladder. The French merchant class therefore demanded that noble titles should be given to successful merchants who would continue in business. They based this demand on the value of their services to the State in creating wealth. The government, after much study, turned it down. It had been suggested that the decision to refuse noble titles to tradesmen sprang from the old principle of divide and rule—from reluctance to allow the old nobility once again to become over-powerful by the addition to it of a lot of fresh and energetic blood from the middle class. But while lacking titles and the chance of various sorts of promotion that went with them, the French merchant class continued to grow in wealth and influence. At the end of our period the middle class took over the State entirely (1789). So in France, Holland, and England the power of the middle class grew. In countries where their power grew in nothing like so spectacular a fashion, if at all, as for instance in Prussia, Russia, or Spain, it was because such countries lagged behind in commercial growth, and so did not have such a numerous or wealthy *bourgeoisie.*

Another result of the increased volume of trade was a whole set of improved methods of conducting it. In our period considerable efforts were made to improve communications: rivers were dredged, canals built, roads repaired, postal services created. Another development far more important after 1660 than before it was the creation of great joint-stock companies. The older trading companies of the Middle Ages had been associations of merchants formed for their own protection in various ways—protection against pirates, unfair competition, etc. But the association itself did not trade on its own account; its function was to protect and regulate the individual trading activities of its members. Very different was the joint-stock company. It set up in business by inviting loans from anyone prepared to lend. It then traded for itself, distributing the profits among the shareholders. For all sorts of reasons this was an instrument far better able to handle big commercial operations. The most famous of those that concerned England were the East India Company, the Bank of England, and the South Sea Company, but the Dutch and French also had many, of which the most famous were their East India companies. The detailed organization of these varied from country to country. With them came the growth of Stock Exchanges.

These companies had always competed with those of other nations, but it may be said that competition grew far more fierce during our period. Two main reasons may be advanced for this, both of them clearly marking off the period before 1660 from that following 1660.

One was the ending of the great price-rise. Owing partly to the tremendous influx of gold and silver from the Americas a severe inflation took place all through the sixteenth century and continued until 1660. During that time prices rose about fivefold. After 1660 prices steadied and then, for twenty or thirty years, fell slowly, although to nowhere near the levels before the inflation. This was caused partly by a falling-off in the production of the American mines, and partly by the increase of trade with Asia, some of whose products had to be paid for in precious metals. The drain of these from Europe caused a relative scarcity of them, hence the fall in prices. It seemed to the great companies that their profits were running a serious risk of diminution by reason of this fall in prices. So they did their utmost to extend the field of their operations and at the same time became more bitter in their competition with each other. The other reason why such competition grew more ferocious after 1660 was that from about that time the governments took a hand in it; they supported the quarrels of their merchants. Previously they had taken little or no part in these quarrels. The entry of governments into these disputes is thus an enormously significant feature of our period. Sir George Clark calls it 'one of the great revolutions of European policy'. During our period commercial disputes played a leading part in causing many wars.

In fact, the leading feature of economic life in the whole of the period 1660–1789 is strong interference in it by the State. Governments interfered because they were concerned about their power over their own subjects and about their power relative to other States. The first needed large quantities of money; the success of monarchs in their struggle with the feudal nobility had come about because the monarchs were rich and could pay for armed forces of a size beyond the resources of a baron. As for their foreign rivals, governments realized clearly enough that they might have to be fought. Without money, there would be no pay for the troops, and hence, in a very short time, no troops. As well as troops, there was just as urgent a need of ships, guns, powder, and dozens of other things used in war; and these required raw materials and skilled workmen, efficient organization, and capital. To make sure that all this was available the State had to become 'the watchful and despotic guardian of the economic interests of its inhabitants'. That is, it interfered on an ever-growing scale in as many aspects of the economic life of the country as it could in order to increase the wealth, and therefore the strength, of the whole. State interference for these purposes on a big scale had not happened before about 1660, so that approximate date can be taken as marking in yet another way a profound change in the history of Europe. As we shall see, before the end of our period there was a considerable body of opinion which regarded that sort of action by the State with disfavour. However, in 1660 most governments could count on a large measure of support from their subjects in these matters.

The merchant community, at least in Britain, had long been accustomed to regulation and protection of their interests by guilds and companies. For them, therefore, it seemed natural to seek the help of the larger unit—the State—which had now become so important and which appeared to be the highest embodiment of the corporate organization with which they were familiar. So we find writers like Thomas Mun asking the State to care for commerce, and officials like Sir George Downing putting many of his proposals into practice. In France direction was inspired more wholly from above by the great minister, Colbert. In most other countries the impulse perhaps owed less to the merchants themselves and more to the State than was the case in England. As for Holland, the merchants there very rarely wanted or tolerated such governmental interference.

State interference in economic matters in this period is usually called 'mercantilism'. A cautionary word is needed about the word 'mercantilism' itself. It was popularized by Adam Smith in his classic work *The Wealth of Nations*, written in the late eighteenth century. He simply meant by it to describe a trading economy as contrasted with an agricultural economy. However, words used by men of genius often become fashionable and then are used by others in so many different ways as to drain them of clear meaning. To such an extent has that happened in this case that at least one great authority (Professor E. A. Johnson) has called the word a 'nuisance'. Another (Mr Charles Wilson) seems to prefer to call at least what was done in France 'Colbertism' (after the great minister chiefly responsible). All that is meant by it in this book is theory and practice, whether inspired by merchants or governments or both, having as aim the wealth and power of a country in our period. Naturally, ideas and practice differed in various places; equally naturally, no statesman ever allowed one rigid set of ideas to dominate his actions all the time. Also, some of the ideas concerned are by no means peculiar to the period 1660–1789.

The chief of those ideas seems to have been the great importance attached to a country's balance of trade. Various writers stressed the importance of selling more to foreigners than was bought from them, so that, as Sir Matthew Decker wrote in 1739, 'Foreigners must pay the balance in treasure and the Nation grow Rich.' So the most favoured transaction was one whereby a foreigner paid for one's goods in bullion. For the English, the worst sort of transaction was to have to pay Dutch ships for carrying goods to or from England; to prevent this a whole series of Navigation Acts was passed, most notably in 1651, 1660, 1662, and 1663. Most countries tried to avoid having to import manufactures because of their cost. To this end, the export of many raw materials was restricted or forbidden, and all sorts of encouragement given to build native industries—encouragement which included money grants and inducements to skilled immigrants. At the same time tariff barriers discouraged foreign imports. The English, for instance, even went to the extent of placing a huge tax on imports from Ireland. One of the most famous tariffs was the French tariff, which was aimed chiefly against Dutch imports and which led to war with that country. But in practice this rigid protection was often considerably modified in many countries. Thus the English relaxed their measures against the Dutch in 1674, while between 1669 and 1678 the French made concessions to the Dutch, Swedes, some of the Germans, and many others. However, such concessions were usually wrung out of the countries concerned by military defeat or some sort of political necessity, not by any change of economic policy.

Governments also assisted in improving the efficiency of the trade and industry of their countries by building canals, such as the French Canal du Midi, the German Oder–Spree Canal, numerous canals near Ostend, and others; by making or repairing roads; and by creating postal services. Workmen were trained in skilled crafts, and the quality of goods supervised by government inspectors.

Colonial policy served the same end. It became the aim of governments to acquire overseas colonies. These, it was hoped, would not only provide cheap raw materials but also furnish customers for the manufactures of the mother country. Protective measures were taken so as to confine colonial trade as much as possible to the markets of the mother country, and to keep foreigners out of it. That led to smuggling and to conflict.

Tariff barriers, colonial rivalry, and a mass of prohibitions and restrictions therefore proved to be a cause of frequent wars. So also did the belief of the mercantilists that the amount of trade was fairly static, so that any increase for oneself could only be at the expense of neighbours. Mercantilist views have often been severely criticized, but there seems to have been some justification for their views on the limited nature of the trade available. As for their anxiety about the balance of trade, which has been the chief target of the critics, a desire to acquire bullion had some sense in it. For in those days large quantities of precious metal were necessary if much foreign trade was to be carried on at all—bills of exchange not then being in wide use, particularly for trade outside Europe.

One last point should be added to this introductory sketch of economic matters, and of some of their political effects, in the period 1660–1789. It is that while capitalism grew very much as a feature of commercial life, its growth was not at first so marked in industry itself. Indeed, industrial methods changed little during most of that period. There was some invention in the seventeenth century but it rarely occurred as a result of the application of science to industrial methods; that had to wait until nearly the end of our period, in spite of the tremendous scientific revolution which occurred in the seventeenth century, and about which something will be said in the next chapter.

2 · Europe in 1660
(2) Some Intellectual Aspects

(a) *ABSOLUTISM AND DIVINE RIGHT*

Side by side with the growth of royal power there grew also a theory which attempted to reinforce and justify it. This absolutist doctrine was expounded by many writers, among whom could be counted professional absolutists like James I, Richelieu, and Louis XIV. According to this theory, kings alone had the right and the duty to make laws and execute them. Richelieu, for instance, said that kings were independent of all spiritual authority (that is, the Church) and of all temporal rivals (such as the States-General). Louis XIV in his *Mémoires* affirmed that it was for the subjects of a king to obey his commands without question. Individual rights always had to yield to the good of the State. Richelieu said that 'the public interest should always be preferred to that of individuals'. Making the point still more emphatically, Louis XIV declared that kings were absolute masters of the lives and property of their subjects. Kings could do as they pleased, and nobody had the right to object, still less to rebel. Subjects therefore had no rights as against *raison d'État*.

Grafted on to this royal absolutist theory was the theory of the Divine Right of Kings. According to this, kings held their absolute power because it was given them by God. Kings were God's lieutenants on earth. One writer (Cassan) said they were 'His living images'. More directly, Bossuet in his *Politique tirée des propres paroles de l'Ecriture Sainte* said that kings were sacred, and to revolt was a sacrilege. 'O kings,' he exclaimed, 'you are gods.' Even writers like Hobbes and Spinoza, who did not especially champion kings, thought that the individual had no rights against the State.

This theory had been invented in opposition to the extreme claims often made by the medieval Popes. It attempted to answer those claims, which were supported by religious arguments, by resting itself on religious arguments. The Catholic idea was still that this mortal life was only a vale of tears which men had to endure so as to be worthy of salvation in the next. The reward for suffering here would be bliss in Heaven. If some of that suffering were inflicted by kings, who owed their position to God, one had to accept it with resignation and humility as one accepted other heaven-sent tribulations, like the plague. The main thing was to ensure one's personal salvation—a notion that was interpreted so rigidly that even charitable works for others were performed, not out of love for others, not out of sympathy with one's fellow men, but because charity was acceptable in the sight of God.

The absolutist doctrine, the religious doctrine of the Divine Right of Kings, and indeed religion itself were all to be powerfully assailed in the years after 1660. The attack might be said to have had two aspects, the one practical and the other theoretical.

On the practical side, the English had already shaken royal absolutism by cutting off King Charles I's head. True, there followed a reaction. His son was restored to the throne in 1660 and many of the English talked at length and with apparent sincerity of the Divine Right of Kings once more. It was often stated in a somewhat watered-down form when clergy of the Church of England preached about the wickedness of resistance to the King. But in 1688 they and most of the nation had to eat their words. For James II tried to make the Catholic religion the dominant one in England, and he went about that policy with such haste and tactlessness that he lost his throne. The exponents of non-resistance to the Lord's anointed showed that they had really meant the sinfulness of resisting a king who would fall in with their wishes, not one who gave appointments in the universities and the army to Catholics. Leaders of both political parties, Whig and Tory, invited James's son-in-law, the Dutchman William of Orange who was a fervent anti-Catholic, to help them get rid of James. Thanks to mass desertion from his cause, James was forced to flee to France. After much embarrassed debate, it was finally decided to adopt a formula which killed Divine Right in England for ever. For the Bill of Rights (1689) said that 'according to the resolution and desire of the Lords and Commons . . . their Majesties [i.e. William and his wife] did accept the crown'. In other words, an English king no longer inherited by Divine Right; he had shrunk to a person who was offered a job by his employers. True enough, it was still no ordinary job; the King was still by far the most important single person in the country. But he was no longer sovereign in his own right: he was the chief servant of the nation. The matter did not end there, for the English had to defend their 'Glorious Revolution' with the pen and with the sword. As we shall see, they proved themselves efficient with both weapons.

Divine Right had already been attacked in theory by various writers, not only in places such as Poland, where the monarch was weak, but even in France. But writers like Joly, who could declare that 'kings are not the absolute masters of the property and lives of their subjects', were not numerous and were little heeded.

The chief theoretical attack on Divine Right and on religion came from the Scientific Revolution of the seventeenth century. This was easily the greatest intellectual movement of that time, perhaps of all time. Religious thought tried to explain the universe in terms of God's purposes. Indeed, thanks mainly to the ancient Greeks, particularly Plato and Aristotle, most European thinkers, whether clerical or lay, had until then tended to think teleologically—that is, they tried to incorporate in the explanation of phenomena reference to the future state or purpose to which any phenomenon tended. Modern science, on the contrary, tends to confine causal explanation to the conditions which must obtain in order that something should come about. Thus the existence of an hotel might possibly be accounted for by events occurring after its erection—that is, the arrival of travellers, for whose needs the hotel has been brought into being—or it could be explained by the efforts of the builders, financiers, and others who had put it there, and these are the necessary conditions for there being an hotel, whether travellers arrive or not. The first explanation is teleological; the second mechanistic.[1] In our period the second mode of thought was to do much to undermine the first, although few scientists had just this aim in view.

To attempt even an indication of all the important intellectual currents of our period would take too much space, and is beyond the

---

[1] The fuller meaning of this word is brought out later in this chapter.

scope of this book. But the Scientific Revolution is of such tremendous interest and importance that some of the subsequent chapters[1] will try to indicate certain effects on political events, on political theory, and on economic affairs in the period 1660–1789. However, first it might be profitable to examine the Scientific Revolution itself a little more closely.

(b) THE SCIENTIFIC REVOLUTION

Men have always tried to alter their surroundings so as to make them more comfortable or convenient in various ways. For a long time they have also tried to understand their surroundings, to make a mental map of the universe. Technological and theoretic activities are the twin aspects of science; they fructify each other. Considerable progress in practical invention and in theoretic understanding had of course been made for many centuries before the seventeenth. But the big break-through to what may be called modern science occurred then.

Modern science is based on ideas which are tested by observation and experiment. Before the seventeenth century there had been many ideas and much observation, but they had rarely been profitably linked. What happens in modern scientific discovery is that the scientist's interest is first aroused by study or observation of facts. He then formulates a hypothesis, or guessed explanation, to account for them. He then tests the hypothesis by specially devised experiments whereby apparatus is set up for the observation of events under known and controllable conditions. The results are often expressed numerically. If they support the hypothesis it can then be called a scientific theory (or 'law'). If they do not, the hypothesis has to be abandoned or modified. Two interesting points emerge here. One is that the scientist concerns himself as far as the tests of the truth of his hypothesis are concerned only with that which is physically measurable. Future states or occult qualities are ruled out, for whether they are relevant or not they can only be surmised. The other is that evidently a great scientist needs to have an almost miraculously fruitful power of imagination and insight to be able to form useful hypotheses.

The greatest name in this Revolution is perhaps that of Newton, whose discoveries occurred at the beginning of our period and perhaps more than any purely political event mark off 1660 from the period

---

[1] Especially Chapters 6, 14, 15, 16, 17, and 18.

before it. But it would be hard to grasp the full glory and beauty of his work if it were considered in isolation from that of some of his almost equally great predecessors. Nor would justice be done thereby to those predecessors.

(i) The Revolution in mechanics and astronomy

The central (and 'strategic' as Butterfield calls it) advance was made in mechanics and astronomy.

Astronomy is probably the oldest of the sciences; the Babylonians had made thorough observations of the heavens. The generally accepted picture of the heavens during the Middle Ages and until the advent of Copernicus was that described by Aristotle, and also by the astronomer Ptolemy, who lived at Alexandria in the second century A.D. At the centre of the universe was the earth, which remained motionless. The heavenly bodies were carried around it attached to concentric spheres. There were eleven of these spheres; the one nearest to us carried the moon, next was that carrying Mercury, then that carrying Venus, and so on for the sun, Mars, Jupiter, and Saturn. Beyond Saturn was the Firmament (fixed stars), the Crystalline Heaven, the Primum Mobile, and the Empyrean Heaven. God dwelt in the last-named. The Primum Mobile revolved around east to west once every twenty-four hours. It imparted motion to all the other spheres. The spheres had no vacuum in between them, and were supposed to be made of some very subtle ethereal stuff which moved without any friction and possessed no weight; later men thought of them as being made of some sort of crystalline material which was invisible. This ether was a perfect material, which, like the spheres and the heavenly bodies which it carried round, never changed and never decayed. Very different was the inferior region beneath the moon (the 'sublunary' region) which we inhabit. It was filled with the four corruptible elements: earth (forming the dry land), water (the ocean), the atmospheric air, and an upper layer of fire. Everything in our world was made of one of these or of a mixture of them. While the heavens were perfect and unchanging, our world did not share this blessed immutability, for everything on it was subject to change and decay.

It was inferior to the heavens in another important respect also. This was as regards motion. The ether had perfect motion; that is, everything moved in a perfect circle. Motion in the sublunary regions was not circular but rectilinear. The four elements all 'naturally' moved in straight lines away from or towards the earth's surface; thus water and earth possessed gravity and had a natural desire to fall towards the centre of the world, and fire and air possessed levity; that is, had a natural desire to move upwards away from that centre. It was an indication of their inferior and corrupt nature that they failed on the whole to do these things, although it was in some respects fortunate that this was so since otherwise, for example, all the earth, which is heavier than water, would sink to the bottom and all our world would be covered by water. As well as this natural up and down motion, the elements also knew 'violent' motion; that is, could be moved in any sort of direction by the application of force, as for example when one lifts a weight. It was thought, however, and this is of the utmost importance, that in order to maintain motion either in the heavens or on earth, a constant force needed to be applied, and that when that force stopped, the body to which it was being applied would also stop. (This supplied Aristotle with a proof of the existence of God, who was necessarily himself the Unmoved Mover in the Empyrean Heaven.) The implication was that a constant force gave a constant velocity and that normally force was required to alter a state of rest.

This neat picture of the state of affairs was very soon found not to correspond with the observed facts. It was therefore altered in various ways which do not much concern us. For instance, it was thought, to account for the actual path of the planets, that they move in epicycles; that is, in small circles about a mean position, while the latter, called a deferent, revolved in a larger circle about the earth. This can be pictured as the sort of path you would get if you had a revolving cart-wheel with a smaller one revolving around its circumference. Ideas of motion had to be modified also; otherwise it was difficult to explain why bodies continued to move when no longer in contact with the force, as, for example, an arrow continues on its way when no longer in contact with the bow. The Aristotelian tradition explained this by saying that the medium through which missiles, etc., travelled—that is, the air or water—had force in it. Another difficulty was that although a constant uniform force was supposed to produce uniform motion, falling bodies were observed to move at accelerating speed. (One explanation of this was that a falling body moved with more alacrity the nearer it got to its proper home; that is, the ground.) Medieval artillerymen also had some puzzles to explain, since their projectiles were supposed to move parallel to the ground and then drop vertically; this must have produced unexpected results.

It will be noticed that a universe constructed on this pattern was filled with 'ghosts'—unseen agencies had to be in tireless operation in order to keep the planetary spheres moving. Although medieval church-men gladly accepted all this as a proof of God's existence as the Unmoved Mover who saw to it that the Primum Mobile functioned, in actual fact Aristotle's system would have needed forty-seven or alternatively fifty-five gods. Either that, or bodies had to be endowed with some sort of 'souls', with dispositions to travel in various directions. After many years of painful thought, a most brilliant body of medieval scholars gradually adopted a theory of impetus; that is, that a moving body acquires impetus which, like heat, does not fade away immediately.

The most famous figure in overthrowing the 'geocentric' (earth-centred) universe was Copernicus, and the most famous one as regards the modern theory of impetus or inertia was Galileo, although, as already hinted, both owed a great deal to predecessors.

Indeed, in the preface of his book which appeared in the year of his death (1543), entitled *De Revolutionibus Orbium Coelestium* (*On the Revolu-tions of the Celestial Spheres*), Copernicus stated that he had been impressed by the fact that not all the ancients had agreed with Aristotle about the immobility of the earth. He put forward the theory that the sun and the stars were motionless at the centre and circumference of the universe respectively, that the earth rotated on its axis every twenty-four hours, and that the earth and the planets revolved around the sun, while the moon revolved around the earth. What is especially interesting about these ideas is that they were not based on any new observations or experiments, but on those of Ptolemy and his successors —so much for the notion that what had previously delayed advance in science was too much theorizing on too little evidence. Copernicus did something much more difficult—he produced a brilliant new concep-tual scheme, a new interpretation of the same facts.

Nevertheless, Copernicus's views did not meet with very widespread acceptance in the sixteenth century. This might seem odd to us, since something like those views is now generally accepted; also, at the time it was claimed that his theories were ever so much neater than the Ptolemaic system, and they did in fact simplify the calculations of astro-nomers and mathematicians. But they were open to serious objections. They did not fit the facts any better than the Ptolemaic system, and some of those facts were not accounted for at all: for instance, there was no parallax (shift in the apparent position of the stars because of the revolution of the earth round the sun) observable in his time. Much more serious was the mechanics of the whole thing. How could the great heavy unwieldy bulk of the earth be turned around? In other words, to accept him would have been to reject the whole of contemporary science.

More observations were necessary. Some of these were provided by the Danish astronomer Tycho Brahe (1546–1601). He built a wonderful observatory and proved that the bright 'new star' which apppeared in 1572 was more distant from us than the moon, and therefore belonged to a region where any change was, according to the old system, impossible. Brahe did not, however, agree with the Copernican system and put forward one of his own which found little favour either then or subsequently. But his recorded observations passed into the possession of his young German colleague, Johann Kepler (1571–1630).

While one reason that impelled Copernicus to believe his own ideas seems to have been an enormous admiration for the sun and a fixed determination to establish its central importance, Kepler was animated by a conviction that God was the geometry-fancier that Plato had thought him to be, and he was bent on finding a geometrical description of the motions of the heavenly bodies. Taking the sun as the centre of the system, as Copernicus had done, Kepler laid down three laws of planetary motion. First, the planets did not move in circles but described ellipses with the sun as one focus. He next stated that planets do not move at the same speed in all parts of the orbit, but faster as they neared the focus; the rule for calculating its speed is that a line drawn from the sun to a planet sweeps out equal areas in equal times. (This was a terrible blow to the old system. Instead of pursuing their former smooth, majestic, regular, circular track, the planets were dawdlers who made up for delays by an undignified rush.) Kepler's third law laid down in what way the time of the planet's orbit is related to the size of that orbit: the square of the period of revolution of a planet is proportional to the cube of its average distance from the sun, i.e. if T is time and D is average distance, then $D^3 \alpha T^2$ is true of all planets. Kepler had thus wrecked the beautiful system of concentric crystalline spheres beyond repair, and by showing what happened mathematically he became 'the apostle of a mechanistic system . . . aspiring to turn the universe into pure clockwork' as Butterfield says.

Even so, Kepler, while working out the mathematical way in which the planets move, still had no idea why they should move in this fashion. His mechanics were still faulty—he thought (and of course he was not alone) that a continuous application of force was necessary to keep a body moving. The new astronomy needed the help of a new science of mechanics.

The man who neutralized the traditional mechanical argument

against the motion of the earth (how could such a weight be moved?) was Galileo Galilei (1564–1643). The achievements of this Italian were simply breathtaking. He is the founder of modern mechanics, and indeed he discovered and established the true method of physical science; he is the central figure in the Scientific Revolution. Galileo's work was of two sorts: he did a great deal of practical astronomy, and also he is the father of the science of mechanics, which itself was of the utmost importance to astronomy.

In the years between 1600 and 1610 Galileo showed that comets and new stars were farther away from us than the moon; therefore, when they faded it was proved that the immutability of celestial bodies was false. In 1609 Galileo heard that a Dutchman had invented a sort of telescope, so he made one for himself and at once began to make the most startling discoveries. The moon's surface was seen to be rugged —not in the least like the perfectly smooth sphere it was supposed to be—and since the moon was thus presumably made of the same stuff as the earth it not only weakened the case for believing in the existence of Aristotle's perfect fifth element, but tended to show that the earth itself was a planet. Worse was to follow. Jupiter was observed to have four hitherto unsuspected satellites circling around it, which showed that some circular motions were not earth-centred, another blow to the belief that the earth was the only natural centre. It also made a sorry mess of the magic number of heavenly bodies, which traditionally had been seven. (A Florentine astronomer, however, attempted to prove that these satellites could not exist by a number of curious arguments, one of which was that 'these satellites of Jupiter are invisible to the naked eye and therefore would be useless and therefore do not exist'. People in his day thought that the heavenly bodies foretold stirring events and governed our lives—to judge by some newspapers plenty of people still do believe this.) Even more shattering was the revelation that the sun had spots which appeared and then disappeared, so even the sublime sun itself was not changeless. It is not very surprising therefore that people who had spent a lifetime laboriously acquiring a lot of misinformation were not too pleased at this; the Professor of Philosophy at Padua refused to look through Galileo's telescope.

Of even greater importance was Galileo's work in mechanics. One of the best-known stories about him says that he tried to disprove the old idea that heavy bodies drop faster than light ones by dropping weights from the Leaning Tower of Pisa. Nobody now seems sure that he ever did this, but in any case two men had already performed similar experiments at Delft about 1590 and shown that a heavy and a light weight released simultaneously reach the ground together, although the demonstration was not entirely convincing because the height (about thirty feet) was not enough.

Of more significance were his measurements of the speed of falling bodies. It was noticed that bodies fall with constantly increasing speed; he set himself to discover the law of that increase. After some thought he made the hypothesis that the speed increased with the time of fall. Then followed the experiments. He took a piece of wood several yards long and made a narrow, highly polished groove in it. A 'brazen Ball, very hard, round and smooth' was next allowed to run along the groove, with the piece of wood tilted; it thus ran down. The distance and time taken were checked. This was done at different distances for 'near a hundred times'. And so it was by this clever device, followed by repetition of experiments under the same and then different conditions, that he arrived at the mathematical deduction that the distance travelled increases as the square of the time. He also found that a smooth ball, after running down one plane, will run up another to a vertical height very nearly equal to that of its starting-point: this led him to the conclusion that a body in uniform motion on a flat, level surface without friction would so continue until some agency caused it to stop. He had very nearly reached the modern law of inertia, viz. a body will move in a straight line at uniform velocity unless some force alters it. (Very nearly, but not quite, for he still pictured the horizontal plane as a plane that went round the earth; he had not entirely shaken off the idea of circular motion.) Galileo also made another important discovery in dynamics. This was the discovery of the true path of a projectile—it has two movements, one horizontal at uniform velocity, and one vertical which follows the laws of falling bodies; the combination of the two gives a parabola.

It is difficult to determine which aspect of these discoveries is of the greater significance: the effects of the discoveries or the way in which they had been made. Their effects were certainly stupendous. They were the chief agent in bringing about the collapse of the Aristotelian system in which the planets had to be kept in motion by an Unmoved Mover. It became clear that it is not motion that needs to be explained, but only alterations in speed or direction, so that once the heavenly system had been set in motion it required nothing more to keep moving for ever. The ghosts were leaving the universe, making way for a clockwork system that went by itself, obeying nothing but a few mathematical laws. Furthermore, since the earth was certainly no longer the centre of the universe, Man himself is in a sense dethroned—no longer was he the central figure in a universe which now obeyed mathematical laws and had no sort of interest in his needs and destiny.

Important as that was in producing a revolution in men's outlook, it is probable that Galileo's methods mattered still more. For in him one can see fully at work for the first time the true methods of modern science. Before him there had been plenty of experiment, but a lot of it had been pointless, such as the over-optimistic toil of the alchemists, or as Butterfield says a 'wild fluttering . . . like a schoolboy interested in everything'. Before him, too, there had been plenty of conceptual schemes. But never before were the two correctly welded together, to use Butterfield's vivid phrase, 'like a great machine getting into gear'. Galileo first formed an hypothesis about the speed of falling bodies, checked it by controlled experiments, and then drew the conclusions from them in mathematical form. More than that, it should be obvious that he had, as it were, mathematicized the business in another way; he first rid the whole problem of difficult and encumbering factors like friction, air resistance and so on, and considered the question of movement in isolation from all that. Hence he could hit on the true law of inertia; only by so doing could he have seen that if all those agencies were removed a body would have nothing left to stop it. So it must go on. This is a profound example of a revolutionary discovery being made not merely by experiments, for, practically speaking, he could not have conducted experiments in which those factors were absent, but by a revolutionary mental picture being made first.

And last, his whole outlook had nothing at all to do with teleology. Aristotle and the medieval Schoolmen had treated terrestrial mechanics from the point of view of their particular metaphysics. They were concerned with analysing motion in terms of the distinction between potentiality and actuality, and the concept of 'natural place'. If the centre of the earth is a natural place for heavy bodies then they move to it. Medieval students of mechanics were really concerned with *why* motion occurred, though the Merton School of physicists (1330–50) did discover the law of descent for falling bodies, called the Merton Rule. Galileo found the concept of natural place unsatisfactory. Instead, he interested himself not in why, but how, motion occurred; he confined himself to those aspects of the problem, i.e. times and distances, which really are measurable and expressible in mathematical terms. Ever since, the physical sciences have done just that. Galileo himself expressed the attitude of the new science perfectly when he said that he knew nothing about the origin of the universe and so on, and preferred not to try to reach the unattainable; he said it was better 'to pronounce that modest sentence "I know it not"'. Galileo thus confined himself to the physically measurable. He also denied reality to secondary qualities. It had been recognized before his time that there is a difference between the primary qualities of some object, such as its physical measurements, its position, etc., and the secondary qualities of that object, such as its colour, bitterness, or sweetness, etc. Galileo held that these secondary qualities are real only in the mind or tastes of the observer, and are the product of the effect of the object and the sensitivity of the organism. They depend anyway on atomic differences; that is, differences of taste, smell, etc., are only the effect on us of differences of the number, weight, etc., of atoms in the object. And the number, weight, movements, and so on of those atoms are themselves subject to mathematical laws. Galileo is therefore the father of the 'mechanical philosophy' which was to dominate the late seventeenth and the eighteenth centuries.

For men went on to argue that if all phenomena were the result of atoms pressing or striking against other atoms, then every physical effect followed from a measurable physical cause, and could be calculated according to the laws of mechanics. Hence the 'mechanical philosophy' as it came to be called in the eighteenth century (the word 'philosophy' was used where we should more often say 'science'). So we have Robert Boyle saying in the late seventeenth century, 'I look upon the phenomena of nature to be caused by the local motion of one part of matter hitting against another.' These notions were developed in a sense by Newton and, as we shall see, taken up and pushed to the most rash conclusions by the eighteenth-century French Encyclopaedists, who imagined that they would be able to explain everything in the world by a few physical and mechanical principles, including problems of law, politics, education, and everything else, so that Man himself and all aspects of his behaviour would eventually be explained in this way.

But this is to anticipate. For although Kepler and Galileo had between them explained a good deal, a bigger problem remained. That was the problem of gravity. Kepler had stated the accurate laws which the planets seemed to obey. But of the reason for their moving in this way he had no notion. And Galileo's researches had put terrestrial mechanics on a sound basis and tended to show that there was need of a cause to keep the planets and their satellites in their orbits and to prevent them from moving off in straight lines through space. So whatever it was that kept the planets in their ellipses, speeding up as they neared the sun, and slowing down as they receded from it, was a mystery. Gravity on this earth also rather complicated matters, for if the earth was not the centre of the universe, it seemed mysterious that falling bodies should still want to go to the centre of it instead of to the centre of the universe. One suggestion was that called 'specific gravitation'; that is, that every heavenly body had its own gravity so that, for example, a piece of the moon would always have the property of falling to its own parent body, and not to the earth. This opinion had at least the merit of explaining why all the matter in the universe did not collect together at the same place.

A clever solution to the whole business was offered by the French mathematician, scientist, and philosopher, René Descartes (1596–1650). His philosophical and astronomical ideas are interrelated. He held that thought, or the world of the spirit, was as real as the material world, but sharply different from it inasmuch as spirit is immaterial and unextended in space; that is, has no sort of physical dimensions. The material world could therefore only be made of that which is physically measurable and thus for him it was quite meaningless to suppose that there could be space without anything occupying it. (He thought that we consist of a material body controlled by a totally non-physical mind, a sort of 'ghost in a machine'. This notion had enormous influence, and still has; one may still hear people talk about the 'influence of mind over matter', although a crippling assault on this sort of theory has been made by Professor Gilbert Ryle in his book *The Concept of Mind*. This book is of considerable interest, which is why no apology is made for its irrelevance here. For instance, since Communist theory is in part based on the influence of the material on the immaterial, a Communist would have to phrase a good many of his remarks a little differently after reading Professor Ryle's book.) According to Descartes, therefore, the universe could not be made up of separate atoms suspended in a vacuum. It is filled with very tiny invisible particles of some primary matter or ether. These particles move round like giant whirlpools, or vortices, as he called them. One huge vortex was centred on the sun, and the swarms of particles careering round the sun carried the planets along with them. The earth had a minor vortex which carried the moon along.

This all seemed perfectly logical to Descartes and to a great many other people, especially on the Continent. Worked out in detail, it seemed to solve the double problem of gravity and of the movements of all the planets. It was attractive for another reason. In this theory of Descartes it is obvious that all motion is being caused by direct contact of one body with another; it reduced the whole universe to an enormous machine expressible and calculable in mathematical terms, and therefore fitted in well with the mechanistic ideas that were becoming so popular. Unhappily, the calculations were wrong.

The correct solution was to be offered soon after the publication in 1673 of Descartes's work. This solution came from Isaac Newton (1642–1727). It might perhaps be most clearly explained in something like a narrative form.

During 1665 and 1666 Newton was at his home at Woolsthorpe in Lincolnshire because of an outbreak of the plague at his university (Cambridge). This is where the famous story of the apple comes in. He was meditating about the problems of planetary motion and his thoughts were disturbed by the soft sound of a falling apple. Of course there is nothing surprising about an apple falling, but it suggested to Newton that the same force of gravity which brought the apple to earth might pull the moon towards the earth, and so prevent the moon from flying off in a straight line. The problem thus was really of two parts: namely, to calculate centrifugal and centripetal forces and then to show that they applied in some fashion on a planetary scale.

If some heavy object like a stone is tied to a piece of string and then swung in a circle the stone attempts to pull away from your hand; its pull can be felt. If the string breaks, the stone flies away in a straight line in the direction it was moving at the time of the break. The outward pull is a centrifugal force. An inward pull is therefore required to keep the stone from flying away; such a pull is called a centripetal force. Now by 1666 Newton was already able to calculate such forces in respect of bodies of any mass moving at any speed in a circle of fixed radius. If the thought inspired by the apple was correct, that is, if the moon were really being prevented by the pull of the earth from flying off into space, the problem now was this: according to what law must the pull of the earth decrease as we go farther and farther away if it is to be just sufficient to keep the moon in its orbit? Put somewhat differently: if the earth's attraction, which makes the apple fall, is suitably lessened by distance, also affecting the moon to just the right extent to keep the moon in orbit, then, bearing in mind what is known about centrifugal forces and also of the laws laid down by Kepler about the elliptical orbits of planets, what is the law of that attraction? Newton deduced that it must weaken inversely as the square of the distance from the centre of the earth. This means that to compare the force of two bodies attracting each other at two different distances, we square each of those distances and then interchange them because the pull at a greater distance is smaller. For example, if we wish to compare the force of the pull at a distance of 5 miles with the force of the pull at a distance of 3 miles, we first square the two figures and get 25 and 9. But because the force at 5 miles is obviously less than that at 3 miles, then the ratio between the two forces is not as 25 is to 9, but as 9 is to 25. That is the point of Newton's Law.

The inverse square rule, he computed, was 'pretty nearly' correct if it was assumed that the earth's gravitational pull really did act upon the moon. But Newton did not at once publish his amazing proof. For one thing, he seems to have become for quite a long time interested in other things. For another, the triumph was not yet complete. This is because in his calculations he had assumed that the earth and the moon are simply points. But they are not; they are of considerable size. Thus he had not yet proved that the external gravitational attraction of a sphere could be computed as though its mass were concentrated at a point at the centre. He was searching for a universal law that every little bit of matter attracts every other little bit of matter with a force given by multiplying their mass together and then dividing by the square of the distance between them—to simplify matters it has not been mentioned until now that whereas the inverse square rule gives the ratio of the force attracting the two bodies, the actual amount of that force Newton supposed to be given by multiplying their masses together. If this sounds difficult, we had better go back to the apple again. If we think of the earth as consisting of a very large number of small bits, then the bits near to the apple will exert a much greater pull on the apple than do the bits that are farther away—very much greater than those, say, on the opposite side of the earth to where the apple is falling. Newton therefore had to calculate whether the pull of the parts of a body arranged in a sphere is the same as the pull exerted by all the matter of the earth if it were concentrated at its centre. The proof that this was so was extremely difficult, but by about 1685 Newton had completed it and found that in fact, granting the truth of the inverse square law, such a surprising result was exactly the case. It was not so on any other assumption. The earth's gravitational pull really was such that it operated as if it were concentrated at a point. Thus the inverse square rule, not fully established in 1665 and 1666, was proved true.

It was now clear that there was no serious objection to the assumption that every bit of matter attracted every other bit of matter throughout the universe according to this rule, and by making this assumption Newton had the entire key to the problem of the motions of the heavenly bodies in his hand. All the motions of the planets and the behaviour of falling bodies were explicable according to the one rule. Not only that: further calculations showed how perfect his theory of 'general gravitation', as we may now call it, was for all the movements of satellites, the orbits of comets, as well as the movements of the tides. All obeyed the same rule. The triumph was stupendous—and complete.

Newton published all this in his great book *Philosophiae Naturalis Principia Mathematica* (*The Mathematical Principles of Natural Philosophy*), usually now referred to as the *Principia*. It appeared in 1687. Had it only contained the theory of universal gravitation and the proofs of that theory, the work would have sufficed to win an immortal fame for its author. But the book contained far more. It began by a statement of his laws of motion, for which he owed a great deal to Galileo and Kepler. The laws are:

(1) 'Every body continues in its state of rest or of uniform motion in a straight line, except in so far as it is compelled to change that state by impressed forces.' This is simple enough to understand now, and probably everyone is familiar with some of its effects; for instance, if a person is travelling very fast in a car and then suddenly applies the brakes, the car slows down very quickly, but his body, which has been travelling at the same speed as the car, continues to proceed—which is why his head might then hit the windscreen.

(2) 'Change of motion is proportional to the moving force impressed, and takes place in the direction of the straight line in which such force is impressed.' An easy example of this is a fall under gravity, because the force is fixed and therefore the rate of change of motion is fixed also; thus in a fall from rest the velocity is 32·2 feet per second at the end of the first second; at the end of the second second it is 64·4 feet per second; and at the end of the third second it is 96·6 feet per second, and so on.

(3) 'Reaction is always equal and opposite to action'; that is to say, the actions of two bodies on each other are always equal and directly opposite. For example, if you push on a trolley, even when it begins to move, we must assume that the trolley pushes back on you with just exactly the force you are exerting on it.

Newton then discussed the inverse square law, proved Kepler's laws of planetary motion, and developed the laws of pendulum motion. He carried on to a full discussion of motion, not in a vacuum or in empty space but in surroundings that offer resistance; in the course of this he proved that the vortices of Descartes were impracticable. There followed a complete account of the motions of the planets, and he showed how irregularities of the moon's path were caused by the pull of the sun, and explained the movements of the tides and comets.

The book is not only an account of the planetary system. It defines mass and the laws of motion, and underlying all the dynamics and astronomy are concepts of absolute space and time which were to prove adequate for scientists for two hundred years. The book does even more. It was to give science the characteristics it has had ever since. This refers to more than method, although of course it is true that he did take the known facts, form an hypothesis which fitted them and which could be expressed in mathematical terms, go on to deduce logical and mathematical consequences from the hypothesis, then once more check these consequences with the facts by means of observation and experiment—and as we have already seen, that is approximately a description of modern scientific procedure. But it does more than establish scientific method inasmuch as Newton also laid down, in a sense, limits to what should and could be attempted by that method. A few of his remarks will illustrate this. He says: 'To derive two or three general Principles of motion from Phaenomena, and afterwards to tell us how the Properties and Actions of all corporeal Things follow from those manifest Principles, would be a very great step in Philosophy, though the Causes of those Principles were not yet discover'd: and therefore I scruple not to propose the Principles of Motion above mention'd, they being of very general Extent, and leave their Causes to be found out.' In other words, he is confining himself strictly to what is measurable, and making no attempt to postulate hidden causes which are not based upon at least the possibility of experiment; as he says: 'Such occult Qualities . . . are uncapable of being discovered and made manifest . . . and put a stop to the Improvement of natural Philosophy.' Even more significantly, he did not say that he has proved that bodies do attract each other at a distance; he merely says that calculations work out accurately on that assumption.

He is thus confining the results of science to mathematical measuring, although it is true that in the preface to the *Principia* he seems to contemplate the possibility of explaining all natural phenomena in terms of matter and motion. In case this point seems a little obscure, one might liken his conception of the scientist's role to that of a clerk in a booking office at a railway station. At the end of the day the clerk could tell very accurately how many people had paid for tickets to different destinations, and how much money they had paid, but could offer no guess as to their character and only a very vague guess about their reasons for making the journey.

The book gained an immediate success in England, and the Newtonian discoveries and methods won very rapid and widespread acclaim. The general admiration was summed up by the well-known couplet of Pope:

> Nature and Nature's laws lay hid in night,
> God said, 'Let Newton be!' and all was light.

It speeded the triumph of the mechanical philosophy, because, although Newton's theory of gravitation was not in agreement with the sort of mechanism expressed by Descartes's notions of vortices, considered as a system of physical nature which embraces all the motions of the heavens and all phenomena of matter in motion, Newton's system was mechanistic. (It should now be clear that the use of the word 'mechanistic' on page 25, while accurate enough, as far as it went, can now be extended; it means asking about previous causes and answering them in the limited and mathematical way that Newton did.)

Orthodox religion was bound to be struck a terrible blow. Newton himself was an extremely religious man, though it is not insignificant that he was a Unitarian. He said that the 'most beautiful system of the Sun, planets and Comets could only proceed from the counsel and dominion of an intelligent and powerful Being', and that God 'endures for ever and is everywhere present, and by existing always and everywhere, he constitutes duration and space'. But his work was used in the eighteenth century as a basis first for deism and then for atheism. He was more successful than he would have liked in chasing the gods from the universe. Men were soon to forget about heaven, and to chase Happiness—blessed word of the eighteenth century and after. The departure of the gods mattered little, because the human intellect had made such dazzling discoveries, was so evidently about to solve all problems, that Man and his all-conquering Reason could now be worshipped instead. Alexander Pope was soon to say:

> The proper study of mankind is man.

At the close of the century some Frenchmen were to be found worshipping the Goddess of Reason, impersonated by a lady of more than dubious reputation, in the Cathedral of Notre-Dame.

(ii) Other sciences

Probably the most important and most startling advance apart from the revolution in mechanics and astronomy was in anatomy and physiology, more particularly the latter. Modern anatomy really began with Jean Fernel (1497–1558), and was considerably developed by several others, of whom the best known was Andreas Vesalius (1514–64). He taught at various universities, including that at Padua, which was especially renowned for its medical teaching, and in 1543 published *De Humani Corporis Fabrica* (*On the Fabric of the Human Body*). This was a book on anatomy based not on the authority of the ancients, but on his own dissecting work. Until his time the chief authority was the great Hellenistic teacher Galen, and ever since the first century doctors were blinded by the undoubted genius of Galen to such an extent that if their own observations differed from his teachings their usual reaction was to conclude that their observations must be imperfect. Vesalius himself accepted most of Galen's work, but did add to knowledge about the bones, the veins, the abdominal organs, and even the brain. His book made a most noteworthy advance too because of the excellence of its illustrations.

The wonder of the succeeding age certainly was the discovery of the true circulation of the blood by William Harvey (1578–1657). Harvey's discovery is of interest to us for two reasons. One of these reasons is purely medical, and therefore need not detain students of history. It is simply that every tissue of the body is dependent on that tissue being bathed directly or indirectly by blood which comes to it as oxygen-bearing arterial blood, and leaves it as venous blood carrying away the products of activity. In other words, any serious advance in medical knowledge is impossible without a correct notion of the way in which the blood circulates. The second reason which makes Harvey's discovery interesting is that it was achieved by methods typical of the Scientific Revolution and added to the 'mechanical philosophy' what seemed like confirmation from a rather unexpected quarter.

The full story—it is a fascinating one—cannot be told here. Briefly, the old opinion was that the blood ebbed and flowed in the veins. Moreover, there was not one sort of blood, but two; one sort ran from the liver through the veins to all parts of the body, but some of this sort found its way through the central partition of the heart (called the septum) and mixed with 'vital spirits' to become another sort of blood, performing in its course through the arteries a vivifying work as compared with the purely nutritive work of the first sort. All this involves all kinds of errors. The direct passage of air from the lungs to the heart was one of these; also the idea that the chief action of the heart was the drawing of the blood into the heart and not its expulsion. The central error was that the blood's 'ebb and flow' was chiefly operated by the right ventricle (the heart has two main chambers, or ventricles, divided by the thick muscle called the septum) and that the blood passed from one ventricle to the other through the septum.

The whole matter had exercised a large number of very clever scholars for some time, and although important advances were made, the correct solution remained as remote as ever, chiefly because the authority of Galen seemed to prevent men from fitting any new facts or observations into anything but a Galenic conceptual scheme. For instance, in 1574 Fabricius wrote a most important book describing certain valves in the veins. These valves operated only to check the outward passage of blood from the heart and through the veins. From this he might have realized that therefore blood in the veins flows towards the heart, on a return journey as it were. However, Fabricius missed this point because he was anxious to preserve the correctness of Galen's teaching, and so produced an explanation which was wholly mistaken. What was needed therefore was fresh observation, it is true, but also a new way of looking at old facts.

This was supplied in William Harvey's book *De Motu Cordis* (*On the Motion of the Heart*) (to give it its abbreviated title) which was published in 1628. It was the fruit of at least nine years of research. He saw Fabricius had missed the point, that the valves must be preventing blood going from the veins to the limbs, and that it must be going through the arteries and returning via the veins. He made a profound study of the fibrous structure of the heart and showed that its real activity was to pump blood outwards, not to draw it inwards. He simply regarded the whole system as a piece of hydraulic machinery, treating the heart solely as a pump, the veins and arteries as pipes, the valves as if they were simply mechanical valves, the blood itself as merely a fluid, thus leaving 'spirits' out of the reckoning altogether. Then, led by a series of steps each based on observations of actual dissections, as he himself said by 'repeated vivisections', he came to the great discovery. He pointed out that if we multiply the volume of blood driven forward by each beat of the heart by the number of beats that take place in half an hour, we find that the heart deals in this time with as much blood as there is in the whole body, or in one hour the heart throws out more blood than the whole weight of a man. It was utterly impossible to explain where all that blood came from and where it could go except on the assumption that it went streaming through the whole body again and again in continuous circulation. He then went on to follow this circulation.

'I finally saw that the blood, forced by the action of the left ventricle into the arteries, was distributed to the body at large and its several parts, in the same manner as it is sent through the lungs impelled by the right ventricle into the right pulmonary artery, and that it then passed through the veins and along the vena cava, and so round to the left ventricle.'

Thus was achieved another complete triumph—by taking existing knowledge, by fresh observation, by a wholly original conceptual scheme, by carefully weighing and measuring and also by treating the body as a piece of mechanism without reference to any occult 'spirits'. It opened the way to very great advances in medicine, but can hardly be said to have done Harvey much immediate good, for many of his patients left him in disgust and mistrust. Yet it seemed to show that the body was as amenable to investigation by mechanical analogy and physical measurement as were the planets.

All that has been said so far is by no means a history of the Scientific Revolution, but merely a bare mention of some of its most famous manifestations; it is hoped that they will suffice to show something at least of the characteristics of that Revolution. But lest the impression should have been created that men like Kepler, Galileo, Newton, and Harvey were solitary geniuses who by themselves made that Revolution, it should be re-emphasized that in fact they were not alone, but the greatest among many clever men; they belonged to their age. To emphasize this point still more, mention can now appropriately be made of some further examples of the scientific progress of the times, all of them in some way significant.

Physics, as well as Navigation, owed a debt to William Gilbert of Colchester (1540–1603). The existence of magnetic phenomena had been known from antiquity, but the growing use of the mariner's compass from as early as the twelfth century made the investigation of magnetism something more than the satisfaction of curiosity. Gilbert, in one of the most masterly experimental studies ever made, investigated the way magnets behaved. He studied the mutual attraction and repulsion of magnets and correctly formulated the rules governing their behaviour. Using Robert Norman's discovery of dip (the angle at which a magnetic needle points below the horizontal), he devised what he hoped would be an important navigational aid, since dip is dependent on latitude. From this he inferred correctly that the earth itself was a huge magnet but he thought, mistakenly as it turned out, that the magnetic poles were the geographical poles. He saw that the compass needle was not attracted to some northerly star as had been supposed by some of his predecessors, but pointed to the North because of the tendency of the needle to lie along a magnetic meridian. The fact that the compass needle did not point to the True North but suffered a declination he explained by the hypothesis of the attractive force of the raised land of the continents. The fact that declination or variation from True North changes year by year was discovered later, in 1622, by Edmund Gunter. (This is useful to navigators; it is one reason why we nowadays get few repetitions of the fate of a ship's captain bewailed by one Edward Wright in 1610—the captain on a voyage to the Azores from England utterly failed to find them 'and after long seeking not able to find it, for shame and sorrow cast himself overboard'.) Galileo himself made many other contributions to Physics; for example, he was the first to assign a rate of vibration to a sound of known pitch, and attempted to measure the speed of light. In 1643 Torricelli constructed a mercury barometer, and then Pascal arranged for his brother-in-law to take a barometer up a mountain in France (the Puy de Dôme), and the height of the mercury was seen to diminish as he ascended because the pressure was becoming less, thus showing that the column was held up by the air, and not by Nature's 'abhorrence of a vacuum', as taught by the Aristotelians. A little later a man called von Guericke, who lived in Magdeburg, made the first air-pumps. This astonished the world, but not as much as did Newton's researches into light. In 1666 Newton showed by experiment that white light was compound, consisting of rays which were refracted to different extents, and that each colour was not a 'qualification' of light but was a property of rays of a particular 'refrangibility'. This was a most fascinating expression of a quality in terms of a quantity, adding therefore fresh support to a purely mechanical philosophy of the universe, since even colour, long regarded as a quality, was now shown to be analysable in quantitative ways. Indeed, all the discoveries mentioned above are noteworthy examples of an untrammelled outlook and were reached by fresh thought and careful experiments.

The huge part played by measurement in the Scientific Revolution should now be obvious—it was largely a matter of correct measurement allied to fruitful conceptual schemes, as we have seen. But that implies the existence of adequate measuring instruments. A good deal of development took place in these. Accurate measurement of length became possible with the vernier scale (1631) and micrometer (1638). Scarcely less important was the accurate measuring of time. The best clocks before about the year 1660 had an error of plus or minus twenty minutes a day. They were improved by Huygens's pendulum, Hooke's balance-spring, and Harrison's method of compensation for variations in temperature (1757). It should be added that Galileo invented the thermometer. Alcohol thermometers were made from about the middle of the seventeenth century. The mercury barometer was in use about 1645, and pressure-gauges soon followed, as did photometry (the measurement of quantity of light), and simple electrometers.

If it was important to have accurate measuring instruments, it was evidently even more important to have adequate measuring methods; that is, an advanced knowledge of mathematics. Luckily, adequate mathematical methods were available when needed. Much of the Greek knowledge of mathematics were available in translations of Euclid. The Arabs invented algebra, and Europeans soon learnt much from them, although about the beginning of the sixteenth century they were still far more at home with geometry, and consequently did a great deal of what would now be done by algebra by using geometry. This made things difficult; for instance such concepts as x, x^2, x^3 were thought of as single lines, areas, and solids, and so the concept of x^4 was exceedingly difficult to work with. But by the end of the sixteenth century mathematicians could solve not only quadratics but also cubics and even biquadratics, and had acquired a reasonable knowledge of trigonometry. Of enormous value to astronomical calculations was the invention of logarithms in 1614 by Napier. Co-ordinate geometry resulted from the work of several seventeenth-century mathematicians, Descartes playing an especially prominent part in this. The differential and integral calculus was invented independently by Newton while staying in Lincoln in 1665–6 and by the German philosopher, Leibniz. The differential and integral calculus is the instrument of almost all higher mathematics. It is concerned with problems relating to rates of change. To give an elementary example, the calculation of the rates of variation of a tangent from any point of a parabola, that is the calculation of two quantities which vary continuously, the one with the other, is a problem of the differential calculus. If this is not very clear, one can imagine the curve of a mountainside. On that the tangent will correspond to the steepness at any point and will be given by the rate at which the height varies with the horizontal distance. If when you climb it and advance one yard horizontally the height increases by one foot, then the steepness is 1/3. The next advance of one yard horizontally may increase the height by only 99/100 of a foot, in which case the slope will diminish by 1/100. But obviously the slope will vary with every tiny bit advanced. The difficult problem is to find the slope with absolute accuracy at any point; it is a problem of the rate at which height varies with horizontal advance. The integral calculus is a sort of reverse problem; given, say, information about rates of change, one has to find how the one quantity varies with the other.

Little progress was made in chemistry. The Aristotelian four elements of earth, air, fire, and water, were believed in even during the eighteenth century. However, long before that, a theory, apparently derived from the Arabs, had it that there were fundamental 'principles' of sulphur, mercury, and salt, but these words were not used in the way understood by modern chemists; that is, as the names of substances. A determined attempt to use chemistry, if we may use the word, for purposes of healing, was made by many people, of whom the best known was von Hohenheim (1493–1541), also known as Paracelsus. He poured scorn on the writings of Galen, but himself was as much an alchemist as anything else; he believed in the theory of transmutation (and in wilder notions). His attachment to the three 'principles' was violently attacked by the greatest of the iatrochemists (those trying to use chemistry for healing), Johann van Helmont (1580–1644). He contended that there were only two elements, air and water. He was famous for an experiment in which he put a willow tree in a tub of earth; although nothing but water was added, the tree gained 164 lb. in weight over five years; this was taken to show that water had been transmuted into solid matter, since the earth in the tub had lost no weight. He also introduced the word 'gas', but this was not in the least understood by him in its modern meaning. Some useful discoveries were made by Johann Glauber (1604–70). He described for the first time the preparation of spirits of salts (hydrochloric acid), sodium sulphate, and possibly chlorine.

The most famous name in this field is that of Robert Boyle (1627–91). His epitaph, which does not improve with repetition, said that he was 'the Father of Chemistry and Uncle of the Earl of Cork'. Some doubt might arise as to whether he should be regarded as the assassin of the old chemistry rather than as the father of modern chemistry. At least, his best-known work *The Sceptical Chymist* (published in 1661 and 1679) rejected the 'forms' of Plato and the 'four elements' of Scholasticism, and equally he rejected the 'principles' or 'essences' of salt, sulphur, and mercury. It had been taught in this connexion that fire resolved things into their different elements, but he pointed out, for instance, that gold withstands fire and quite certainly yields nothing resembling salt, sulphur, or mercury, yet it can be alloyed and also dissolved and recovered in its original form. Instead, he suggested something much more like the modern definition of a chemical element. In spite of the recognition which he has received in this connexion, it may be doubted if his ideas were truly modern, or even particularly fruitful. For Boyle was essentially a physicist, and he was really trying to explain and prove that the processes of chemistry were explicable in terms of our old friend the mechanical philosophy; he believed that all substances were made up of the same fundamental particles. This was really not taking him towards the modern conception of a chemical element, but away from it. However, there is no doubt about the value of his attitude and of much of his work. To mention one or two examples: he prepared phosphorus, isolated methyl alcohol from the products of the distillation of wood, and studied the form of crystals as a guide to chemical structure. 'Boyle's law' is well known—that the volume of a given quantity of air is inversely proportional to the pressure. There is thus no doubt about the importance of Boyle as a figure of the Scientific Revolution.

Finally, although it remains true that chemistry did not make any very great strides until the end of the eighteenth century, and biology until the nineteenth, it is perhaps worth mentioning, if only as indicative of the great scientific activity of the times, that even in biology John Ray (1627–1705) made great advances in the scientific classification of plants and animals.

The seventeenth century, then, truly saw the beginnings of what it is probably correct to regard as the most important new thing in the history of the world since the coming of Christianity. While it would be inappropriate to describe its later developments in a political history book, it is hoped that enough has been said to illustrate the nature of that Revolution.

But we are here chiefly concerned with political events; our interest is not so much in the history of science as such but in its effects on other things. Something of the ways in which the new scientific ideas were disseminated, and of their effects on political and other events, will appear in the narrative.

3 · The Despotism of Louis XIV, 1661-1715

Voltaire described the late seventeenth century as 'Le Siècle de Louis Quatorze', and indeed to such an extraordinary degree was not only France but also Europe dominated by the power and the personality of Louis that, before saying anything about that power, it will not be irrelevant to say something about its possessor.

The easiest and most obvious thing to say about him is that there never has been a more kingly king; nobody has ever known better how to look and play the royal part, the 'métier de roi'. Not tall, but of handsome and dignified appearance, he filled all with admiration. That masterly gossip, Saint-Simon, wrote in his *Mémoires* that Louis had 'an exterior so unique and incomparable as to lend infinite distinction to his slightest actions . . . proportions such as a sculptor would choose to model, a perfect countenance and the grandest air ever vouchsafed to man, a natural grace and singular charm which has never perhaps been equalled'. Louis also had beautiful manners, those of a true gentleman; he was courteous to all, including (what was rare in those days) servants. Not for him the loutish displays of ill-temper and guttersnipe abuse which often disgrace upstarts of the Napoleon sort; as Saint-Simon says, he had 'a courtesy always grave, always dignified, always distinguished'. These are attractive qualities, but they do not make a man great. There is no doubt, however, that Louis had at least one of the attributes which characterize most great men—a staggering capacity for hard work. (He also found time for a long succession of mistresses.) A real flaw in his character was his insatiable appetite for flattery, however absurd, 'which he swallowed with unfailing relish', as Saint-Simon says. So far there is agreement about him. Estimates of his wisdom vary. At the worst, he has been called 'the most criminally stupid man in history' (by David Ogg). Perhaps it is better to form one's own opinion after studying Louis's actions, and this will first involve an examination of the sort of power he wielded.

Louis is often called a despot. In theory, there is some justice in this, for nowhere was the theory of Divine Right pushed further than in France. He was held to be the absolute master over his subjects' lives and property. He could rob them, kill them, sell a whole province to the king of England if he wished, and they would have no right to offer criticism, much less resistance. As we have seen, Bishop Bossuet called him a god, and in fact he was worshipped by his courtiers in a way that was almost blasphemous. The Church in France upheld strongly the view that to resist him would be as bad as to resist God, for he was appointed by God; it held to the view that, if he made one suffer, humble resignation was the only correct attitude. Happiness in this life was in any case not something to be expected but something to be shunned because it distracted souls from worship of God. Grim were the punishments that could fall on anyone rash enough to question either political or religious authority. Death could be the penalty for even being suspected of talking against the royal authority, while blasphemers could have their tongues pierced by a red-hot iron.

So much for the theory. In fact, Louis did not behave with a total lack of responsibility; he did not sell provinces to the king of England. He recognized that there was some truth in Bossuet's warning to kings that 'although their power comes from on high . . . they must employ it with fear and restraint, as a thing of which God will demand an account'. It should be noted too that restless writers challenged the Church's submissive attitude with more and more impunity as Louis's reign went on. So Divine Right of Kings was not so ridiculous in practice. (Nor was it in theory much more ridiculous than many other political theories—it does not seem possible to construct an unassailable theory to support any system of political beliefs. Political theories almost always are made in general terms, but are really intended as weapons for or against particular political circumstances. Divine Right was an answer to Papal claims, and in a religious age it anyway seemed perfectly natural to ascribe anyone's position, whether king or peasant, to God's wishes.)

So we can now turn to Louis's government in practice. The King attempted to guide and direct the whole business of government himself. Indeed, in his *Mémoires pour l'année 1661* he blames himself for the 'fault' of not doing this sooner. In 1671 he wrote an account of his activities in which he describes himself as conducting the whole administration down to the smallest details: he says that he knew at any given moment the number, etc., of his troops, and gave all the orders for them; that he dealt with all foreign nations, read all dispatches and personally answered some of them and directed secretaries about the remainder; that he directed all the income and expenditure of the State, and so on. On 9 March 1661 he announced that henceforward nothing would be done in connexion with any sort of State business without his order. In the sense that he attempted to survey everything this stupendous claim had a large measure of truth in it. But one man cannot even make all the necessary decisions in a big State, still less carry them out himself. Louis was the very active head of a huge administrative machine, which was itself only partly of his own creation.

It is here useful to distinguish between the government, that is the small number of men who met and made all major decisions of policy, and the administration, that is the officials who carried on the day-to-day tasks connected with their departments, such as the army, taxation, and so on. In this sense, the government consisted chiefly of a council, usually called the *Conseil d'en haut*. Its composition varied, especially very early in the reign, when it often included an army marshal (Turenne more than any other). Later it consisted almost always of three men, who were at first Fouquet, Le Tellier, and de Lionne. In September 1661 Fouquet, the dishonest *surintendant des finances*, was disgraced and replaced by Colbert, and later Le Tellier was replaced by his son, the Marquis de Louvois. They met under the chairmanship of the King as often as he thought it necessary, and discussed any important matter of policy and then decided on a course of action. The membership of the *Conseil d'en haut* caused a great deal of pained surprise among the nobility, for they were all chosen from the middle class. But the reason was simple, and Louis explained it himself (in his *Mémoires*):

'Il n'était pas de mon intérêt de prendre des sujets d'une qualité plus éminente. Il fallait, avant toutes choses, établir ma propre réputation et faire connaître au public, par le rang même d'où je les prenais, que mon intention n'était pas de partager mon autorité avec eux.' ('It was not in my interest to take subjects of a more exalted station.

Above everything else, I had to establish my own reputation and to let the public know by the very station in life that I chose them from, that it was not my intention to share my authority with them.')

To make them even more dependent on his pleasure, Louis never gave the members of the *Conseil*, as such, any formal title or letters patent appointing them as ministers, as had previously been done; he simply asked them to attend and thus could get rid of them again, if he wished, by not asking them to attend.

For similar reasons Louis did not permit the Chancellor to have any great authority. The Chancellor had always been regarded as one of the very great officers of State—the more so since the *Conseil d'en haut* played little part in legislation, because all the ordinances of the King had to be sealed, and the Chancellor was the keeper of the Royal Seals. The Chancellor was also head of all the law courts, but neither he nor his royal master could do very much there because the officers of the courts bought their posts and were therefore virtually irremovable. Under Louis the high administration of justice saw little change. It was not so with the finances. The monarchy had in the past wavered about their control, sometimes the finances were under a *surintendant*, sometimes under a council. After the disgrace of Fouquet the office of *surintendant* was not revived, but by degrees the finances fell entirely under the control of Colbert, with the title of Controller-General.

Apart from justice and finances, all the other great administrative departments were under the direction of four Secretaries of State. Le Tellier was in charge of war, La Vrillière looked after the affairs concerning the *R.P.R.* (*Religion Prétendue Réformée*; the French Protestants or 'Huguenots'), Lionne saw to diplomacy, and in time Colbert took charge of all the rest—all the marine, finances, King's Household, agriculture, industry, commerce, colonies, buildings. Thus, in practice, the government controlled the administration closely, because the members of the *Conseil d'en haut* were Secretaries of State as well, and directed nearly all the great administrative departments themselves. Two other administrative devices are worthy of mention. The first was a meeting held twice weekly, of the four members of the *Conseil d'en haut*, in their capacity as Secretaries of State, with the other Secretaries of State. Any decision reached was sent out as an order from the King and this body, which was called the *Conseil des Dépêches*. Thus the King could take the advice of the *Conseil d'en haut* or of the larger *Conseil des Dépêches*. He was in no way obliged to work with the advice of either; indeed some orders went out after a consultation between the King and only one of the Secretaries. The other council of note was the *Conseil de conscience*. This was rarely anything but a meeting between the King and the priest who recommended Church appointments and promotions, and that usually meant a talk between the King and his confessor. Such was the governmental machine and, though it might sound cumbersome, it was flexible and efficient.

As for local government, this was supervised by agents of the King, the *intendants*, of whom there were about thirty. These had their origins in the sixteenth century, and at first were given temporary commissions to investigate local finances and justice. Under Louis XIV they became permanently attached to a taxation district (or *généralité*), and an *intendant* rarely moved from his own *généralité*. A *Mémoire* of 1663 or 1664 (the date is uncertain) drawn up by Colbert clarified their powers. From then on the *intendants* closely supervised the finances, which were assessed and collected by the officials known as *trésoriers de France* and *élus*; in this they were helped by officials called *subdélégués*. They also looked after justice, and were also supposed to guard against any abuses committed by any influential persons, whether they belonged to the nobility or the Church or to officialdom. Later, Colbert instructed them to extend their authority to municipal government as well. The *intendants* became almost local kings, but they were themselves under the close scrutiny of the central government, for each Secretary of State supervised several *intendants*. In practice, a disproportionate share of this burden fell upon Colbert.

It will have been noticed that the foregoing sketch of the French system of government, a system that remained fairly constant during the remainder of the period of the *ancien régime*, that is, until the Revolution of 1789, repeatedly mentions the name of Colbert. An examination of the activities of Louis and his government shows that most of what was constructive was the work of Colbert.

Colbert worked fifteen hours a day, and achieved so much that even so he must have been working at high pressure. Most of his effort was aimed at making France and Louis rich. He realized that a poor country was a weak one, and he realized too, casting a jealous eye at the Dutch, that in comparison with theirs, French commerce was pitifully small. The Dutch had about 16,000 ships, even the English had then about a quarter of that number, while France's mercantile marine numbered a beggarly five or six hundred. Colbert thought that it would only be possible to increase French commerce by taking some from the Dutch; he therefore thought of commerce as a 'money war'. He also thought that France could not be strong unless it had what is nowadays called a favourable balance of trade. France must sell more abroad than she bought, and must carry her goods in her own ships to avoid having to pay ruinous freight charges to the ubiquitous Dutch carriers. In this way France would build up a large store of hard cash without which the State could not be strong. (It has long been usual to describe this and some allied notions as 'Mercantilism'.)[1] He promised to make Louis the 'master of the world'. It was natural therefore for him to regard productive industry as of prime importance.

French industry was chiefly concentrated in the towns, where most of it was organized by *corporations*, who regulated it through their own tribunals known as *jurandes*. There was also a good deal of 'free' industry, some of it in the towns, but most of it in the countryside, where it was often in the hands of capitalist organizers. Industry lacked capital, so Colbert by tireless propaganda persuaded some of the moneyed people in the country to lend to industry—he tackled not only financiers but anyone with money, even bishops. Another serious weakness was a shortage of skilled labour. Colbert tried to remedy this in two ways. One was to induce skilled foreign artisans to live in France (much to the annoyance of the governments of their own countries). His recruiting agents were the French ambassadors, who applied themselves to this unwonted task with such success that thousands of craftsmen came to France—tapestry and paper workers from Holland, silk workers from Italy, engineers and shipbuilders from England, miners from Germany and Scandinavia, and so on. The other way was to have Frenchmen trained. So he set up or re-endowed various schools, like the Academy of Painting and Sculpture, which gave instruction in drawing, geometry, etc., the Academy of Architecture, which gave lessons in mechanics, masonry, etc., and the School of the Gobelins, which taught industrial drawing.

He also founded State industrial enterprises; these were regulated by the Royal Ordinance of 1673. The usual system was for the State to advance money to capitalists, and in this way Colbert encouraged not only existing industries such as the cloth industry, already established in such places as Abbeville, but was instrumental in founding such new manufactures as those started by Dalliez de la Tour, who collaborated with Colbert in founding factories for making anchors, cannons, tin, etc. A lot of money was advanced by the State in this way, sometimes as much as half a million *livres* in a year, but a great deal more was spent

---

[1] See Chapter 1.

on industrial enterprises such as foundries and tapestry-making. Art was encouraged by the same means, mostly for the embellishment of the numerous royal residences, so much so that Colbert complained (it was done merely because the King liked art), but the money at least helped to make French art supreme in Europe, although to spend ten times as much on this as on helping French industry did not please the dour minister. He did not realize that this entailed such improvements in design that industry benefited from it indirectly. Colbert also tried to regulate the quality of goods. This met with opposition, but he held on his way and at least helped to give French goods a better reputation abroad. He tried to bring all trades under *corporation* control. This was partially successful in the towns but an almost total failure in the countryside.

These enterprises prospered, but not for the benefit of the workmen, whose wages were low and whose hours were long. Colbert tried to stop them from organizing themselves, but failed: there were even strikes (e.g. in 1677 and 1679) in the royal dockyards themselves. Attempts to strengthen the *corporations*, the better to bring all industry under government supervision, were not wholly successful inasmuch as he also sapped them by State competition. The whole system was too rigid to be permanently successful, but Colbert certainly increased the wealth of France.

His young industry needed protection and fresh markets. A moderate tariff was introduced in 1664, but this was very greatly increased in 1667, the earlier dues being doubled and in some cases trebled. This was aimed directly against the Dutch; it was a sort of declaration of economic war which soon in fact helped to cause a shooting war. Attempts to find fresh markets were made through commercial consuls, whose number Colbert greatly increased, especially in the Levant, by special trade missions to cities such as Hamburg, and by commercial treaties such as that with the Hanse in 1665. To supply these markets he tried to found big commercial companies, but he encountered little enthusiasm among Frenchmen for these; their reactions varied from the cold apathy of the Marseillais to the point-blank hostility of the men of Rouen. Still less was the general desire to advance money for these projects, and the pressure which Colbert applied to those with money to part with some of it gained a mediocre result. Slightly more successful were his colonial activities. For instance, the French settlement in Canada in 1663 only numbered about 2,500 people. A royal regiment was sent there, and the colony furnished with a governor, an *intendant*, and a council, and Quebec was supplied with a bishop. The colony certainly grew in size, although this was not necessarily the result of this abundance of temporal and spiritual guidance, whose efficacy was dubious (at least there were so many crooks in Canada in the next century that large numbers were hoping to be conquered by the English so that they might be spared an investigation by the French authorities). Exploration was encouraged and the land adjacent to Lakes Huron and Superior seized for France. Colbert also founded a West Indies Company in 1664, and, because all this needed protection of another sort, he made strenuous and successful attempts to improve the navy. This in 1661 was a moribund force of about twenty warships, some of which were unfit for service. Colbert at first bought battleships abroad, then had them made in France after organizing the necessary industries. He founded the naval ports of Brest and Rochefort (Toulon and Dunkirk were founded later by Vauban). By 1667 France had a hundred well-found warships, and ten years later nearly three hundred.

It would not have been much use to create and protect all this wealth if none of it reached the government. In fact, finance was the Achilles' heel of the French monarchy, and remained so until the Revolution of 1789. One glaring weakness was the bare-faced dishonesty of almost everybody connected with the taxes—when Colbert took over their direction the taxpayers paid about 81 million *livres* a year, of which about 54 million vanished before reaching the Treasury. This was by no means the worst feature of a system so disastrous as to play a major role in the collapse of the monarchy in the next century, so a sketch of that system would here be appropriate. Depending on one's sense of humour, it may also provide a little comic relief.

The chief direct tax was the *taille*, which in about a third of France (the *Pays d'États*, i.e. provinces more recently added to France which still retained their own Provincial Estates) was a land tax, from which land cultivated by nobles or owned by the Church was exempt. In the remainder of France (the *Pays d'Élections*) the *taille* was personal, and nobles, clergy, and many officials were exempt. The tax fell entirely on those least able to pay because, quite apart from these exemptions, the assessors (*élus*) placed the chief burden on those with the least influence, that is the poor. Collection was organized by middlemen or tax farmers. These were financiers who agreed to pay the government a fixed sum, and who then extorted as much as they could from the taxpayers. The most notorious of the indirect taxes was the *gabelle*, a tax on salt. In some provinces it was not levied at all; the others did not pay an equal amount. Everybody had to buy a fixed quantity, whether they wanted it or not, from government agents. The cost was high. Coarser grades for industrial purposes were cheaper, but to prevent people from consuming these sorts, officials often mixed poison with them; sometimes mistakes occurred with fatal results to the consumers. Utter lack of uniformity and of common sense marked most of the other indirect taxes. The *aides* (taxes on drinks and some other products) varied in amount from province to province. The *traites* (customs duties) were levied on goods entering or leaving the kingdom, in some cases on goods passing from one province to another, and also on those passing from one to another of the three main areas into which the country was divided for the collection of customs (called *l'étendue des cinq Grosses Fermes*, *le pays réputé étranger*, and *le pays étranger effectif*). These taxes were farmed out to tax-farmers, who practised great extortion, so that goods paid huge taxes on being moved about the country. France was not therefore a free trade area within itself, and in this most important respect lacked one of the most obvious characteristics of a modern State. Another device for raising money, which was practised on such a large scale that it has been described as the war-chest of the Bourbon monarchy, was the sale of offices, more especially of financial and judicial posts. This was done in two ways, an official taking up a post after the resignation of another had to pay a tax, and also the king created fresh posts in batches, and sold them to financiers, who in turn sold them to anyone wishing to buy. This absurd and ruinous system created a horde of officials who were usually both incompetent and unnecessary.

Various features of the financial system of the *ancien régime* thus stand out glaringly. The worst was that the privileged Orders of Nobles and Clergy, those, that is, usually best able to pay, paid nothing or very little, while the chief burden was placed on the poorest people. Also there was not even fairness within those narrow limits, some people and some provinces paid more than others. And while this system was hopelessly unfair, it was just as inefficient, for large amounts of the money so levied went to private financiers and not to the government. In time of real emergency, such as a war, the poor would be bled white, but the monarchy would be at its wit's end for money because it had no effective means of tapping the real wealth of the country. No French government before the Revolution of 1789 was able to make any fundamental reform of this state of affairs, for the confusion was too great and the vested interests too numerous and too powerful: a reform would have meant a revolt. In these circumstances, Colbert did as much as anyone could. One of his first moves was to tax large numbers of people who had been evading the *taille* by false claims to nobility (in Provence alone he found 1,257 of these impostors). He dismissed many officials, and made far better bargains with the tax-farmers, and redeemed many of the *rentes* which paid a high rate of interest. For the rest, he managed to enforce a relatively high standard of honesty throughout the whole system. All this was really nibbling at the problem; even so the results showed how rich a country France really was, for by 1667 the taxes yielded 95 million *livres*, of which the Treasury actually got 65 millions —more than twice the amount received in 1661.

That was a very gratifying result for the King; it was the chief reason why he was able to cut such a figure in France and in Europe. But really the results of Colbert's commercial and industrial efforts were more impressive. Symptomatic of this was the very great increase in the size of the mercantile marine, which grew to be four-fifths the size of the English, and a seventh of the Dutch. Industrial activity in France certainly increased enormously and the colonies for the most did well; for instance, the population of Canada increased fourfold. The finances, on the other hand, remained fundamentally hopeless, and Colbert, so far from being able to make the privileged classes pay the *taille*, so far from being able to stop the crying abuses of the local assessors who forced the poor to pay more than even such an unjust system legally demanded, could not alter such absurdities in the customs arrangements as that whereby some French territories on the eastern border were separated from the rest of France by a customs barrier while enjoying free trade with their foreign neighbours.

The government was no more able to effect any very striking reforms of the legal system, which was if anything a bigger muddle than was the fiscal. In addition to royal law, there were three other sorts: Roman law, which held sway over about half of France, more especially in the south, and which was greatly admired in the universities; feudal law, for although the kings had defeated the nobility's political ambitions they had been obliged to let them keep control over feudal law courts; and canon (i.e. Church) law, as lawsuits arising out of such matters as marriage were dealt with by ecclesiastical courts. The monarchy struggled to overrule and displace the first and third of these, but made no serious attempt to do anything about the second. Apart from this hotchpotch, there were in France no less than eighty different codes of civil law alone. All the government managed to do about this was to issue the *Ordonnance civile* of 1667, which did nothing to alter the laws themselves but merely codified procedure. The same thing applies to the *Ordonnance criminelle* of 1669: procedure was codified, but the laws were untouched, leaving barbarous punishments and not giving the accused the chance of a fair defence. Similarly the *Ordonnance du commerce* of 1673 and the *Ordonnance de la marine* of 1680 did little more than codify existing practice; and much the same is true of the *Code noir* of 1685, which did do something to alleviate the condition of the slaves in the colonies. True, the *Ordonnance des eaux et forêts* of 1669 was a much more useful affair; the forests were of vital importance to the fleet, and this measure resulted in their more efficient exploitation as well as in more revenues for the government. But the overall picture was of a government unable to do very much to reform the laws; this royal 'despotism' was, for example, too much afraid of the Church to legalize the lending of money at interest.

In the actual administration of what passed for justice, the government was still more helpless. Some magistrates flatly refused to obey the laws, and most of the magistrates were not only refractory but ignorant, dishonest, and biased in favour of the local nobles. As for the seigneurial (lords') law courts, their administration remained a crying scandal. Royal commissions, of which the most famous was the *Grands Jours d'Auvergne* (1665–6), investigated some of these and revealed how wickedly the nobles only too often treated the helpless peasants under their jurisdiction; some of the nobles were themselves found guilty of robbery and murder and of torturing peasants to death. Some of the offenders were executed, and the others were more careful afterwards. Yet practically no impression was produced on the majority of the magistrates; the constant succession of royal orders to them simply proved that nobody took any notice. It was therefore useless to rely on royal orders being carried out by the magistrates. The King increasingly used the *intendants* for this purpose, and their efforts were supplemented in Paris by the creation in 1667 of a 'Lieutenant-General of Police.' Similar officers were afterwards used in some of the other big towns.

A government which had such a very imperfect control over its subjects nevertheless attempted to exercise a very thorough control indeed over their minds. This involved a struggle with the Protestants as well as with some of the Catholics of France, and also an attempt to direct thought and culture generally.

The story of Louis's treatment of the Huguenots (French Protestants) is a mean and miserable one. They had been a menace to the existence of the French State in the sixteenth century, and had again taken up arms against the government even after the granting by King Henry IV of toleration by his famous Edict of Nantes of 1598. But since Richelieu dealt with their military power in the 1620s and then allowed them to go on worshipping in their own fashion, they had ceased to give any more trouble, and remained quiet even during the time of the *Frondes*, which showed that they could no longer be regarded as a danger to the security of the State. They were on the contrary one of its chief assets, because their ranks contained thousands of the most intelligent and hard-working people in the country, men who played a vital role in creating its prosperity. That was part of their undoing, for many of the Catholics were jealous of their commercial success and the *corporations de métiers* (guilds) petitioned the King to suppress them; similar petitions came from the clergy, and even from the Provincial Estates of Languedoc. At first Louis preferred to leave them in peace, especially in view of their loyalty during the *Frondes*, and hoped that in time they would all be converted to the Catholic faith. Their position weakened with the voluntary conversion of the great marshal Turenne in 1668.

This would not have mattered so much but for the fact that Louis himself became more pious. In his young days he had been a very active sinner, but as he grew older, like so many other sinners who grow too old to enjoy sinning as much as they did when younger and stronger, and who then display a very elevated anxiety about its evil effects on others, Louis showed a keen interest in religion. This interest was encouraged by his confessor, Father La Chaise, who led the clamour of the French clergy, which is understandable enough, and by the endless persuasion of Louis's mistress, later his wife, Madame de Maintenon, herself a pious convert from the Huguenot faith; there is possibly nothing irreconcilable between her status and her religious convictions, although to some modern eyes the combination might lack attractiveness. It was a slow business—Louis was not so very old in 1680—but gradually he was won over, and repressive measures against the Huguenots began.

Between 1679 and 1683 a whole host of Edicts attacked them in various ways. The law courts (the *Chambres de l'Édit*), which had contained a mixture of Catholic and Huguenot judges so as to ensure them a fair hearing, were suppressed in 1679. Then various employments were forbidden to Huguenots, heavier taxes were imposed on them, their academies were shut, their pastors were forbidden to stay longer than three years in any one place, their children were encouraged to leave their faith, and, when all this did not produce results fast enough, troops were billeted in their homes who inflicted insults and even torture on them, and many of their churches were shut. Previous attempts to bribe them to abandon their faith had not achieved much:

this persecution was more effective and thousands declared themselves converted. Then in 1685, anxious to glorify his reign, and to ensure his own salvation by some really signal act of piety, Louis revoked the Edict of Nantes. His other motive was that he could not bear to countenance the existence of Frenchmen who did not share his opinions, although the preamble to the Revocation stated, improbably, that he was fulfilling the intentions of his grandfather, of glorious memory, and that in any case the Edict of Nantes was no longer necessary since there were very few Huguenots left. Louis's Edict forbade the practice of the Protestant faith, whether in private houses or elsewhere, ordered all Protestant ministers to leave the country within a fortnight on pain of being sent to the galleys, forbade other Huguenots from leaving it, forbade all Protestant schools, and ordered all Huguenot children to be baptized as Catholics.

The text of the Edict also said that Huguenots were not to be molested, but in fact a bitter persecution of those who still refused conversion began. Hundreds, including women, were sent to the galleys, and many were executed. Then the Huguenots took to flight in thousands. Defying the law, about 200,000 of them, out of a total population of approximately nineteen million, fled abroad. This was a terrible blow to France, for the refugees included large numbers of highly skilled artisans and professional men; they included, for instance, three-quarters of the skilled silk workmen of Lyons, half the skilled workers in Rheims, and nearly the whole of the labour force of the hat-making industry of Nîmes. Nearly all of French industry—carpets, gloves, jewellery, shipbuilding, watch-making, and so on—was seriously affected. (Some of the watch-makers went to Switzerland, and it is from then that one dates the prosperity of the industry there.) France's loss was other countries' gain. They went chiefly to Protestant countries, Holland, England, Brandenburg (the government of the last-named even had the impudence to open a sort of immigration office for them in Paris). This hospitality was caused in part by a genuine sympathy, but also by a keen desire to get such valuable citizens, and foreign governments offered inducements such as temporary exemption from taxation in order to attract them. This act also cost the French government a great deal of goodwill abroad, where it was generally regarded with horrified amazement, so that besides largely ruining Colbert's efforts to build up French industry, Louis wrecked his own diplomatic position.

Was it worth it? Most of France thought so. Bossuet went as far as to call it a latter-day miracle, and Mme de Sévigné said in a letter of

28 October 1685, 'no king has done or ever will do anything more honourable'. It is true that some, like the great Marshal Vauban and the courtier Saint-Simon were appalled (the latter called it 'frightful'), but most Frenchmen did not like the Huguenot minority.

It is more difficult to judge if the Revocation was successful. The Huguenots in the Cevennes area were never crushed; they maintained a civil war against the government to the end of the reign and were bold enough to measure swords with no less a person than Marshal Villars; they proved such a terrible nuisance that in 1699 the government was obliged to relax the measures taken against them and the *intendants* were instructed accordingly. It has also been claimed that the King failed in a much more disastrous sense, that the Huguenots remained a permanently hostile body who got their revenge by helping to cause the French Revolution of 1789 by ceaselessly fomenting discontent against the monarchy, that August the Tenth was the belated revenge for 18 October 1685. It would be very pleasant to believe in this if one likes revenges, and if one likes to contemplate villainy brought low at last, although the sufferings of Marie-Antoinette, for example, did not hurt Louis XIV, and are more calculated to induce tears than satisfaction in the beholder. This Huguenot revenge, however, is a myth. The majority of the Huguenots, those who did not choose exile, were thoroughly demoralized; deprived of pastors and of middle-class members, the Huguenot faith was chiefly adhered to for a long time by obstinate, ignorant, and superstitious peasants, and when under Louis XV conditions became much easier and *bourgeois* adherents reappeared, the Protestant Church in France became worldly and easily accommodated itself to the régime. After that it played no significant part during the time of the Revolution, produced no martyrs at all under the Terror, and later comfortably came to terms with Bonaparte's and every subsequent French régime. Louis XIV's policy, then, was nearly, if not completely, successful.

The relationship between the pious performer of the deed of 1685 and his father in Christ, the Pope, was for a long time anything but harmonious. The two soon got into a quarrel over the *régale*. This was an old privilege of the French monarchy whereby the king enjoyed the revenues of a vacant bishopric (the temporal *régale*), and also had the right, in the interval before a new bishop was appointed, to appoint to benefices within the gift of the vacant bishopric (the spiritual *régale*). This right of the king did not extend over all the country until a royal Edict of 1673 declared it to be universal (apart from some areas which

had purchased exemption). There was not really anything very startling in this and, in fairness to Louis, he was not concerned about the
money involved, which was trifling. Nothing much might have been
heard of the matter had not two bishops resisted the decree. This was
somewhat unexpected. In truth, most of the bishops tended to support
the King, and furthermore the era of piety in France was passing (as is
suggested by the fact that while between 1620 and 1662 sixty Carmelite
monasteries were founded, after 1663 not one was). But the saintly
Bishop of Pamiers, Caulet, and his colleague the Bishop of Alet objected
strongly. The King was supported not merely by the majority of the
bishops, however, including the Archbishop of Paris, but also by the
parlements and even by the Jesuits. A squalid squabble then ensued, in
the course of which the government was petty and mean enough to
reduce the Bishop to penury by confiscating his revenues. Caulet died
in 1680, but the quarrel continued over the administration of the
diocese; officials of the King and those in sympathy with the late
Bishop kept it up. This absolutist government found itself drifting into
a very awkward situation, for the Bishop's party was supported by the
Pope, who threatened to excommunicate anyone appointed to benefices
in the diocese by the King, and this raised again the whole question of
control of the Church. It was therefore decided to discuss the matter at
a general assembly of the French clergy specially convened for the
purpose in 1682, when the government showed itself decidedly nervous
in case the clergy would not produce a majority vote in its favour over
the *régale*.

The outcome was the Four Gallican Articles, the drift of which was
to declare the invalidity of any Papal decrees which the King did not
approve of. Despite all the heat and smoke, the King had no very
strong desire for a real quarrel with the Pope, and in fact the quarrel
was patched up; Louis let it be known that he would not insist on the
rigorous application of the Gallican Articles, and for his part the Pope
agreed to an extension of the *régale* in France. French Gallicanism
therefore slumbered for a while.

Louis was determined to be the despot in Church matters; he
persecuted the Huguenots and quarrelled with the Pope. In his treatment of the Jansenists also he displayed intolerance, if not on the same
scale. This is a somewhat complicated story, but since it illustrates
further the would-be despotic nature of Louis's government and also
throws some light on the ultimate collapse of the *ancien régime*, it is
worth a cursory glance.

The Jansenists may be simply and conveniently described as enemies of the Jesuits, and the quarrel was a clash between the doctrines of Predestination and of Free Will. Predestination is usually associated with Calvinism, but in fact stemmed from Saints Paul and Augustine, who both inferred that salvation could come only from God's gift of Grace, which descended quite apart from men's own efforts or will, so that only a predestined few on whom this Grace did fall would be saved. Salvation was for this few and had nothing to do with anyone's efforts. Such a belief spelt despair for the hapless majority, and so the Jesuits, among others, tried to soften the iron doctrine. One of their number, Louis Molina (1535–1601), wrote a book in 1588 which propounded that Grace was efficacious only if the Will accepted it, and his colleagues generally accepted this notion and taught that salvation is within the reach of all men and may be obtained by deserving effort. As practical missionaries and as confessors to large numbers of very human sinners, the Jesuits were well aware that a doctrine which gave sinners some hope was more likely to make a wide appeal, and there is no reason to doubt their sincerity. Nevertheless, their teaching narrowly missed being declared heretical by the Pope in 1605.

Their 'Molinist' teaching came under fire from a different direction, the pen of Jansen of the University of Louvain (1585–1638), whose book *Augustinus* strongly reaffirmed the official doctrine, and who may be regarded as the founder of the Jansenist Movement, if it was a movement at all. The Jesuits were next attacked by Antony Arnould, whose father had been a famous opponent of the Jesuits in the University of Paris, and by his sister, Angélique, who became the Superior of a convent at Port-Royal-des-Champs, near Paris, in 1602. In 1625 she moved to Port-Royal in Paris, and was joined in 1633 by Saint-Cyran, a friend of Jansen, who became chaplain to her nuns. Port-Royal thus became the home of an extreme form of asceticism and gloom and of the staunch defence of Predestination which seemed to Jansenists to be synonymous with the Divine authority. The nuns, however, enjoyed Saint-Cyran's pessimistic sermons rather more than Richelieu did, for the latter put Saint-Cyran in jail (his reasons were actually political, as Jansen was hostile to Richelieu's alliance with the Swedes), and stopped the educational work for which the nuns were becoming famed.

The Jesuits were not likely to take Arnould's criticism lying down, but were obviously unable to attack their more orthodox enemies on doctrinal grounds. Their chance came with the publication in 1643 of Arnauld's book *De la fréquente communion*, a work in which the author attacked the Jesuits for the allegedly loose way in which they tolerated sins as long as the sinner confessed and took the Holy Communion after every offence. The Jesuits at once circulated the rumour that the book was an attack on the Eucharist itself (they knew that most people do not read books but are ready to listen to scandalous lies). They also managed to induce the Faculty of Theology at the Sorbonne to extract from the book five propositions which were declared heretical and duly condemned by a Bull of Pope Innocent X in May 1653. The Jansenists agreed that the propositions were heretical, but strenuously denied that they could be found or were implied in the book. But, although they were strictly speaking the more orthodox, as being nearer to the teachings of St Augustine, they had been outmanœuvred. At this point they found a most formidable new champion.

This was the famous mathematician, Pascal. Port-Royal-des-Champs had become the home not only of nuns; in the same neighbourhood there had gathered a community of earnest seekers after a more holy life, and to it had repaired Pascal in 1655. In 1657 appeared his book *Lettres provinciales*. This was one of the most savage and successful attacks ever written. Its target was Jesuit laxity. The Jesuits had certainly made a complete system out of casuistry; that is, they had tried to make religion as easy as possible for their converts by adopting principles of which the two chief were the principle of most favourable circumstance: that is, where there was an omission in a canonical rule the most favourable interpretation of an offence may be taken, or, in other words, if no punishment is specifically mentioned the conduct may be excused; and the principle of probability: of two opinions, the one probable, the other more probable, the first may be accepted unless it was obviously ridiculous; that is, the most favourable interpretation possible may be placed on conduct. Some Jesuits were said to push this to almost criminal lengths, that is, were laxists. Pascal's book was an attack on these. The book was a brilliant success; Jesuit casuists were crushed, unfairly—since very few of them, if any, could rightly be accused of laxity, and since the casuists were only trying to make religion a possibility for those with ordinary human weaknesses.

The success of the *Lettres provinciales* did not save the Jansenists from persecution. Louis XIV did not like them, partly because he simply could not understand their theology and partly because of the fact that the Jansenists furnished him with ugly reminders of the *Frondes*. Thanks to a misunderstanding, they received the fatal approbation of Cardinal de Retz, arch *Frondeur*, and still in exile. Hardly less embarrassing was the support of a notorious mare from the same stable, the Duchess of Longueville, turned pious in her old age. In fact, the Jansenists tended to come from the same lawyer class as the members of the *parlements*. Members of the two Port-Royals were compelled to sign the Formulary condemning the five propositions. An uneasy sort of truce in this unedifying conflict was reached in 1669, and the Jansenist position was temporarily strengthened because of Bishop Caulet's support of the Pope in the *régale* quarrel (he was a Jansenist). After that, darkness closed in on the Jansenists. In 1678 one of their leaders, Quesnel, had published his *Réflexions morales*, an extreme statement of their point of view, and this incurred the hostility of such powerful people as Fénelon and Mme de Maintenon. Then in 1701 they asked the Archbishop of Paris to decide whether a confessor could absolve ecclesiastics who maintained as a matter of fact that the five propositions could not be found in Jansen's book.

This rash act was their complete undoing. The Pope declared against them, Quesnel was arrested, but escaped, and the King got the Pope to issue the Bull *Vineam Domini* in 1705 which condemned their attitude to the five propositions. It was still necessary, however, to get the Bull received by the French clergy and registered by the *Parlement* of Paris (according to the very Gallican Articles of 1682 which Louis had taken so much trouble to get accepted by the French clergy). And the *Parlement* in particular was not anxious to let any writ of the Pope run in France. Thus Jansenism is connected with both *Frondeur* associations and Gallicanism. The French clergy finally accepted the Bull with some reluctance, and accordingly Port-Royal in Paris and Port-Royal-des-Champs were suppressed. The King even had the buildings of the latter utterly destroyed in 1709, and the Jesuits, triumphant, dug up some of the bones of dead Jansenists from the graveyards and scattered them. The next move was the Bull *Unigenitus* of 1713 which condemned Quesnel's *Réflexions morales*. Uproar followed. A strong minority of the French bishops were against its acceptance, more because of Gallican than Jansenist leanings, and they had the support of the *Parlement* for the same reason. Thus Jansenism allied to Gallicanism was opposed to Molinism and Ultramontanism, and a new *Fronde* seemed about to break out. Louis wavered, then on 13 August 1715 he accepted the Bull; but on 30 August he died.

Louis had acted despotically in destroying Port-Royal and in pursuing the Jansenists after that, but he failed either to obliterate Jansenism or even to silence the Jansenists. The policy and its failure proved a great deal more costly to the régime than did the failure against the Huguenots. For the wretched struggle continued. In 1730 the Bull was declared to be the law of the land, and two years later the

THE DESPOTISM OF LOUIS XIV, 1661-1715

police closed the cemetery of Saint-Médard, which contained the tomb
a certain Deacon Pâris where hysterical Jansenist miracles were said to
take place. By then most people had become rather tired of the whole
business, but it was revived again in 1752, when the Bishop of Amiens
and the Archbishop of Paris ordered their clergy to refuse the Sacraments to any not provided with a ticket saying that he accepted the
Bull. This roused many of the clergy to fury, not only because many of
them were Jansenist in sympathy, but also because they fiercely resented
the dictatorial attitude of the higher clergy. There was another horrible
rumpus, which the government finally managed to calm down.

The damage done was serious. The Church was divided and discredited at the precise moment when it should have presented an
unbroken front to an enemy far deadlier than any Jansenists, the bitter
onslaughts against it coming from the pens of the *philosophes*, who were
by then at their boldest. So not only the Church, but religion itself, was
undermined, and this partly because of the Church's own internal
quarrels. Furthermore, the Church and its dogmas, now held up to
ridicule, were themselves a great support of the régime; Divine Right
looked as ridiculous now as any squabble about Grace. The eighteenth
century has been called (among a lot of other things) the 'Century of
Disrespect', and for the Church, an old institution, to incur disrespect
was to cause other old institutions to be called in question, among them
the monarchy. Louis's treatment of the Huguenots did not harm the
monarchy; but his hounding of the Jansenists, aided by the Jesuits and
some of the upper clergy, did.

Louis's government was not content with trying to force everyone to
be Catholic and a particular sort of Catholic at that; it tried to control
all thought about everything. A censorship existed which controlled the
publication of all books, even of science and law, but especially of
theology. Undesirable foreign books were stopped at the frontiers.
There were eighty-four printing presses in Paris, a number that was in
Colbert's opinion 'excessive', and the government stopped some of
them. This failed to prevent the circulation of anti-government pamphlets. Whenever the authors were caught they were sent to the Bastille or
the galleys, or banished. More positively, the government did its best
to organize thought and culture generally so that everything should
serve safely to glorify the King and the régime. It was this that made it
take a great interest in the various academies; for instance, the *Académie
Française* was by 1671 lodged in the royal palace of the Louvre under
the King's kind 'protection'. A close watch was kept on the others such

as the Academy of Sciences, the Academy of Painting and Sculpture, and the Academy of Architecture (the membership of the last was nominated by the King). All these bodies in the official view existed to flatter the King. At first the government was fairly successful in this, but as we shall see for various reasons its grip on opinion later failed.

Something has now been said about the power that the government wielded both in theory and practice, and something too about the way the King and his ministers dealt with some of the bigger problems within France such as those connected with the finances, trade, and religion. Before turning to Louis's performances on the European stage, however, we must make some sort of estimate of what this government added up to; to what extent was it a despotism at all?

It will already have been noticed that judged by twentieth-century standards, when governments wield enormous power over their subjects (every State is indeed Leviathan now), Louis's government was quite a weak affair. It could do nothing to alter the unfair system of privilege which permeated French society, nothing to make the system of taxation fair, nothing to make France a unified country in economic matters, nothing to give one and only one system of law throughout the realm. So although Louis was accused of despotism by some contemporaries, this accusation was based on the fact that he ruled with far less reference to the claims of nobles and *parlements* than his predecessors had usually been obliged to do, and of course on such tyrannous acts as the Revocation of the Edict of Nantes, as well as his habit of harshly demanding obedience from those near him. Yet if his powers are compared with those of a modern government, he is seen to have a relatively feeble control over the nation. France under Louis was only half-way to being a fully developed State. It took the Revolution of 1789 to blast the inequalities and anomalies out of the way and make France a truly modern State.

Our inquiry is not finished yet. France did not contain in Louis's time so many millions of citizens equal before the law. It was a country whose inhabitants were fairly sharply divided into different social groupings, and in that sense there was not one France but several. So an examination of the Old Régime is not complete until we have glanced at the King's relationship with the various social classes and at the nature of his control over each.

The most influential by far of all these groups was the clergy. The clergy was the only group really meriting the description of a separate Order. The Church was enormously rich, although the King had practically no means of taking more money from it; it paid very little in taxes, and most of what it did pay was a voluntary gift determined by itself. It had its own General Assembly which treated with the King practically as one equal with another, and such was its prestige, stemming both from its wealth and of course from the respect accorded to its sacred character, that only a very rash king would have dared to do anything that might offend all the clergy. Luckily for the King, however, the Church was not as strong as it seemed. For one thing, it was hopelessly and bitterly divided within itself. This is not only a question of quarrels between Jesuits and Jansenists or between Ultramontanists and Gallicans, serious though these quarrels were; there was also a very deep rift between the upper and the lower clergy. The bishops wielded tremendous and almost despotic powers over the humble parish priests, and furthermore enjoyed very much bigger incomes, and the lower clergy hated their inferior and humiliating status and the grinding poverty in which many of their number lived. Besides that, the King controlled Church appointments, so that nobody could hope for promotion if they displeased him; all the upper clergy were in the King's pocket.

The next social group was the nobility. They no longer really constituted an Order, because they never met together as a body, and there were so many different sorts of noble that there was no trace of unity among them; not merely great and lesser nobles, but nobles of ancient lineage and those of recent creation (the latter could be hereditary or life creations), nobles of the robe (ennobled lawyers), *nobles de cloche* (municipal officers), and also a numerous brood of false nobles, that is, persons fraudulently claiming to be noble. Most of this vast band were either, like Condé, too frightened of the royal power to dare to try any more *Frondeur* activities or were too poor to be dangerous; this was so because trade was becoming a more important source of wealth than land, and the nobles were usually prevented by the law or their own pride from taking part in business. They therefore experienced a steady progress towards bankruptcy, and from this plight they usually tried to extricate themselves by crowding to Paris and to the royal court, in the hope that the King would pay their debts (he sometimes did) or give them profitable appointments, usually showy but useless offices about the royal households, or, for their younger sons, offices in the Church. This is why the King was so easily able to keep them dangling round the royal palace at Versailles, where they sought royal favour and generally impoverished themselves even further.

It is hardly possible to say something about Louis without at least a mention of Versailles. Louis disliked and, since the *Frondes*, distrusted Paris, so he had a palace built at Versailles, a smallish town a few miles from Paris. The building and gardens are certainly one of the most impressive sights in Europe, which is not surprising as it cost fifteen million pounds and employed the labours of 30,000 workmen. There, attended by 15,000 guards and servants at a cost of a tenth of the annual revenues of the country and surrounded by hordes of nobles and assorted hangers-on, Louis put on a show that made the French monarchy seem a semi-divine affair in the eyes of France and of the rest of Europe. It was to this magnificent if draughty palace that the nobles hurried in the hope of favour, and that is how they were tamed, and, in fairness to Louis let it be added, also taught good manners. But this picture of all the nobles meekly and almost blasphemously worshipping the King and fighting to attend the various royal occasions of getting up, eating, and dressing (all of which operations Louis performed with due ceremonial and attended by numbers of nobles) should not be painted in over-prominent colours. The nobles could still be dangerous if only because of their military commands, and the military provincial governors were powerful enough for Louis to be apprehensive about them. This is why he deprived them of some of their authority and shortened the duration of their commissions. The nobility of the robe, although effectively deprived of control over governmental acts by the Edict of 1673, which obliged the *parlements* to register edicts before offering a remonstrance, had been after all a menace during the *Frondes*, and Colbert was still frightened enough of them to see to it that both their number and the amount of their incomes were diminished.

Below the nobility was the middle class, the large number of those engaged in business of all sorts, in finance, the law and medicine, and in literature and the arts. They were independent in the sense that for the most part they asked few favours of the King, practically monopolized control over the towns, and had a great deal of economic power. Even Louis had to show tact to the bankers; in times of stress on his purse he could sometimes be seen walking arm-in-arm with bankers like Samuel Bernard. They provided a lot of money in taxes, but Louis had nothing at all to fear from them. They on the contrary had everything to fear from a state of anarchy such as the *Frondes*, and realized that only a strong government could preserve France from that sort of thing. Moreover, the King drew his government from their ranks rather than from the nobility; he was at once their patron, their protector, and their ally.

It only remains to add a very significant point about the King's relationship with the privileged Orders, nobles and clergy: it was a fatal mistake, ultimately, for the King to go on allowing them to acquire all the best posts, to occupy the greatest social ranks, and to be almost immune from taxation—all this as the price of their continued obedience—for in the end it meant that the monarchy was associating itself with a régime of privilege for the few and hardship for the mass of the nation. It was thus running the risk of falling with them if they should ever fall, and there was such a risk. A great political revolution can occur when the political and economic institutions of a country no longer correspond with realities. In France by 1789 the real France, the working millions of peasants, the thousands of the *bourgeoisie* who possessed the wealth and talent, joined forces and flung off the privileged few who occupied the highest position in the social scale without doing anything to justify it, and in the process the monarchy sank as well. Louis's government was not sufficiently broad-based in popular support; he relied on troops to keep order; he used as many troops against his subjects as against his foreign enemies. Versailles was a fairy palace built on the back of a sleeping giant, if such a metaphor may be permitted.

Sleeping, or just tied up, it was much the same thing. The vast majority of the population, that is the millions of peasants, counted for nothing at all except as labour to support their superiors. Sometimes, goaded by hunger, they revolted, but the revolts were always put down, and like their brother workers in the towns (who were themselves not numerous) they had no means of improving their lot unless they could seize the chance to be better organized, or unless some of the upper classes organized them and used them as allies. Since they did not count, we can leave them for a century or so, until they did.

Louis was just as interested in making himself supreme in Europe as in France, but this operation was not to be performed without fighting. At his accession, the French troops and fleet were quite inadequate for the task of imposing his will on Europe. They were built up to a state of immense strength, however, by Louvois and Colbert. In 1667 the army numbered only about 72,000 troops, of whom about half were fit only for garrison duties. By 1678 Louvois had increased this number to no less than 279,000. Nor does that figure give the full measure of the improvement; a number of measures also improved the quality of the army. Improved weapons were issued to the infantry and cavalry. Ten officer-cadet schools were founded. Their products, in spite of a preference for amusement rather than study, became reasonably good junior officers. As for senior officers, nothing much could be done because they usually bought their promotions, and this went on in spite of Louvois's efforts to stop it, nor could much be done to improve the rank and file because they came from the sweepings of the country. An attempt was made to form some sort of local militia, but it was never very useful. However, the cavalry was improved by a good remount service and much more so by the creation of companies of *carabiniers*. More striking too was the improvement in the artillery brought about by a closer State control over the manufacture of cannons, and also by the formation of additional regiments for this arm. While a good field army was thus built up, the frontiers were made practically impregnable by the fortresses constructed by a military architect of outstanding genius, Vauban.

The navy was similarly improved, chiefly by Colbert. As we have already noticed, in 1661 the fleet had about 20 ships, some of them useless. By 1683 the number was 217, most of them battleships (though most of these were third-rate, i.e. having 60 cannon or less—first-rates had over 74). As for the sailors, the galleys in the Mediterranean were filled up with slaves (mostly Turks bought in various slave markets) and criminals, among whom were imprisoned Huguenots. The rest of the fleet was provided for by a much better method: all sailors and fisher-men were put on a register and conscripted from that as need arose. This aroused intense opposition and even occasional revolts, but it served rather better than the press-gang methods used by the English, although the French had to resort to these sometimes. Colbert also worked fiercely to establish better discipline among the officers, who were in the habit of neglecting their warships in favour of private buying and selling, taking extensive shore leave without permission, and doing all the things which made the *ancien régime* in every country so pleasantly inefficient. After that sort of behaviour, they found Colbert's new *intendants de la marine* most unwelcome. Naval ports were founded by Colbert at Brest and Rochefort, and by Vauban at Toulon and Dunkirk.

France, then, at Louis's accession, was not really an exceptionally strong military monarchy, but by about 1670 was transformed into the most formidable Power in Europe, able to conduct the most impressive —and aggressive—foreign policy.

4 · France and Europe, 1661–97

(a) THE ANGLO-DUTCH WAR AND THE WAR OF DEVOLUTION

At the beginning of Louis's reign the Dutch were in fact part of the French alliance system, and Louis was much more interested in attacking the secular enemy—Spain. This would have seemed sensible enough to anyone in 1660 because, although Spain had just suffered a shattering defeat at the hands of the French and the English, she had been a deadly enemy to the French for centuries, and furthermore France still was nearly surrounded by Spanish territory. To make the French situation perpetually safe against Spain seemed therefore a legitimate policy for the French King, and in Louis's eyes it also offered something equally dear to him—the chance to win military glory.

The chief risk in such a policy was not the feeble power of Spain, but the chance that other countries might take active steps to prevent France from becoming too strong. Fortunately for Louis that risk for the moment was slight, and he prudently took good care to make it slighter. He first advertised to the world that nobody could trifle with him (he very roughly forced humiliating apologies from the King of Spain and from the Pope for insults which his Ambassadors in Rome and London had received at the hands of the Pope's Corsican guards and the Spanish Ambassador in London respectively in 1662–4; Louis's preparations for an invasion of Italy so terrified the Pope that the latter even consented to erect a monument in Rome commemorating his own ignominy). Louis then carefully re-knit his alliances with various small members of the League of the Rhine, and brought in Denmark, Brandenburg, and Saxony. These were all the more eager to ally with him because in 1663 Louis advertised his power at the expense of a much more formidable opponent than the Pope: the Turks had tried to invade Moravia and Silesia and Louis sent 6,000 French troops against them to assist the common cause of Christendom, and these troops covered themselves with glory. Thus he was free to attack the Spanish Netherlands. This was the weakest part of the French frontiers, and to gain territory there was most desirable. It was also dangerous, because the English did not care to have such a strong country as France occupying seaports which could menace England, and the Dutch preferred the French to keep their distance.

Luckily for Louis, the English and Dutch were drifting into another war against each other. The Second Anglo-Dutch War (1665-7) was caused mainly by the same commercial rivalry that had led to the war of 1652-4. Collisions between English and Dutch traders continued to occur in the East Indies and in West Africa. The English East India Company and the Royal African Company claimed that the Dutch had cost them hundreds of thousands of pounds, and these Companies clamoured for war. Other causes of bad feeling were that Charles had been expelled from his refuge in Holland at Cromwell's bidding, and Charles furthermore resented the Dutch government's exclusion from power of his relatives of the House of Orange. The Dutch on their side strongly resented the English occupation of Tangier and were rash enough to seize several English ships off West Africa and also to capture Goree and several other English settlements (January 1665). There was some justification for this, for by the end of 1664 the English had captured the whole of the Dutch settlement of New Netherland, had caused ruinous losses to a Dutch convoy off Gibraltar, and later seized all Dutch vessels in English harbours. A naval war even more terrible than the first therefore broke out.

This gave Louis a chance to put forward a claim to large parts of the Spanish Netherlands. He had already claimed that the renunciation of rights to any of her parents' territory made on behalf of Louis's Spanish wife, Maria Teresa, at the time of her marriage to Louis was invalid because the sum of half a million crowns payable to France in compensation for this had never been paid. Philip IV of Spain needed French help in a war against Portugal, so he did not at first demur at this, but when the Spanish government rejected his claim Louis helped the Portuguese (1663-5). The Spanish Netherlands thus appeared to be at Louis's mercy, but he was at this point worried about the possible reactions of both Holland and England. He was, in fact, nominally the ally of both of them and the outbreak of the Second Anglo-Dutch War in 1665 seems to have puzzled him. At first he remained neutral, but after the defeat of the Dutch at the Battle of Lowestoft in June 1665, he decided to help the Dutch, and left the Netherlands question for the present in order to polish off the English. His fleet never did manage to give the Dutch much useful help before the war ended. Very soon both English and Dutch were exhausted and this suited Louis very well. King Philip IV of Spain had died in 1665, leaving an ailing son by a second marriage, who became king as Charles II. Louis now (1667) advanced a fantastic claim concocted by one of Turenne's secretaries (named Duhan) to the provinces of Brabant, Antwerp, Limburg, Upper Guelderland, Malines, Namur, Cambrai, and Artois, and to one-third of Franche Comté and a quarter of Luxemburg. This was based on the so-called law of 'Devolution', which prevailed in part of the Netherlands, whereby the daughter of a first marriage could not be disinherited in favour of the son of a second. But this only applied to private property, and to pretend that it applied to sovereignty over great provinces was as ridiculous as it was novel; so few people were convinced by it that one may safely say that the chief value of the claim was merely to give the title of 'The War of Devolution' to the military action for which it was the pretext.

Louis's preparations included some of a much more practical sort. He renewed his treaty with the Portuguese in March 1667, thus providing the unhappy Spaniards with another difficulty, and in the same month managed to persuade Charles II of England not to interfere with the invasion of the Netherlands in exchange for French neutrality in the Anglo-Dutch War. As the Dutch were nominally, at least, his allies already, Louis had nothing to worry about in that quarter, so in May 1667 about 50,000 French troops under no less a person than Turenne poured over the frontier and began making conquests in the Spanish Netherlands with ludicrous ease. Charleroi, Armentières, Tournai, Douai, and Lille were taken. This thoroughly frightened the Dutch. They were already more than anxious to end the English War, which was inflicting terrible losses on their commerce (for instance, on 8 August 1666, the English fleet inflicted damage estimated at over a million pounds by destroying the town of Brandaris, together with about 160 merchant vessels lying in the Vlie). The English, too, were tired of a war which had proved far more costly than they had bargained for, but they proved dilatory in peace negotiations. To help them reach a conclusion, the Dutch raided the Medway and destroyed several warships laid up there by Charles II as an economy measure (10 June 1667). This drastic hint proved effective, and peace was signed between the two Maritime Powers at Breda on 21 July 1667. Both sides had some grounds for satisfaction, for the Navigation Act was somewhat modified in Holland's favour. The Dutch kept Pularoon and Surinam which they had captured from the English, but the English kept New Netherland and the Dutch still had to salute the English flag. This at least left the Dutch free to try to do something to check the alarming advance of the French.

They were at first, however, baffled by the immense diplomatic skill of Louis XIV, who renewed his alliances with the Rhine princes and with Brandenburg and, much more startling, signed a treaty with the Emperor on 20 January 1668 by which it was agreed that if, as seemed likely, Charles II of Spain died without children, France would get the Netherlands, Franche Comté, the Kingdom of Navarre, Naples, Sicily, Morocco, and the Philippines, while the Emperor was to have the remaining Spanish possessions. This is doubly interesting as the first Partition Treaty and because the Emperor by it evidently recognized Louis's claims to Spanish territory through his Queen. Louis therefore seemed unassailable, but the Dutch had a stroke of luck. In England, Clarendon's government fell, and the Cabal which followed him, despite King Charles's personal wishes, sought an alliance with the Dutch against Louis (January 1668). In April this became the Triple Alliance because it was joined by Sweden. The English also persuaded the Portuguese to make peace with Spain so that the country was now in a slightly better position to oppose France itself in the Netherlands. Rather than face the Alliance, Louis agreed to make peace, and this was done at Aix-la-Chapelle on 2 May 1668. Louis agreed to return Franche Comté, but gained several towns—Bergues, Furnes, Armentières, Douai, Tournai, Lille, Oudenarde, Courtrai, Charleroi, Ath, Binche, and Menin. These were important gains, but, although outwardly expressing satisfaction, Louis was furious at having been thwarted by the Dutch, and his rage was not calmed when they struck a medal to commemorate their check to Louis. He resolved to wipe them off the earth. To do that he would first have to break up the Triple Alliance, which, although of enormous significance as showing what would be likely to happen to him if he alarmed Europe too thoroughly, was not a very solid structure.

(b) LOUIS'S DUTCH WAR

Louis was an expert at forming alliances of his own and at breaking up other people's. Nevertheless, for him the situation in Germany was beginning to look ugly. The German princes were becoming more frightened of him than of the Emperor, and so the League of the Rhine[1] which France dominated was showing signs of cracking. The Elector of Mainz began forming instead a League of Electors, but by immense efforts Louis managed to achieve the neutrality of Brandenburg and the alliance of Bavaria, and he capped this by obtaining the benevolent neutrality of the Archbishop of Cologne and so a route to Holland which spared him the trouble of violating the Spanish Netherlands. The Elector of Hanover and the Elector Palatine of the Rhine followed suit, and at this the Emperor gave up in despair the idea of opposing Louis. He himself promised neutrality.

With Germany thus brilliantly rendered harmless or even useful, Louis negotiated with England. He encountered little reluctance there, for the first overtures came from Charles II. The latter was anxious to help the Catholics in England and still more anxious to free himself from a parliamentary control which had become more and more irksome. He had no love for the Dutch either, so he calculated that a Dutch war would be popular especially among the merchant interest in England; it would thus serve all his aims very well if he received money from France for a war with the Dutch. The money would free him from parliamentary control, for it was by its control over taxation that Parliament so often thwarted him. There was no difficulty about reaching agreement, apart from the wild nature of some of Charles's demands (he even asked for the whole of Spanish America). A secret treaty was signed at Dover on 1 June 1670 by which the English provided 6,000 troops and the French thirty warships to the common cause. Charles was to be paid three million *livres* annually during the war, to receive Sluys and the island of Walcheren, and with help from Louis (6,000 troops and two million *livres*) to make England Catholic 'as soon as the welfare of his kingdom will permit'. This is usually held to be a disgraceful arrangement on Charles's part, but to his credit he never very seriously tried to put it into effect, and it is difficult to see that it is any more disgraceful than the Covenant by which Parliament during the Civil War had agreed to accept another minority religion—Presbyterianism. Charles at least also stipulated, with an eye presumably on

---

[1] See Chapter 1.

the safety of his own country, that Louis should not attack the Spanish Netherlands. A second secret Treaty of Dover was negotiated by Buckingham on 2 February 1671, and given more publicity in England; it had no mention of the Catholic clauses, but gave England two more Dutch islands. It should be noted that Charles had not really betrayed English interests in planning this attack on the Dutch; on the contrary, the biggest enemy to English commercial expansion at that time was certainly Holland.

It only remained to find a good excuse for starting hostilities, but a ferocious tariff war between the French and the Dutch succeeded in achieving this no better than did the frantic attempts made by the needy Charles to goad the Dutch into fighting. At length Charles ordered a sudden attack on a Dutch convoy on 22 March 1672, and on the 28th he declared war, in the same month publishing his Declaration of Indulgence for the benefit of religious minorities in England.

On the face of it the war seemed certain to end in the annihilation of the Dutch. The English and French fleets greatly outnumbered the Dutch, and the disparity between the land forces was even more ridiculous. The English alone had 132 ships of the line against the Dutch 110. The French army numbered about 160,000, all first-rate troops led by some of the finest generals in the whole history of warfare —Condé and Turenne, not to mention Vauban and Luxemburg. The Dutch army consisted of about 25,000 foot and 2,500 horse, and the officers were mediocre. So the French swept all before them, and the Dutch were only able to save the province of Holland itself by flooding the country (June). Their position was quite hopeless and so they begged for peace, but the only terms that Louis and Louvois would accept would have meant the virtual extinction of the Dutch as an independent people; they included the retention of all conquests, a huge indemnity, freedom of worship for Catholics, and the removal of barriers to French trade. This roused the Dutch populace to fury, and a revolution broke out.

The position of John de Witt[1] had been extremely precarious for some time. The Act of Exclusion which debarred the Prince of Orange from supreme power was highly unpopular, and in an attempt to repair this injustice de Witt in April 1666 proposed that the States of Holland should take charge of the education of the young Prince who was declared a 'Child of State'; it turned out a disquieting experience for the Grand Pensionary to look after this cold, proud, and secretive pupil.

---

[1] See Chapter 1.

Perhaps this, together with his growing unpopularity even among the Republican *bourgeoisie* (many of them resented the monopolizing of power by the de Witts and their family connexions), explains his nervous move in August 1667; the 'Eternal Edict' was passed whereby no Captain- or Admiral-General of the Union could also be Stadtholder of a province. This Edict was only accepted with very great reluctance by most of the provinces, and it did not succeed in its object of retarding the advancement of the young Prince, now growing into manhood. For William was appointed Captain-General of the Union, amid much popular rejoicing, in February 1672, before the war had started, and as soon as the first disasters befell the Dutch he was made Stadtholder of Zeeland and of Holland (July). The huge failure of de Witt was of course that he had misread the international situation; he hardly believed that Louis really meant to annihilate his old allies; he could not stop the war and had not succeeded in building up the Dutch forces enough to give them any sort of chance against the French either. For this he was to pay a terrible price; his brother Cornelius was arrested, and when John went to visit him in prison in The Hague a frenzied mob forced its way into the prison, and John and his brother were literally torn to pieces (20 August 1672). With them perished the long ascendancy of the Republican party. This suited William very well; probably he had had nothing to do with the murders, but he did nothing to punish the murderers.

Yet John de Witt had deserved better than this cruelty. Had people only realized it, the French campaign had already failed, and that thanks largely to him. For one thing, the French advance was brought completely to a halt by the flooding, and the decision to flood the country, carried out in face of opposition from the Dutch themselves, had been de Witt's, not William's—the latter was the poorest general ever produced by the House of Orange. For another, the Dutch had also made total defeat almost impossible by their naval victory over the combined English and French fleets at the Battle of Sole Bay on 7 June, for after that the aggressors never managed to stop Dutch commerce from continuing to supply the sinews of war; and that victory was won by Ruyter, one of de Witt's supporters, whom William promptly disgraced as soon as he could. De Witt's brother had also distinguished himself in that battle. Lastly, de Witt's diplomacy had already altered the French position for the worse, for, thanks to his efforts, the Emperor and Brandenburg signed a treaty on 23 June by which they agreed to send 24,000 troops to help the Dutch. He was certainly not to blame for the invasion. The thought that a lout bought one of his fingers for a glass of beer and that his great heart was left for a time on the counter of an ale-house can still move us to pity and indignation, and makes it hard to feel any warmth for William III, the most unattractive hero of modern times.

In William the French found a remorseless, tireless, implacable enemy. He failed in an attempt to take Charleroi, but on 30 August 1673 he secured a far better alliance with the Emperor, who agreed to send 30,000 troops. He even persuaded the Spaniards to promise 8,000, so that the defection of Brandenburg that June counted for less. In fact, it was no longer for the French a matter of smashing the Dutch, a task anyway beyond their capacity because of the flooding, but of facing a European coalition. They evacuated the United Provinces and turned on the Germans, earning a good deal of bad feeling by devastating the Palatinate; the Imperialists retaliated by meting out similar treatment to Louis's ally, the Archbishop of Cologne. This worried Louis very little—which cannot be said of the defection of his chief ally, England, in 1674. The English were deeply suspicious of their King's designs; Parliament made short work of his Declaration of Indulgence and broke up his government by the Test Act in 1673. Alarmed, Charles decided it would be safer for him to make peace with the Dutch, and this of course he had no difficulty in doing. By the Treaty of Westminster of 19 February 1674 the English flag was to be saluted in the English Channel and the North Sea, the Dutch paid an indemnity of 800,000 crowns, the disputes in the East were to be settled by an arbitration tribunal, and the English regained New York, which the Dutch had managed to capture. These were not particularly good terms for the Dutch, but the advantage of peace with England was enormous, not only because it removed a powerful enemy, but also, as it turned out, because it set in train more disastrous diplomatic results for the French.

This defection of England encouraged some of the German princes, who were tired of the rough tactlessness with which Louvois treated them, to listen to the Emperor's advances, with the result that the German Diet declared war against Louis in May 1674. He retained as allies only Bavaria, Sweden, and the Duke of Hanover, while opposing him was the structure known as the Grand Alliance of The Hague. However, this did not prevent the French under Condé and Turenne from winning victories. They quickly recaptured Franche Comté and occupied most of the Spanish Netherlands. When threatened by superior numbers, Turenne, in a campaign of quite dazzling brilliance over the winter of 1674-5, retreated behind the Vosges, and to the disgust of his opponents, who thought that he would follow the leisurely habit of the day and spend the bad weather in winter quarters, marched behind those mountains out of sight of his unsuspecting enemies, reappeared through the Belfort Gap to fall on the Imperialists, and defeated them in three battles. To balance this, Louis's ally Sweden was badly defeated by Brandenburg at the Battle of Fehrbellin in 1675 and also suffered naval defeats at the hands of the Danes. His own attempts to persuade the Poles to help them failed, partly because the latter were at war with the Turks and partly because they were treated tactlessly by the French Ambassador. Nothing daunted, Louis turned to the Turks instead, but they were busy fighting the Russians. He was consoled by success in the Mediterranean, where the French captured Sicily (1676).

So the French did well enough in the fighting, although the original objective had not been gained. What brought this rather senseless bloodshed to an end was the turn of events in England. After leaving the war, Charles II had at first kept up a very friendly attitude to Louis and continued to receive money from him, but anti-French feeling in England grew rapidly, and, for this and other reasons, Charles decided to grant permission for the marriage in November 1677 of William of Orange to his niece, the Princess Mary. This seemed to herald an Anglo-Dutch alliance and thus helped to persuade Louis to seek peace. William had shown no great desire for this marriage, but an alliance with England would help him to still the clamour for peace in Holland, and he obtained Charles's promise of help at the time of the marriage. For his own part, Charles saw it as all part of the fantastic intrigues which then distinguished English politics, for it strengthened his hand against the Opposition, most of whom were in any case in the pay of France, and, besides that, it was all part of his game played at the expense of Louis, for despite this Treaty with the Dutch signed on 10 January 1678 Charles agreed to accept money again from Louis in May. Luckily, all this dishonest and tortuous nonsense was brought to a sudden end by the conclusion of peace, which Louis wanted and which William, because of pressure at home even from his own party, could no longer resist.

It is useful to call the peace settlement 'The Treaty of Nymegen' (the spelling varies), but it actually consisted of several treaties signed in that town and two more elsewhere. Two were signed on 10 August between Louis and the Dutch whereby Louis returned Maastricht and agreed to free trade between France and the United Provinces (thus the French tariffs of 1667 were abolished). A third treaty signed on

17 September 1678 with Spain gave to France, Franche Comté, Cambrésis, part of Hainaut, part of maritime Flanders, and the remainder of Artois. The fourth treaty was signed on 5 February 1679 between the Emperor on the one side and France and her ally Sweden on the other; by this France got Freiburg but gave back Philippsburg, and promised to give back Lorraine to its ruler (Charles V) except for Nancy and Longwy, but reserving rights for the passage of troops (Louis did not keep the promise). Lastly it was necessary to end the northern war in which the Baltic Powers had been engaged as allies of the two sides in the war in the West. In this war Sweden had suffered heavy defeats at the hands of Brandenburg and Denmark, but such was Louis's enormous authority in all Europe that Sweden at the Treaty of Saint-Germain-en-Laye on 29 June 1679 received everything that she lost to Brandenburg except a small piece of land on the right bank of the River Oder. By the Treaty of Fontainebleau of 2 September 1679 she regained everything that she had lost to Denmark.

Opinions differ about the value of these settlements to France. Louis, it is true, had not gained his revenge against the Dutch. They had won trading freedom, and he was from henceforward to find William of Orange his worst enemy. His territorial gains have been described as important for the future defence of France, but Spain had long been a neighbour so feeble that it is hard to see the use of fighting to take from her places like Franche Comté (which was in a ruined condition anyway), while to do this at the cost of making a bitter enemy of the Emperor and many of the Germans seems merely foolish. On balance it seems he had gained nothing; he strengthened his frontier but made his neighbours much more likely to attack it. Perhaps this is too critical a judgement, for Louis had certainly gained two things he valued highly: military glory, and, especially by the way he had protected his defeated ally Sweden, tremendous diplomatic prestige.

(c) *LOUIS AT THE HEIGHT OF HIS POWER; THE REUNIONS 1679–85 AND THE WAR OF THE LEAGUE OF AUGSBURG 1688–97*

Louis emerged from the Settlement of Nymegen with his influence and prestige greater than ever. From a dazzling eminence he seemed to survey a weak and divided Europe, a Europe he could treat pretty much as he pleased. He was able to resume his mastery over Germany with a deceptive ease; the Emperor was up to his eyes in difficulties with the Turks and the Hungarians, so the German princes hastened back into the French fold. Brandenburg, Saxony, and Bavaria were his allies; as were also the Electors of Mainz, Cologne, and Trier. The time-honoured method of having an ally who could cause distraction in the rear of Germany was not discontinued for, although he lost influence in Poland, he more than made up for that by cultivating the friendship of the Turks. Holland was exhausted by the war, and the *bourgeois* there were foolishly seeking future safety by a policy of friendship with Louis. Spain was in its usual mismanaged condition and could not protect its commerce from the attentions of even the Elector of Brandenburg, whose frigates were pleased to find someone they could defeat. As for England, after the Titus Oates and Exclusion crises, Charles II was glad enough to rule without Parliament and to accept five million *livres* a year from Louis to help him to do it (November 1681). There was thus nobody in sight who could stop the depredations of the world's most exquisite bandit, the Sun King of France.

As in the 'Devolution' racket, Louis concocted a wonderful historico-legal excuse for pursuits which differed from those of Dick Turpin or of Billy the Kid chiefly in scale. The Treaties of Westphalia and Nymegen had ceded to Louis various territories with their dependencies, and it was the unhappy vagueness of this that furnished Louis with his pretext. Lawyers and historians were employed on research into just what those dependencies were supposed to be. Nobody really knew, but the researches found attractive answers every time. On the basis of these antiquarian labours, therefore, Louis in rapid succession marched troops into the Bishopric of Strasburg, lands belonging to the three Bishoprics of Metz, Toul, and Verdun, the province of the Saar, then Saarlouis, most of Saarbrücken, the Principality of Montbéliard, a few places in the Spanish Netherlands such as Alost and Grammont, and, choicest gain of all, the town of Strasburg, which was occupied in October 1681. These places were worth having, but Louis displayed very little sense in seizing Zweibrücken, which was of no great use in itself but which belonged to the King of Sweden, so that this most useful of allies became an enemy overnight. Sweden made an immediate alliance with Holland, but not much could come of it. Louis increased his subsidies to Charles II of England, the Emperor was busy with the Turks, and Brandenburg, jealous of Sweden, renewed its alliance with France (22 January 1682). So serious were the Emperor's troubles that he called on Christendom for help, but the Most Christian King continued his profitable aggression in the Spanish Netherlands. After a defeat inflicted on the Turks by the Polish hero Sobieski at

Kahlenburg (12 September 1683) the Spaniards, hoping for help now from the Emperor, declared war on Louis on 23 October 1683. William of Orange took his chance and organized the Alliance of The Hague with the Emperor, Sweden, Spain, and some of the German princes, but such poor opposition was offered to Louis in the Netherlands that

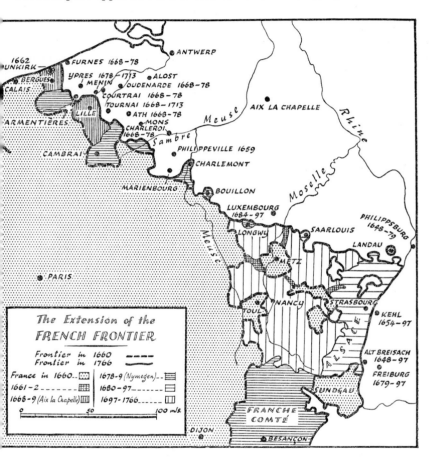

The Extension of the FRENCH FRONTIER

Frontier in 1660 -- -- --
Frontier in 1766 ————

France in 1660	1678-9 (Nymegen)
1661-2	1680-97
1668-9 (Aix la Chapelle)	1697-1766

0   50   100 mls.

the States-General of the United Provinces forced William to make peace and this obliged the Emperor to follow suit. The outcome was the Truce of Ratisbon on 15 August 1684 by which Louis was allowed to keep all he had seized before 1 August 1681, including Strasburg. The arrangements included a truce for twenty years, but it was highly unlikely that Louis would observe it; why should he, when aggression had proved so easy and profitable?

At about this time Louis seemed to have decided to throw reasonable calculations overboard. He was at the very height of his power and influence, and up to the Settlement of Ratisbon his foreign policy had been successful inasmuch as he had made useful territorial gains and seemed utterly irresistible, the greatest king in all the world. He certainly disdained the opinion and the power of everyone else in Europe. In 1685 he stupified the entire continent by his Revocation of the Edict of Nantes. He had always been a dangerous enemy: this piece of despotism made him look like a monster. While the exiled Huguenots were doing their best to stir everyone up against him, the diplomatic situation was altering very much to his disadvantage for quite different reasons. One was the complete defeat of the Turks. The League of 1684 that had been formed against them was joined two years later by Russia and in 1687 the Venetians captured the Morea from the Turks, unfortunately blowing up the Parthenon in the process, and followed up this success by taking Dalmatia. Still worse (for the Turks) were the successes of the Imperialists; they took Pest in 1684 and Buda in 1686, and in the following year utterly routed the Turkish army at the Battle of Mohacs. The result was that Hungary now fell completely under the control of the Emperor, and became a German colony. The Emperor in one brief campaign had added more to his empire than Louis managed to add to his in fifty-five years, and besides being more powerful than formerly was much more able to take an active part in checking the French King. To make matters worse, Louis also lost his grip on North Europe. For in 1682 Denmark and Brandenburg formed an alliance against Sweden, whereupon Louis told the former that they could expect no help from him. The next thing to happen was that Brandenburg and Sweden drew together, for Louis had also annoyed Brandenburg by reproving its Elector for showing friendliness to Holland, and the result was that Louis lost all his northern allies. Brandenburg and Sweden in January 1686 formed an alliance for the defence of the Protestant religion, and in the same month Brandenburg joined the Emperor in an alliance. By 9 July 1686 the League of Augsburg was formed to stop further French aggression, and it contained all his former enemies and some of his former friends—the Emperor, Holland, Brandenburg, Sweden, and many lesser German princes. As if that were not enough, Louis offended the Pope by a silly quibble over Ambassadors' privileges in 1687 and then, apparently looking for trouble, quarrelled with both Emperor and Pope about the candidature to the vacant Archbishopric of Cologne. On 24 September 1688 Louis issued a long statement offering all sorts of concessions if his opponents would convert the Truce of

Ratisbon into a permanent peace, and stipulating a cessation of hostilities for three months while negotiations along these lines could be conducted, but in fact he broke his own suggestion and in the following month moved his troops into Avignon, invaded the Palatinate, began the siege of Philippsburg, and occupied most of the Electorate of Cologne. The evil genius pushing Louis into this reckless course of action was Louvois, who counted on rapid victory. Louis's action in thus needlessly precipitating a war was described by the Prussian envoy as 'light-hearted', but one could think of harsher terms for it.

If the influence of Louvois had so far been disastrous, Louis himself seemed determined to be the chief architect of his own ruin. In 1689 he infuriated the Germans by another devastation of the Palatinate. Enormous damage was inflicted for no very obvious military purpose, and his troops seized the left bank of the Middle Rhine. At once Brandenburg broke off negotiations with him, and Bavaria joined the coalition. As if he did not already have enough enemies, he declared war on Spain on 15 April 1689 because they had allowed the presence of German troops in the Spanish Netherlands. The circle of foes was now nearly complete as he had declared war on the United Provinces on 26 November 1688, so it only remained to offend the English, and this he did not fail to do. We have previously seen[1] that the English King James II fled to France in December 1688 and that Louis's reception of him was kind. It soon went far beyond kindness, for three months later Louis aided James in an attempt to recover his kingdom by attacking Ireland. William of Orange, Louis's bitterest enemy, was now King William III of England and was naturally eager to swing the strength of England against Louis. The English Parliament might very well, however, have refused to permit this, but the attack on Ireland settled it as far as they were concerned and William was able to declare war on France, as English king, on 17 May 1689. Louis was face to face with a coalition of every important Power in Europe.

The war that followed, the War of the League of Augsburg, was not quite as calamitous for the French as appearances at its start might lead us to expect. The huge coalition against them suffered, as such groupings almost always do, from mutual jealousies and absence of central direction. Several of the members were poverty-stricken and could not afford to keep an army for long in the field, with the result that most of the necessary cash had to be found by England. The French plan was therefore to fight defensively at first in Europe but to strike hard at the

---

[1] See Chapter 2.

English. The French admiral, Tourville, did in fact get the better of the Anglo-Dutch fleet at the Battle of Beachy Head of 10 July 1690, but on the same day the invasion of Ireland ended in disaster, thanks to William's victory at the Battle of the Boyne, and James II had to return to France. This was hardly compensated for by the victory of the French marshal, Luxemburg over the Imperial general, Waldeck, at Fleurus, nine days earlier.

Luck ran against the French, for Savoy joined the allies. Louis's personal burden was made heavier by the death of Louvois in 1691, but he was by then very experienced. His energy was undiminished and he surprised the allies by seizing Mons and Liège in April and June 1691, and by invading Piedmont. He even went so far as to revive the notion of an invasion of England; he was encouraged in this by the near-treachery of some of the English grandees, who were taking the precaution of allowing for all eventualities by keeping up a brisk and secret correspondence with him, and by the unpopularity of William in England. This enterprise died a sudden death when the French fleet, outnumbered, was defeated by the English under Admiral Russell in the Battle of La Hougue (or Hogue), 29 May to 3 June 1692. After that the French fleet was unable to make much difference to the course of events, but the French nevertheless did great damage by the use of privateers, of whom the most famous was Jean Bart, while the battle fleet itself, prudently restricting itself to commerce raiding, destroyed an enormous Anglo-Dutch convoy off Cape St Vincent in June 1693, the allies losing ninety-three ships. Things continued to go badly for the allies on land: William again being handsomely defeated, this time by Marshal Luxemburg at Neerwinden in May 1693 (William's military efforts seem as a rule to have had the effect of making the reputations of the enemy commanders). Marshal Catinat defeated the Savoyards at Marsaglia, near Turin, in October 1693. On the other hand, the French lost possessions in India and Africa.

Thus neither side could gain a decisive advantage and everybody was sick of the war. Louis offered peace terms, but the allies rejected them as not being favourable enough. So the hostilities continued, but on a diminished scale. Louis was even obliged to sell jobs to Huguenots in order to raise money, and he also imposed a new tax, the *capitation*. Everybody from the King's eldest son downwards, except the clergy, was supposed to pay it, but not everybody did. The English were not faring much better; Cromwell's land tax was revived (1692) and a tax placed on windows. (The English can count themselves fortunate that this piece of governmental folly was withdrawn in the 1820s, quite soon

by tax-gatherers' standards.) To make it easier to mobilize for government purposes the financial resources of the country, the Bank of England was founded in 1694. While the French finances were tottering
and English trade dying, neither side could afford hostilities. Louis
again offered peace, but the negotiations collapsed because he refused
to recognize William as the rightful king of England as a preliminary of
negotiating. Peace eventually came because Louis in the end agreed to
this, and also because the military situation worsened for the allies by
the defection of Savoy in June 1696, which made the Emperor give up
his campaign in North Italy. Even the English by then had difficulty
in finding money to pay the troops, and all the belligerents, except
Spain, agreed to meet. Louis had already signed an agreement at Turin
in 1696 with Savoy, by which he returned Pinerolo and Casale and
agreed to a marriage of his grandson to a daughter of Victor Amadeus
of Savoy; the general peace was concluded at Ryswick in September–
October 1697, consisting of several treaties between France and Holland,
England, the Emperor, and Spain.

The terms showed a considerable deterioration in Louis's position in
Europe. The French tariff against the Dutch was lowered, and Dutch
troops allowed to garrison fortresses along the frontier between France
and the Spanish Netherlands (called accordingly the 'Barrier Fortresses'). The most powerful exponent of the doctrine of the Divine
Right of Kings admitted the right of the English to depose their own
king and appoint another. He returned nearly all of Lorraine, though
he kept Strasburg, thus still leaving a seriously weak gap in France's
eastern frontier. The Electorate of Cologne was given to Bavaria,
though Louis's candidate was restored to his own possessions, while the
question of the Palatinate was settled in favour of the Neuburg family
and the claims of the Duchess of Orleans were bought off with a
pension. Last, Louis gave up Catalonia and also returned to Spain
Luxemburg, Mons, Ath, Courtrai, and Charleroi. These were very
serious losses; Louis ended the war without important territories he had
previously possessed. This is a little surprising in view of the fact that
on balance the French forces might be said to have had if anything
rather the better of the fighting, but as against that consideration must
be set the greater exhaustion of France and also the fact that Louis was
anxious to make peace because he wished to be able to deal with the
question of the Spanish succession, for the childless King of Spain was
by then at last clearly near to death.

5 · Northern and Eastern Europe, 1660–1700

Before following the story of Louis's last and greatest war, one should look at the States of North and East Europe, or the impression might be gained that Europe began and ended with France, England, and Holland. Such an impression would not in fact be so wildly wrong. One of the prime reasons why the latter part of the seventeenth century is so much 'Le Siècle de Louis Quatorze' is that the other parts of Europe were in his time very weak—a state of affairs unique to that period. In the preceding two centuries the dominant Power had been the Habsburgs, and France had been fighting for survival. Now Spain was but a shadow of a great Imperial Power, while the Emperor in Mazarin's day had seen himself successfully defied by the German princes, over whom he exercised indeed rather less influence than did Louis. To the South-east the Ottoman Turks, once the terror of Europe, were clearly past their peak. In the East, Poland was in the process of disintegration, the great power of Prussia was being born, while Russia was still backward and unable as yet to face a Swedish army with much hope of success. France in Louis's time was thus able to play the dominant part to a large extent not merely in Western Europe but all over it. With the rise of Russia and Prussia in the eighteenth century, however, Western influence in Eastern Europe suffered a marked decline, and in the nineteenth century, apart from the Napoleonic interlude, a severe eclipse, which continues in the twentieth century.

(a) SWEDEN AND DENMARK

If Russia in those days was frightened of Sweden, so were most other countries in that area, and with good reason. From small beginnings Sweden had gone up like a rocket. She had brushed aside the claim to her throne by the kings of Poland. She had made nonsense of Denmark's ancient claim to supremacy in the Baltic. Various treaties at the end of different wars against an assortment of victims marked her advance. At the Peace of Stolbova in 1617 she took Ingria and Karelia from Russia. The Treaty of Bromsebro in 1645 saw her wrenching from Denmark the Norwegian provinces of Jemtland and Herjedalen, the islands of Gotland and Oesel, and a fresh confirmation of her immunity from the tolls levied by Denmark on ships passing the entrance to the Baltic. As security for this last-named gain she kept the Danish province of Halland for thirty years. Westphalia gave her Western Pomerania, Bremen, Verden, Wismar, Stettin, and the island of Wollin in 1648. In 1657 at Roeskilde she took Scania from the Danes. It is true that her next war was lost, thanks to the intervention of the Maritime Powers of England and Holland, and the Treaties of Oliva, Copenhagen, and Kardis (1660–1) saw some check to this headlong advance. Nevertheless, she still held a magnificent position, at least in appearance, and for the first time in the seventeenth century was at peace with all the world.

Her position, however, was precarious, and in any case she was not content with it. She blocked the path of several Powers, notably Russia and Brandenburg, and any great increase in their strength would mean ruin for a small country with a mediocre economy. Among other sources of weakness for Sweden was the power of the nobles, who still tried to assert their authority against the Crown. Worse, the government had made reckless gifts of lands to the nobles, and was so short of money that it even had to sell cannon from the fleet. The young King Charles XI was a minor, and the Regents failed to make any impression on the mountainous National Debt. In these straits the Chancellor, a charming, elegant, cultured, and utterly incompetent person called Count de la Gardie, hit on the bright notion of trying to make money by double-crossing Louis XIV. Louis in 1672 was on the eve of his great attack on Holland, and therefore wanted Swedish help. La Gardie thought that he could elicit large subsidies from the French and do nothing in return ('do naught else for it than sit still', as one of his colleagues put it). So on 3 April 1672 a treaty was concluded with the French, although the Swedes assured the Dutch that no harm against them was contemplated.

The young King Charles XI came of age a few months later and thus inherited along with a weak and ill-managed country a foreign policy

which was to bring Sweden practically to the brink of total ruin. Nor did he seem the right man to improve matters; he was reputed to be unable to read or write, and his favourite pastime was field sports. He strengthened his own position by a sweeping 'reduction' in 1674, but the country was still quite unable to fight a war out of its own resources, and Louis XIV insisted that the Swedes should put an army in the field to menace the Emperor before he would pay any subsidies. Louis was a much more experienced performer at the game of diplomatic poker than La Gardie or his raw young master. Charles himself, eager to emulate the military exploits of his great predecessors, was in any case bound to comply. In the event, a Swedish army landed in Pomerania after La Gardie had done his best (which was not good enough) to wriggle out of a war. As the army failed to gather enough supplies there, it crossed the frontier into Brandenburg, so by December 1674 Sweden found herself at war with the Great Elector as well, and a few months later the Dutch duly declared war also. The campaigns that followed showed to what depths a few years of rule by nobles and Regents had brought the country of Gustavus Adolphus. The Swedish fleet put to sea and succeeded only in demonstrating that it could not navigate, while on 28 June 1675 a Brandenburg army at the famous Battle of Fehrbellin routed double its own numbers of Swedes. At this point the Danes decided the times were auspicious, and joined Sweden's enemies.

Denmark had endured at the hands of Sweden a long succession of painful defeats, and had been toppled from the important position she had enjoyed in the Baltic. These disasters had been caused at least in part by gross internal weakness. The nobles owned half the land of the country, but refused to pay any taxes, dodged military service, monopolized all the best posts in the country, and reduced the powers of the King, through their control of the *Rigsraad* (Permanent Council). Like a tiger converted into a hearth-rug, the Danish monarchy had been pacified completely. After 1660 King Frederick III, however, was respected and admired for his recent defence of Copenhagen against the Swedes and, for a man whose chief interests were supposed to be studious, soon made surprisingly practical use of this remaining advantage. By an adroit alliance with the clergy and burghers and by threats of force, he carried through a bloodless *coup d'état* which transferred a great deal of authority from the nobles to himself (October 1660). In January of the next year he neatly dispensed with his new allies by withdrawing all their powers too and making himself a dictator. Good use was made of this revolution to reform the State. The government was reorganized, the country divided up into districts ruled over by sheriffs appointed by the King, offices thrown open to anyone of ability, and, after the King's death in 1670, the new king, Christian V, helped by a statesman of exceptional ability, Peter Schumacher, created Count of Griffenfeld, by further measures transformed Denmark. A new aristocracy of service was formed, the finances improved, the army and navy increased, and measures taken to further commerce. In short, a good deal was done within the limits of the possible to make Denmark a tolerably powerful country.

It could never hope to cut much of a figure on the international stage. Its best interest was to keep the peace and keep quiet, and Griffenfeld had the sense to see it. But King Christian V was young and anxious for a fight, so Denmark attempted in the next few years, in what is called the War of Scania (1675-9), to recover her lost provinces by force.

Sweden's plight was indeed hopeless without this fresh adversary, for the Brandenburgers captured Stettin, Rugen, Stralsund, and the mouth of the Oder. The Danes did manage to capture Central and Southern Scania, but Charles XI of Sweden displayed feverish energy and won a few victories. It was not to him, however, that Sweden owed a magical recovery. The war in the West came to an end at the Settlement of Nymegen in 1678-9, and Louis XIV almost contemptuously insisted that Sweden should not be a loser even though she had been an indifferent ally, both in performance and in intention. Accordingly, by the Treaties of Saint-Germain-en-Laye in June 1679 with Brandenburg, and of Fontainebleau in September 1679 with Denmark, Sweden regained all her losses except for a small strip of land on the right bank of the Oder ceded to Brandenburg. The events of the previous quarter of a century had thus served to show that France, Holland, and England were the true lords of the Baltic area whenever they cared to use their fleets or diplomacy there. North-east Europe was just a sideshow to what happened in the West, a state of affairs that depended on several conditions and which would end if the Western Powers were locked in a life and death struggle with each other or if Sweden or any of its neighbours somehow contrived to grow significantly in strength. In fact, the West was soon to engage in the huge War of the Spanish Succession, while in addition to that, Sweden and two of her neighbours achieved such a growth.

Defeat in the recent war had done a great deal to discredit the nobles of Sweden, while the young King Charles XI had shown himself to be, if a somewhat wooden-headed strategist, a hero worthy of his family. Helped by the other Estates, he immediately tackled problems created by the nobility. Very large amounts of alienated Crown land were recovered from them in a great 'reduction' decreed in 1680; all such domains having a yearly rental of 600 dollars or more were seized, and the three non-noble Estates (clergy, burghers, and peasants) declared the King an absolute ruler, responsible to God alone. The nobles, cowed by fear of the mob and of the royal guards, meekly accepted the new situation. The *Rad* (Council), which they had dominated and which in turn had dominated the Estates, was thus bloodlessly, but not painlessly, overthrown, for Charles forced the nobles to disgorge over four million dollars, a sum big enough to enable him to be independent of grants from the Estates too, and big enough to make possible sweeping reforms. Industry was encouraged, especially cloth, iron, and shipbuilding, as these were necessary for the armed forces. The army, by an arrangement called the *Indelningsverk* (a system by which Crown lands were assigned for the support of soldiers), was made a permanent regular force; it numbered 38,000. In time of war every tenth peasant would be conscripted into the army, while in peace-time the rural districts had to supply land for the upkeep of an equivalent number of troops, usually hired mercenaries. Similar provision was made for the fleet, which was raised to thirty-eight warships. Charles also made some reforms in the laws and their administration, and, in 1686, a new ecclesiastical law brought the Church far more under the control of the King than it had ever been before. Even art, literature, and science flourished, though owing nothing directly to a King whose chief pleasures included inspecting troops and riding horses to death. Charles also gave Sweden nearly twenty years of much-needed peace, and when he died in 1697 he left his country very much stronger than he had found it.

That was just as well, for he also left as successor a youth of fifteen, who after a brief Regency assumed power (November 1697), a circumstance which seemed heaven-sent to the numerous enemies of Sweden, who now gathered for an easy kill. Prominent among this sanguine and, as it happened, ill-advised band was Russia.

(b) RUSSIA AND THE REFORMS OF PETER THE GREAT

Russia in 1660 was not very well known by the rest of Europe and was still a very backward country. She had been long retarded by disasters like the Tartar invasion in the thirteenth century, and had also been cut off from the rest of Europe to a considerable extent by the fear and jealousy of her neighbours. As late as 1547, for instance, the Livonians prevented the Tsar from importing engineers, mechanics, and artists from Germany so as to stop the industries and army of Russia from profiting by Western ideas. That sort of dog-in-the-manger attitude did not, however, prevent the Russians from gaining some information about the West. The English had traded with them for a long time. Foreigners joined the Russian army, and some lived in Moscow in what the

Russians called the 'German suburb' (they seemed to have thought that all foreigners were Germans). The Tsars had also begun to enter into normal diplomatic relations with foreign governments.

The GROWTH of RUSSIA in EUROPE

Boundary in 1645 ═══
Gains under
    Alexis.....1645–76..
    Peter......1682–1725.
    Anna....–1730–1740.
    Elizabeth...1741–1762.
    Catherine II.1762–1796.
    Russian share in first
    Partition of Poland..
0   1   2   300 mls.

The reign of Alexis (1645–76) was of some importance for two reasons. For one thing, Russia gained more territory. Russia supported the Cossacks of the Ukraine against their Polish overlords, and the Swedes, who were also at war with Poland. The upshot of a long struggle was the Treaty of Kardis (1661) by which Russia averted the danger to herself that would have resulted from a further growth of Sweden at Poland's expense, and the Treaty of Andrusova (1667) by which Russia gained from Poland Smolensk and Little Russia, including Kiev, east of the Dnieper.

The other thing that marked the reign was a bitter religious dispute. The Patriarch of the Russian Church put into effect various reforms in the liturgy which had been suggested by a Greek scholar (the Russians belonged to the Greek Orthodox Church). This led to the great *Raskol* (schism) because many Russians regarded the innovations as foreign; they loathed foreigners and 'abominable German customs'. The *Raskol-niki* (Old Believers) were never crushed. However, the reforms at least meant that many Russians could open their mind to changes. After the death of the Tsar Theodore III (1676–82) they quietly allowed another innovation. Women had been hitherto secluded, but the Tsarevna Sophia acted as Regent for her young brothers, Ivan and Peter. Some modernization had begun which a subsequent, more famous ruler, Peter the Great, was able to extend.

Peter's early life undoubtedly sheds light on his later character and actions. While Sophia ruled for him and his imbecile half-brother Ivan (Peter was only in his tenth year in 1682), he spent most of his time in a village outside Moscow amusing himself with military games in the company of a gang of young louts. He disliked the company of his mother Natalia, but must have picked up some Western ideas from her, for she had been the favourite pupil of the scholar Matvieeff, who was greatly influenced by them. Peter learned something of geometry and fortification from a Dutchman (Timmermann), and showed a great interest in ships, which he sailed on a lake eighty miles from Moscow. He also seems to have picked up some knowledge of the German and Dutch languages, and possibly gained something from two foreign friends, General Lefort (a Swiss) and Patrick Gordon (a Scot). Apart from that he appears to have been taught little; in short, his education would have been rather more suited to an artisan than to an autocrat. In other respects, however, his impressionable years included experience of a sort likely to come the way of the high-born, namely intrigue and violence. He lived in constant fear of assassination, and the scholar Matvieeff was actually hacked to pieces by members of the old Moscow Guard, the *Streltsi*, while holding Peter's hand, a deed whose memory may have been a cause of the convulsions from which Peter suffered in later life. However, he survived. A palace revolution in 1689 overthrew Sophia, and after about 1694 Peter took over the reins of government himself, the death of Ivan in 1696 removing the last possible obstacle.

Peter was a barbarian but he was also a genius, and throughout a long reign (he died in January 1725) this cruel, debauched 6 foot 4 inch giant worked at the task of regenerating Russia with all the force and speed of a runaway train. Reforming measures poured from him, and yet during most of this time he was at war too, the reforms in fact springing from the needs of war. It is therefore merely confusing to list all, or most, of these measures chronologically. The work which made Russia a European Power at one bound is of such importance and interest that it merits more than a cursory glance, so an attempt will be made to outline it in something approaching a logical rather than a chronological order, although it should be emphasized that the reforms were dictated piecemeal by military needs rather than by any grand overall scheme.

The basis of the whole business is of course the building up of Russia by borrowing or imitating Western knowledge. This itself meant a total revolution in the attitude of the Russians towards the West which, in spite of the slight innovations we have already seen being made in previous reigns, the vast bulk of the ignorant population regarded with an almost hysterical xenophobia.

External symbols as well as matters of more real significance were altered. One of the first things he did was to force his people to wear Western clothes instead of their cumbersome robes, and, what excited even more horror, to shave off their beards or pay a fine. Peter himself on 27 August 1698 began the work with a large pair of shears on the faces of some of his nobles, a performance which caused alarm as well as despondency for the beard was regarded as sacred, and to lose it had previously meant running the risk of excommunication. The Russians were also obliged to stomach a closer view of these outlandish fashions from those among whom they were more usual, for a *ukase* (government Decree) of 1702 allowed foreigners into the country in large numbers: Peter was anxious to bring in foreign technical experts. He also tolerated the *Raskolniki* (Old Believers), who often were good workmen, on condition that they paid double taxes; for a country needing all the help it can get cannot afford the luxury of religious intolerance. To mark the new order he altered the calendar: the new year in Russia was henceforward to begin on 1 January instead of 1 September (*ukase* of 1699). Another enormously important westernizing measure was a Decree of 1704 emancipating women; compulsory marriage was stopped. Just as startling was his coronation of his (second) wife as empress in 1724. The first hospital, with a medical school, in Russia, was opened in 1706, and the legal code was reformed in 1718, the most interesting measure being the adoption of primogeniture. Even the wretched serfs were not wholly neglected, although Peter could not do much for them as he needed the services of their noble masters in administrative and military posts, and so had to leave them control over their serfs in exchange. He did at least decree that masters who too grossly abused that control should be shut up as lunatics, and a *ukase* of 1721 stopped the selling of serfs separately; they were only to be sold in families. Perhaps the most famous of these westernizing measures was the creation of a window, or rather a door, opening to the West. In 1704 he founded a new capital for his empire on the Baltic coast. By the banks of the River Neva, out of a desolate marshy waste, gradually arose the great town of St Petersburg, and directing the workmen in person was the Tsar himself, who during this time lived in a little hut. The new town was not only meant as a new capital, but as a fortress to protect the country from Sweden, and it contained foundries for making cannon. It was also intended to be a port for merchant as well as naval ships (by 1712 it harboured a fleet of line-of-battle ships and war galleys) and furthermore was intended as a way of making entry into Russia easier for foreign experts. In time the whole court moved there and the town possessed monuments and an Academy of Sciences.

All this aroused much opposition, partly because it was too imitative of the West, so before sketching the remaining, and more important, part of Peter's reforms, we could here glance briefly at the nature of that opposition and how Peter dealt with it. The Tsarevna Sophia in 1698, supported by some nobles, persuaded the Moscow Guard (the *Streltsi*) to rise in revolt. The rising was put down easily enough by foreign mercenaries under the Tsar's friend Patrick Gordon. Their punishment was infamous; a horrible account of it is given by an Austrian diploma-tist, von Korb, who was in Moscow at the time. He speaks of Moscow as being adorned with corpses, and Peter himself, in between wild bouts of drinking, helped the torturers. 'The whole month of October was spent in lacerating the backs of culprits with the knout and with flames; no day were those that were left alive exempt from scourging, or else they were broken upon the wheel or driven to the gibbet or slain with the axe. . . .' Nothing could be proved against Sophia so she was left in her monastery, nor against Peter's wife, but he shut her up in one as well. Nor did opposition and cruel reprisals end there. Years later, in 1718, he butchered his own son, the Tsarevitch Alexis. Alexis was not in sympathy with his father's character or policy, but may be acquitted of treason, although he almost certainly would have undone a lot of Peter's work if he could. He fled to Vienna, but was lured back, and, in spite of a solemn oath that no harm should befall him, Peter had him flogged to death. It is difficult to read the details of these enormities without horror. The only defence one can give of Peter is that he feared that his life's work would be undone, but this is a defence that would only commend itself to those holding that the end always justifies the means.

It is a relief to turn to Peter's better side. It was all very well to persuade foreigners to come into Russia, but it would be more satis-factory if the Russians could learn how to do things for themselves. Education was needed, and Peter glimpsed that the first one in need of it was himself. In 1697 and 1698 he made a journey to the West for the purpose of picking up what is nowadays called 'technical know-how': significantly, the chief stops were made in countries famous for shipbuilding—Holland and England. (Venice was on the list too, but he had to go home to deal with the *Streltsi* instead.) In Holland he stayed five months, mostly in shipyards, and then went to England, where Deptford drew him like a magnet. He learnt a lot about ships and much else besides; Bishop Burnet in his *History* says that 'he is mechanically turned, and seems designed by nature rather to be a ship carpenter than a great prince'. Nobody was very sorry to see the departure of a guest who amused himself by getting drunk, smashing furniture, and extracting his followers' teeth.

When he returned home it was his subjects' turn to receive the benefits of education, although he had in fact made a start even before he left by sending fifty young and reluctant nobles abroad to acquire knowledge. (This was not a complete novelty; the Tsar Boris had sent some abroad about a century earlier, and they had all, after sampling civilization, refused to return.) Schools for navigation and mathematics were established in 1705 in Moscow, as well as some with a rather more cultural syllabus. A School of Artillery and a School of Engineers were founded in 1712. It was soon found that the pupils lacked the previous elementary education necessary to follow the instruction in these places, so, in 1714, professors were ordered to go around the country-side teaching arithmetic to the sons of the nobility; the nobles were forbidden to marry, and were refused government employment, unless they were educated. Of education for the masses there was practically nothing. Peter founded the Academy of Sciences in 1724 to provide education at university, secondary, and primary levels, but his interest in education went beyond formal instruction; in 1703 he gave Russia its first newspaper and in 1707 he reformed the alphabet. He also started a natural history museum and helped in the production of books.

If Peter knew that knowledge is power, he knew also that wealth and efficient organization are equally necessary if a State is to be strong, so he laboured just as hard to provide Russia with a thriving economy and an efficient system of government. About ninety per cent of his subjects were peasants, and the main agricultural area was Central Muscovy. They used very primitive methods and Peter's attempts to persuade them to improve these were a failure, though he did make the Baltic landowners produce more flax and hemp for export. Far better results were obtained in industry. The iron works at Tula were enlarged for the making of cannon, foundries were established at Olonets and St Petersburg, and eleven more foundries set up in the Urals. By 1725 Russia's production of iron was 20,000 tons a year, and some of it was exported. Ambitious steps to create textile industries were also made, and, by 1725, more than two hundred factories were producing cloth. Some of these were State-aided, but Peter also tried to force merchants to invest part of their profits in industry. The labour was found by drafts of peasants, and after 1731 merchants could buy peasants. The latter were not serfs, properly so called, for they were attached to the factory, not to its owner. Skilled labour was a different matter, and the lack of this was in part made good by importing foreigners and by an apprentice system introduced in 1711. Other industries were encouraged too, among them carpet-making, leather, and even sturgeon-fishing, while the timber industry was also made more productive. The results were good. The great fairs at Moscow and Astrakhan attracted foreign traders, and commerce was further helped by the development of the ports of St Petersburg and Archangel and by the construction of a canal linking the Volga and the Neva. The trade of Russia multiplied, as can be inferred from the vastly greater volume of ships putting in at the Baltic ports—100 in 1720 and 650 by 1725—and as can be seen by the figure of Russia's exports, which were 4,200,000 roubles in value by the time of Peter's death.

The object of this was of course partly to provide the government with more money to support a bigger army, but to find this was always very difficult, although Peter more than doubled his revenues by means of a poll-tax, by taxes on a variety of things such as beards and windows, and by means of the State monopolies of salt and tobacco. This increase at least sufficed to allow Russia to play a much bigger part in international affairs, but huge resources still need to be efficiently handled, and the task of providing the country with a governmental system able to do this proved to be as difficult as any of Peter's reforms.

Government in Russia started at the top, and Peter himself worked like a dynamo. Nevertheless, it was still necessary to do things to improve the power, status, and efficiency of the Head of State. One measure was the abandonment of the office of Patriarch of the Russian Church. (The Patriarchs had greatly hindered the Tsars in the past.) This was easily done, for the Patriarch died in 1700 and Peter did not appoint a successor. After 1701 monks were little more than salaried State servants, and after 1721 the Church was placed under the control of a government-appointed body, the 'Spiritual Department'. Peter intended to run no possible risk—admittedly it did not seem a great one in Russia—of any sort of challenge from the Church: no Thomas Becket or visit to Canossa for him. In 1721—22 October, it is a momentous date—he assumed the title of Emperor of All Russia; the Russian Empire was born. The Head of State was untroubled by rivals and had a resounding and impressive title, but there remained the problem of the possibility of the Crown falling into incapable hands. Peter met this by the Ordinance of 1722 which declared the principle of primogeniture as applied to the succession to be stupid and dangerous, and vested in the reigning Tsar the sole right to nominate his successor; he quite wisely nominated his own wife.

One man cannot run a country single-handed, and Peter at first had no real central administrative machine to help him, the Senate being useless and in any case only an advisory body. Local government was cumbrous and chaotic. An early start was made. Between 1701 and 1703 Directories of Mining, Coining, Artillery, and Naval affairs were created. (Here can be seen the basic necessities of a government at war.) The *Duma* of *Boiars* (nobles) was dispensed with and a Chancery took its place. But these were somewhat makeshift arrangements. In 1711 an Administrative Senate was appointed to deal with finance and justice, and in 1713–15 he formed 'Collegia' on the Swedish model, nine in number, which were in effect ministerial departments, each controlled by a President (usually a Russian) and a Vice-President (usually a foreigner). Such were the Tsar's attempts at reform in central government. For the purpose of local government, Russia was in 1708 divided into eight huge areas ('Governments') headed by Governors, and each Government afterwards divided into Provinces (the total was forty-three) run by Presidents (*Voivodes*), assisted by a Council of Assessors called *Landräthe* whose members were elected by the gentry, although the Presidents remained responsible also to the central government. This did not complete the arrangements; in 1720 Courts of Justice were established in every town as well as Burgomasters and Town Councillors.

All this might sound very neat and efficient, but, as the Emperor Joseph II was later to remark, in Russia everything starts and nothing is finished. In this case Joseph was right, for most of it collapsed by 1728. Peter was obliged to wage ceaseless war against the incompetence and dishonesty of his subjects, and was even obliged to invite informers to step forward and denounce their superiors in the administration if they detected peculation, which they did only too frequently. Peter was forced to execute the Governor of Siberia, Prince Gagarin, for plundering public funds. He did make an important constructive reform in this direction, however, and that was that he transformed the status of the nobility; henceforth they held their land only on condition of performing State service, either civil or military. By these means an aristocracy of service was built up, but at the expense of allowing the nobility a firmer grip on their serfs. (The position of the nobility is dealt with more fully in Chapter 16.) These aristocrats were never very efficient; in any case there was no real co-ordination between the various administrative organs created by the Tsar; none, for instance, between the Colleges and the Senate, or between these and the local bodies. In the end, everything depended on the Tsar.

What does all this add up to? Opinion is fairly unanimous that if anybody can be described as the founder of the power of modern Russia, it is Peter. Frederick the Great said that he worked on Russia like nitric acid on iron, and the remark is peculiarly apt, for he did leave ineradicable marks on a country whose real mentality remained nevertheless much as before. Voltaire said that under him Russia made more progress in fifty years than any other nation had made in five hundred. At one bound Russia under its tempestuous ruler became a European Power, for all this mighty effort was directed towards creating a huge army and fleet with which Peter sent Russia off on a career of conquest that ever since has received only temporary setbacks. The army was increased to 210,000 men and the navy had forty-eight warships as well as nearly eight hundred galleys and smaller craft by the end of the reign. With this force Peter achieved some success against his neighbours, as we shall see.

(c) POLAND

Another country which was to attack Sweden in 1700 was one which was to gain nothing from this attempt to dismember a neighbouring State and which was itself, ironically enough, to be partitioned among its neighbours so thoroughly that by the end of the eighteenth century it disappeared entirely from the map. Yet in the sixteenth century Poland had been a huge country, stretching from the Baltic nearly to the Black Sea, and from the Oder and the Carpathians to east of Smolensk. This sprawling giant, in fact, contained within itself weaknesses which were to prove fatal. Notorious among these was the constitution, and since the weakness of Poland has troubled the world from that day to this it would be appropriate here to outline its salient features.

In 1572 the male line of the Jagello dynasty, which had ruled Poland, became extinct and the Constitution thereafter adopted, while retaining a monarchy, in effect made the country an oligarchical republic, with all real power in the hands of the *szlachta* (gentry). The Polish *szlachta* wielded absolute power over their serfs, and the kings were not strong enough to bring them to heel. The crazy Constitution therefore only reflected the anarchy of the country and then in turn became an additional cause of it. Over seventy per cent of the population were serfs crushed by the gentry. The middle class was small, and the gentry, although quite numerous, were in turn dominated by about a hundred great noble families, and of these again seventeen stood out above the rest. The greatest one of all was the Czartoryskis; it was usual to refer to it as 'The Family'. At the root of the Constitution was a contractual theory of the State, and at every monarch's accession there was drawn up an agreement which the king had to sign, the *Pacta conventa*, and which reduced him to a figurehead. He could not refuse his signature, for the monarchy had become elective. Even discussion of a successor during the lifetime of a king was forbidden. The king was elected by the supreme legislative body—the Diet (*Sejm*). This consisted of two Chambers: the House of Deputies, which contained nothing but gentry elected by local 'Dietines' which in their turn were filled by gentry; and the House of Senators, which contained archbishops, bishops, some of the chief governmental officials, and some of the more important members of the nobility. To be valid, every law had to be passed by both Houses as well as the king, but few laws stood much chance of this, because of the most amazing feature of the Constitution, which was the *liberum veto*; that is, every law needed unanimous support, for a single adverse vote from one deputy sufficed to stop it. Worse, one such adverse vote not only blocked the law in question but every other law which that session of the Diet might have managed to pass; this was called 'destroying' the Diet. In such circumstances it would have been a near miracle if any law were passed, and in fact of the fifty-five Diets held after 1655, forty-eight produced no legislation. Thus we have the spectacle of a king controlled by a Diet which itself could do nothing, and just to make really sure that the king remained under the thumb of the Diet, Senators-Resident lived with the king; after 1717 he had to abide by their decisions.

Administration was in an even worse mess than the legislature, for the king had little control over the officials, while the judiciary too presented the same spectacle. Most of the courts were dominated by the gentry. Local government was little better, for the countryside was dominated by scores of 'Dietines', which again were mouthpieces of the gentry. One peculiar Polish institution might seem to be especially designed to wreck what little chance of sensible direction might emerge from the institutions just mentioned, namely the 'Confederations'. These were unions, usually of gentry, for certain specific ends, and a 'General Confederation' covered the whole country. Its authority was greater than that of any other body and it could overrule the king. During an interregnum it did take over, and even the functioning of the ordinary law courts ceased and 'hooded courts' nominated by the Confederation took their place. However, the great merit of a Confederation was that the *liberum veto* did not apply to it; a majority sufficed. So in times of emergency it was sometimes possible to by-pass the legalized anarchy of the normal Constitution and achieve some results.

Not that Poland could usually hope for much government even through a Confederation. The revenues were microscopic; the king could sourly contemplate (the normal word 'enjoy' seems too painfully ironic) an income one-seventy-fifth that of the King of France. The army was a smallish force of cavalry with little pay, less discipline, and no artillery. There were, in the single caustic phrase of von Moltke, 'no forts, no navy, no roads, and no ambassadors'. The country was large but thinly populated and possessed no geographical obstacles, such as mountains, which might serve to hinder an invader. There was no religious unity, for while about half the population were Catholics, about one-third were members of the Greek Orthodox Church, and the remainder included Jews and Protestants. There was no ethnic unity either, for of the country's total of perhaps rather more than eleven million, only about a half were really Poles; there was a big minority of Little—and White—Russians.

This means that it is hardly appropriate to call Poland a 'State' at all. It was a vast area in a condition of anarchy. A loose comparison might be made with the Holy Roman Empire, which itself was not really a State but a collection of independent countries admitting nominal allegiance to an elected Emperor. In Poland the greater nobles wielded power much as did such figures as the Electors. The difference was that in Germany some of them managed to create smaller States which grew to formidable proportions, whereas in Poland the greater nobility, while crushing their serfs and also dominating the lesser *szlachta*, never made independent States for themselves.

Yet although Poland was to be dismembered in the eighteenth century, it still had some life left in it in the seventeenth. The war with Sweden which we have already noticed went badly for Poland and, by the time of the signing of the Treaty of Oliva in May–June 1660, she not only had to renounce for ever her claim to the Swedish throne, but also had to give up sovereignty over East Prussia to the Elector of Brandenburg, and this after having lost large areas of territory on the Baltic coast to Sweden earlier in the century. Sweden was perhaps the most terrible enemy of Poland, but she was by no means the only one. Russia was almost as bad, and in the end was to prove a great deal worse. True, Poland just before our period begins actually invaded Russia in an attempt to gain the Russian Crown for her own King, Ladislaus IV, but at the Treaty of Viasma in 1634, by which the Tsar gave up his claim to the Polish Baltic Provinces, to White Russia, and to Severia, she had to give up her claim to the Russian Crown.

The following reign, that of John Casimir (1648–68), was, however, disastrous for the country. The Cossacks of the Dnieper area of the Ukraine in those days owed allegiance to Poland. They were a wild lot, living by plundering their neighbours, but they possessed fighting qualities of a sort that could have been invaluable to Poland. Unhappily, the Polish nobility tried to exploit this freedom-loving people as if they were serfs, and the result was that the Cossacks rose under their *hetman* (a sort of viceroy), Bogdan Chmielniki, in May 1648, routed a Polish army, and then, fearing that they might still not manage to retain their independence, decided to throw in their lot with the Russians. They asked for, and of course were only too gladly given, Russian protection (1654) in exchange for some measure of autonomy. The result was that Poland lost, and Russia gained, a great source of strength. The Russians had won control over the Ukraine without effort and they did not respect the autonomy of the region for long. This was the beginning, not the end, of a chapter of disaster. In the next year came the Swedish invasion helped by Brandenburg, but

Poland was saved by her own efforts and by those of Austria and Denmark; Brandenburg was bought off by the cession of East Prussia. Even so, Poland at Oliva lost Livonia to Sweden, and seven years later (1667) at the Truce of Andrusovo gave to the Tsar the lands beyond the Dnieper. All this, followed by a rebellion of the nobles when he tried to limit the *liberum veto*, was just a bit too much for the King, John Casimir, and he abdicated in September 1668. He was the last Vasa King of Poland. During the interregnum that followed, the royal power, such as it was, was exercised by the Bishop of Gnesen, while various foreign factions intrigued to get their particular candidates elected. In the end the Polish gentry got tired of all of them and elected instead one of their own number, King Michael; but he died in 1673 after a reign of only four years, a reign which saw the loss of the fortress of Kaminiec (in Podolia) to the Turks.

Yet the plunge into total darkness was to be briefly and gloriously postponed. The next king, John Sobieski (1674–96), became a Polish and indeed a European hero. There were plenty of enemies all around Poland that had stripped her of provinces, but in fact John Sobieski's imperishable fame rests on his overthrow of the enemy of all Christendom—the Turks.

(d) THE TURKISH EMPIRE AND THE SIEGE OF VIENNA

The Ottoman Turks were Asiatic Muslims who had conquered all the Balkan area and in 1453 had rounded off this by capturing Constantinople, the old capital of the East Roman Empire. In 1517 their ruler, the Sultan, assumed also the Caliphate—that is, headship of the Muslim faith—and a little while later the great sultan Suliman the Magnificent pushed Turkish conquest deep into Europe by his defeat of the Hungarians at the Battle of Mohacs (1526).

The Turks owed these successes to two main causes: the disunity of Christendom and their own military prowess. Indeed, they seem to have been singularly devoid of any other sort of prowess. They left administration of conquered provinces to locals and did not bother themselves much with commerce, which was to a great extent conducted by Greeks. Their own government at the top was a weird and bloody nightmare of palace intrigue and assassination. Their army, the first regular standing army in Europe, was wonderful, but even this owed not a little of its success to the famous corps of Janissaries, who were all taken as children from conquered Christian peoples and brought up as soldiers dedicated to their profession and given privileges and a high status in return. The fact that the Turkish Empire stretched from the Pillars of Hercules in a great sweep across North Africa and Asia Minor and to the very gates of Vienna thus has in it more than an element of the paradoxical, and, so far as it is explicable at all, they won this Empire by a good army with the best artillery in the world. They held it by skill at playing off subject races against each other and perhaps also because their rule in some respects compared favourably from the viewpoint of the conquered with rule by any Christian Power at the time, for the Turks never indulged in religious persecution.

This Power, always held to be an interloper in Europe, had been a frightful menace, but in the seventeenth century bore all the marks of a fatal decline. The viceroys of the various provinces took little notice of the government at Constantinople; the regular army and the Janissaries were readier to fight for their own pay and privileges than for the State (they executed Sultan Osman II in 1622, for example), and the officials became as useless as they were corrupt. Most serious of all, after the reign of Suliman the Magnificent (1520–66) there followed for nearly a century a collection of sultans who positively strain credulity. One was an imbecile, another executed a Grand Vizier merely because he had incurred the hostility of the harem, and it was normal practice for sultans to execute all their brothers as a precautionary measure. However, things could be very different if a capable sultan or two came along, and the next best thing actually happened. Sultan Mohammed IV (1648–87) was almost as eccentric as his father who had preceded him, and who had been executed because not even the Turks could put up with him any more; but he had the wisdom to give the direction of affairs to an extremely able Grand Vizier, Mohammed Kiuprili, who founded what was really a dynasty of famous and able rulers.

Kiuprili imposed his will by a reign of terror in which the mortality rate among inefficient, corrupt, or merely disgruntled, admirals, pashas, beys, and Janissaries (who were hanged, strangled, decapitated, and otherwise disposed of) was very high; in which even important churchmen were not spared; and in which on one occasion the wives and children of the chiefs of a rebellion in Aleppo were skinned alive in front of the wretched men before they themselves were beheaded. In six months he had infused some discipline into the Empire and gained the complete trust of the Sultan. Not only was the Turkish decline arrested, but the Ottoman Empire could now hope for fresh conquests.

Their main line of advance was up the Danube Valley, and here their

The OTTOMAN EMPIRE in EUROPE

During the latter part of the Seventeenth Century

Mountains mostly over 1500 ft. -----
Boundary of Empire in 1660 -----
Ottoman gains in 1664, 1669, 1672 -----

300 m/s.

chief enemy was not Poland at all, but Austria. Between these two Powers lay Hungary and Transylvania, and the Habsburgs viewed with alarm Kiuprili's grip on Moldavia and Wallachia, and his claims to Turkish sovereignty over Hungary. A long period of war therefore opened between the two Empires. The second Kiuprili invaded Hungary, Moravia, and even Silesia, but was heavily defeated by the Austrians, helped by a French contingent, at the Battle of Saint Gotthard in 1664. A truce was then made at Vasvar (August 1664), which was supposed to last for twenty years, by which Austria got western Hungary and Turkey got eastern Hungary and recognition of her claim to suzerainty over Transylvania. This was a distinct gain for the Turks, but actually the Austrians received the greater part of Hungary. Their control over this immensely valuable acquisition could only be maintained if they could manage to suppress the native Magyars (a difficult task), and also if they could keep the Turks at bay. Ironically enough, in this task they were saved by Poland.

John Sobieski was an old enemy of the Turks. The defeats suffered by Poland in the reign of King Michael in 1672 and the Treaty of Buczacs in October of the same year had been so humiliating to Poland that Sobieski, who was then Grand Marshal of Poland, and many of the nobles, disavowed the treaty. Sobieski then marched against the Turks and heavily defeated them at the Battle of Khoczim (in Bessarabia, 11 November 1673). Later that year he was elected King of Poland and, since Poland still felt intense hatred of the Turks, he could count on an unusually high degree of support for anti-Turkish action. Yet to defeat the Turks would simply mean fastening Habsburg rule more securely on Hungary, and for this Sobieski had scant enthusiasm. For the present, however, he had to fight the existing Turkish war, and in 1675 he again defeated the Turks at Lemberg. In spite of this he was unable to shake their hold on Podolia, and in 1676 both sides were exhausted enough to be glad to make peace at Zurawno. By this the Turks retained their conquests, but at least the Poles no longer had to pay the tribute which King Michael had agreed to pay them. For the next few years the Turks were busy in a war with Russia. They got the worst of it, and in 1681 Kara Mustapha, who had succeeded his brother-in-law Ahmed II Kiuprili as Grand Vizier, was happy enough to make peace at the expense of handing over to the Russians that part of the Ukraine which he had just wrested from Poland at the Treaty of Zurawno. Nothing daunted by this set-back, Kara Mustapha, whose ability was in inverse proportion to his ambition, determined to make his name glorious in Turkish annals by no less a feat than the conquest of Vienna and the extension of the Turkish Empire to the Rhine.

The moment was well chosen. The attention of Europe was fixed on Louis XIV, who was just adding to a long list of gains at the expense of his neighbours by grabbing Strasburg. Even the Emperor, who had most to fear from a fresh Turkish advance up the Danube, was forced to spare some of his attention to the menace from Louis. The Emperor was in trouble in Hungary. Habsburg rule was bitterly unpopular there. The Austrians severely persecuted the minority of Protestants in Hungary, who therefore looked enviously on their more fortunate brethren living under the tolerant rule of the Turks. Worse, the Austrians offended them by their partition of the country under the Truce of Vasvar, and still more by their policy of trying to Germanize the country and rule it from Vienna. So great was the discontent that the Hungarians had revolted in 1666 under Francis Rakoczy, but they failed to get the help that they had expected from France, and the rebels were treated with pitiless cruelty by the Austrians. The country fell completely under Austrian officials, the aristocracy were taxed heavily, and Protestant pastors were sent to the galleys. This reign of terror caused the brave Hungarians to revolt again, this time under a Magyar aristocrat called Tokoli (1674). The Turks and the Poles were for different reasons sympathetic to the Hungarian cause, but as they were at that time engaged in fighting each other neither could help the Hungarians. The Emperor made a last-minute attempt to propitiate the Hungarians. Their government was reorganized more in conformity with their wishes, and the more irksome taxes were removed. Calvinists and Lutherans were given toleration and full rights of citizenship, and Hungarian nobles given posts in the government. All this sweetness and light, however, did not fool the Hungarian leader Tokoli, who proclaimed himself Prince of Hungary under the overlordship of the Sultan.

This time the Turks were ready to give help. The Sultan collected an enormous army, whose numbers are generally given at about 200,000 men (though John Sobieski afterwards said they numbered 300,000), and, advancing into Hungary, was joined by Tokoli, who up to then had bluffed the Austrians into relying on him. Near Buda the Sultan handed over the banner of Mohammed to Kara Mustapha and went off hunting. By 7 July 1683 the latter had defeated the scanty forces sent against him and reached the gates of Vienna, from which the Emperor and a large number of inhabitants had prudently fled. A small garrison of about 14,000 troops was all that stood in the way of the Turks.

This sad state of things caused the utmost alarm throughout Europe, but it must be regretfully said that nothing very much in the way of practical help seemed likely, at least not from the bigger Powers. England under Charles II took no notice, Holland's Estates would not permit William of Orange to do anything, Spain was too busy trying to defend herself against the aggressions of Louis XIV. As for the Most Christian King himself (although he offered to leave the Emperor's western frontier unmolested), he sneeringly observed that Crusades had gone out of fashion. Even his small concession had strings tied to it, for it was conditional on the Dauphin's being admitted to the Imperial succession, and in any case the French King was for the moment avoiding too forward a policy because he was afraid of annoying the English. However, the despairing appeals of the Emperor and of the Pope did not fall on deaf ears only. To her eternal credit, Venice offered help, even the Germanic Diet, after first confining itself to recommending public prayers, voted money, and the offer of troops was made by Maximilian Emanuel of Bavaria, John George of Saxony, and the young George Lewis of Brunswick-Lüneburg (afterwards King George I of England). Even more useful than the help of these relatively humble rulers who came forward to the defence of Christendom while more important Powers were coldly pursuing, as usual, their own crooked ends, was the intervention of one of whom European opinion was afterwards to be best expressed in the text, 'There was a man sent from God whose name was John.' Just as another John had come forward in the sixteenth century, Don John of Austria, 'the last knight of Europe' as Chesterton wrongly called him (had Chesterton never heard the name 'Sobieski'?), to win the Battle of Lepanto, so now advanced John Sobieski, King of Poland, with 40,000 troops from a country which in a long and pathetic history has never lacked heroes. His aim was not merely to smash the Turkish army besieging Vienna, but to detach the Magyars from their alliance with the Turks and to expel the Turks totally from Europe.

The latter were at that moment enjoying the prospect of a certain and easy victory, and the senior officers were enjoying it in fair comfort —their dug-outs were elaborately furnished—and unhurriedly, for they saw no reason to launch costly assaults against a city whose walls were being, patiently and skilfully, undermined by the excellent Turkish engineers. This delay was to prove their undoing, for it is certain that they could have taken the place before help could possibly have arrived had Kara Mustapha and his senior generals attacked instead of amusing themselves during a protracted siege. As it was, morale among their horde steadily dropped, as it often does among inactive troops, while the lower ranks told each other that the whole business was unlucky because it infringed the Truce of Vasvar.

The bad luck soon arrived. By 5 September John had reached the Danube and joined forces with the Imperialists. Three days later the troops of Saxony and Bavaria arrived and with a combined army of about 60,000 men he hastened on. Avoiding the dangerous route along the plains, he climbed the Kahlemberg, a feat which took three days and reduced men and horses to a state of exhaustion, the whole force being kept moving only by the iron determination of the King. On 11 September rockets from the top of the mountain told the city that help was at last at hand. Even then the Turks outnumbered the Christians by three to one, and the nature of the terrain was such as to make the success of the relieving force seem quite hopeless. Nevertheless, the long and fierce battle fought on 12 September resulted in a total victory for the Polish King—thanks to the courage of the Christian troops, to the skill of John Sobieski, and, it must be admitted, just as much to the boundless tactical ineptitude of Kara Mustapha. The defeat was turned into an utter rout when an eclipse for a short time hid the crescent moon; wild panic at this ominous omen swept through an already demoralized force, and the remnants of the shattered Turkish army fled, leaving 10,000 dead and a mountain of baggage behind them.

Sobieski wrote that the booty would take eight days to gather up, but was personally just as pleased by the capture of the banner of Mohammed, which he sent off to the Pope. (He also mentions, with charming glee, that he had captured the Grand Vizier's tent, which, he says, 'was so large that it might have contained within its circumference the city of Warsaw'.) Of course he also gained an almost hysterical welcome of the sort that our times seem to reserve for film-stars: 'crowds of people tried to kiss my hands, and even my feet and clothing; most of them had to content themselves with touching my coat'. Such was his reception by the common people, but from the great he soon found that jealousy and suspicion took the place of gratitude. The Emperor hurried back to Vienna but received him coldly, and the Poles were even refused fodder for their horses. The pursuit of the Turks was not energetically followed up, partly because it was suspected that Sobieski wished to conquer Hungary for himself.

Nevertheless, the hero-king joined in the Holy League which was reorganized by the Pope in 1684 and which also included Austria, Venice, Malta, and, after 1686, Russia. Sobieski had inflicted another defeat on the Turks in 1683, but he was elbowed out of any share in the victories that followed—only regaining some previous losses—and in 1686 had to make a peace with Russia by which the latter kept all the gains made in 1667. The profits of war fell mainly to the Emperor, for in 1686 Buda was taken and the defeat of the Turks in the next year at the Battle of Mohacs led to the invasion of Moldavia, Wallachia, and Croatia; the Emperor's grip on all Hungary became sure after the defeat of the Transylvanian rebels, and the Crown of Hungary was declared hereditary in the Habsburg family, while Transylvania shared the same fate. The Venetians, too, captured the Morea and Dalmatia. The Turks' still stubborn resistance under the able third Kiuprili (who had succeeded Kara Mustapha, executed for his failure) was finally broken after the disastrous defeat at the Battle of Zenta (August 1697), and the Turks sued for peace. The Peace of Karlowitz, 26 January 1699, was humiliating for them. Venice took Dalmatia between the Kerka and the Narenta, the whole of the Peloponnese except Corinth, the Aegean Islands, and St Maure. Russia, by a peace not concluded until 1702, received the fortress and district of Azov. Poland received Kaminiec, Podolia, and western Ukraine. The lion's share went to the Emperor, who received Transylvania, the whole of Hungary except the Banat of Temesvar, and the greater part of Croatia and Slavonia.

This treaty marks a great moment in the history of Europe. The threat to Christendom from the Turks, which had been the nightmare of three centuries, was dispelled once and for ever. From then on the nature of the problem was changed, but a Turkish problem still lingered into the twentieth century. As Carlyle remarked, 'the Grand Turk . . . has staggered about less and less of a terror and outrage, more and more of a nuisance, growing unbearable, ever since that day'. The shrinkage of Turkish power left a vacuum which would somehow be filled, or, to change the metaphor, plenty of Powers would rush in to seize the remaining spoils.

This nearly concludes our survey of North and East and South-east Europe in the second half of the seventeenth century. We are left with an overall impression somewhat as follows. The whole area at that time did not contain a single State in any way comparable in power to the monarchy of Louis XIV on land or to the English or the Dutch at sea. The two latter Powers, if they chose to act in concert, could upset the balance of power in the Baltic any time they wished, while Louis XIV, with contemptuous ease, could restore it again by mere diplomatic pressure. In the centre was moribund Poland, which the French made contact with only when they wished to frighten Germany. In the South, the Bogy-man of Europe was showing the symptoms which were to earn him the title of the Sick Man, and in any case it is difficult to take very seriously the frequently expressed view that the siege of Vienna had ever really constituted a mortal threat to Christendom itself; it takes more than a feat of imagination to picture Kara Mustapha capturing Vienna and then going on to defeat, say, the armies of Louis XIV. The Turks had been of great service to the French, at least since the days of Francis I, in furnishing a very real embarrassment for the Emperors whenever the latter were at war with the kings of France: henceforward they could hardly do even that.

Huge changes were to occur in the eighteenth century not only in the importance of the countries in these areas relative to each other, but also in the importance of the whole area to Western Europe. The ancient State of Poland was to crash in total ruin, the moon of Islam to suffer further eclipse, the Empire of the Vasas to shrink back to its Swedish homeland. Instead, Austria and Russia were to dominate in the East and South, and indeed the power of Russia was to dominate the North too; both, but especially Russia, were to grow to such a stature that so far from having to trouble about the West they could run Eastern Europe in accord with their own wishes and in defiance of those of the West. Russia had a still bigger future, but great though she was to become under Peter and his successors, her power was to be matched by the startling growth of a State which we have so far hardly mentioned. It is at the first steps of Brandenburg-Prussia in its upward march that we must now briefly look, before this survey of Eastern and Northern Europe can be regarded as complete.

(e) BRANDENBURG-PRUSSIA AND THE REFORMS OF THE GREAT ELECTOR

It must be granted that Brandenburg is more worth looking at in this period for what it was to become rather than for what it amounted to in the seventeenth century. The State which was to grow so great, to swallow all Germany, and then in the twentieth century to fight the whole world twice and to conquer from the Atlantic to the Caucasus and from the Arctic Circle to the gates of Cairo, was in 1640 a sorry little ruin.

It consisted of roughly three groups of widely separated territories which had been amassed by the House of Hohenzollern. Cleves, Mark, and Ravensberg were in the Rhineland area; Electoral Brandenburg was a poor, sandy-soiled group of five 'Marks' (marches, or borderlands), having Berlin as a centre; eastern or 'Ducal' Prussia was held as a fief from the King of Poland. Most of the territory of the Hohenzollerns therefore lay east of the Elbe, land reconquered from the Slavs and hardly worth the trouble of reconquest—poor soil, no industrial centres, no large city, no useful outlet to the sea, thinly populated by poor and ignorant nobles engaged in oppressing even poorer and more ignorant peasants. All that these scattered territories had in common was the family which held sway over all. Even to say 'over all' is to say too much. During the Thirty Years War the Elector of Brandenburg had sought safety by diplomatic adroitness, or rather maladroitness; he tried neutrality as well as half-hearted alliances at different times with the Swedes and then with the Catholics. The fruits of this ineptitude were the hearty contempt of all the Powers, disaffection in his own East Prussia, and hordes of foreign soldiers roaming at will over most of Brandenburg. Nor does that end the sad story, for the Elector had very little control over his own subjects; he was dependent on the Estates of the various territories for taxation and these were so stingy even in wartime that the only army he could afford was made up of a few thousand ruffians well qualified to loot the Elector's own subjects but incapable of defending them against foreign invaders. Such was the mess inherited by the new Elector, Frederick William, in 1640.

His problems were thus interrelated. Without control over taxation he could never have a useful army, and without an army his dominions would remain tiny, weak, and contemptible. It speaks volumes for him that he was ready to try to do something about all this. He not only tried; he won a measure of success which his subjects recognized during his lifetime by referring to him as 'The Great Elector'. Nor has posterity wished to question this estimate.

He saw at once (though he did not say so until years later) that 'alliances are good, but forces of one's own still better. Upon them one can rely with more security, and a lord is of no consideration if he does not have means and troops of his own.' He began by throwing most of the undesirables out of the army. There were so many of them that the army was reduced thereby to about 2,500 men. This act, however, earned him the gratitude of his subjects, who were so glad at being rid of their tormentors that the Estates of Brandenburg and elsewhere gratefully voted him the money to keep this little force properly, and even to increase it. This he did to such purpose that by 1648 it had

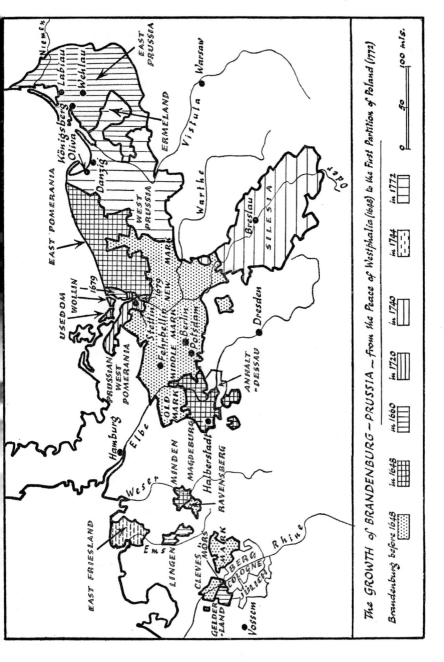

The GROWTH of BRANDENBURG-PRUSSIA — from the Peace of Westphalia (1648) to the First Partition of Poland (1772)

increased to about 8,000. After the Thirty Years War the Estates resumed their niggardly attitude, but the Elector was by then strong enough either to negotiate with them or to overawe them. The key agreement was the famous arrangement of 1653 made with the Estates of Brandenburg. In return for a large grant to his treasury (530,000 *thalers* to be spread over six years), he gave the so-called Junkers (noblemen) tremendous concessions. They were themselves afterwards to be exempt from taxes, were the only class allowed to acquire estates, and were given complete control over the peasants on their domains. Frederick William soon made good use of their money. His little army was at least big enough to enable him to override any further opposition of a dangerous sort, and so he imposed fresh taxes. With the proceeds he still further enlarged the army, which by 1660 had swollen to 27,000, and though it shrank again for a time after the Peace of Oliva, it had grown by his death in 1688 to 30,000 men.

It had grown in quality too. For one thing, he modified the old system under which the colonels made independent contracts with him whereby they provided a given number of men in exchange for a fixed inclusive payment to themselves, while retaining complete control over recruitment, payment, and promotion of the troops and appointing commissioned subordinate officers themselves. Also the Elector gave to Freiherr von Sparr command over all the troops, and under him a sort of General Staff came into being which diminished the importance of the colonels, as did the appointment of Claus Ernst von Platen to the post of General War Commissioner (*Generalkriegskommissar*), responsible for provisioning, billeting, and payment of the soldiers.

All this required a sound system of taxation under the Elector's control, and that also meant two things which he did not possess; namely, an efficient civil administration and a prosperous country. After the necessary preliminary of forcing the Estates formally to accept his full sovereignty he reorganized the whole system of government. Under the General War Commissioner were placed local ones called Tax Commissioners, or, more usually and more appropriately, War Commissioners, who encroached not only on the functions of the old municipal and other local officials appointed by the towns and the Estates, but also on his other officials, the Governors and Chancellors and their subordinates in each province. All these were in turn responsible to his central Council of State, Chamber of Finance, and Supreme Council of Justice. The quality of all the officials was improved and he also set up a postal service.

Even more useful were his efforts to encourage a sound economy.

Industry, trade, and the cultivation of the soil were in a piteous condition; Berlin was practically in the middle of a desert. The chief need was, in fact, human life and labour and, since the population had shrunk, he did all in his power to encourage immigration. (This policy, continued by his successors, was so vigorously pursued that by 1770 about a sixth of the total inhabitants of the country were immigrants or their descendants.) The most famous, and the most noble, example of this was his Edict of Potsdam of 8 November 1685 in which he said, 'In view of the sympathy which we ought to, and do, feel for our brethren of the reformed evangelical religion in France, who have been driven by persecution to leave their homes, we . . . desire to offer them a free and safe refuge in all our lands and possessions.' It should be noticed that this welcome, which resulted in 20,000 valuable new French subjects for the Elector in two years, was not extended purely to strengthen his dominions, for the Elector, an ardent Calvinist ruling over Lutherans, genuinely believed in religious toleration as a matter of conviction. These French refugees were valuable in all sorts of industries and professions as well as in providing the Elector with five regiments for the army. Nor were they the only assets thus acquired by the Elector's broadmindedness and generosity, for numerous highly skilled Dutch workers entered his dominions also. These taught the Brandenburgers how to drain their lands, manage dairy farms, and cultivate potatoes; they also stimulated the government into building canals, especially the Frederick William Canal which linked the Elbe and the Oder. So, thanks to them and the French, industries were created or revived, notably the woollen industry. The Elector's vision ranged overseas too, for under his encouragement was formed in 1682 the Brandenburg African Company, and a fair trade thus started on the Guinea Coast. There was also formed something which we can courteously entitle the Brandenburg-Prussian Navy, but it consisted chiefly of privateers, and died an early death.

All this effected an amazing transformation; the ridiculous Hohenzollern dominions became in a very few years something to reckon with. But though the Elector's handling of foreign affairs was marked by very great skill and persistence, it produced good but rather disappointing results.

True, he did amazingly well out of the Thirty Years War, and that was due as much to the existence of his useful little army as to his own cleverness and the patronage of Mazarin. He emerged with Cammin, Halberstadt, Minden, and the reversion of Magdeburg, all rich territories which helped to make him the most considerable Protestant

German Prince. For some time after that he was fully occupied in building up the strength of his dominions with the help of his great minister, Schwerin.

A crisis arose in 1655, however, when the Swedes attacked Poland. This imposed an agonizing decision on the Elector, for while a Polish defeat might bring him profit in the shape of the corridor (Polish or 'Royal' western Prussia) which separated his small portion of Pomerania from East Prussia, a Swedish success would probably mean that he could say 'good-bye' for ever to his chances of gaining the bulk of Pomerania. To make matters worse he could at that date still not rely on being able to control his own nobles and he still lacked a powerful ally. In the end he joined Sweden, and his troops played a not undistinguished part in the capture of Warsaw in July 1656. His reward was the Treaty of Labiau in November of the same year, by which the Swedes gave him complete sovereignty over East Prussia, to which they had a claim, and Ermeland. In the very next year, when Sweden was in difficulties with her Danish campaign, he coolly abandoned his ally and signed instead the Treaty of Wehlau (September 1657) with Poland, by which Poland was to recognize his sovereignty over East Prussia, though not over Ermeland (he got Elbing instead). He then organized an alliance with the Emperor and the Dutch which resulted in the military discomfiture of the Swedes. Once again we are reminded that these Powers in Eastern Europe had to dance to the tune of the great Powers of the West; after Sweden had been overawed by the Dutch fleet, Mazarin took good care that his Swedish allies should not suffer too much. In the Peace of Oliva in 1660 all the Elector gained therefore was sovereignty over East Prussia, but without Elbing. His skill, persistence, courage, and treachery thus won a substantial reward, though it fell short of his expectations.

His subsequent adventures in the field of foreign policy were marked by the same utter selfishness, faithlessness to allies, and single-minded determination to put the aggrandizement of his State before any other consideration; but since he failed to add any more territory to his dominions, little is to be gained by following the details of the turns and twists of the Elector's actions. He did give his State something which had enormous if intangible value—military glory. He remained neutral in the War of Devolution (1667–8), but when Louis XIV launched his attack on the Netherlands in 1672 Frederick William went to their defence. French successes soon made him change his mind and he concluded a separate peace with the French at Vossem in June 1673. When, however, the Empire declared war on the French in 1674, he about-turned yet again and sent a contingent against them. It achieved no success at all against Turenne, but the Elector won imperishable glory against the Swedes (allied to France). On 28 June 1675 he totally defeated a vastly larger Swedish army at the Battle of Fehrbellin. This was the first great victory of the Prussian army. Swedish power crumpled because of that and the assaults of numerous foes; but again the Elector was disappointed for, after conquering western Pomerania and the port of Stettin, he was obliged to give it all back again at the Treaty of Saint Germain-en-Laye in June 1679 on the insistence of Louis XIV. After that he did little of note except, by his alliance, to help Louis XIV in his 'Reunions' (yes, he had changed sides again).

His reign is nevertheless of the first importance. He did not make Brandenburg-Prussia a great State but he laid the sound foundations of greatness.

His successor, the Elector Frederick III, known as King Frederick I after he obtained the title of King in Prussia in 1701, did not, however, build anything very substantial on those foundations. For years he devoted all his energies towards the attainment of his ambition, or rather obsession, which was to get the title of king. There were numerous and serious obstacles barring his path, but after a treaty by which he undertook to help the Emperor, who was about to fight the War of the Spanish Succession against the French, he was given the Imperial permission to adopt the style not of King of Brandenburg, for the Emperor wanted no such title in the Empire, but of King in Prussia, which was outside the boundary of the Empire. (In fact, he was usually called King *of* Prussia, and it would be pedantic to revive his more correct title.)

Great were the festivities and rejoicings (30,000 horses were needed to drag all the requirements for the coronation and celebrations to Königsberg), and greatly did Frederick enjoy his new dignity—he even rose early in the mornings so as to have more time to relish the title—but we must leave Prussia, as it will be convenient to call the dominions of the Royal House of Hohenzollern from now on, and look instead at the gathering storm in both Western and Northern Europe. For in Sweden a young boy's accession to the throne seemed to her enemies the chance to dismember that country once and for all, while in Spain the death of King Charles II, without leaving a child to follow him, was the signal for all the Great Powers to dispute his Empire. By comparison with these, Frederick I of Prussia counted for very little, and indeed, in the eyes of some, only made himself smaller rather than bigger by a perhaps slightly childish hankering after a resounding title. Maybe he was not so very silly, for titles do carry great prestige, and did especially so in that age. His honour marked out Prussia as the most important German State, except for the House of Habsburg. Probably there was also an attraction in being a king at a time when Bossuet was proclaiming that kings were gods.

Yet at that time, too, the possessor of the clearest brain that ever came out of the county of Somerset, and perhaps one of the most influential that ever came out of any English county, was stating very decidedly that kings were not gods.

Before discussing the quarrels of the kings of Europe we must turn to study what John Locke was saying about their rights—divine and otherwise.

6 · Science and a Mental Revolution: The 'Enlightenment', or the *Philosophe* Movement in the Seventeenth Century

In most of Europe in the years immediately after about 1660 kings enjoyed a wonderful position. Peoples saw in kings the only hope of protection from exploitation by barons at home or from subservience to some conqueror from abroad. The melancholy exceptions to this—and what an awful object-lesson they provided!—were Poland, where they put the Crown up to auction for all-comers, and Turkey, whose sultans often met a violent end; both countries paid dearly for their failure to imitate everyone else and have a strong central government under a king.

Rather more flourishing exceptions to the rule appeared to be Holland and England. Holland was a republic but one that was only too happy to give royal powers, if not a royal title, to the House of Orange as soon as the storm-clouds rolled near. As for the English, it is true that a fanatical and unpopular minority had seized power and cut off King Charles I's head, but very soon the leader of that disrespectful gang was wearing the purple and putting his own head on the coins, and after his death the English went delirious with joy at the appearance of the august passenger of the battleship *Naseby*, now tactfully rechristened *Royal Charles*. After that a lot was said about Divine Right of Kings, until James II made the English realize that what they had really meant was Divine Right of a nice non-Catholic king. Much vain ingenuity was used after the Revolution of 1688 in an attempt to make out that nothing much had happened, while William III assumed not only the title of king but in many people's eyes also the magical power of curing disease by his royal touch. (In fairness to William it should be added that his remark to one such optimist, 'God send you better health and more sense', indicated a lack of conviction on his own part.) So even Holland and England appeared to be not really such striking exceptions to the prevailing king-worship, and England certainly was not an exception to the general spectacle of strong centralized governments, although we must realize here an extremely important point, and that was that in no country did governments have in practice anything like as much control over their subjects as is usual nowadays.

Kings, then, were everywhere respected because they were useful: they preserved their countries from escapades like the *Frondes* and offered the only hope against powerful neighbours. They owed their unique authority to something much more subtle than a realization of their usefulness. They were hedged with divinity too. We have already seen that the Catholic Church in France, for instance, deified Louis XIV; while the courtiers worshipped him as a god, Bishop Bossuet was calling him one. To the Church he was literally God's lieutenant and was answerable to God alone. For his subjects there was no right of protest, much less of rebellion, and the same veneration for kings was held in Protestant countries quite often too. Had not Luther said that it was the duty of all Christians to 'kill, stab, strangle' as many rebels as possible, for rebellion was a sin as well as a crime?

The Christian Churches, and especially the Catholic Church, had an enormous influence over men's minds and consciences, for the Church claimed that it had been directly appointed by Christ Himself to care for men's souls. Thus men everywhere, if they were not to fall into risk of damnation, had a duty to obey a double authority; the king in the political, and the Church in the religious, sphere, and this authority rested ultimately on Divine Revelation as recorded by the Holy Scriptures. So before royal power and before this theory men were supposed to bow, and most of them did; kings were not only necessary but divine.

This was a glorious position indeed, but a great deal more precarious than it seemed. For one thing, the nobility were not obliterated at all.

Although they had lost any hope of waging war on their kings, at least singly, kings everywhere had in effect won their obedience, albeit often grudging, as part of a bargain. The nobles were left still on a dizzy social eminence. In France they tended to monopolize all the most important positions in the country while they enjoyed almost complete immunity from taxation, while in Eastern Europe the various monarchs deliberately increased the social and fiscal privileges of the aristocracy *vis-à-vis* the remainder of their subjects in return for co-operation in the fields of military and administrative service. There might yet therefore come a time when the nobles would regret the tacit bargain and strive to regain some of their former real power. What meanwhile of the attitude of other classes? Might there not likewise come a time when the merchant classes would become dissatisfied with a system which barred the road to a really distinguished career for men of high ability merely because they were not born noble? In the France of Louis XIV, at least, no such complaint would be truly justified (although there were persistent demands from successful merchants that their services should be rewarded with honours and titles),[1] for in fact some of Louis's most important ministers were drawn, as we have seen, from the middle class, to the disgust of nobles like Saint-Simon. The labouring masses, who did all the hard work and got nothing, often revolted and were duly crushed by troops. They could not achieve much until they could find leaders.

Risks such as these lay far in the future. A far more deadly set of enemies, however, had already taken the field to begin a series of murderous onslaughts on the entrenched positions of both Church and monarchy. Europe is a continent, for ever, figuratively speaking, on the march, never resting long, always probing new ideas, a continent of intellectual nomads. While the twin glorious edifices of the Old Régime, the Church and the kings, seemed after much travail to have at last arrived at a position not only of eminence but also of changeless permanence, the sappers and miners were already hacking at the very foundations of that position. After the Reformation came the rationalists, after the *Frondes* came the scientists, as the new enemies of Church and king. The Old Régime was subjected to a new sort of danger from enemies who fought not with the sword but with ideas and books, though the struggle was to be transferred to the battlefields too. The closing years of the seventeenth century saw an intellectual revolution in Europe.

---

[1] See a brilliant article by Mr Richard B. Grassby in *Economic History Review*, vol. XIII, no. 1, 1960.

It is possible here to give only the merest sketch of that revolution's beginnings, but its importance must not be underestimated for it largely dominated the history of the eighteenth century. It dealt the Churches a crippling blow. It helped to wipe out the French monarchy at the end of the century, and played no small part in that great and good event, the independence of the United States of America. It contained the origins of most of the significant hall-marks of modern civilization—or at least of Western civilization—namely toleration, democracy, and liberty. It even had a good deal to do with the creation of modern industry.

This thrilling mental revolution is probably all of a piece, but it will be convenient to try to distinguish its chief sources. They were four, having in common at least one feature—a weariness of obedience to authority, specifically the authority of Church and king, wielded over men's minds and bodies. The four were: the influence of foreign travel following the opening of the ocean routes by Columbus, Vasco da Gama, and their successors; a disgusted reaction against the wars, persecutions, and cruelties which had been caused by religious intolerance; a further revolt of individual human reason against the intellectual claims of Church and State, a revolt which can be traced back to the Renaissance of the fifteenth century, if not earlier; and, probably most important of all, the Scientific Revolution of the seventeenth century.

The first may sound slightly surprising, for two centuries had passed since the *Santa Maria* had sighted Watling Island, but it took a long time for the effects of these discoveries to germinate in men's minds. It was the late seventeenth century which saw a flood of books about travel. The mere fact that the books were about travel was revolutionary in itself. The great classical writers of the most glorious part of the reign of Louis XIV kept their plays, for instance, neatly within the narrow boundaries of the unities of time and place, and the literature which glorified Louis XIV was written by men who preferred to keep their own bodies within a similarly neat boundary. Racine, Boileau, Molière, Fénelon—these giant exponents of the classical tradition moved about as little as possible. While they were still penning their immortal masterpieces, a torrent of books about all sorts of far-off places—and the farther off the better, China, Siam, Persia—came rushing from the presses. Everyone took up the craze and read all the books they could lay their hands on about these strange lands and their still stranger inhabitants, as soon as they found that the flood of books about Europe which had preceded them contained not enough marvels to stimulate their appetite. Books with titles like *Le Gentilhomme étranger voyageur en France* and *Description of Rome for the use of foreigners* were therefore soon followed by such works as *On the Ceremonies of the Chinese*. There might not appear to be any harm in that, but the trouble was that many of the writers made it clear that such things as customs, morals, habits, and religion itself, varied infinitely from place to place and that peoples who had never heard of Christian morals nor of the Christian faith seemed to manage pretty well without either. The implication was that the Christian Church was something much less than the fruit of God's direct revelation of Himself to mankind, that it was perhaps just a product of the local climate. As La Bruyère said, 'Some . . . by extensive travel lose whatever shreds of religion remained to them.'

Nor did the damage end there. After real travel books came a spate of writings which owed more, and often everything, to the imagination of the writers, books purporting to be all about the Wise Chinese or the Sage Egyptians or the Noble Savages (such as Hurons) and about the admirable denizens of utterly fictitious lands (such as *The Isle of the Severambes*). The whole point of these Utopias was the usual point of Utopias; that is, the writer draws a picture of a virtuous and enlightened people and the reader is tacitly left to contrast it with the crimes, follies, and irrationalities of real life in Europe. The chief target, however, was the Church, and the chief function of all the virtuous Siamese and Redskins that were dragged in was merely to attack the Church, at first by implication, and then, as the writers grew bolder, directly. So by 1710 we find a writer like Tyssot de Patot saying, 'It pains me to think of the dark and narrow alley-ways of religion', and the far more renowned Comte de Boulainvilliers saying that Christianity is no better than the religion of Mahomet—'Every nation has its own type of wisdom. Mahomet symbolizes the wisdom of the Arabs. Christ symbolizes the wisdom of the Jews.'

The Church probably did not need to worry overmuch about such light-weight stuff, even though it was helping to change public opinion. But both Church and kings, and in particular Louis XIV, had a large number of opponents whose critical guns fired much heavier shot.

One of the greatest of these opened fire early in the seventeenth century, in 1625. Appalled by the endless barbarities, wars, bloodshed, and atrocities which as usual were disfiguring Europe, the great Dutchman, Grotius, wrote a book which is immortal as being the first real contribution towards modern international law. In his *De Jure Belli et Pacis* he says that there is a law which should apply at all times, and this law is Natural Law, a law graven in the hearts of all men by Nature and telling them that they should behave with mercy and justice even in time of war. He is not here at first sight saying anything at all which could harm religion, but while not denying the existence or even the primacy of the Law of God, he yet treats Natural Law as distinct from it; in other words, the implication is that the Law of God has totally failed to stop wars and atrocities, and Grotius was thus inviting men to wrestle themselves with their own destinies, leaving the Law of God as revealed by the Churches to concern itself only with the hereafter. This theme was taken up by a writer only slightly less influential in the seventeenth century than Grotius, namely Samuel von Pufendorf; two of his books produced in 1672 and 1673 emphasize Natural Law and the importance of relying on our own Reason (which reveals Natural Law to us), and to leave Revelation, the laws of God as taught by the Bible, to the theologians. These two writers are damaging to the claims of religion rather than to any specific king, but the Revocation of the Edict of Nantes let loose an impassioned attack on Louis. Some of it, understandably enough, was written in a white-hot rage and had little permanent effect. In any case the indignation was not universally felt; the Lutherans of Germany and Scandinavia, and the Calvinists of Switzerland, kept silent. The main storm came from Dutch, French, and English pastors, and too much should not be made of it because there was nothing peculiar to the seventeenth century, not even to seventeenth-century France, in literary outbursts against persecuting tyrants; the Massacre of St Bartholomew in the previous century had been promptly followed by loud cries from Hotman and other writers that the States-General ought to depose a government of assassins.

The frenzied outbursts of such writers as Pastor Claude and Pierre Jurieu did Louis lasting harm, but at least they came from Christians. They received rather two-edged support from a colossus of the world of letters who introduced a new note into the whole controversy. This was Pierre Bayle (1647–1706), who, if he was a Christian at all, was a very unusual one. The first part of his savage attack on Louis in such works as his *Commentaire philosophique sur ces paroles de Jésus-Christ: 'Contrains-les d'entrer'* (this was an answer to Catholic apologists who had sought to justify the Revocation of the Edict of Nantes by quoting Jesus' words in St Luke, Chapter XIV) suited the Protestants very well. When he went on to claim that the individual conscience should never be coerced in any circumstances he did not please the Protestants quite so well, since most of them felt little inclination to tolerate anyone else. Then, horror of horrors, Bayle argued that any dogma, even if clearly supported by Holy Scriptures, must be rejected if it clashed with 'the clear and definite conclusions of the natural understanding'. So Bayle set up natural Reason as superior to any other authority, that of the Bible and the Churches included.

Bayle was a terrible foe, made more terrible by the fact that the supreme place he allocated to Reason was allocated to it by hosts of others; he was one of a distressingly numerous swarm whose intellectual parentage may be definitely traced back to the Renaissance and thus, of course, back to Classical Greece and Rome. Reason, to them all, was the faculty that man possesses which places him above other creatures and which enables him to inquire, to explore the mysterious and shed light on it, to criticize anything at all, to accept nothing as authoritative unless it has been thoroughly investigated. It is easy to see how deadly this notion would be to a Church based on Authority, even on a Divine Authority, all the more deadly because many of its most effective exponents were devoted sons of the Church and imagined they were using Reason in its defence.

Not all such thinkers aimed at the Church itself. A good many blasts were directed against superstition. Bayle himself, together with others such as the Frenchman Fontenelle, the Dutchman Bekker, and the German professor Christian Thomasius (this last, who lived from 1655 to 1728 may be regarded as the founder of the German *Aufklärung*— Enlightenment—of the eighteenth century) poured scorn on miracles, oracles, the belief in comets as portents of great events to come, and on witchcraft. (Their efforts did not prevent Marshal Luxemburg from being put in prison in 1680, charged with having made a pact with the Devil.) To attack superstition might have been salutary; the trouble was that none of them made the slightest attempt to draw any distinction between superstition and the Church; they treated them as one and the same thing. Other writers, not especially concerned to attack anything, nevertheless undermined Christianity by open unbelief—the freethinkers, deriving their inspiration from Epicurus. One of them (Dehenhault) said, 'L'homme meurt entier comme entier il est né', and others took up the denial of the immortality of the soul. The general attitude of the freethinkers was that they subjected everything to the searching light of Reason, and rejected it if it failed to pass Reason's tests. By 'everything', of course, they principally meant the claims of Revealed Religion, which were invariably found wanting.

These freethinkers can be regarded as a branch of the Deists. Deism originated in Renaissance Italy, and became prominent in France in the seventeenth century (as well as in England where Edward Herbert composed the 'Deist's Profession of Faith' in 1624). The Deists violently rejected Revelation and the authority of the Church. Rejecting any belief in Revelation meant not only rejecting belief in Christ as God; it meant as a logical consequence rejecting belief in the meaning and purpose of Christ's mission; that is, in the Atonement. The net effect is to push God out of human affairs, for, once God's intervention in them for the purpose of Salvation was no longer believed in, the Deists felt quite happy to use their Reason as a guide to virtuous conduct. Thus they arrived at a belief in 'natural' religion, an extremely vague notion, by which they seem to have meant that Reason will enable us to obey Natural Law; in fairness to the Deists it must be added that they were embarrassed by their inability to define 'Nature' in any satisfactory way. Briefly, then, Deists believed in God but not in Christianity. The most violent exponent of their notions was an Englishman called John Toland, who wrote in 1696 a book called *Christianity not mysterious*, a book which savagely attacked Christian beliefs. The most famous Deist was of course Voltaire.

Toland's somewhat vulgar outbursts did not have the same success as attacks by more distinguished intellects. Bayle himself was far more effective, and his most famous work was his *Historical and Critical Dictionary* (*Dictionnaire historique et critique*), the first volume of which appeared in 1695. It was meant as an encyclopaedia and is justly celebrated for being the first European attempt of that sort; the famous French *Encyclopédie* of the mid eighteenth century owed it a great debt. It dealt with all sorts of topics, but here we are concerned only with the fact that while giving a mass of useful information it was consistently hostile to the Church, becoming a sort of unbelievers' Bible. He never missed a chance of emphasizing that nothing can be known beyond any doubt. In other works too Bayle directly poured scorn on Christian beliefs, one of his favourite targets being the doctrines concerning Salvation. He anticipated a famous theme of Voltaire's here by arguing that a just God would not be so grossly immoral as to create sinful people and then to condemn them to an eternity of suffering because they were sinful.

The poor Church, then, was having a worse time than anything it had known since Luther pinned up his Ninety-five Theses. Unhappily for it, some of the most sincere believers, even defenders of the Church, produced work which damaged it. Among this sort of writer we cannot place Spinoza (1632–77), who was a lapsed Jew, not a Christian of any sort, and who published a famous work—the *Theological-Political Treatise* (*Tractatus theologico-politicus*)—in 1670. This was a devastating attack on Churches and on kings. He advocated Reason as the best guide to political conduct and said that men would never be happy until they realized the stupidity of religious wars and of persecution. Passionately convinced of the need for individual liberty as against Church or State authority, Spinoza failed as a propagandist partly because of the very profundity of most of his philosopy; he was at least a century before his time. For this reason the fruits of his philosophical thought—and he was one of the world's greatest intellects—lie outside the scope of this history. Most of Spinoza's political thought was naturally clear enough, but nobody at the time seems to have had much idea of what he was driving at in his views on moral philosophy. To most contemporaries he seemed like the worst and wickedest sort of blasphemer and even Bayle said he was a lunatic. A better reception was accorded the works of far less profound men. Among them, for instance, was Malebranche, a sincere Christian who tried to defend the Christian position by the use of Reason, but only succeeded in thereby subordinating God himself to human reason, for which unhappy result he was duly saluted by the ironical Bayle. Much the same occurred in the work of the great Biblical scholar, Richard Simon, a brilliant philologist who published a searching Biblical commentary. He treated the Bible like any other work, exposing contradictions and pointing out evident interpolations. His innocent ambition was merely to place Biblical scholarship on a firmer basis, but what this devout son of the Church succeeded in doing was to expose the Bible itself to the searchlight of Reason allied to learning. He thus gave poor Bossuet some more sleepless nights.

Most of all this seems purely destructive and negative. However, all these 'rationalists' were concerned with supplying something to take the place of the authority of the Church and of kings, something a bit more systematic than a destruction of the claims of the former by the use of Reason. Gradually, from the time of Grotius onwards, one can see their main constructive notion taking shape. It is really the idea that there is in Nature an essential harmony; to put it another way, that there is an entirely rational tendency in the social order. This is what is meant by Natural Law. What was needed therefore was to sweep away the superstitious claims of Revealed Religion, to sweep away the wretched kings with their endless wars. Once all that dead lumber had gone, Reason would be free to show us the Natural Law, at last unimpeded by artificial obstacles. Since Nature is meant to be harmonious, men would then live harmoniously together, would be free to find their happiness here on earth. Even their selfishnesses would cancel out and all would live as brothers together. This glorious, though unpractical ideal, was eagerly spread abroad by Bayle, Fontenelle, the second Lord Shaftesbury, and others, but by none more successfully than by John Locke (1632–1704).

Locke drew his own inspiration more from the Scientific Revolution than from this older Renaissance pattern of thought, so a consideration of his enormous influence will be more appropriately made as part of the last of the four elements making up the mental revolution of the seventeenth century which was to be so damaging to the claims of the Church and of the kings; that element being the Scientific Revolution.

We have already seen (in Chapter 2) some of the intellectual effects of that Revolution. Newton and others seem to have dethroned religion to some extent if only by chasing gods out of the planetary system, by making a teleological type of thinking appear unfruitful and out of date, and perhaps most of all, by the very completeness of the triumph of his theories of gravitation. Newton gave people the best of inducements to carry their respect for Reason to fantastic lengths. Science damaged religion in other ways too. For instance, in the literal sense, it charmed men away from bothering about religion at all. Many examples of this were given by the Secretary of the French *Académie des Sciences*, Fontenelle (1657–1757), who himself did a good deal to popularize the taste for science. One of his functions was to deliver the funeral orations of a large number of the scientists of the period, and in many of these he described how scientists had often started out in life with the idea of entering the priesthood but had been overcome by the fatal charm of geometry and had promptly given up their previous plans and taken up scientific studies instead. But possibly more serious harm was eventually done in quite a different way. Science after all was concerned with what was physically measurable. By enabling men to understand their material, measurable surroundings far better than ever before it held out a promise of the happiness to be obtained on this earth, not in the hereafter. It fired men with an enthusiastic belief in the possibility of progress here and now. The chasing of this will-o'-the-wisp, happiness, by piling up material possessions—happiness by 'progress'—was born in the seventeenth century; at least before then there was no general belief in any idea of progress. People had tended to look back with longing to the vanished perfection of former times. We find the typical outlook expressed by Chaucer in the late Middle Ages; in a beautiful poem called 'The Former Age' he says:

> A blysful lyf, a paisible and swete,
> Ledden the peples in the former age.

But in the nineteenth century we find the poet Tennyson talking about 'one far-off Divine event to which the whole creation moves', and in the twentieth the air is thick with the promises of politicians offering more prosperity.

It would be a mistake, however, to suppose that the battle of the idea of progress was initiated by Science. That battle was fought out in France in the reign of Louis XIV, and took for the most part the form of a literary debate between those who held that the ancients (of classical antiquity) surpassed, especially in artistic excellence, anything that could possibly be produced in more modern times, and the moderns, who pointed with pride to the literary masterpieces produced in the France of their own day by such geniuses as Racine, Corneille, and Molière. Nevertheless, that the battle was won by the moderns was due largely to Science, for the moderns were able to state the undeniable truth that in matters of scientific knowledge the seventeenth century far outshone all previous ages.

It must not be supposed, either, that the scientists were normally concerned to attack religion. We have already seen that Newton himself was profoundly religious (he wrote far more on religious topics than on scientific ones). Similarly, Newton's only serious scientific rival in the matter of gravitational theories, Descartes, was just as fervent a believer. However, the latter harmed religion in yet another way while actually seeking to defend it.

He was in fact deeply anxious to prove the existence of God and the immortality of the soul and was seriously worried about the implications of the very mechanistic theories to which he had made such a great contribution. Those theories seemed to reduce everything to a question of matter in motion, including Man himself, who appeared to be nothing but a soulless automaton, just another mass of atoms, measurable like everything else. Descartes managed to his own satisfaction to endow Man with a soul, but the mischief lay in the method underlying his philosophy. He was determined to let Reason be his only guide, and to build up afresh a system of philosophy resting on utterly unassailable foundations, immune from the assaults of Reason or of anything else. This could only be done if he began by rejecting absolutely everything that passed for knowledge, or at least everything open to the slightest doubt. That, he found, seemed to mean everything whatsoever; we cannot even accept the evidence of our senses because they notoriously mislead us only too often. Happily, there seemed to be one glorious exception to the universal uncertainty. He held that at least it was certain that he had thoughts. About the reality of thoughts there could be no question. As he himself puts it in his famous book, *Discourse on Method* (1637), 'While I wanted to think everything false, it must necessarily be that I who thought was something; and remarking that this truth "I think, therefore I am" was so solid and so certain that all the most extravagant suppositions of the sceptics were incapable of upsetting it, I judged that I could receive it without scruple as the first principle of the philosophy that I sought.' 'Cogito ergo sum' ('I think, therefore I am'). He did indeed receive it as a certain principle and a most marvellous structure of thought he went on to build on it. Into that we need not enter, for what is significant here is the utter completeness of the initial step, the 'Cartesian doubt'. This clean sweep of all previous notions, of course, did more harm to the traditional authority of the Church than to anything else, and thus it was that Descartes, a sincerely religious man whose ideas had an enormous vogue, was yet one of the most deadly enemies of Christianity.

By far the largest part in translating the scientific attitude into an attack on the Church and on the Divine Right of Kings was, however, played not by Descartes, great though the latter's influence was, but by the English philosopher John Locke (1632–1704).

Locke's influence from that day to this has been truly stupendous, both in the realm of philosophy and in that of political thought and action, but in some ways that influence was at its peak in the century with which we shall be concerned, the eighteenth. In that it was overwhelming, as is testified by Voltaire, who said that Newton and Locke were 'the Castor and Pollux [or twin gods] of the new dispensation', and by the fairly unanimous opinion of historians since, of whom it will be sufficient to cite Leslie Stephen, who called Locke 'the intellectual ruler of the eighteenth century'.

Locke wrote in a clear, simple style, and his writings are marked by a robust and earthy common sense; the fact that, as philosophers go, he is not particularly difficult to understand is one reason for his wide influence outside the circle of professional philosophers as well as within it. Even so, a few statements about his life and character might be of help towards grasping his thought.

He was born in Wrington in Somerset, the son of a lawyer. He went to school at Westminster and from there to Christ Church, Oxford.

There he studied philosophy and did not think much of the form of Aristotelianism at that time in vogue. He admired Descartes's style, without, however, thinking quite so highly of his opinions. He took his B.A. and then his M.A. degree and was elected to a life Senior Studentship at his own College. In 1659 he became a lecturer in Greek and later taught Rhetoric and Moral Philosophy. These activities failed to satisfy him, for he next started to study medicine and by 1674 he had qualified to practise as a doctor. From that time he came very much more in contact with the practical affairs of the outside world. After serving on, of all things, a diplomatic mission to Brandenburg, he came to the notice of the first Lord Shaftesbury and entered his service as his personal physician, and as a sort of political secretary. From then on, naturally, his life did not lack excitement, for he shared all the political vicissitudes of his employer at the time of the Exclusion Bill (though still spending some time at his old College; no wonder one of his colleagues noted in his diary that 'John Locke lives a very cunning and unintelligible life here'). Shaftesbury's intrigues resulted in a prudent flight to Holland in 1683, and Locke sensibly went there too. He became friendly with the English supporters of William of Orange, and so returned to England almost immediately after the Revolution of 1688, where he still took occasional part in public affairs, but spent most of his energies on his philosophical studies and writings.

From the foregoing it will be correctly inferred that three aspects of Locke's training and career might be expected to have a marked effect on the character of his thought. He was trained in the old Scholastic philosophy as well as in a scientific study, and both affected him profoundly, although he rejected the former and valued the latter. In addition, he had been very much concerned with practical politics on the side of the Shaftesbury faction and was therefore a strong supporter of Whig principles and in particular of the Revolution of 1688. So as a scientist and a Whig he produced philosophic and political theories, attacking both traditional Christian philosophy and the Divine Right of Kings; he was the father of British empiricism and the prophet of the Revolution of 1688.

His great philosophical work, *Essay Concerning Human Understanding* (1690), was written with the object of determining once and for all what constitutes knowledge, what sort of things human beings can know, and what they cannot, 'to examine our own abilities, and see what objects our understandings were, or were not, fitted to deal with . . . vague and insufficient forms of speech, and abuse of language, have so long passed for mysteries of science . . . they are but the covers of ignorance'. In other words, this is an attack on metaphysicians and theologians, who in Locke's opinion have caused a great deal of misery in the world by making assertions dogmatically about matters of which we can have no real knowledge at all. The mistake they have made, he really thinks, is caused by overrating the ability of the human intellect, by speculating about things we can never actually know, and then giving out those speculations as great truths. 'We began at the wrong end, and in vain sought for satisfaction in a quiet and sure possession of truths that most concerned us, whilst we let loose our thoughts into the vast ocean of being; as if all that boundless extent were the natural and undoubted possession of our understandings, wherein there was nothing that escaped its comprehension.' If he can show that such speculations are not based on knowledge at all then 'in things whereof we have no certain knowledge, we ought to moderate our persuasions'.

Locke was a profound admirer of science, and in particular of Newton. What he therefore set out to do was to employ, he hoped, techniques of philosophical analysis as strict as the methods of science to secure the foundations of those methods with which the scientists had won such dazzling successes. His aim was to study, not as they were doing, the material world, but the instrument of knowledge, the mind itself. By sticking to what is really observable and thus perhaps poten-tially measurable, as they had done, Locke was embarking on an attempt to chart the human mind. After these preliminary remarks about his intentions, he went on to make a sweeping attack on 'innate ideas', the notion, that is, 'that there are in the understanding certain innate [inborn] principles stamped upon the mind of man, which the soul receives in its very first being, and brings into the world with it'. This attack could only have had for its target the great metaphysical systems of the medieval schoolmen, which rested on axioms for which no evidence could be found, and Locke is thus undermining the logical grounds on which theology rested. It would perhaps be fairer to emphasize that that was bound to be the result of Locke's ideas, rather than his consistent aim, for he was uneasy at the notion of demolishing proofs of God's existence even though he once remarked that meta-physics was 'fiddling'. (Locke is clear, but it is very hard to summarize him accurately because he was not always consistent.)

The main part of the *Essay* then followed. He maintained that all true knowledge is of one of two sorts only. The first is from experience, from the evidence of our senses: 'Let us then suppose the mind to be, as we say, white paper, void of all characters, without any ideas [he means of course that as we are born without innate ideas then we must start off with blank minds]; how comes it to be furnished? Whence comes it by that vast store which the busy and boundless fancy of man has painted on it with an almost endless variety? Whence has it all the materials of reason and knowledge? To this I answer, in one word, from experience: in that all our knowledge is founded, and from that it ultimately derives itself.' This was the 'great source of most of ideas', and this process of external objects conveying ideas to the mind he calls 'sensation'. The other sort of knowledge, 'the other fountain, from which experience furnisheth the understanding with ideas, is the perception of the operations of our mind within us, as it is employed about the ideas it has got . . . and might properly enough be called "internal sense". But as I call the other "sensation" so I call this "reflection".' What it all boils down to is that we have ideas from observation, through the senses, and further ideas by thinking about the first ones; the second sort would thus be impossible without the first, so ultimately all our knowledge is derived through the senses.

We need not follow him in the long discussion and classification of these ideas which he embarks on after making these points. Instead it is more relevant here to state the implications of Locke's theory of ideas. It will be noticed that he is talking about the mind as a sort of container which starts off in life quite empty and then with experience becomes filled with a 'vast store' of ideas, all separate and distinct, like seeds in a packet. The influence of Newton is here apparent. Locke hoped to perform for the mind and for human conduct the same sort of service that Newton had done for the universe as a whole, and as an essential preliminary is trying to get an exact picture of the operations of the human mind. Once this was achieved, and the study of human beings thus put on a scientific footing, it would be possible to make a scientific study of human conduct and even of human passions, for the single ideas are surely subject to as definite and as simple laws as the atoms in physics. So at last laws of history, of politics, of moral conduct, of artistic matters, of the passions and of the imagination, of legal systems, of education—of all that chiefly interests man—could be confidently formulated. This would reveal the real harmony of Nature, concealed until now by ignorance or idleness or wickedness or superstition. That was how his enthusiastic admirers understood Locke. Just as the physicists had achieved such astounding triumphs by treating the universe as atoms in motion, so would Locke's followers build up a complete human psychology by treating ideas as so many atoms in the mind which join together and behave in a perfectly definite and codifiable way. Most seductive hope of all, the new laws governing all human behaviour would be just as all-embracing, and at the same time just as blindingly simple, as Newton's theory of gravitation.

Thanks to Locke, therefore, the most influential writers and thinkers of the eighteenth century imagined the Golden Age was just around the corner and practically within reach. Men were objects in Nature just like trees and, by the proper study of them Newtonian successes (but this time in the sphere of social and political relations), the true answers to all human problems, would be found. In a harmonious Nature men would live in happiness. Unfortunately, Locke's theory of knowledge, for reasons it would not be relevant to discuss here, contains some fatal errors, and the attempt to use an atomistic model for the items of knowledge is one of the worst of them. A great deal of practical good was brought about by these errors all the same, but the central idea that everything in the world could be accounted for mechanically, that there could be precise engineers for human souls and bodies, was then only a dream, if a very happy one.

No such morbid doubts troubled Locke's eighteenth-century disciples, however. To them Locke seemed not only to have pointed out the correct path, but to have made a successful step or two along it, more especially in the question of morals. He thought he had proved that morality needed no religion to support it. Looking around the world at the actual facts, he said that morals varied infinitely from one place to another; what was thought good in one place was held in disgust in the next. The only common feature was that every society regarded as good whatever rules 'are absolutely necessary to hold society together'. There was nothing so very new in the notion that morality did not depend on religion; Bayle was saying already, 'Morals and religion are completely independent of each other.' Locke, however, went on to point out the basis of a new morality. If we look within ourselves we find that 'things are good or evil only in relation to pleasure or pain. That we call "good" which is apt to cause or increase pleasure, or diminish pain, within us.' 'What is it,' he asked, 'that moves desire? I answer, happiness, and that alone.' Thus the keynote of the new moral system is to be the observed fact that men pursue pleasure and avoid pain. This was later regarded by Locke's admirers as a sort of key to the understanding of men's motives, a sort of Newtonian law of psychology, which would be invaluable to guide the legislators. (Alas! it is useless and very nearly meaningless.) It is extremely interesting to notice the importance that Locke gave to the word 'desire', that state of the mind which is moved by the need of happiness. He says 'Desire is a state of uneasiness', and 'the only spur to human industry and action is uneasiness'. Without that feeling of uneasiness we therefore would do nothing; from it come our hopes, our fears, our passions. Later on, some of Locke's followers in France were to push this notion to extremes; for instance, Helvétius declared that people of a passionate nature are of a higher order than the placid, contented ones, and the odd result of this is that Locke and such people as Helvétius, while being the apostles of the Age of Reason, are also in part the parents of the Romantic Movement, which is often regarded, because of the value it placed on the emotions and passions, as a reaction against too much emphasis on Reason.

It should not be inferred from all the foregoing that Locke was irreligious or even a Deist. On the contrary, he was a most sincere Christian, but, although he granted the validity of metaphysical arguments for the existence of God, he does not say much about them, and this part of the *Essay* had little effect. The *Essay* as a whole remained the most devastating blow struck in the seventeenth century against the theoretical basis of religion, the most powerful influence weaning men away from a religious outlook and luring them on to a happy future in which the essential harmony of Nature would at last be revealed by the light of Reason.

Locke was more fortunate than most philosophers. His political views were if anything more influential than his philosophical ones. If only because they profoundly influenced the events leading to the French Revolution and because some of the chief ones are now incorporated in the Constitution of the U.S.A., they are worth study, although that is not the full extent of their importance. They are to be found in his two *Treatises of Civil Government*, probably written in 1678, and in *A Letter concerning Toleration*, written some years later.

The two *Treatises* were written in defence of the attitudes that were to find practical expression in the Revolution of 1688. The first was an effective answer to a book by Sir Robert Filmer, published in 1680 but written several years earlier, called *Patriarcha: or the Natural Power of Kings*. This is a most extreme statement of the Divine Right theory. According to Filmer, the House of Lords could only offer advice to the King, while the Commons scarcely had any rights at all. The King alone could make laws, and was perfectly free from all human control. He owed this enviable position to the fact that God bestowed the kingly power upon Adam and it descended to his heirs, who are the modern kings. This seemed to Sir Robert perfectly good and natural; the authority of kings was that of a father over his children. Locke had little trouble in refuting all this, which he did with a wealth of argument drawn from the Bible itself. Adam, he pointed out, could have only one heir, so if his descendant could be found all kings would have to surrender their powers to him, and he happily demonstrated that this was by no means the only hole in Sir Robert's case.

Locke's victory was too easy. It is surprising that instead of blasting Filmer he did not tackle a bigger opponent, namely Thomas Hobbes. Theoretic support for an absolutism, almost indistinguishable in practice from Divine Right, did not in fact rest wholly on religious arguments, and in his book *Leviathan*, published in 1651, Hobbes provided such a support, and one far more difficult to answer than Filmer's. He said that men in a state of Nature are impulsive and entirely selfish, every man's hand is turned against every other man, men left to themselves are worse than wolves. Out of the conflict of myriad selfishnesses, therefore, arises a continual state of war, so the condition of man in a state of Nature is uncomfortable and dangerous—'nasty, poor, brutish, and short'; no justice exists, only 'force and fraud'. To avoid this intolerable state of affairs, which would soon have resulted in the extinction of the human race, men therefore banded together into separate communities in each of which a social contract or covenant was made. This was done by large numbers of them agreeing to choose a sovereign to rule over them. They make the covenant with each other, not with the sovereign himself, who is not a party to it and not in the least bound by it, and thus no right of rebellion exists. Total power must be given to one sovereign, or else he will not be strong enough to keep down anarchy. In this theory, the sovereign could be one sovereign body, a parliament for example, but Hobbes himself preferred a king. Whatever the type of sovereign, he must have total and absolute control over life, opinion, and property—this last because in the state of Nature there could be no property; it is created by the government, which may do with it as it pleases. So government is 'a monstrous machine', made by man, 'that great Leviathan called the Commonwealth or State'. The only rights Hobbes leaves individuals come logically out of all this; they are the right to resist for self-protection, the right to refuse to fight for the government, and the right to disobey a government incapable of defending its subjects.

There is a good deal of sense in much of what Hobbes says, since it was supported by a scientific background quite as impressive as Locke's and could claim to be no less based on actual observation. Obviously, the *Leviathan* is much more awkward to deal with than improbable talk about what might have happened to Adam and Noah. However, although Charles II thought highly enough of his old tutor to keep a portrait of him on his walls and to award him a pension (which he forgot to pay), Hobbes was regarded as irreligious to an extent which few people could at the time stomach, so his writings did not enjoy much influence, and this might be the reason why Locke chose instead to demolish the arguments of a far less profound thinker. Besides, the second *Treatise of Civil Government*, though it does not refute Hobbes specifically, could be regarded as an answer to him.

Locke begins it with his own version of the state of Nature and of the origins of government. The state of Nature he defines thus: 'Men living together according to reason, without a common superior on earth, with authority to judge between them, is properly the state of Nature.' In his opinion they did in this state live by their reason and more or less obey the 'natural law'. They are thus quite the reverse of Hobbes's warring brutes, but still found the absence of authority an inconvenience; so to avoid such dangers as might arise, and chiefly so as the more easily to defend their property, men enter into a contract. Property for him is of cardinal importance. He says that every man has a complete right to retain the fruits of his own efforts (including, oddly enough, those of his servants); that is, to whatever things he finds in their natural state and then 'hath mixed his labour with'. Property thus pre-dates governments, and so far from having rights over men's property, governments are created by men to safeguard it: 'The great and chief end of men uniting into commonwealths, and putting themselves under government, is the preservation of their property.' Governments, under this theory, were to have very limited powers indeed, and Locke says an absolute government is not a government at all because in that case there is by definition no check on the sovereign, who is thus still 'in a state of Nature'. To avoid this evil, he taught that it was necessary for the legislature and the executive to be quite separate, so neither would be able to act like a tyrant. (If unfortunately they conflicted, then, says Locke, the argument could legitimately be decided by force; what he really had in mind is the action of the English Parliament in rebelling against Charles I.) This theory of the separation of powers as a way of preserving the liberty of the subjects was advocated in France by Montesquieu and became also one of the most important features of the Constitution of the U.S.A.

Governments for Locke, therefore, are deliberately created by the majority for the protection of their property and can be removed if they break the contract; all governments can only exist by the consent of the governed. This talk of majority, however, does not imply democracy, since Locke did not consider the poor as parties to a contract to defend property, so they were not citizens. This was regarded in some quarters as a complete answer to the claims of the Stuart kings and later as a complete justification of the Revolution of 1688. As already indicated, it had a huge success in England, France, and America.

That success was largely due to Locke's enormous prestige as a philosopher, and his success as a philosopher he mainly owed to the boundless prestige of science; his philosophy seemed plainly to be scientifically based. So, through Locke, science had tremendous effects on politics.

The odd thing about this is that Locke's political philosophy was not derived from science at all; people just thought it was. There is nothing scientific in anything he says about the state of Nature or the Social Contract; both are figments of the imagination, not the result of external objects impinging on our senses. There was nothing original in these notions either. Locke is talking the language of St Thomas Aquinas, who said, 'Every law framed by man bears the character of a law exactly to that extent to which it is derived from the law of nature.' (The Church had not always supported royal claims.) The entire notion of a state of Nature and Natural Law, on which the whole of Locke's second *Treatise* is based, has for its parentage, therefore, not science, but the medieval schoolmen and their successors. As for the Social Contract, Locke himself was uneasily aware that no evidence for the making of it existed; he puts up a feeble defence for its historicity by saying that 'Government is everywhere antecedent to records' (Chapter VIII), but nevertheless there must have been a contract. This attempt to prove an historical event by the absence of evidence, rather than the existence of evidence, can hardly be called convincing.

Locke's political views thus owed their prestige to a scientifically based philosophy by which in fact they are contradicted, but nobody in the eighteenth century seems to have noticed this. The success of Locke in thus demolishing the claims of the Stuarts to rule by Divine Right and in replacing those claims by the rule of the property-owners, but not of the poor, who, having no property, could not have taken part in a contract to defend it, suited the magnates who made the Revolution of 1688, but that success was achieved by a sort of logical confidence-trick. That of course does not alter the fact that, as an answer to tyranny, the idea of government by consent has been a noble and beneficial one; the only trouble is that anyone who tries to defend it on logical grounds is skating on very thin ice. In modern Britain, for example, it is obviously untrue that people 'consent' to the actions of their government or to being citizens in the first place. It is true that a majority can remove a distasteful government, but that is a very different, and a very good, thing.

Of his *A Letter concerning Toleration* (1689) it may be said that the strongest of the arguments he uses in favour of religious toleration is more genuinely related to the influence of science, and to his views on human knowledge. He points out that the limits of human knowledge are so narrow and the probability of error on speculative matters is so great that we cannot be certain that our opinions are correct and other people's wrong, and therefore we are not justified in persecuting opponents. 'We should do well to commiserate our mutual ignorance and endeavour to remove it in all the gentle and fair ways of information, and not instantly treat others ill as obstinate and perverse because they will not renounce their own and receive our opinions.' Locke was not, however, in favour of tolerating all opinions; for example, he held it wrong to tolerate practices in the name of religion which were clearly immoral in any case (like human sacrifice); he also refused to tolerate atheists on the illogical grounds that atheists would not keep promises, and so would loosen the bonds keeping society together; and he refused toleration to those who would not tolerate others—thus giving the English government an excuse to continue persecuting Catholics.

It must not be supposed that all this attack on the beliefs of the Churches and on the Divine Right of Kings went unanswered. Bossuet did his best to refute it, as did others, but they were swimming against too strong a current. The mental revolution of the seventeenth century was to do irreparable damage to the *ancien régime* in Europe and to its religious foundations.

The attack on the Divine Right theory had a most impressive practical ally. This was, of course, the English Revolution of 1688, which shattered Divine Right in England. The correctness of the English point of view had already been tested on the battlefield in the War of the League of Augsburg, and to his utter disgust Louis XIV at the Peace of Ryswick in 1697 was obliged to recognize the justice of William's title to the throne of England and had to promise not to help the Stuarts again. This was possibly a bigger blow to Divine Right than any theorizing by Locke or anyone else, although Louis did not accept the verdict as final. In a very short time the claim of Divine Right was to be fought out again on the battlefields of Europe and was to be settled in the War of the Spanish Succession, to which, therefore, we turn next.

7 · The War of the Spanish Succession, 1702–13

(a) CAUSES

The Peace of Ryswick in 1697 had brought England glory as well as profit. The King whom England had appointed in place of the one she had dismissed had triumphantly vindicated the Revolution carried out in the name of the sovereignty of the nation, and had forced Louis, the most illustrious exponent of Divine Right, to recognize the justice of that Revolution. Accordingly, the House of Commons thanked William for 'the honourable and advantageous' Peace of Ryswick and for 'restoring to England' the position of the keeper of 'the Balance of Europe'. A very short time later at the end of 1701, the Commons, who had not always supported William's foreign policy, delivered to him a special address which required the King to add an article to the Treaties of Alliance then being negotiated with the Dutch and the Emperor for the purpose of a fresh war with Louis. The article stipulated that no peace should be concluded with France until reparation was made for the indignity offered to the nation by the French monarch in declaring the Pretender to be King of England, Scotland, and Ireland. From that it may evidently be seen that Louis had broken his promise, but it would be ridiculous to infer from it that therein lay the only, or chief, cause of the War of the Spanish Succession. The causes of that war must be sought in the weakness of Spain and the colliding ambitions of France on the one hand and of the Emperor, the English, and the Dutch on the other; in any case English ambitions were by no means confined to defending their Revolution.

Just over a hundred years after the Armada was sighted off The Lizard and Philip II of Spain seemed near to conquering England and putting his daughter on the throne of France,[1] the Kings of those two countries signed a treaty partitioning the Spanish Empire. The fall of Spain had been abrupt. It is true that Philip II's schemes had failed, and the attempt to execute them had seriously overstrained the strength of his country; but Spanish power in the first half of the seventeenth century had continued to appear formidable, and Spain played by no means an insignificant part in the Thirty Years War. By the end of that war, however, Spain had seen her best troops smashed by Condé and Turenne, and was obliged to acknowledge the independence of her wealthiest provinces in the Netherlands. Besides this she lost control of Portugal, which gained her independence in 1640. The most severe blows were still to come. The war Spain fought against France and England, which ended in 1659, put an end to the greatness of Spanish military and naval power. Thereafter, the decline of Spain was even more spectacular, and we have seen already the pitiful helplessness she displayed in the face of the further aggressions of Louis XIV in the Spanish Netherlands.

As well as weakness caused by an over-ambitious foreign policy, there was in Spain serious economic weakness. The Crown itself went bankrupt for the third time in 1692, and the economy of the country was not in much better condition. Production had declined sharply; cities like Toledo, Seville, and Granada, formerly renowned for their manufactures, were complaining of poverty (the wool manufacture at Toledo had fallen off by about three-quarters in the first two-thirds of the seventeenth century). Trade internally had almost disappeared, while that with the Indies was pathetically small. The population fell catastrophically in numbers from about 9,000,000 in 1500 to about 5,700,000 in 1700,[2] though the number of beggars rose (the population of Madrid declined by a half, but the number of beggars to join the frantic breadqueues rose by 20,000). Naturally this economic weakness was reflected in a weakness in the armed forces, which consisted of starving soldiers

---

[1] Such an ambition was, of course, only feasible because of the civil wars in France in the second half of the sixteenth century.

[2] This small number compared with the huge population (*c.* twenty million) of France is a great factor in the relative weakness of Spain.

and a few moribund battleships (there were supposed to be only three of the latter in existence by 1693).

It is one thing to indicate the economic weakness of Spain, but quite another to account for it. Indeed, Spanish history as a whole has in it the elements of mystery, even for Spanish historians, who talk of the 'problem of Spain' and the 'historical enigma' of the country, and who are greatly occupied with a discussion about the national psychology. The 'Spanish character', if there is such a thing, is often held to be to blame for the economic backwardness of Spain. As early as 1512 the Florentine envoy said of the Spaniards: 'They are not skilful in the arts, whether mechanical or liberal . . . the natives do not devote themselves to trade, which they regard as degrading . . . the whole nation is opposed to industry . . . the artisans only work when driven to do so by necessity, and then they take their ease until they have spent their earnings.' More recently, the *New Cambridge Modern History* (Volume VII, Chapter XII) adds that the Spaniards had 'a fanatical preoccupation with the affairs of the next world rather than with prosperity in this'. So, briefly, the Spaniards preferred religion to work. This might well be true, and it would not be so very surprising if it were, because the country had been occupied for eight centuries in driving out the Moors. A crusade lasting for so long naturally sharpened fanaticism. It also put a premium on the military virtues, to the detriment of work, particularly manual work. One of the modern Spanish ministers, Señor Ullastres, talking to reporters early in 1959 (the interview is quoted in *The Times*), added to this the fascinating suggestion that 'grazing, the one economic activity which Spain had early developed, had a great deal that was military about it—the movement, the riding, the manœuvring of large bodies'. Señor Ullastres then offered another interesting remark, that 'Spain was only partly a European nation; Spaniards had a great deal of Arab blood in them, and this had affected their temperament.' The whole history of Spain is therefore evoked to explain such things as the economic weakness of the country at the end of the seventeenth century.

Probably that is the only way to explain it. For fanaticism led not only to a contempt for commerce but also to the expulsion of the Moriscoes in 1609, and they were the most industrious section of the population. As for sheep-farming, which was preferred to agriculture, the Guild of the Sheep-farmers, the famous *Mesta*, was able to do considerable damage to agriculture by driving their sheep over the land and by destroying its fertility by cutting trees down for pasture. A grave source of weakness was the reliance on bullion from the Indies, which gave the Spaniards a taste for luxury and a reluctance to work, and also caused a terrible inflation which ruined trade by pricing Spanish goods completely out of European markets. Worse still, the gold of the Americas lured men out of Spain by the thousands, and this is the chief cause of the decline of the population. It will not have escaped the reader that, in common with many who have tried writing on this subject, we have thus offered a contradictory account of the Spanish character; first, it is said that they preferred religion to the things of this world, and second, that many of them rushed off looking for gold. The truth is that 'the Spanish character', like anybody else's, contains contradictions, and also it is safer not to talk about the 'character' of whole nations at all; there are just millions of different individuals, some of whom have certain resemblances to each other.

We are on somewhat firmer ground if we turn from attempts at economic explanations, important though they are in this case, to a consideration of the way Spain was managed, or, rather, mismanaged. The weakness of Spain in the latter half of the seventeenth century may also be attributed to the total incapacity of the King, Carlos (Charles) II. King Ferdinand remarked to the Florentine envoy, Guicciardini, whose opinions of Spain in 1512 are quoted earlier, that 'the nation . . . was unorganized' and that 'great results would be obtained should any one arise who could hold it well in hand'. Charles II certainly did not hold the nation well in hand. He ascended the throne as a sickly child of four, and remained a chronic invalid during the whole of his reign of thirty-five years. The government was perforce left in the hands of the Queen Mother and her favourites, and of a number of prime ministers. None of these displayed any ability or energy, and so Spain, 'a monarchy without a monarch', was misruled by an inefficient and corrupt bureaucracy and by the nobles, whose influence became important. If Spain had had a Louis XIV things might have been very different. What it got instead was a King whose life was nearly always in danger, a King with so many diseases that the doctors were driven to supposing that his constant sufferings were caused by witchcraft. The King was furthermore childless, so his health was of keen interest both to the countries which hoped to secure all or a share of his vast dominions and to those, principally the Dutch, English, and French, whose merchants carried on an enormous amount of trade with Spain and her colonies.

Claimants to the Spanish inheritance were numerous. Among those with no chance of getting anything were the Duke of Savoy and several Spanish noblemen. The serious candidates were three: the Habsburgs, the Bourbons, and the Wittelsbachs; the first because the younger daughter of the Spanish King Philip III had married the Emperor Ferdinand III, and the second because his elder daughter had married King Louis XIII of France; the Bavarian claim rested on the marriage of Margaret, a daughter of Philip IV of Spain, to the Emperor Leopold I in 1666, and the only surviving child of this union, Maria Antonia, had married Maximilian Emanuel, Elector of Bavaria. The Bavarian claim was on behalf of the son of Maria Antonia and the

TABLE SHOWING DESCENT OF THE THREE CHIEF CLAIMANTS
(SHOWN IN CAPITALS) TO THE SPANISH THRONE

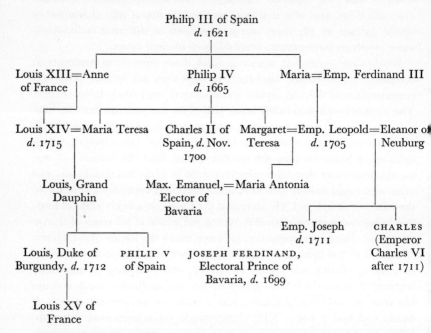

Elector, the Electoral Prince Joseph Ferdinand (see table above). This last claim was legally the best, particularly in view of the fact that the French had signed a renunciation of their claims to the Spanish inheritance on the marriage of Louis XIII, and another similar renunciation on the marriage of Louis XIV to Maria Teresa, daughter of Philip IV of Spain. The French did not accept the validity of these renunciations, and the whole complicated business was made still more complicated by the attitude of the English and Dutch, who, while not putting forward any candidates of their own, had much to fear if France, for instance, received it all; for in that case France would be a menace to both in the Spanish Netherlands, might possibly be able to shut the Mediterranean to them, would seriously or even disastrously alter the Balance of Power in Europe against them, and be in a position to cut them off from the lucrative trade they enjoyed with Spain and its Empire.

Nobody was anxious for a great European war, however, and so Louis, who was in the meantime fortifying his chances by active diplomacy in Spain, agreed to discussions with William III of England. Agreement was reached in mid October 1698 by the 'First[1] Partition Treaty', signed at The Hague. The French were to get Naples and Sicily (the 'Two Sicilies'), and, in Northern Italy, Tuscany, and Finale, together with the Spanish province of Guipuzcoa (on the French frontier). All the remainder was to go to the Electoral Prince of Bavaria, except that the Austrians were to be fobbed off with the offer of Milan to the Archduke Charles, second son of the Emperor. This bit of work pleased the Maritime Powers, who saw their worst fears averted, and Louis, who although surrendering the greater part of the prize, was consoled by huge gains easily obtained and by the knowledge that to try to gain all would have meant a big and possibly disastrous war. It aroused fury in Madrid, for the dominant desire of the Spaniards was to keep their great Empire intact no matter who ruled it; the English Ambassador said that lacking anyone else they would have accepted the Devil himself. Consequently the King of Spain roused himself for once and made a Will, leaving the whole inheritance to the Electoral Prince (14 November 1698). The emotions roused throughout Europe by this attempt to save the Spanish Empire from dismemberment were mixed, but of brief duration. For on 5 February 1699 the young Joseph Ferdinand died, officially of smallpox, though voices were not lacking which accused the Emperor of having had him poisoned; the Emperor probably had done nothing of the sort, in spite of his vehement protests at the Will. At all events, both the Partition Treaty and the Will were now pointless.

William III and Louis therefore agreed to a Second Partition Treaty signed by the English and French on 3 March and rather grudgingly by the Dutch on 25 March 1700. William's bargaining position was not strong, for Parliament was driving him to thoughts of abdication by cutting down the size of the army, but Louis was fairly moderate in his demands, possibly because of the sudden growth of Austrian power as manifested by the recent victories of Prince Eugene over the Turks and by the consequent gains of Austria at the Peace of Karlowitz in

---

[1] Usually so called, in spite of the Treaty of 1668 (see p. 75).

January 1699 (see page 112). So by the Second Partitition, Spain, the Spanish Netherlands, and the Indies were to go to the Archduke Charles; France was to get Milan in addition to the territories named in the First Partition Treaty; it was understood that France would be allowed to exchange Milan for Lorraine. This arrangement, from the point of view of the Maritime Powers, at least had the virtue of keeping France out of the Spanish Netherlands and of handing the Indies to a Power which presumably would leave their trade open to the English and Dutch. Louis expressed pleasure at such important gains, though he kept up a very skilled diplomatic activity in Madrid with a view to a complete inheritance if that should turn out to be feasible. But once again the Emperor and the Spaniards were furious. The Emperor still hoped to secure the entire Spanish Empire for his son, and imagined that this attitude might persuade the King of Spain to make the Archduke his sole heir. His dismay at subsequent developments is therefore understandable, the more so because the King of Spain's impulse, once he had recovered from the extraordinary rage induced by the news of the Second Partition Treaty (a rage matched by his wife's; she smashed everything in her room) was to turn to the Emperor for sympathy and support. But the governing clique in Spain decided that the best way to preserve the Empire undivided was to place it under the rule of a French king, and they so persuaded Charles II. On 2 October 1700 the King signed a second Will, bequeathing his entire dominions to Philip, Duke of Anjou, the second grandson of Louis XIV, with the condition that the Crowns of France and Spain should not be united and that if the bequest were not accepted on behalf of either Anjou or his younger brother, the Duke of Berry, then it should be offered to the Archduke Charles. A month later (1 November) the unhappy Charles II died.

This put Louis in real difficulty. If he refused, then Spain would in effect pass under the control of Austria, and the nightmare of Habsburg encirclement which France had fought desperately to break in the sixteenth century would become once again a reality. If he accepted, he would have a war with Austria for certain, and probably one with the Maritime Powers as well. If he tried to adhere to the Partition Treaty, a war with Austria was more than likely. Louis and his advisers did some very hard thinking, the result of which was dramatically made known on 16 November. The door opening from his Cabinet-room to the huge room which overlooks the fountains of Versailles, the *Galérie des Glaces*, was flung wide, Louis emerged with his grandson, surveyed the assembled company for a moment, and then said, 'Messieurs, voilà le roi d'Espagne!' and the enraptured Spanish Ambassador said soon afterwards that the Pyrenees were no more.

This meant that war with the Emperor was more or less a foregone conclusion, but the latter did not at first feel strong enough to risk it without the support of the Maritime Powers. This was slow in coming. Indeed, the first reaction of the English merchants was satisfaction that the Partition, which would have directly given France control of the Mediterranean, was now a dead letter; it seemed preferable that France and Spain were not after all to be united. William tried strenuously to alter this frame of mind, and was assisted by pamphleteers, prominent among whom was Daniel Defoe. His most useful agent in this matter was Louis himself, who committed a series of blunders so foolish as make it seem that he positively desired a war against as many opponents as possible.

On 1 February 1701 he got the Paris *Parlement* to register a decree reserving the rights of Philip V of Spain to the French throne, and four days later French troops entered the Spanish Netherlands and quickly disarmed the Dutch garrisons there. Nevertheless, even this news, which produced something like a panic in London and a run on the Bank, found William so weak, since Parliament still refused to vote subsidies for a war, that after demanding compensation from Louis, and not getting it, he felt obliged to recognize Philip V on 17 April. But the Tory majority in the Commons had ceased to represent the merchant class or even the public at large, which now clamoured for war, and an election held in September brought in a Whig majority eager for it. In the meantime (June) William had prorogued Parliament and in the next month opened negotiations at The Hague with the Austrians. Agreement was reached by the Treaty of The Hague, called the Grand Alliance, on 7 September 1701. By this the Maritime Powers agreed to the claims of the Archduke Charles to the whole of the Spanish dominions in Italy, although in fact the Emperor had every intention of getting the whole Empire, but on condition that they could keep any conquests they made in the West Indies and, more significantly, that the security of their trade and navigation was assured. Thus the Emperor was fighting for territory and the Maritime Powers were fighting for the trade of the Spanish Empire in the West. The Austrians did not wait for the completion of these negotiations but opened a campaign in Italy against the French.

Louis's next action was all that was required to bring the English, already consciously preparing to fight for the commerce of the New World and their own commercial supremacy, to a boiling-point of indignation against him. On 16 September 1701 the exiled English King James II died at Saint-Germain. Louis thereupon recognized his son as the 'rightful' King of England, and his assertion that this did not affect his recognition of William as King in fact, while conceivably sincere, was one whose subtlety the English public were in no mood to appreciate. It was regarded as an intolerable insult by the nation which had in 1688 pronounced its right to choose a king for itself and whose Parliament had moreover just regulated the succession by the Act of Settlement (1701). The country went wild with rage at the notion that Louis XIV could give England a king of his choosing as he apparently had done for Spain. Meetings all over the country passed resolutions supporting William, and Parliament voted enough money to supply an army of 40,000 and the same number of sailors. William never lived to see even the beginnings of the downfall of his lifelong adversary. A fall from his horse proved too much for his enfeebled health, and he died on 19 March 1702, happy in the belief that very hard times lay ahead for Louis. The latter and his court for a moment imagined that this might after all alter English policy, which shows how profoundly Louis misunderstood the Revolution of 1688. It did not make any difference who sat on the English throne. Those who ruled the country, and those who represented the commercial classes, were determined to fight for the Balance of Power in Europe, for the economic and commercial supremacy of England in the Americas, and for the right of the nation to choose its own king; of these motives it is likely that the second was the strongest.

(b) THE WAR

At the outset it might not have appeared to a knowledgeable observer that Louis had been so very rash in virtually provoking a great European war. His fleet was sadly outnumbered; he had about 100 battleships and that number was soon reduced, whereas the allies had 227, and so seemed assured of complete command of the sea. Yet his army was very nearly as numerous as those of all the allies together (about 200,000), and his marshals, Villars, Vendôme, and Berwick, were very able men, even if some of the others, such as Villeroi, Tallard, and Marsin, turned out to be mediocre. Louis no longer had the good fortune to be served by any ministers of the calibre of Colbert or Louvois, and so a heavy burden of work fell on the King himself, a burden made all the more heavy because he soon found that the young King of Spain and his advisers were inept and he had to lend a hand in the direction of Spanish affairs also. On the other hand, his ability and experience were great; Louis was also placed very favourably on interior lines, and Austria was wide open for a quick knock-out blow. The latter was menaced in Italy by the Spaniards, who could easily be supported by the French, for Louis had secured the alliance of the Duke of Savoy. To the west of Austria lay Bavaria, which was soon to join Louis and was separated from him only by Baden, an ally of the Emperor whose extinction by the French army was practically a certainty. After that it was hard to see how the Austrians could hope to defend themselves against invasion by the combined French and Bavarians, and they could expect no help from the English and Dutch, who would be hard put to it to defend themselves in the Netherlands. The Dutch were hardly a serious military nation at all, while the English appeared an amateurish crew, who, apart from the freakish episode of Cromwell's time, had done nothing much to add to their reputation as land fighters since the glorious days of the longbow—and Agincourt was a memory nearly three hundred years old.

The allies nevertheless did have advantages, not all of them as yet revealed. The Austrians in Prince Eugene had at least one first-rate general, and the Dutch, although too timid to let their soldiers go far from the defence of their homeland, possessed in the Grand Pensionary, Heinsius, a man of courage and great diplomatic skill. The big surprise of the war was to be the renaissance of the English army under one of the greatest soldiers of all time, John Churchill, created Duke of Marlborough in December 1702.

Marlborough (1650–1722) has not escaped accusations of dishonesty, which, if true, may be disregarded, for he certainly gave his country good value for money. More seriously, he also spent some time as a prisoner in the Tower of London for treasonable correspondence with the exiled Stuart King, but that too was a form of life-insurance with which many others attempted to cover themselves. These faults he outweighed by an unbreakable self-control, patience with fools, which he often needed, courtesy, and calmness; and he was thus exactly fitted to the difficult task of keeping the allies together.

As a soldier, he was that rarity, a master tactician and a master strategist, and in addition had the imagination to use new and successful methods. The armies of the time were based on slow, defensive techniques, in part a hangover from the days of the pike as the chief weapon of the infantry. This was essentially a defensive weapon, for the infantry could only hope to withstand the shock of a cavalry charge by grouping themselves into massive and unwieldy formations. The other factor making for defensive ideas was the generally recognized superiority of the cavalry, and since they relied on forage for the horses this led to the necessity of establishing magazines of supplies, and this in turn to wars of sieges, pitched battles being avoided as much as possible. Marlborough realized, however, the implication of the invention of the flintlock musket (a much improved type) and of the ring-bayonet and the socket-bayonet (1678) which had made the pike obsolete. In fact, it was abandoned wholly by the French, and was rarely used by the English, before the War of the Spanish Succession started. Therein lay his originality, for he saw that the infantry could defend itself far better with the musket and had no need of such thick columns. This made possible a far more mobile and manœuvrable formation of four or even three lines. So it was possible to use the infantry for attack, the offensive weapon being not so much the musket, which was not readily reloaded in attack, but the bayonet. Thus Marlborough pinned down his enemies with furious infantry attacks, keeping his cavalry until these attacks had softened up the enemy so much that they could not, even with their muskets, withstand the shock of a cavalry charge. With this tactical genius went an offensive strategic spirit; it now became his object to seek out the enemy and destroy him in battle; and, with that strategic spirit, a strategic genius which enabled him to grasp the essentials of a war fought on a continental scale.

His task at the opening of the campaign of 1702 was extremely complicated. In Italy, Prince Eugene was outnumbered and hard pressed by a Franco-Spanish army under Marshal Vendôme. It was essential to give some help to the Austrians at the earliest possible moment, but to strike at the Spanish communications with Italy with naval power was practically impossible, for Portugal had joined the enemy side in June 1701, and the allies thus possessed no base from which it was easy to operate in the Mediterranean. To bring help from the Netherlands overland was likewise out of the question, for Marlborough was faced there not only by 90,000 French troops under Marshal Boufflers, but with the timidity of his Dutch allies. The only comforting feature was that the approaches to Austria through the Black Forest area were for the moment blocked by the Emperor's ally, the Margrave Louis of Baden, though how long he could hold out against Villars, the ablest of the French marshals, was doubtful. If Bavaria joined the enemy the Margrave would be overwhelmed from both sides.

'Corporal John' (as Marlborough was called by his troops—the French referred to him as 'the handsome Englishman') decided to do what he could to smash Boufflers in the Netherlands while at the same time ordering (he was in supreme command of the direction of the war) Admiral Rooke to capture Cadiz for use as a base. In spite of the Dutch, whose nervousness four times prevented him from dealing really effectively with the French, Marlborough in 1702 managed to push the enemy out of the valleys of the Maas and Lower Rhine. Rooke, meanwhile, failed completely at Cadiz, but made up for it by a sudden attack on Vigo, destroying fifteen French warships and taking an enormous amount of treasure. But time was running out, for in September 1702 Bavaria joined the enemy and on 14 October, Villars defeated Louis of Baden at Friedlingen and by the following May had crossed the Black Forest and joined forces with the Bavarian army near Ulm. As the wretched Austrians were also being threatened by a revolt of the Hungarians, a quick dash by Villars to Vienna might have knocked them straight out of the war. This he saw clearly enough, but the Bavarians idiotically insisted on going off to try to capture territory for themselves in the Tyrol, which they failed to do. So the chance was missed, as an Austrian army under Marshal Styrum joined the Margrave.

These allies just as foolishly missed a chance of defeating Villars, which they might have done had not they also separated their forces. The result was that Villars defeated Styrum on 14 October 1703 at Höchstädt. This gave another chance to carry out the attack on Vienna, but the Elector of Bavaria quarrelled with Villars over the project. The latter was therefore recalled to France and replaced by a commander of inferior ability, Marshal Marsin. The situation was still horribly precarious, however, for another French army under Marshal Tallard had in the meantime entered Bavaria. The enemy had missed his chances so far, and it was by then too late in 1703 to campaign any more that year; but in the campaigns of the following year the overthrow of Austria seemed assured, the more so as in 1703 Marlborough, thanks to the Dutch, had achieved nothing. The only bright news was that in May 1703 Portugal, by the Methuen Treaties, joined the allies, and on 23 October Savoy did likewise, though how either event could save Vienna it was impossible to see. It seemed that the French would soon be able to turn all their forces against the English and Dutch in the Netherlands who would thus be hopelessly outnumbered.

The really pressing task for 1704 was evidently to relieve Austria, but Marlborough had also to arrange operations in a more distant theatre. This was in Spain. The treaty with Portugal was clearly advantageous in an economic sense, for the Portuguese agreed to accept English cloth and to sell wine in return; this involved throwing open to the British the huge Brazilian market. In the military aspect too it was obviously useful to have the use of Portuguese harbours. But King Pedro of Portugal, fearful of possible attack from Spain, had also by the offensive treaty signed at the same time as the defensive one, made the allies agree to send a force of 12,000 troops to Lisbon and to proclaim the Archduke Charles as King of Spain. This, at least from the point of view of the Dutch and English, was to extend the political aims of the war in a manner never envisaged at the start of it. The original Grand Alliance had as one of its purposes to secure most of Italy for the Emperor, but it was only in the Treaty of 16 May 1703 with Portugal that they engaged on the far more difficult task of 'contributing all their endeavours unanimously that the most serene Archduke Charles, second son of his imperial Majesty, be put into the possession of all Spain', and moreover promised that 'neither peace nor truce shall be made but by mutual consent of all the confederates, and they shall not be made at any time while the most Christian king's grandson, the Dauphin's second son, or any other prince of the House of France, remains in Spain' (Article XXI). Wars breed their own needs, and so war aims alter because of the changing military and political circumstances which the fighting produces. This undertaking was to prove a bad one, for the Spaniards revered their chosen King, and so the task of trying to remove him, although obstinately pursued, was impossible to fulfil and was to prolong the war needlessly.

To meet this new situation Marlborough ordered Rooke to escort the Archduke to Lisbon, together with troops. After that Rooke was to attack Toulon, aided by land forces belonging to the Duke of Savoy. The Duke was unable to spare them, so Rooke retired to the Straits and made a sudden and successful attack on Gibraltar (4 August), and three weeks later hammered a French relieving force so badly that for the rest of the war the French did not dispute the English control of the Mediterranean.

Help for the Austrians was soon forthcoming too, and that by one of the most daring plans in the history of war. Marlborough realized the only thing to do was to take his army to the Danube, and had to conceal this from most of the Dutch, who were terrified at the removal of their chief defence from the French, who had armies along the Moselle and at Strasburg, under Coignies and Tallard respectively, while another army, commanded by Marshal Marsin, lay at Ulm, covering a smaller Imperial army. This means that practically all of Marlborough's route

left him open to a dangerous flank attack. His army was twenty miles
west of Cologne on 16 May, entered Bonn on the 23rd, and was at
Coblenz by the 25th. All was going like clockwork; the troops had
never been so well cared for. They started the day's march about three

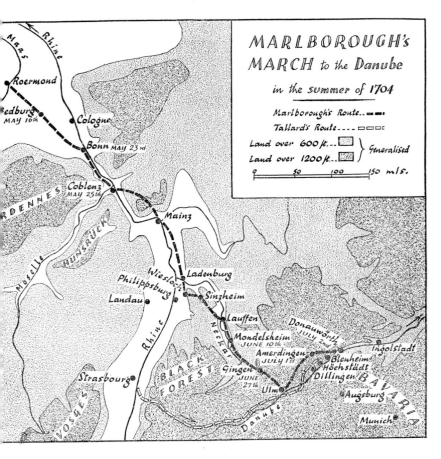

MARLBOROUGH's
MARCH to the Danube
in the summer of 1704

Marlborough's Route..
Tallard's Route....
Land over 600 ft... } Generalised
Land over 1200 ft...
0   50   100   150 mls.

in the morning, did about twelve miles, and rested from about nine
onwards in places carefully prepared for them by allied commissioners,
who brought up food and so on to the agreed sites. The enemy thought
he was intending to invade France by way of the Moselle and were
therefore amazed when, instead of turning up the Moselle at Coblenz,
Marlborough headed for Mainz. The enemy were equally wrong in
supposing that his intention then was to enter France by the Rhine-
crossing at Philippsburg, for the allies turned again towards Sinzheim,

a move that baffled and dismayed Tallard, who had moved up to block the advance via Philippsburg. Marlborough headed instead towards Lauffen, and on 10 June reached Mondelsheim, where he was joined by Louis of Baden, and by Prince Eugene, who had fortunately been placed at the head of the Austrian army in that theatre. Thereafter the Duke and the Prince formed one of the most generous and harmonious teams of allied commanders known to history.

The combined forces continued and reached Gingen on 27 June. At Gingen it was decided that Eugene should cover the armies of Villeroi and Tallard, and prevent them from joining Marsin and the Elector of Bavaria, while the two last-named were watched by Marlborough. Thus Eugene with 30,000 men faced Villeroi near Strasburg (with double his number), while Marlborough first came in contact with his adversaries near Dillingen (about twenty-five miles north-east of Ulm); the Duke's 70,000 men outnumbered his opponents by approximately 10,000.

Even so he did not fight the enemy there. Instead he took another of his daring risks and moved away north-east to attack the fortress town of Donauwörth, a place more than valuable because with it he could open the road to attack the Elector's capital (Munich), and if need be secure a better way of retreat for himself. It was dangerous, however, because, seeing this, the Elector was already reinforcing it; and it had to be taken by storm, for a siege would delay matters long enough for Tallard, now rapidly advancing, to come up. The Duke would then be caught between the army of Tallard and the Franco-Bavarian army under Marsin. He therefore rushed to Donauwörth, taking advantage of the fact that he was over half a day's march nearer to it than Marsin was, leaving Amerdingen early on the morning of 2 July, with Marsin close behind him.

The town itself was dominated by an oval-shaped hill called the Schellenberg, and the Bavarian Marshal had placed his 14,000 men on it.

The battle, which began at five in the afternoon, is a classic example of Marlborough's tactics. He attacked the strongest part of the defences, on the western side, because an attack would be least expected there. Up the steep slope went the British infantry, and a ferocious struggle with the defenders began, so ferocious that in the hand-to-hand fighting men tore out each other's eyes with their finger-nails. But the attack failed, as did the second and third; the hill was too strong to take in that fashion. The point is that Marlborough knew that too. The attacks were not meant to succeed. Their purpose was to threaten that side of the hill so savagely that D'Arco, the Bavarian commander, should fear that they might succeed, and so put nearly all his reserves there to support the defence. This he obligingly did, and got a numbing shock when the troops of the Margrave of Baden, forming Marlborough's right wing, their approach entirely unnoticed, appeared on his left. At that moment the Margrave attacked and Marlborough flung in his fourth infantry assault. Caught between two fires, the Bavarians broke and fled. In the battle and the merciless pursuit that followed, they lost 10,000 men against the Duke's 1,400 killed and 3,800 wounded.

Donauwörth quickly fell, since it was not defensible against an army occupying the Schellenberg. With it the Duke got a bridge over the Danube and the chance of invading Bavaria, whose Elector, in a panic, entrenched himself in Augsburg, while Marsin sent to Tallard for help.

Tallard responded at once to this appeal, and by 29 July reached Ulm, which put Prince Eugene into the impossible position of having now to watch him as well as Villeroi. He misled both by heading first north, to make Villeroi think he was still the object of attention, and then by disappearing in the direction of Donauwörth the better to support Marlborough.

Again anxious to bring the enemy to battle, Marlborough devastated part of Bavaria, and after getting rid of his ally the Margrave of Baden, who was a nuisance, by telling him to go off to besiege Ingolstadt, he wrote to Eugene asking him to join him. By 10 August, Tallard, Marsin, and the Elector, whose forces had now come together, set out to cross the Danube, and soon reached Höchstädt. From there they moved three miles down the river to the village of Blenheim, arriving on 12 August. They outnumbered Marlborough and Eugene because of the absence of the Margrave of Baden and his army, and were delighted to suppose that Marlborough would have to retreat, the more so as they took up a very strong defensive position. There would be no battle, and Marlborough, only a few miles away, would have to slink off with the campaign virtually lost after all.

There was a battle. A British defeat would have meant the downfall of the Emperor, and an England left to face overwhelming odds herself. A decisive British victory would mean the Revolution of 1688 made safe for ever; it might bring with it victory in the whole war. The overthrow of Louis XIV's France by the British would be the foundation for English maritime, commercial, and colonial supremacy in the world. The battle would take too long to describe adequately, but some indication of its broad outlines seems justifiable. Besides, as a battle, it is an exciting piece of generalship.

The Franco-Bavarian army was strung out on the top of a rise. On its right was the broad Danube and, from the village of Blenheim close to the river, the line stretched three miles at right angles to the river, to the village of Oberglau, and a farther mile and a half to the village

The BATTLE of BLENHEIM 13th AUG. 1704

Franco-Bavarian Infantry	Franco-Bavarian Cavalry
Allied Infantry	Allied Cavalry
High ground mostly wooded	Riverine marshes (shown only on left bank of Danube)

0 ... 1 ... 2 ... 300 yards

of Lutzingen. Tallard's troops occupied the position from Blenheim to Oberglau while those of Marsin and the Elector defended Lutzingen, Marsin himself being in the former village and the Elector in the latter. In front lay a marshy area through which ran a stream called the Nebel, while the Lutzingen area was wooded and difficult country for an advancing army. All three villages were so heavily defended as to seem virtually impregnable fortresses, and a successful advance could thus only be hoped for between them. But a successful advance there would ruin the attacker, who would be walking into a trap—he would be caught by flank attacks from the garrisons of the villages. A failure would be worse still, as a retreat by a defeated force to the Nebel would quickly become a total rout. Small wonder that the Franco-Bavarian army slept well on the night of 12 August, and that Tallard complacently credited his foes with enough sense to make off as soon as they could.

While the French slept, Marlborough and Eugene were marching, Marlborough on the left and Eugene on the right. By six in the morning (after they had marched four hours) the mist rose and the enemy had the shock of seeing the advance-guard of cavalry surveying them. Even then, in fact a full hour later, Tallard thought it was only a party covering the main retreat; but the advance continued, and the truth at last sank in. Hastily Tallard's troops formed line of battle. Eugene, who was to attack on the far right, had farther to go and over rougher ground, so from about half past eight until half past twelve there was an artillery duel while Marlbrough waited to begin his attack.

The defence was well planned. There were nine battalions of infantry (a battalion was about 800 men) in Blenheim, and eighteen more in reserve near it. In Oberglau were fourteen battalions, and near it thirty-two squadrons of cavalry. Between the two villages he had forty-four squadrons of cavalry (about 5,500 men) and nine of infantry. At Lutzingen, under the Elector, were fifty-one squadrons with twelve battalions. Between Lutzingen and Oberglau were thirty-two squadrons and twelve battalions under Marsin. Thus the villages were very heavily defended, while to advance between them meant being caught by their garrisons. Marlborough's method of tackling this problem was something like the plan for the Schellenberg, but on a far bigger scale. While Eugene distracted the enemy by attacks near Lutzingen, Marlborough's troops were to attack the villages, not with much hope of taking them, but to pin down their garrisons and supporting troops by ferocious attacks with smaller numbers. He could then safely send his main body in overwhelming numbers to smash Tallard's forces between Blenheim and Oberglau, and once these were disposed of the garrisons of these two villages would in turn be surrounded.

That roughly is what actually happened, though unfortunately there is not space to give all the thrilling details here. The battle, then, really began with a horrible attack on Blenheim. Lord Cutts, the leader of this attack, sent in only one battalion, which lost a third of its number in the first French volley. But the French commander in the village lost his head because of the determination of the attack, and in the blinding smoke thought a much larger English force was being used. He pulled all his eighteen supporting battalions into the village, and there for the rest of the battle 12,000 troops could hardly find standing room. The English kept them busy with a second attack, which failed like the first; it failed, that is, in the sense that it could not take the village. Much the same result was achieved at Oberglau, though there a very critical situation was saved only by the unselfish support hurriedly sent by Eugene, although his position was also critical.

With the garrisons pinned down safely, the time had come for the knock-out in the centre. At half past four in the afternoon it duly came. At his disposal for this, Marlborough had ninety squadrons and twenty-three battalions against the fifty to sixty squadrons and nine battalions of Tallard. After an initial reverse, Marlborough cut down every single man of the heroic nine French battalions with grapeshot, and at the irresistible advance of his cavalry the French cavalry broke and fled, thirty squadrons of them so blindly that they ended up in the Danube. Marsin and the Elector retired too, and the garrison in Blenheim surrendered. Marlborough's forces in this stupendous victory lost 4,500 dead and 7,500 wounded, but the enemy lost over 38,000 in dead, wounded, prisoners, and deserters. The victory was shattering, both to that French army and to any real prospects of their winning the war. The legend of French invincibility was broken too, and though the war went on for another eight years, Louis XIV never during that time hoped for more than an honourable peace. That is why it seems worth while to give more space to the battle than can be devoted to whole campaigns in the rest of the war—that, and the same pleasure as comes from viewing a work of art or studying a great game of chess, though how much more complex than any chess game!

The allies, however, failed to make the most of this victory. Their only big success in 1705 was the capture of Barcelona by Lord Peter-borough, and the possibility of success in Spain was made rather point-less by the death of the Emperor in May of that year. His successor, Joseph I (1705-11), as yet had no son and might therefore be succeeded by his brother, the Archduke Charles. If the latter were put on the throne of Spain by allied victories there, the allies would presumably have fought to destroy the supremacy of Louis XIV only to substitute for it a renewed supremacy of the Habsburgs. The war had become almost pointless. Louis offered terms at the end of the year, but they were rejected, and in 1706 the allies again won great victories. On 23 May, Marlborough utterly defeated Villeroi at the Battle of

Ramillies, went on to conquer the Spanish Netherlands, and was even able to make a temporary advance into France itself. Eugene won a huge victory at Milan, and the allies temporarily occupied Madrid. Louis XIV, at his wit's end, offered even more advantageous terms, of which the main features were that Philip V should only have the Two Sicilies and Milan, while the Archduke Charles was to have all Spain and the remainder of the Empire. These were refused also, and Louis's last hope seemed to lie in the possibility of decisive intervention by the King of Sweden, Charles XII. In the end nothing came from that quarter either, and Louis had somehow to scrape up the resources to carry on the fight.

Things did not go quite so disastrously for him in 1707. His armies in Spain under Marshal Berwick cleared the allies out of Valencia, Aragon, and Saragossa, for which the allied capture of Naples was hardly compensation. Meanwhile Marlborough's authority in England, based in part on the dominating influence of his wife, Sarah, over the English Queen Anne, was reinforced by an election in 1708 which gave a majority to the pro-war Whigs, whose lack of realism caused them to adopt the slogan 'No peace without Spain', although nobody could begin to guess how Spain was to be captured or what good it would do England to put on the throne of that country the heir presumptive to the Habsburg dominions. Marlborough, however, in 1708 came near to smashing France. In the Netherlands, his victory at Oudenarde on 11 July once more opened the door to France, and in December he actually captured Lille; Ghent and Bruges fell soon after.

France was now in a pitiful condition. Already in 1707 Vauban in his book, *Dîme Royale*, had estimated that the population of the country had dropped by nearly half a million; trade was on its death-bed, the bankers could lend Louis no more, thousands of the poor were starving, and there was a clamour for peace. Louis's answer was to disgrace Vauban and to levy fresh taxes, but his Controller-General of the Finances, Desmaretz, warned him that a total collapse of the State was very near and that he feared a 'terrible revolution'. Louis thus offered peace terms once more. This time they amounted to a complete surrender. He offered to surrender Spain, to give a line of barrier fortress towns for the defence of the Netherlands, to recognize the Protestant Succession in England, even to give the Emperor Strasburg and Alsace. All this was not enough for the allies; they added the unworthy demand that Louis should use his own troops to help to expel his own grandson from Spain. Louis, beaten but not dishonoured, refused.

The allies made a profound mistake in rejecting such a favourable settlement. In 1709 France roused herself to a last desperate effort, and a large army was collected under the command of Marshal Villars. Marlborough defeated it at the Battle of Malplaquet, but, though he outnumbered the enemy, lost far more men than they (11 September). Although fresh offers of peace from Louis were once again haughtily rejected, things did not improve for the allies. The allied cause in Spain soon became hopeless. The English army led by Stanhope was heavily defeated on 10 December 1710, and two days later an Austrian force was smashed at Villaviciosa by Marshal Vendôme. The bad news from Spain added very much to the growing impatience with the war in England. The English government's unpopularity increased most alarmingly after a foolish attempt to prosecute a clergyman called Dr Sacheverell; this Tory priest became the idol of the mob, and the Queen, who was receiving floods of petitions asking her to dismiss the government, obliged by sacking Marlborough's chief supporters in the government, Sunderland and Godolphin being the most important of them; she appointed in their places Shrewsbury, Harley, and St John. These enemies of the Duke won an election in 1710, so that the Duke, while remaining in his post of Commander-in-Chief, no longer had any influence in the government, which indeed wanted peace. His own desire to continue the war has been said to have been caused by his lust for continued power as military commander, and by offers from the Emperor to have him made Regent of the Spanish Netherlands; if these allegations are true this must rank as the most disgraceful of the Duke's faults.

The Tory government in England felt it hardly creditable, however, to make peace without its allies, but the logic of the situation was reinforced by the death of the Emperor on 17 April 1711. The new ruler of the Habsburg dominions was thus the Archduke Charles, and so it seemed more than ever idiotic to carry on a war in Spain in order to hand that country over to him, and thereby re-create the Empire of Charles V which had dominated Europe in the sixteenth century. This reasoning was reinforced by the evident fact that the allies could not conquer Spain. Not that even a Tory government entirely overlooked the main war aims of Britain; for though the war in Europe was allowed to languish, the English attacked strongly in North America and in October 1710 captured Acadia (Nova Scotia). Early in the next year secret negotiations were carried on with the French, and an agreement was reached by 11 October. This forced the Dutch to see that they must fall into line as they could hardly continue hostilities for long without English support, and they agreed to meet for peace discussions at Utrecht on 12 January 1712. The Whigs in England made a last attempt to prolong the war, but they failed, and their failure was made irretrievable by the dismissal of Marlborough. Prince Eugene's continued fighting against the French in 1712 came to grief partly because of the ability of Villars, and partly because of the downright treachery of the English government in betraying his plans to the French, so that peace could at last be made.

(c) THE PEACE OF UTRECHT, 1713-14

The treaties signed at Utrecht in 1713 naturally enough gave the lion's share of the spoils to England. At the head of the list came the French King's pledge that he recognized 'for ever' the Protestant Succession in England and his promise to expel the Stuarts from France and never to help them to regain the British throne. Thus Louis had to sign an agreement which implicitly condemned the Divine Right of Kings at least so far as England was concerned. The principles of the Revolution of 1688 and of John Locke had signally triumphed over Versailles and Bossuet, and government by consent of at least some of the governed achieved a victory of enormous propaganda value. A more practical gain was that the French had to destroy the fortifications of Dunkirk and fill up the harbour since the port had been used as a base for privateers which had preyed on English shipping. In the New World the French ceded to the English the island of St Kitts, the territory around Hudson Bay, Acadia (Nova Scotia), and Newfoundland. They also undertook that the French and Spanish Crowns should always be separate. Lastly, the French promised not to seek commercial privileges in the Spanish dominions, and granted most-favoured-nation terms for English commerce with France. (That is, duties on English goods entering France would be as small as the duties on similar goods of any other nation.) Great as these concessions all were, the gains made at the expense of Spain were almost as considerable. Spain surrendered Minorca and Gibraltar, and this of course implied future English mastery over the West Mediterranean. The Spaniards also granted to England the famous Asiento, which was the exclusive right to import Negro slaves into the Spanish American possessions for thirty years at the rate of 4,800 a year, a very profitable and disgusting business. A further concession was the right to send one ship of 500 tons to trade every year for the next thirty years at the trade fairs in the Spanish Indies. (That was not very much in itself but it made a useful cover for smuggling a great deal more.)

Protection of the Dutch was provided by two measures. They were needed, for the treaty possibly marks the end of Dutch greatness; the country was greatly weakened by its wars with England and then France. One transferred the Spanish Netherlands to the rule of Austria, which, being a stronger Power, could presumably protect the area more effectively from French aggression than Spain had been able to do. The other provided that a barrier of fortresses on the French side should be garrisoned by the Dutch—it included Ypres, Menin, Ghent, Furnes, Tournai, Mons, and several other towns. However, the French regained control of Lille, Aire, Béthune, and Saint-Venant. The French restored Savoy and Nice to their ruler, Victor Amadeus, and also gave him the throne of Sicily (this was Spanish territory, but the Spaniards obeyed their French masters). The Spaniards also gave to Portugal a small colony (San Sacramento, north of the River Plate).

Hostilities between France and the Emperor dragged on for a little while, but were brought to an end by the preliminary Treaty of Rastatt in March 1714, and confirmed on the whole at the Treaty of Baden in September of the same year. By this, the Electors of Bavaria and of Cologne had their territories restored to them, France retained Alsace, including Strasburg, and the Emperor, besides gaining the somewhat dubious honour of being the new ruler, and defender, of the Spanish Netherlands, became in effect the ruler of Italy by the cession of Naples, Milan, and Tuscany. The perfectly useless island of Sardinia was foisted on him by the English, although he would have preferred Sicily.

All this—there were fourteen treaties in all—can be lumped together and referred to as the Utrecht Peace. It is obviously a rearrangement of Europe on a very great scale and may be regarded as settling not only the War of the Spanish Succession, but the whole crisis stemming from 1688. What emerged fairly clearly was the huge influence England was now able to wield on the continent of Europe, and the apparent decline of France.

The influence of England was indeed so great that some French historians particularly are fond of describing it as an 'English preponderance'. Perhaps there is some element of exaggeration in this; nevertheless, the English obviously controlled the West Mediterranean, and by giving Sicily to little Savoy, instead of to the Emperor, seemed to make fairly sure that their mastery could not easily be disputed there. At the other end of Europe, France was held in by Austria's possession of the Spanish Netherlands, while a watch was kept on both of them by giving Neuchâtel and High Guelderland to Prussia. The Straits of

Dover were safe for English shipping because of the demolition of Dunkirk, and by provisions which prohibited Austria from using the River Scheldt for navigation, thus ruining Antwerp for the benefit of London and of Amsterdam. Later, when Queen Anne of England died (1714), the new ruler was George I, Elector of Hanover, and this little German State had an alliance with Denmark, so the English position in the Baltic was strengthened. Add to all that the various trade concessions in the peace settlement itself, and also the alliance and trade treaty with Portugal, and it is obvious that England did indeed have a remarkably strong position, if not a preponderant one.

France on the other hand had received a terrible defeat, even when allowance is made for the fact that, after all, a French prince still sat on the throne of Spain. We have already referred to the terrible distress caused in France by the wars. What was just as striking was the decline in the authority of Louis XIV himself. As already noted, he was defied by the Jansenists, and the principles of Divine Right which supported him were receiving scant respect from the pens of Bayle and other rationalist writers (see previous chapter). The Huguenots after the Revocation of the Edict of Nantes naturally never ceased to denounce him, but, more than that, kept up, chiefly in the Cevennes, a war against his troops. He was driven as early as 1699 to sending to his *intendants* instructions to relax the application of the laws against them. In another sphere, there were outcries, to which he had to yield, against excessive government control of economic life, and several seaports recovered the complete direction of their own affairs. At the centre of the monarchy, in Versailles, the words of Fénelon, who spoke of France as a great desolate hospital, were outdone in sheer daring by Father Masillon, who preached to the King's face that 'it is the supreme will of peoples which has made kings all that they are'. Even the King's strict outlook on morality was not accorded by many people the flattery of imitation; by the end of the reign Masillon said that immorality instead of being regarded with horror was almost a mark of distinction. By the time of his death the great old King had forfeited not only a good deal of the respect and obedience of his subjects but their affection as well. He died on 1 September 1715 at the age of seventy-seven. As soon as the eagerly awaited news was heard, people gave themselves up to wild rejoicing; dancing, drinking, and singing were the order of the day. Some of the songs were cruel, one of them speaking of him as 'the sworn enemy of peace' and going on to say, 'Pray not to God for his soul, for such a monster never had one.'

This looks as if Louis was a failure. Some inkling of that may have been present in his mind when, on his death-bed, he sent for his successor, the little boy who was to be Louis XV, and said to him, 'J'ai trop aimé la guerre; ne m'imitez pas en celà', and then told him to look after his people. If he had added that he had also loved his own glory and importance too much, he would have given a fair criticism of his own reign. But although he would have been wiser to stop his aggressions about the time of the seizure of Strasburg, and though he went on to involve France in a ruinous defeat, it should not be forgotten that he left France a frontier that gave her immunity from invasion for a very long time. He had no notion whatever of seeking to obtain the 'natural frontiers' of France; how could it for him have 'natural' frontiers, when it was not an entity on its own but his personal possession?

Louis also before his death realized that the policy of fighting Austria was a mistake, the chief result of which was to give the English too great a say on the Continent. He began to turn to the idea of a *rapprochement* with the House of Habsburg, for if France and the Austrians were friendly they could in effect rule the Continent between them and almost exclude English influence. He realized that it would not be easy to undo the hostility and suspicion of centuries, and the idea died with him; later it was to be reconsidered by Cardinal Fleury and eventually revived by the Austrians themselves.

The great war had quietly achieved something of a different sort. We have already observed in passing that at one time during it Louis had hoped for help from Sweden, which did not come. While Louis was fighting to preserve France from invasion, neither he nor his opponents could possibly exert so much influence in the north of Europe, itself the scene of a great war which had for one of its results a further growth in the power of Russia and Prussia and a corresponding decline of Western influence there, a decline which became more marked as the eighteenth century grew older.

8 · The Great War of the North, 1700–21

The interplay of character with larger historical forces rarely fails to grip the imagination. This war—as this necessarily brief account will try to show—provides an outstanding example, for it revolved round one of the most amazing persons in the history of the world, King Charles XII of Sweden, the 'Terror of the North'.

The King was only a boy of fifteen when his father, Charles XI, died, but the Swedish Estates after a few months declared him of age to rule (November 1697). It was a highly reasonable assumption that such a very raw youngster could not possibly be an opponent to be feared, and the chance of aggression at Sweden's expense was irresistibly attractive to Peter the Great of Russia.

Russia at that moment was engaged in fighting the Turks, and after a calamitous start had captured Azov, on the Black Sea (1696). Peter did not make a full peace with the Turks, as did his allies (at Karlo-witz), but only a truce. However, he prolonged this with them in July 1700 in order to get his share of the Swedish Empire.

For Sweden was menaced not by Russia alone but by a whole coali-tion, of which the author may be said to have been Augustus II, Elector of Saxony, who had also been elected King of Poland in 1697. He is supposed to have got the idea from a disgruntled Livonian noble-man called Patkul who had been deprived of his estates by the Swedes, and who became his adviser. The plan was to partition the Swedish Empire between Poland, Russia, and Denmark. Brandenburg was also approached, but showed little immediate interest. The whole conspiracy came as a complete surprise to the young King of Sweden.

The allies started in February 1700 with a Danish invasion of Holstein, whose Duke was friendly with Sweden, and a Polish-Saxon attack on Swedish Riga. A Russian army of about 40,000 men under Marshal Golovin, accompanied by the Tsar, toiled slowly westward with the intention of besieging Narva, in Estonia. They expected their youthful victim to be quickly overwhelmed.

Unluckily for these aggressors, the young King of Sweden was a born warrior who loved fighting, enjoyed the hardships of campaigning, and regarded all difficulties as something provided by a kindly Providence to give him a chance to prove his genius for war. He treated his troops well, except that he expected miracles from them, and they in turn had a boundless faith in his ability to lead them to victory (and that confidence makes troops love a commander far more than any sort of good treatment on his part could). The young King had an extremely good natural tactical ability and could pick out rapidly any weakness in his enemies' positions. Having picked it out, he attacked like a hurricane.

He first showed his mettle by knocking out Denmark in two weeks. King Frederick IV of Denmark (1699–1730) had counted on the superiority of his fleet to give him immunity from Swedish attacks, but this was a gross miscalculation, for an English squadron sent by King William III in accordance with England's treaty obligations nullified the Danish superiority and so enabled Charles to cross the Sound and menace Copenhagen to such purpose that the Danes on 18 August 1700 were glad enough to sign the Treaty of Traventhal. By this, Denmark recognized the Duke of Holstein's rights in ducal Holstein and promised not to help the enemies of Sweden. This happened without the knowledge of Peter the Great, who fondly imagined that Charles would have his hands entirely full with Denmark, and consequently sent his own declaration of war a few days after the treaty, in circumstances that were all the more inauspicious for him because the Saxon army did not succeed in taking Riga. Instead of being tied up by the Danes, Charles was hurrying his army eastwards, and by October was in Estonia, thinking first to relieve Riga. Hearing that Narva was also besieged, he left Riga to look after itself and by 19 November was nine miles from Narva. Peter only then learned that his foe was anywhere near him, and the surprise was so complete that Peter himself, and his Marshal, promptly fled in panic, leaving their army under Prince de Croy. On the next day a blinding snowstorm almost hid the armies from each other, and this pleased Charles since it was blowing towards the enemy, who were thus, as he told his troops, unable to see how few the Swedes were (they actually had less than 9,000, possibly as few as 7,000, against the 35,000 or 40,000 Russians). The Swedes attacked with the ferocity of wolves, and in half an hour the Russian army was obliterated, losing 15,000 dead and 20,000 prisoners.

The GREAT WAR of THE NORTH 1700-21   (Boundaries as in 1700)

Charles then decided to deal with the Poles. For this he has been much criticized on the grounds that he should have finished off Peter first, but invading Russia was a suicidally dangerous affair, and it would have been still more dangerous while the Poles were in the field. It has been suggested that he also feared intervention by the Maritime Powers against him. Accordingly Charles, after wintering in Estonia, began his Polish campaign in June 1701. On 8 July he smashed a Russian-Saxon army of 30,000 men at Dunamunde and then captured Courland. The next year saw a few more thunderbolts for his unhappy foes. Charles set off for Warsaw in January 1702, took it on 14 May, routed a vastly more numerous army of Saxons and Poles on 2 July at Klissow, and in the same month captured Cracow. In 1703 he heavily defeated the Saxons at Pultusk, and in 1704 declared Augustus deposed. In his place Stanislaus Leszczynski, a Polish noble, was elected King of Poland in July 1704. This career of conquest in Poland still left Charles far from being master of all that huge country, however, and while Charles was marching across vast plains and annihilating Polish armies, his chief enemy was hastily taking full advantage of the opportunities presented by Charles's continued presence in Poland.

As early as the beginning of 1703 Peter the Great had recovered from the shock of the disaster at Narva, and invaded Ingria. He managed to defeat two smaller Swedish forces, and by December had captured the little town of Nöteborg, which he renamed Schlüsselburg ('key city'), for it gave him control of the River Neva, and in May of the following year he was able to have a start made in the building of St Petersburg, which was to give him the long coveted 'window' on to the Baltic and to Europe at large. He followed up these successes by taking Dorpat and Narva in the next year (1704). Well pleased with these successes, Peter was prepared to make peace, but Charles would have nothing to do with it. Peter then went to the help of the Poles, who certainly needed it, and in 1705 the Russians, after occupying Courland, wintered at Grodno. A rash attempt by Augustus to attack the Swedes near Grodno went hopelessly astray in February 1706 and this entailed a forced retreat for Peter also; the latter was glad enough to escape with the loss of his heavy artillery and baggage. Charles did not press his pursuit too far. Instead, he went off to try to finish Augustus, and chased the ill-starred originator of the attack on Sweden right into his native country of Saxony. To reach Saxony he had to cross Silesia, but he did that with no respect for anybody's feelings, and on 20 October 1706 forced Augustus to accept his terms by the Treaty of Altranstädt. Augustus had to give up his alliance with Peter and to recognize Stanislaus as rightful King of Poland. In addition, he had to keep the Swedish army in Saxony at his own expense until the Emperor and the Maritime Powers had guaranteed the Peace.

The emotion aroused in various parts of Europe by the presence in the middle of Germany of the, by then, legendary hero-king and his army of hard-bitten veterans, was profound. Louis XIV hoped that Charles might yet save him from the worst effects of the series of disasters that had befallen the French arms, and which showed no sign of ending. Charles did grant an interview to a French Ambassador, but nothing came of it, partly because the fervently Protestant Swedish King regarded the Most Christian King with sour disapproval. Louis's hopes were matched by the alarm of the Emperor and the Maritime Powers, for the Emperor had too openly sympathized with Charles's enemies, and might pay for it by being crushed by the invincible Swedish army; the Maritime Powers naturally dreaded the prospect of such a disaster to their chief ally. It was therefore decided to send no less a person than Marlborough himself to use his very great diplomatic ability to persuade Charles not to attack the Emperor. The two most famous soldiers in Europe met at Altranstädt in April 1707. Marlborough tried in vain to soften the crop-haired, taciturn, and unsmiling King by an extravagant compliment (he said his ambition was to study the art of war under Charles), but could get nothing out of him; much less could the Duke persuade him to join the allies against Louis XIV. However, the Duke guessed correctly that Charles's thoughts were straying in the direction of Russia. At last Charles forced the Emperor to agree to stop ill-treating his Protestant subjects, and, satisfied with this and with the condign punishment he had already inflicted on Augustus, he stopped playing the part of piper to whose tunes all of Europe had to dance and abruptly departed to settle accounts with Peter the Great.

Peter had been straining every nerve to face the coming struggle, had gathered reinforcements, regained a good deal of his influence in Poland, and devastated the countryside along Charles's likely line of advance.

Early in September 1707, Charles left Silesia with an army of 24,000 cavalry and 20,000 infantry, and had soon swept through Poland and advanced to near Minsk, Peter retreating before him. Charles's aim was Moscow, but after reaching Mogilev, on the Dnieper, on 8 July 1708, he got an offer of help from the Hetman of the Ukraine, who feared that Peter would stifle the remnants of his country's independence. Charles waited a time for the Ukrainian revolt to break out, but it did not, so he carried on until he got to the Russian frontier at Tatarsk, where he saw nothing but desolated countryside and burning villages ahead. He should now have waited for his subordinate general, Loewenhaupt, to come up with fresh troops and a large quantity of supplies, but foolishly decided to set out south for the Ukraine instead. This was to commit about half a dozen strategic blunders all at once: he cut himself off from supplies, did a flank march in face of the enemy (and he was no Marlborough), and scattered his own forces instead of concentrating them. Loewenhaupt did join him in October 1708, but only after having lost nearly half his men and all the precious supplies in fighting with the Russians. As a result of this and of similar disasters to another of Charles's generals, the Cossacks lost heart and Charles thus found himself with no hope of supplies in the Ukraine either.

In the remainder of the campaign Charles had many opportunities of making a safe retreat, but that was totally outside his calculations. He regarded himself as invincible, and he underestimated Peter and his Russians. He certainly allowed Peter to play successfully on his vanity, for while he was safely camped at a town called Romni, which contained ample shelter and provisions for his soldiers, he was lured away to go to the help of a force of his which was suddenly attacked by the Russians in a place called Gadiatz (December 1708). This was insane, for the winter was an extraordinarily severe one. Even in Venice the canals froze, as did the River Rhône in France, while in the Ukraine it was said that casks of spirits froze solid and birds died in mid-air. The march from Romni to Gadiatz took heavy toll of the Swedish heroes, who were ill-clothed and underfed; 3,000 died on the way and hundreds lost fingers and toes through frostbite. The pathetic thing about these ghastly sufferings was their pointlessness, for of course Peter's troops rushed into both towns while Charles was between them and destroyed most of the buildings and all the provisions they contained. That frightful winter passed somehow, although Charles's army was reduced to 20,000, of whom 2,000 were crippled, and most of the remnant of their powder was unusable.

Charles allowed none of this to affect his spirits in the least, but, desperate for provisions, he laid siege to the town of Poltava, after two amazing little battles in which with forces of 400 and 300 men he scattered two Russian armies of 7,000 and 5,000 men respectively. Poltava contained a lot of provisions, but instead of giving in at once, as Charles expected, the Russians defended it. Six horrible weeks went by with Poltava still untaken, and a huge Russian army under Peter lurked near by, afraid to attack the dreaded Charles. However, in a skirmish on 17 June 1709 Charles was badly wounded in the foot, and this was a disaster to the Swedes because he could no longer lead or adequately direct the Swedish troops, who depended, for their ridiculous and repeated successes against vastly superior numbers, on the tactical eye and irresistible dash of their King. As soon as he heard of Charles's incapacity, Peter decided to seek a battle. This duly took place on 27 June. Even though Charles had to be carried about on a litter, he contrived to be so much in the thick of it that he had twenty-one of his bearers killed in turn about him, and he nearly won the day. But the battle was muddled and the Swedes were finally overwhelmed by numbers. All the army was lost except about 1,000 who fled with Charles to the territories of the Turks; he reached the town of Bender, on the River Dniester, and was well received by the Turks.

It is because the Battle of Poltava was a muddle that no attempt has been made here to give a detailed description of it, for to give anything like a clear account would take too much space. The battle was certainly a momentous one. It saw the end of Sweden as a Great Power, and was to result in the loss of Sweden's Baltic Empire. Much more important, it was the birth of Russia as a Great European Power, whereas a big Swedish victory at Poltava might well have broken Peter's country beyond repair.

Peter made nearly as many mistakes as Charles had done in the years immediately after Poltava. Charles induced the Turks to fight Russia, and in the Russo-Turkish War which began in March 1711, Peter made so many blunders that he would have lost his entire army but for the absurd mistake of the Turkish commander, who parleyed instead of wiping out Peter's army, as he could easily have done. Finally the Sultan, after the war had dragged on for two years, asked Charles to leave Turkey. Charles refused, and so a Turkish army of 12,000 men attacked his house, which he defended for eight hours with only forty men, killing ten of the attackers with his own sword. But he was captured, and the Turks and Russians made peace at Adrianople in July 1713.

Charles then rested for many months and left Turkey in September 1714, arriving amid his enraptured subjects in December. They had need of the 'Terror of the North', for in his absence the Russians had conquered Livonia and southern Finland, while the other Powers had rushed in to get what they could; the Prussians had seized Stettin, the Danes part of Schleswig, and the Hanoverians Bremen and Verden (exchanged from Denmark in return for helping the latter to overrun Pomerania). However, the Swedish armies in all this had lost too many men, and not even Charles could stop a big army of Danes and Prussians from capturing Stralsund in December 1715. To add to Charles's misfortunes, he also fell foul of Britain because his chief minister proposed to help a Jacobite rising in England. So negotiations for peace were made in 1718, but these proving abortive, Charles resolved to strike at his enemies through Norway, since he could not cross the Sound, and in December of that year was killed by a stray bullet while besieging Fredriksten.

Sweden could do no more. In November 1719 she made peace with Hanover (Treaty of Stockholm), at the cost of the cession of Bremen and Verden to that Power. Another Treaty of Stockholm in January 1720 was made with Prussia, by which Sweden ceded Stettin and part of Pomerania. In the same year two treaties saw the end of hostilities with Denmark, by which the Danes renounced their claim to Rugen and Wismar, while the Swedes gave up their claim to a share in the Sound dues. Peace with Russia was not achieved until 1721. By the Treaty of Nystad in September of that year Russia gained Livonia, Estonia, Ingria, the Finnish province of Keksholm, and the fortress of Viborg.

Sweden had ceased for ever to be a Great Power; she had gone up like a rocket—and come down like one. Nor after this did Denmark aspire to play an important part in international affairs. The chief heir to the Swedish Empire had been Peter the Great, and it is the policy of Russia which in the eighteenth century was chiefly to mould the policies of the two little countries that had played such a big part on the European stage in the seventeenth. The struggle for the hegemony of the Baltic fought out between Denmark and Sweden thus ended in their common eclipse.

Russia was to play a big part in Baltic affairs, but it would be quite wrong to pre-date the rise of that country; Russia had become under Peter a Great European Power, but not the greatest of them. England and France could still exert an influence in the Baltic as great as Russia's, if not greater, and oddly enough these two countries, foes for centuries, were at the moment of Peter's triumph settling the affairs of all Europe in unwonted friendship.

9 · England and France defend the Utrecht Settlement, 1715–31

If England had emerged from the Utrecht Settlement with a preponderant position it soon became obvious that the most strenuous efforts would be needed to keep that position, and still more to improve it. None of the losers in the War of the Spanish Succession would be inclined to accept the verdict as final. Spain, for instance, fiercely resented the loss of so many of her former provinces, especially the Italian ones, and resented just as keenly the commercial privileges which the English had extorted. As for Gibraltar, the tourist in Spain in the present day may still see assertions of Spain's right to it chalked up on walls—a method of obtaining its return which has so far been no more effective than the military and diplomatic attempts made in the eighteenth century. Even one of the nominal winners in the war soon came to the conclusion that England had handed him a booby prize. The Emperor looked askance at being given the task of defending the Austrian Netherlands without any hope of making use of the country's trading potential, which was sacrificed to preserve the prosperity of his allies in Amsterdam and London, and at being given Sardinia, which was of no use, instead of Sicily, which was a highly desirable island. One consolation for the English in all this was, however, the pleasing fact that at least that disgruntled pair could never logically be expected to combine against the Peace of Utrecht, for the simple reason that Spain wanted the very Italian provinces now held by the Austrians.

There were soon to be two other major consolations. The first was that on the death of Queen Anne in 1714, the new ruler of England was, under the Act of Settlement passed in 1701 to ensure that England always got a Protestant monarch, George, Elector of Hanover, who became King George I of Great Britain. This brought a danger of costly entanglements in the defence of Hanover or to support its policies, but it also brought worth-while gains. For Hanover exempted English goods from customs duties, and because of its friendship with Denmark obtained a big reduction for English shipping in Danish Sound dues. Also, Hanover was profiting by the collapse of Sweden, and its increased power might hold out prospects of an English preponderance in the Baltic and North Germany. The other major consolation was something very startling indeed. In 1715 Louis XIV died, leaving as his heir a little boy aged five. Louis had appointed a Council of Regency, but this was at once pushed aside by the young King's uncle, the Duke of Orleans, who got the Paris *Parlement* to declare him sole Regent. The new Regent was a charming and utterly debauched man. He was also very intelligent and ambitious. At first he kept the services of many of Louis XIV's advisers and was also inclined to follow Louis's foreign policy. Later, under the influence of the brilliant Abbé Dubois, who soon became his chief adviser, he came to see the advantages of working hand in glove with the English, for they could support his weak position as a sort of usurping Regent and would be invaluable allies in case the young King should die (his health was not robust). This was so because in strict order of succession the Crown of France should then go to Philip V of Spain, but after him the Regent had the strongest claim. The hopes of the Spanish King would be opposed by none so bitterly and strongly as by the English, chief architects of the Peace of Utrecht which declared the same man could never be king of France and Spain. In that eventuality the strongest supporters of the Regent's claim would be the English; they were his natural allies. But if such a very odd alliance would benefit the Regent, how much more valuable it would be to the English, who would thus find themselves supported on the Continent by French diplomacy and perhaps by French armies!

The English grasped that in a flash. All their statesmen of course could see that France had to be contained somehow, though they differed in their notions about how that was to be done. The more old-fashioned of them preferred to contain the French by the old

Marlborough method; that is, by reviving the Grand Alliance. That is approximately what was first tried, and it had the hearty approval of such statesmen as Townshend and Robert Walpole. A burst of frenzied English diplomacy therefore resulted in alliances with Holland, Spain, and the Emperor, all between December 1715 and May 1716, but they were not a very useful collection because they were mutually incompatible, and the negotiations with the Emperor over Sicily had to be kept secret from Spain. The pro-French group led by the highly astute Stanhope, who furthermore had the backing of George I, accordingly found it easier to turn to the Regent, who was in any case apprehensive about the English agreement with the Emperor. The result was an alliance with the French signed on 28 November 1716, and made into a Triple Alliance by another with the Dutch in January 1717. The biggest gainer by far in this was unquestionably England, for the French agreed not merely to give no help to the Stuart Pretender (James, son of James II) but to assist England against him if necessary, to destroy the fortifications of Mardyck, to guarantee Hanover in the possession of Bremen and Verden, to guarantee the Dutch Barrier Treaty, and implicitly (though not in so many words) to cause the English no bother anywhere in Europe. France therefore had in effect agreed to underwrite the Peace of Utrecht for the benefit of England. It seems that if there really was an English preponderance in Europe after Utrecht it rested more on this treaty with the French in 1716 than on the Utrecht Settlement itself, and was therefore a highly precarious preponderance, for there was nothing much to prevent the French from withdrawing their support at any time, particularly if the young French King showed every sign of growing up to healthy manhood, and, more immediately, if the Regent's position as such should appear to be unassailable.

The value of this alliance to England was soon to be amply demonstrated. Before it was signed a worrying situation had arisen in the Baltic. The chief minister of Sweden, Baron Görtz, was trying to interest Russia and Prussia in an anti-Danish policy (Sweden would get Norway, which belonged to Denmark, and would thus be compensated for the loss of its Baltic provinces). This was all very alarming to Denmark's ally, Hanover, and so caused a fine flutter in London. Stanhope's answer had been in part the renewal of the alliance with the Emperor, but he had to pay a high price for it, including English help in getting him Sicily instead of Sardinia (this is the treaty of May 1716 already referred to). However, many English politicians recoiled in alarm from so many commitments, involving, as they might, the obligation to fight in Northern and Southern Europe at the same time, all, apparently, for the English King's miserable little German Electorate. The result was what is usually called the 'Whig schism'. It should here be explained that the new English King gave all the Tories, although they were far more numerous than the Whigs, a very cold shoulder indeed because after the Tory chief minister's abortive attempt to get 'James III' put on the throne on the death of Anne, he did not trust the Tories and chose only Whigs for his ministry. But a large section of Whigs resented wasting the country's strength for the sake of Hanover, and the quarrel erupted as a sequence to Stanhope's diplomatic entanglements on behalf of that State. The victory went to Stanhope and his associate, Sunderland; several prominent Whigs, including the Walpoles, Townshend, Devonshire, and Pulteney, were ejected from the ministry in 1717. That at least left Stanhope free to deal with the schemes of Görtz and Peter the Great. He dealt brutally with Görtz. The latter was trying to interest the French in his Northern League, and in the course of his journeyings incautiously entered Holland, where Stanhope got the Dutch to arrest him. Shortly afterwards, the English alliance with France was signed, and the Tsar at once took a more careful attitude.

This was the very welcome first fruit of the Alliance for the English, but the danger in the Baltic was only momentarily averted; the English were immediately glad of French help because of renewed danger from that quarter, and because of what looked like a worse threat from the other end of Europe at the same time. The trouble-maker this time was the Queen of Spain.

Elizabeth Farnese, who hailed from Italy, was the second wife of the King of Spain, and was acutely and painfully aware that on her ailing husband's death her sons would inherit nothing, for the King had sons by his previous marriage. That would involve Elizabeth too in an abrupt descent into insignificance. Besides ceasing to be the wife of a king she would not even be mother of the next. This energetic and ambitious woman decided to get for her sons independent principalities in Italy, in particular the dominions of her own family, of which Spain had formerly been overlord. Spain had recently recovered some of her strength because of expert help from France during the war. Elizabeth, however, pushed the French aside and made an Italian, Alberoni, predominant in Spain, and between them they hastened to do what they could to make the Spanish armed forces fit to make military gestures. As it turned out, their preparations were not enough to meet all eventualities, although they made a promising start in the latter part of 1717. Using as an excuse the arrest by the Austrian authorities of the Spanish Grand Inquisitor in Milan, Elizabeth and Alberoni dispatched an expedition and seized Sardinia. A little later, in July 1718, a much bigger Spanish force attacked Sicily. It looked as if Spain was aiming at more than just a little bit of Northern Italy—aiming, in fact, at control of the western Mediterranean as well.

This was a very nasty situation for the English, made worse by the fact that there was no sense in being too rough with Spain because that might involve losing the precious trade concessions obtained from her at Utrecht. The situation was soon revealed as being nastier still. Alberoni, aware that his latest expedition would probably get him into trouble with the English and the French, and knowing that Spain's military chances against these two were exactly nil, had endeavoured to cover up his smash-and-grab raids in Italy by giving the Triple Alliance and the Emperor something to think of elsewhere. He stirred up Jacobite plots (favouring the Stuart Pretender) in England, nego-tiated with the Russians and Swedes in the hope they would give trouble in Hanover, stirred up the Hungarians and the Turks against the Emperor, and for the benefit of the French cooked up a plot against the government of the Regent. These improvised diversions all looked fairly hopeful at first, but soon fell through. Charles XII of Sweden was killed in Norway in December 1718, Görtz, who returned home, was executed, the plots in England and France failed dismally, and the Emperor was not unduly bothered.

Nor had the vigorous Stanhope been idle. In August 1718 he completed an alliance with the Emperor, who now fell in with his famous 'plan', which he had previously been hawking in vain, for pacifying Europe: the Emperor was to get Sicily instead of Sardinia, but was to renounce the claims to the throne of Spain which he still maintained; Sardinia would go to Savoy; and Philip V of Spain was to be persuaded to abandon once and for all his claims to his former Italian possessions, except that Elizabeth Farnese was to be consoled by the possibility of Parma, Piacenza, and Tuscany for her eldest son, Charles. This conversion of the Triple Alliance into a Quadruple Alliance was not Stanhope's only way of turning some heat on to Spain, for an English naval squadron under Admiral Byng was already on its way to Italian waters. The Admiral met the Spanish fleet off southern Sicily, at Cape Passaro, and, although the Spaniards enjoyed the tech-nical guidance of an English naval captain who had joined their service, their fleet was destroyed. Early in 1719 the French rallied to the support of their new ally. The French government was a little nervous of its own public opinion if it should attack a Bourbon king in Spain, but proved Spain the aggressor by exposing the plot engineered on Alberoni's behalf by Cellamare, the Spanish Ambassador, and so felt it could put extreme pressure on Elizabeth Farnese. A French army invaded Spain and did a great deal of damage, especially to naval installations near San Sebastian. Philip of Spain soon realized that the game was up, and offered to come to terms. He had to dismiss Alberoni, become a member of the Quadruple Alliance, and give up his claims to the French throne, as well as acknowledge the Emperor's title to his Italian possessions. This was a brilliant success for Stanhope, though of course since the way was now open to a reconciliation between France and Spain it would imply that neither would have so much need to keep in well with England, and a weakening of England's influence on both would follow some time in the future. Anyway, all the points in dispute were not as yet settled so it was decided to hold a congress of the Powers at Cambrai.

That seemed hopeful, but the North remained unsettled. It was a cardinal object of English policy to pacify Northern Europe if only because of the opportunities that continued hostilities there had given, and would go on giving, to nuisances like Elizabeth Farnese to get one or other of the belligerents to attack Hanover or to help Jacobite plots against George I. Here again the French alliance was invaluable. An English fleet under Admiral Norris was sent to the Baltic, but failed to do any damage to the Russians, and in the end it was French diplomacy that persuaded Peter the Great to come to terms with Sweden at Nystad in 1721, and this, following the treaties which Sweden had just made with Denmark, Prussia, and Hanover, finally brought peace to the North.

But the English and French did not give Europe peace at Cambrai, and were not destined to do so until 1731. During the next ten years they themselves were faced by internal difficulties, and to them was added more trouble from Elizabeth Farnese and from the Emperor.

The internal difficulties were financial. All countries, thanks to the War of the Spanish Succession and to the military operations like those of Admiral Byng, were staggering along under a burden of debt. This made them abnormally dependent on loans from financiers. The influence of financiers was reinforced by peculiar views on money and credit which were then in vogue. Most governments then held 'mercantilist'[1] views in matters of trade. That is, they sought a favourable

---

[1] See also Chapter 1.

balance of trade and did what they could to encourage exports and discourage imports, which, it was hoped, would result in bringing gold into the country. That in itself seems perfectly sensible, particularly in an age of incessant war, since wars could not be financed without large quantities of gold and silver. But if their views on the desirability of a large export trade had much to commend them, the same cannot be so readily admitted about some of the ideas then current about how to achieve this, more especially of the opinions held by some about the proper roles of money and credit.

Very curious ideas about money were put forward in two treatises written in 1705 and 1707 by a Scotsman, John Law. He said that abundant production and trade depended greatly on the possession of an abundant currency; the more money there was and the faster it circulated the more would industry and trade flourish; furthermore, the best money was paper resting on land, or, better still, on great trading companies as security. (Absurdly enough, the paper had as one of its attractions the fact that being worthless it could not depreciate!) By manipulating paper, too, ministers would be able to make State debts vanish. His notion is not perfectly clear, but if what he meant boils down to paying off debts with floods of printed paper based on dud security, then of course he is perfectly right; it is a slightly sophisticated way of welshing on one's creditors by a thinly disguised bankruptcy. Anyway, so desperately short of cash was the French government that they listened to this highly seductive if obscure reasoning, and by January 1720 Law was Controller-General of the French finances.

Law seized his chance with the eagerness of a fanatic or of a sincere quack, and immediately launched huge commercial enterprises; a great Company to trade with the Americas (the Mississippi Company) was prominent among them, but he also had schemes for trading with Senegal, the South Seas, the Indies, and China. Shares in all these projects could be bought for State bills (in effect, that is, for receipts for money lent to the government), so the State debt certainly did go down. Things seemed so very promising that crowds rushed to buy in the hope of a quick fortune. Law was besieged by would-be investors, including one duchess, who, despairing of getting an interview with this magician any other way, had her carriage upset outside his house and had to be carried in to recover. The usual fortunes were quickly made by the usual queer people—one noble French family was taken aback at the theatre on seeing that the affluent-looking lady occupying the next box was their cook. The whole business crashed as dramatically as it had arisen. Doubts about the soundness of Law's enterprises were whispered in Paris by English agents (the English government did not relish his sympathy for Spain in the matter of the return of Gibraltar, and chose this way to get rid of him). Apart from English-inspired rumours, Law was basically unsound; he was paying dividends not out of profits, for it was too soon to earn many, but out of money subscribed by later investors to his later companies. The inevitable crash was all the more spectacular because by the time it came at the end of 1720 Law had taken over direction of most of the French taxes and a great deal of the economic life of the country. Selling resulted in a blind panic, and Law beat a hasty retreat to Brussels.

Ironically enough, the part-authors of his downfall were caught in much the same way, and partly as a result of the loss of confidence caused by doubts about Law's schemes. The English South Sea Company, which had been formed in 1711 for the purpose of trade with South America, offered the government a conversion scheme whereby the public could exchange holdings of government securities for issue of South Sea stock. As inducements it offered a premium (in effect, a gift) of seven and a half million pounds and promised to charge the government a lower rate of interest than it had to pay to the public. In case this was not tempting enough it also privately offered large bribes to some of the ministers. On the face of it this looked remarkably generous, but in fact the Company expected a big rise in the value of their own shares and if that did not happen they could fix the rate of exchange of their stock and government securities in their own favour. The Company would thus be the sole holder of government short-term debt purchased on the cheap, and the public, which thought it must be a wonderful Company to be able to enjoy the government's confidence and to offer the government what to the uninitiated looked like very generous terms, rushed madly to buy South Sea stock, whose price then soared by June 1720 to ten times the face value. Here again the crash was as speedy as it was inevitable. Prudent speculators, who could see that stock bought at such a price could never be worth having no matter what profits the Company made, began to sell, and this, together with the shady activities of a number of other companies which hastily sprang up to take advantage of public gullibility and the mania for get-rich-quick schemes and the prosecution of one such company, led to panic selling, and of course the price of South Sea stock plummeted downward. Many were ruined and the public cry for vengeance was so insistent that for a while it looked as if not only the financial structure of the country was in peril but the régime as well.

The results of these financial crises in the two countries were more political than economic. In France, indeed, Law's schemes did provide commerce with a stimulating influence, and in England, after some of the victims had been compensated and the holdings of State debts in the possession of the Company had been transferred almost entirely to the Bank of England and the East India Company, the amount of harm done was slight. French society, however, had received a shaking, and loss of confidence in the Regent's government meant the abandonment of governmental reforms initiated by him and a return to the ministerial system of Louis XIV in place of his system of government by councils. In England the chief political effect was to make practically a clean sweep of the government faction led by Stanhope and Sunderland and their replacement by their rivals, the Walpole-Townshend group. In 1723 the Regent and Dubois died, and so by then France too was under different direction.

But that is to anticipate. The Congress of Cambrai was achieving nothing, and Spanish patience was running short. Bitter messages were sent to England demanding the return of Gibraltar. This was all the more awkward because Dubois seemed to be slipping away from English control, for he had caused the young King of France to be affianced to the Infanta of Spain, not that there could be an early marriage, for she was a baby. Stanhope in desperation had held out hopes to Spain, but he died in 1721, and the best the Spaniards could get was a personal letter from George I on 14 May 1721 in which he gave an empty assurance to the Spanish King that he would bring the matter of Gibraltar to the notice of his Parliament at the first convenient opportunity. If England was thus decidedly embarrassed by the attitude of Spain and the ambiguous position of France, she was even more worried about the Emperor. The latter was refusing to give the Spaniards any satisfaction in Italy either, and was also giving the English trouble by toying with a scheme for large-scale trading operations from the Netherlands. In these circumstances it is not surprising that some of the English ministers, led by Townshend and Walpole, favoured taking a strong line against him, though some such as Carteret preferred treating him gently. The English needed French diplomatic help pretty badly, and luckily they were soon to get it.

This was not wholly because of the change of government in France after the death of Dubois and the Regent in 1723, for Dubois had been really persuaded that the English alliance was necessary and had no genuine intention of giving it up. But his death improved the English position. The new directors of French policy, the Duke of Bourbon and Cardinal Fleury, did not see eye to eye, for the former favoured Spain and the latter England. Fleury's policy triumphed because the Duke in 1725 mortally offended the Spaniards by sending the little Infanta, by then only five years of age, back to Spain; this was not quite as stupid as it might seem, for there were urgent reasons making it desirable for the young Louis XV to be married with no more delay. In the meantime the crisis boiled up because, of all things, the two enemies, Spain and the Emperor, were coming to the conclusion that they might make more headway if they united against England. Spain's grievances have already been touched on. The Emperor's were of long standing too.

The Emperor had two gigantic schemes on the stocks, and the English did not smile on either of them. They were the Pragmatic Sanction and the Ostend Company. The first was in part an attempt to alter the succession to the hereditary Habsburg possessions. By the 'Disposition' of 1703 the Emperor Leopold I declared his elder son Joseph as his heir, to be followed by the younger son Charles. If the latter had no male heirs, then the next in succession were to be Joseph's daughters and not Charles's; a fair arrangement which only meant that, in default of the brothers having sons, the female offspring of the first took precedence over female offspring of the younger son. Neither brother actually had any sons, but Joseph had two daughters (Maria Josepha and Maria Amalia, who married in 1721 and 1722 the Elector of Saxony and the Elector of Bavaria). The Pragmatic Sanction sought to reverse the succession in favour of Charles's daughter, Maria Theresa, and since this arrangement was very much the concern of all Germany, and indeed of all Europe, it could not be regarded as effectively binding until the support or approval of as many States in and outside Germany as possible had been obtained. Naturally they were for the most part reluctant to acquiesce without some compensation in return. The Pragmatic Sanction was promulgated in 1713 and by 1723 had been accepted by most of the Habsburg dominions. (It should be remembered that the Habsburg ruled not over a unitary State, but over a bundle of separate territories having separate rights and customs; their only effective connexion with each other being a common ruler.) For the rest of his reign Charles spent a great deal of effort and made many concessions in order to collect as many signatures to the Pragmatic Sanction as possible, and has been criticized from that day to this for doing so; Prince Eugene said it would have been better to put his trust in a strong and efficient army, and modern writers often take the view that he was 'chasing shadows', presumably because most of the promises subsequently proved worthless. However, these criticisms

Plate _1_. Sir Isaac Newton (_see p. 36_).

Plate 2. Louis XIV—from a painting by Rigaud (*see p. 50*).

Plate 3 (opposite). Peter the Great, Emperor of Russia— from a painting by Kneller (*see p. 96*). (*Reproduced b gracious permission of Her Majesty the Queen.*)

60

Plate 4. John Sobieski, King of Poland (*see p. 110*).

Plate 5. John Locke—from the painting by John Green-hill (*see p. 133*).

Plate 6. John Churchill, Duke of Marlborough—from a painting after Kneller (*see p. 151*).

Plate 7. Charles XII, King of Sweden, 'The Terror of the North' (*see p. 167*).

Plate 8. 'Financial speculations in France'— a drawing by Bernard Picart satirizing all concerned in the speculative mania in France and England at the time of John Law and the South Sea Bubble. It depicts Fortune, on a chariot driven by Folly, distributing the shares of the various companies to the credulous—and in the process ruining true commerce and leading her victims to ruin and the madhouse (*see p. 181*).

Plate 9. 'The Sergeant King'—Frederick William I, King of Prussia *(see p. 201)*.

Plate 10. Frederick the Great reviewing troops (*see p. 231*).

Plate 11. François-Marie Arouet, generally known as Voltaire (*see p. 251*).

Plate 12. Jean-Jacques Rousseau—from a print by Garncrey (*see p. 261*).

Plate 13. The New Palace 'Sans Souci') at Potsdam, home of the Prussian kings, built 1745–7 *(see p. 274)*.

Plate 14. 'The Cake of Kings' (*c.* 1772)—from an engraving after Le Mire, satirizing the First Partition of Poland. Here Catherine II, Joseph II and Frederick II point to their shares while King Stanislaus of Poland clutches his crown *(see p. 310)*.

Plate 15. Madame de Pompadour—from the painting by Boucher (*see p. 342*).

Plate 16. Benjamin Franklin—from a bust made by Houdon in 1778; now in the Metropolitan Museum of Art, New York—gift of John Bard, 1872 (*see p. 368*).

Plate 17. Capture of Yorktown, 1781—from a painting by M. Couder. General Rochambeau and Washington giving orders for the last assault on the town. La Fayette appears among the group of officers (*see p. 366*).

Plate 18. The capture
of the Bastille,
14 July 1789
(*see p. 378*).

Plate 19. The flight of Louis XVI stopped at Varennes (see p. 381).

ignore two overriding facts. The first is that Charles simply did not have enough resources to build up a large army, and even if he had, no army could have enabled him to defy all Germany and the rest of Europe, had that been necessary. The second fact is that the criticism misses half the target altogether, for the Pragmatic Sanction was a great deal more than a matter of the succession of Maria Theresa. Charles, conscious of the Partition Treaties which had divided Spain and wishing no such partition ever to carve up his inheritance, placed at the head of the Pragmatic Sanction a declaration of the indivisibility of the Habsburg lands and made that a fundamental law of them. This object was successfully achieved in so far as the risk that the dominions would break up of their own accord, which they could do, if only because in his time some of them could not legally be passed to a woman, was averted until 1919. The unity of the Habsburg dominions was therefore, on a long-term view, easily the most important part of the Pragmatic Sanction, and few impartial observers would dare to claim that the break-up of that Empire in 1919 has been other than a world disaster.

It has been noticed that lack of resources was one reason forcing Charles to rely on promises instead of on the army. He was not such a fool as to be unaware of that himself. That is the motive of his second scheme. He took active steps to increase the commerce of his Empire, including the opening-up of the ports of Trieste and Fiume, the setting-up of a High Council of Commerce in Vienna, and the establishment of an Eastern Company for trading with Turkey. The pride of the collection was his Ostend Company in Belgium, founded in 1722. The Dutch and English viewed any revival of Belgian trade with the liveliest alarm, and indeed had already got the River Scheldt closed. There was no international agreement barring trade from Ostend, but the Dutch, who had for the last three or four years dropped into the neighbourly habit of sinking Belgian ships at sight, took up an even more hostile attitude.

The English were more divided. George I and the Walpole-Townshend group were opposed to an extension of Charles's influence in Germany and were not disposed to favour trade rivalry either, though it was partly the dependence on England occasioned by his weakness in Germany that pushed the Emperor into trying to become stronger by means of the Ostend Company. Carteret was more disposed to be sympathetic, at least to the Pragmatic Sanction, and there was an underlying feeling among English statesmen that it was unwise to push their ally about too much, and Dutch appeals to join in attacks on the Ostend Company at first therefore met with little response. Gradually

ENGLAND AND FRANCE DEFEND UTRECHT

a more anti-Habsburg policy emerged; Carteret was pushed out of the government and replaced by Walpole, a man of peace who was nevertheless unable to avoid foreign entanglements. He made an alliance with Prussia in 1723, and although he did not want serious trouble with Austria soon found he had it anyway.

The crisis came swiftly to a climax once again because of Elizabeth Farnese. Spain still wanted Gibraltar and Minorca, and Elizabeth still had not obtained lands in Italy for her sons, while the Congress of Cambrai was still talking away and deciding nothing. A Dutchman called Ripperda who had taken the place of Alberoni as her chief adviser was sent to Vienna to negotiate secretly with, of all people, the Emperor, in January 1725. In the following month the return of the Infanta from France to Spain infuriated Elizabeth Farnese and made her even readier to do any sort of deal with the Emperor, who for his own part despaired of getting the approval of the Maritime Powers for his Ostend Company. Accordingly a treaty was signed in March 1725: the Emperor at last gave up his claim to Spain and the Indies, while Philip gave up his to his lost Italian provinces and guaranteed the Pragmatic Sanction. The Emperor promised to give diplomatic help for the return of Gibraltar to Spain, while Spain recognized the Ostend Company and gave it, in defiance of Utrecht, commercial concessions. No agreement, however, was obtained from the Emperor to suggested marriages for Elizabeth's sons to Maria Theresa and an Austrian Archduchess, so Spain had the worst of this arrangement. Elizabeth was still in such a rage with France that she was prepared, more from passion than as a result of any rational calculation, to offer the Emperor even more commercial privileges. She also talked of dismembering France, a feat which the Spanish armed forces could have achieved about as easily as an invasion of the moon. The result of this ill-judged generosity was therefore another treaty in the following month (April); this time it was a treaty of alliance, and a marriage of one of the Emperor's daughters to one of Elizabeth's sons was vaguely promised. Diplomatic approaches were also made to Russia and to Sweden, so the outlook for Hanover was bleak.

The English statesman countered this very quickly by an agreement with France at Herrenhausen in November 1725, by which, in return for English help in preventing the partition of France (of which no possibility existed), the French guaranteed all existing English commercial privileges with Spain and also the possession of Gibraltar and Minorca. The reply was yet another treaty between Spain and the Emperor, the First Treaty of Vienna, November 1725, which this time promised two marriages and military help to Spain. They were soon to learn that against English sea-power the Emperor could not help Spain to get Gibraltar or Minorca, nor even protect the ships of his Ostend Company. Walpole and Townshend, after completing their 'Hanover Alliance' by the addition of Holland, put three naval squadrons to sea. One under Admiral Wager spread terror in the Baltic and persuaded Sweden to return to the English fold, another under Hozier blockaded the Spanish treasure-fleet in Porto Bello and thus made it impossible for Spain to fight a war at all, while a third under Admiral Jennings actually seized the Spanish port of Santona and blockaded the Spanish coast.

These measures gave the Emperor insight into the value of an alliance with Spain, and his Ambassador in Madrid obtained Ripperda's dismissal in May 1726. But he doggedly signed a treaty with Russia on 6 August 1726, a treaty into which Russia was forced by fright at the English naval demonstration, and by the need to get Austrian neutrality in a forthcoming war with Turkey. This turned out to be the most permanent and important result of all the diplomatic activity of these years. Long after all the other strange alliances reached between the Emperor and Spain, and between England, France, and the others of the Hanover Alliance, had crumbled to dust, that treaty of 6 August 1726 between the Emperor and Russia was to continue, hanging like a black cloud over Eastern Europe, and over Poland in particular, for who could hope to defend Poland against Russia and Austria combined? It is probably correct to date the beginning of the eclipse of the influence of the Western Powers in Eastern Europe from that treaty. The Emperor was also helped by Prussia, whose King now deserted the Hanover Alliance and made a treaty with him (October 1726). England was therefore fortunate in seeing the direction of French policy taken over by Cardinal Fleury, who was in favour of continuing the alliance with England. Not that Fleury desired to have the Continent run for England's benefit. Since the death of the Regent, France no longer had such a strong reason for supporting England, although it must be remembered that France without the English alliance would have been diplomatically isolated. But Fleury was a very clever statesman, and furthermore desired peace. His policy was therefore to use the influence of France to give Europe peace, thus removing the *raison d'être* of both systems of alliances; he looked forward to their eventual dissolution and then if possible to a reconciliation of France with Spain and even with the Emperor. Thus he would make France predominant in Europe to the exclusion of England. However, until he could effect such a reconciliation with at least one of them, he had to work with, and only in appearance for, England.

His agents worked fast and well. The disillusioned Emperor agreed to the Preliminaries of Paris in May 1727, under which he was to suspend the Ostend Company for seven years and to give up his commercial concessions from Spain. This was for the unhappy Elizabeth Farnese the end of her chief hopes. The siege of Gibraltar was not prospering, and while the Spanish guns kept on banging away with little inconvenience to the garrison it looked as if the King of Spain was about to have a fit of insanity. If that occurred, he would be replaced by the Prince of the Asturias, who viewed Elizabeth with a jaundiced eye. She therefore had to give in quickly and in March 1728 agreed to negotiate at a congress to be held at Soissons, though before it met she had to lift the siege of Gibraltar and restore their privileged commercial position to the English.

The Congress of Soissons, which assembled in June 1728, was not without its comedy. The Emperor began with a wistful request for some concessions for his Company at Ostend, but got only an Anglo-Dutch ultimatum. At the same moment Elizabeth bluntly asked him for definite action over the marriage of her sons, and got a blunt refusal. Beside herself with fury, she went straight to the English and French with the suggestion that together they should all make war on the Emperor. This was too ridiculous, but the pacific Fleury's gentle stalling tried her very limited stock of patience so much that she did a deal with the English instead. By the Treaty of Seville, 9 November 1729, she gave Townshend all he asked for—Gibraltar, Minorca, and the commercial concessions, as well as the return of English prizes; while in exchange the English promised to give military support, and to transport Spanish troops to take Parma and Tuscany for her sons. The French signed this rather than be left out in the cold, but on the absurdly disadvantageous terms of agreeing to help if need be in the war with the Emperor, in return for a guarantee of the French frontiers, which were in no sort of danger from any quarter; Fleury privately had very little intention of fighting.

Neither had Walpole, unlike the tough Townshend, who contemplated a war with the Emperor with cheerfulness. But Townshend had served his purpose, and Walpole recommended his dismissal in May 1730, after which he employed his talents in agriculture. Walpole was determined to pacify both Spain and the Emperor and if possible to return to genuine friendship with them. He was in rather too much of a hurry to do this, for in March 1731, without consulting the French, he signed the Treaty of Vienna by which the Emperor gave up the Ostend Company altogether while England mollified him by guaranteeing the Pragmatic Sanction. The basis of all this English success had really been the friendship of France, and all France had got out of it was the prestige of seeming to arrange European matters. Now she was coldly denied even that, with the result that friendship with England was abandoned even faster than would otherwise have been the case, which naturally meant a tremendous relaxation of the English grip on Europe. So Walpole had bought his triumph rather dearly. However, nothing of the sort was apparent to him, and he was able to persuade the Spaniards and the Emperor to patch up their differences at another treaty in July 1731, allowing Elizabeth's son Charles to occupy Parma, Piacenza, and Tuscany with 6,000 troops and confirming his right to those territories.

The Utrecht arrangements were thus finally settled, and England in particular seemed to have succeeded all along the line. But as this had been done with French help, which in future would not be forthcoming, the English might have to defend their gains by themselves. Also, these years of busy diplomacy had as an almost unnoticed by-product the alliance between Austria and Russia of August 1726, and, if England and France were divided, the two Eastern Powers would be able to do as they pleased in Eastern Europe. Within two years they had discovered this congenial fact for themselves.

10 · The War of the Polish Succession, 1733–8

The diplomatic comings and goings caused by Elizabeth's impulsive method of running a foreign policy had not really achieved very much, and Elizabeth herself had gained only a small bit of territory in Italy, but they had helped to divert the eyes of Europe from the most significant political development of the first thirty years of the century, and that was the rise of Prussia and Russia. True, Prussia's foreign policy during all that time had won her exactly nothing, but the strength of the State was being built up by King Frederick William I, and was to startle Europe in the War of the Austrian Succession, which began in 1740. Russia too had grown tremendously in power under Peter the Great, although a series of short reigns after his death in 1725,[1] by not particularly brilliant rulers, delayed the full effects of Peter's work. Even so, Russia had made the highly important treaty of 1726 with Austria which, since it carried implications about the position of Austria in Germany and the Balkans, and that of Russia in the Balkans and in Poland, became in effect a sort of political system for all of Eastern Europe.

It soon produced results, the first of which was the adhesion to it of

---

[1] Catherine I (1725–7), Peter II (1 27–30), Anna (1730–40), and Ivan (1740–1).

Prussia in 1728, and this was followed by the victory of the Emperor in Germany, for on 11 January 1732 all the German Diet except Bavaria, Saxony, and the Palatinate accepted the Pragmatic Sanction. Russia for her part negotiated a commercial treaty with the English, who were always ready to turn an honest penny in the Baltic (or a dishonest one in South America, as we shall see), on 17 May 1727. Really the English by this, by their cold-shouldering of Fleury and by their renewal of the alliance with Austria, sold the pass in Eastern Europe altogether, for France, the traditional ally of Poland, could no longer protect that country by herself. Fleury saw the danger clearly enough, and would have preferred to come to an understanding with Austria, which would have thus kept down the influence of Russia in Eastern Europe and maintained that of France there and everywhere else. But he was a very old man indeed (in 1733 he was eighty years of age) and was unable to prevent more energetic and less clever men, who could see no farther than their noses, from having a hand in the direction of French foreign policy, and that meant a return to the old anti-Habsburg policy. The result of that, of the estrangement between England and France brought about by Walpole's ineptitude, and of the *entente* between Austria and Russia, was the War of the Polish Succession.

The French did what they could to counter the rising influence of the Emperor in Germany, and of the Emperor and his Russian ally in Poland, and actually succeeded in making a treaty of alliance with Bavaria and Augustus II of Poland in 1732 (really two treaties, May–July). This was not difficult, because Bavaria was traditionally a rival of the Habsburgs, while Augustus of Poland personally loathed the Emperor. But the alliance was very shaky because the aims of Augustus and France were contradictory. Augustus wished to make the Polish throne hereditary in his own family; so strong was this ambition that he was cheerfully prepared if necessary to give away parts of Poland as bribes to his neighbours in order to achieve it. Unfortunately, the French King had married Maria Leszczynska, daughter of the penniless and exiled Stanislaus, ex-King of Poland, and the French wanted Stanislaus to be re-elected King of Poland on Augustus's death. They would thereby regain their influence completely in Poland and at the same time provide a throne for Louis XV's father-in-law. The French wished also for Turkey to form part of the alliance, the better to counter the position of Austria and Russia, but Augustus was not very interested in that idea. In any case the whole shaky scheme fell flat, for the Austrians and Russians answered it by the Treaty of Loewenwolde of

13 September 1732, by which they agreed to put a cousin of the Emperor on the Polish throne. Augustus treacherously torpedoed it also by agreeing with Frederick William of Prussia, who had become a party to the Treaty of Loewenwolde, to suggest a scheme to the latter's allies whereby all three would get parts of Poland if they would guarantee the Polish Crown as hereditary in Augustus's family. Augustus had thus double-crossed the French. On his death, which occurred on 1 February 1733, the Russians and Austrians double-crossed Prussia as well, for they were not charmed by the notion of giving any of Poland to Prussia; they wanted to control it all themselves, an easy enough matter when the weakness of Poland is remembered (see Chapter 5). They agreed to put the new Elector of Saxony on the Polish throne, to let Russia have Courland, and to leave Prussia out in the cold.

Frederick William, in a decided huff, therefore allowed Stanislaus, who was hurrying to his homeland, to cross Prussian territory to get there. Stanislaus was elected King of Poland by the Diet in September, but in the following month Russian troops entered Poland and he had to flee to Danzig, whereupon a few hundred Polish nobles at Warsaw elected Augustus of Saxony as King, a decision which they had no difficulty in arriving at because the town was filled with Russian soldiers.

The French preparations had, however, included measures more practical than the expedient of sending Stanislaus to Poland. The anti-Habsburg party in France, under the inspiration of the *Garde des Sceaux*, Chauvelin, bustled about with immense energy. An alliance was made with Savoy in September 1733. Another was made with Spain on 7 November—the Treaty of the Escorial, often called 'The Family Compact'. The French offered Naples and Sicily to Elizabeth Farnese's son Don Philip and the return of Gibraltar to Spain, and were to receive the commercial concessions in the New World held by the English. (The last two parts were wisely kept secret.) Yet another treaty was made with Bavaria a week later. Sweden and Turkey also offered to join the alliance, for those old enemies of Russia were delighted at what seemed a heaven-sent chance to smash her with the help of such a powerful ally as France.

Fleury looked at all these lively preparations for the inflicting of a crushing blow on Austria in Italy and elsewhere with scant enthusiasm, his thoughts running far deeper. It was dangerous to inflict too deadly a wound on Austria, for that would probably bring in the English, because of their need to support their traditional, and biggest, ally; Fleury did not want to re-create the nightmare of the old Grand

Alliance *à la* Marlborough. He carefully kept up the show of flattering friendship with Walpole, and began to get the measure of that peace-lover. He began to guess that Walpole might not help Austria at all. In that case, the old Anglo-Austrian alliance, rather a delicate growth since its revival by the Treaty of Vienna in 1731, would wither of itself. If that happened, incredible though it might seem that Walpole would be so foolish as to let Austria be defeated by France, and if France did not press Austria too hard, then Austria would be permanently estranged from England and be grateful enough to a magnanimous France to accept the idea of a Franco-Austrian alliance. France would then be supreme in Europe and England pushed out, thus realizing the last ideas of Louis XIV. But England in the meantime must not be given too much cause for alarm, or she might be driven quickly into the arms of the Emperor, which were already outstretched to receive her; the Emperor was clamouring for English help from the summer of 1733 onward.

Accordingly Fleury, so as not to alarm the English by sending a big expedition to the Baltic, which was the only possible way of helping Stanislaus, sent a small naval squadron and three battalions of soldiers to the relief of Danzig, a force so grotesquely inadequate that the French Ambassador, Count de Plélo, was overcome by shame and, a man of honour, deliberately sought death by leading a charge with a small force against the Russian hordes. He found it. That finished Stanislaus's chances in Poland. Fleury also poured cold water on the negotiations with the Turks. The result was that Sweden remade her alliance with Russia, and the Turks did not move. Fleury also soft-pedalled the war with Austria. French troops seized Lorraine with no difficulty, but did not attempt to go farther east or to join the Bavarian forces, while in Italy the French efforts were feeble. He had his reward. The Emperor's repeated attempts to elicit some help from England were rejected, in January 1734 and again in July 1735, by Walpole, who watched his ally go down with the complacent remark that 50,000 men had been killed in Europe that year (1734) but not one Englishman.

Without money, men, or ships from England to help him, the Emperor saw little hope of defending himself successfully against the French war machine even when it was running at half throttle, and the preliminaries of peace were signed at Vienna in October 1735, but a final settlement was not reached until the Treaty of Vienna was signed on 18 November 1738. The delay was caused by fresh diplomatic moves, through which Fleury was able to take advantage of the growing hostility between England and Spain to isolate them both; he also managed to sack the over-zealous Chauvelin, who had done so much to form the coalition against Austria, in February 1737. He was thus able, at last, to arrange a Franco-Austrian settlement, which amounted to a pacification of West and South Europe by those two Powers. Stanislaus gave up his claim to Poland, but got instead Lorraine and Bar, which after his death were to revert to France—a gain of huge importance to the latter. The Duke of Lorraine was given Tuscany instead. Elizabeth Farnese's son Charles was given Naples and Sicily, which was a glittering prize offset only by the fact that Elizabeth's ambitions in Tuscany thus received a definite quietus. The Emperor kept Milan and Mantua, and Piedmont got the two small towns, Novara and Tortona. All of Europe was still not pacified, however, for the Turks and the Russians were once again at war.

Russia was able to resume the historic drive against the Turks largely because the commercial treaty with England, the understanding with Sweden, and the treaty of 1726 with Austria gave her a free hand in the North, and especially in Poland, where Augustus III was nominally King but had to follow Russian orders. Consequently the Russians took the offensive against Turkey in 1735, and in 1736 their troops took Azov and invaded the Crimea. The Emperor was eager for his share too, so his troops, although tired and crestfallen after their recent defeats at the hands of the French, made some progress at first and invaded Wallachia, Serbia, and Upper Bulgaria. The French soon altered all this. Their Ambassador in Stockholm obtained the victory of the pro-French, and anti-Russian, faction in Sweden and that country thus escaped from Russian influence and signed an alliance with France on 10 November 1738. The French Ambassador in Constantinople, Villeneuve, was even more successful. He played such a useful part in reorganizing the Turkish armed forces that the dispirited Austrian troops were driven back, and the Emperor was glad enough to make a hasty peace at Belgrade on 1 September 1739, without consulting his Russian allies. A very expensive peace it was for him, too, for the Turks recovered Belgrade and the possessions in Serbia, Bosnia, and Wallachia that they had lost at the Peace of Passarowitz in 1718. Thus isolated, the Russians felt constrained to follow suit, and they too on 18 September 1739 signed a peace treaty at Belgrade by which they received Azov but returned all their other conquests except a strip of land between the Rivers Bug and Dnieper, and were left still without access to the Black Sea. The Russians seem to have felt uneasy even then, for they sent an envoy to Paris to negotiate an *entente* with the French, and as Fleury had already negotiated a commercial treaty with Turkey, France now appeared to have become as much the arbiter of Europe as she had ever been in the hey-day of Louis XIV (Frederick the Great of Prussia afterwards said as much). However, Fleury, the author of this happy situation, who was certainly one of the cleverest men in Europe, was alarmed by what he called 'too high a degree of power of Russia in the North' and said her 'union with the House of Austria is extremely dangerous'. Furthermore, the rise of the power of Russia, obvious to Fleury at least, was being quietly matched by the rise of the power of Prussia. Within a few months the increased stature of Prussia was to become painfully obvious to all Europe.

11 · The Anglo-Spanish War of 1739; the rise of Prussia under Frederick William I; and the War of the Austrian Succession, 1740–8

(a) THE ANGLO-SPANISH WAR OF 1739

The great conflict which convulsed Europe almost as soon as the ink was dry on the Treaties of Vienna and Belgrade grew out of a trade war between England and Spain and out of the action of King Frederick II of Prussia, who gave dramatic evidence of the rise of his own country by suddenly attacking Austria in 1740.

If England was worried by the loss of her preponderant position in Europe, which had been brought about by the shortsightedness of Walpole and the skill of Fleury, few in London gave any sign of it. On the contrary, the English had by no means constantly relished the effort involved in maintaining it, an effort which to many had always seemed to be devoted to Hanoverian rather than to strictly English interests. What is more surprising is that few seemed to be very interested in the French commercial treaty with the Turks with which Fleury had rounded off his triumph in that quarter on 8 May 1740, and which was a disaster for London. But by that time the English were engaged in a war to increase their trade in a very different part of the world.

Trade was not the only cause of the war between England and Spain which broke out in 1739. The Spaniards were still furious at the loss of Gibraltar and Minorca, and there were disputes about the boundaries of the neighbouring colonies of Florida (Spanish) and Georgia (English). But trade counted for far more than these. The English had for a long time done a very great deal of smuggling in Spanish America, which until 1700 the Spaniards did little to stop. After that date the Bourbon monarchy was more active, and coast-guard ships seized English ships wherever they could—not always with impunity, for whole fleets of English merchant ships, sometimes as many as thirty vessels at a time, occasionally destroyed the coast-guard ships, and it was difficult to recruit crews for defence against the English (and Dutch). The South Sea Company itself, which had the concession for the annual ship and the importation of Negroes, also smuggled, though on such a modest scale that the Spanish authorities never complained about it. Under the Asiento agreement the Company was supposed to pay money to the King of Spain, and disputes arose about this too. The quarrels had been going on for years, but came rapidly to a head after 1737. In that year the Spanish government made a strong effort to enforce the anti-smuggling regulations, and about a dozen English ships were seized.

There were storms of protest in London, Bristol, Liverpool, and other British ports, and a petition was presented to Parliament. Walpole's government took the matter up, and the Spanish government proved anxious to avoid trouble; indeed, Walpole did not want it either, and if the decision had rested with the two governments there would have been no war. But the London merchants were determined to force a war with Spain, and they were backed up to the hilt by the opposition, which was ready to use any means to discredit Walpole. In response to mob clamour, inflamed by stories about the captured ships (actually five of them had been captured by ordinary pirates, not by the Spaniards) and about cruel treatment accorded English sailors, the English government sent a squadron of battleships to Gibraltar. Walpole also negotiated with the Spaniards, who agreed to pay compensation of £95,000. Unfortunately the South Sea Company refused to pay a counter-claim of £68,000 which it owed the King of Spain, and the popular clamour was redoubled, egged on by Pulteney, Carteret, Chesterfield, Pitt, and the Lord Mayor of London. They had already urged the public to a pitch of hysteria by the stunt of producing an alleged victim of the wicked Spaniards, one Captain Jenkins, to give evidence in the House of Commons about how the Spaniards had mutilated him by cutting off one of his ears (1738). They now intensified their efforts to such purpose that Walpole's colleagues took fright and began to desert him, so in June 1739 Walpole yielded, though the declaration of war was not sent until 19 October.

The English were obviously not going to war about a matter of a few ships and a few thousand pounds of compensation. They were dissatisfied with the trading concessions obtained at Utrecht and wanted all the trade of South America. Possibly they could have done much as they pleased with Spain, but naturally this was a matter that deeply interested France also, and Fleury, although not keen on a war with England, could hardly allow the Spaniards, who were his allies since the Family Compact of 1733, to go under. At the end of 1740 a French squadron was dispatched for the defence of the West Indies, and though Fleury still did not join more actively in the conflict, the English and French were soon fighting each other in the War of the Austrian Succession.

The Emperor Charles VI died on 20 October 1740. By that time every State of any consequence except Bavaria and the Palatinate had guaranteed the Pragmatic Sanction (Spain in 1725, Russia and Prussia in 1726, Holland and England in 1731, Denmark and most of Germany in 1732, Saxony in 1733, France in 1738, Charles Emmanuel of Sardinia in 1739). There was thus no obstacle to the accession of his daughter Maria Theresa, who was proclaimed Archduchess of Austria, Queen of Hungary, and Queen of Bohemia. Better perhaps than all these guarantees was the recognition of her rights by France on 10 November 1740, and everyone was all the more thunderstruck when King Frederick II of Prussia suddenly invaded the Habsburg province of Silesia on 16 December 1740.

He had inherited the Prussian Crown on the death of his father, Frederick William, in May 1740. He had been putting out claims to the Rhenish Lands of Berg and Cleves, but on the death of the Emperor he claimed Silesia instead, offering in exchange to assist in the election to the Imperial Crown of Maria Theresa's husband, Francis. He had little expectation that this outrageous demand would be satisfied and was already negotiating with both England and France in order to play off one against the other, calculating that France would almost certainly have to support the Spanish desire to reconquer their lost Italian possessions. He knew also that Bavaria was preparing to enforce her claims to the Imperial throne and that Sardinia was hoping to enlarge her territories at Maria Theresa's expense, while the English were well enough disposed towards him because they hoped he might stir up trouble for France in Europe. The diplomatic situation was therefore confused, but Maria Theresa was evidently going to be troubled by many besides Frederick, and those most likely to help her already had trouble enough of their own. Frederick judged that his own attack on Silesia would be the signal for others to do the same, but allowing for that correct calculation, it still might seem suicidal for a small and poor State of two and a half million people to attack a Royal House which ruled over a total of about twenty-two millions. That it was not suicidal was due to the military gifts of the young aggressor, and also to the army which his father had built up. So it will be instructive to study how that was done, for the army was the fourth biggest in Europe, although Prussia was only the tenth State from the standpoint of territory and thirteenth in population. Clearly, to make that possible was not purely a military problem; the whole State would have to be organized to the topmost possible height of efficiency as well.

(b) THE RISE OF PRUSSIA UNDER FREDERICK WILLIAM I

Prussia's first King, Frederick, had died in 1713. Although he has been regarded as slightly ridiculous in his frantic pursuit of the kingly title and in the naïve ecstasy with which he relished the pomp of that rank, it should be recognized that in an age when ceremonial and precedence were so highly valued he had done Prussia a very great service by obtaining the title. Henceforward the rise of his House was accelerated by the prestige of the Royal Crown, and the Hohenzollerns were soon recognized as the only serious rivals to the Habsburgs in Germany. Frederick the Great himself described obtaining the Crown as 'a masterpiece of statesmanship' and said it was an inspiration and challenge to the first King's successors, a challenge to try to make themselves worthy of their exalted rank. Nor did the first Prussian King bequeath nothing but a name to his successors. He gradually increased the army, which he found with a strength of about 30,000 men, until it had grown to about 40,000. However, he spent fortunes on keeping up a magnificent court, imitating Louis XIV as well as he could, even to keeping a titular mistress in whom he had not the slightest personal interest, with the result that in spite of increased taxes, the debt mounted steadily and the large army could only be maintained with the help of foreign subsidies. That made him dependent on the governments which paid them; the Prussian army, big though it was, and though it showed good fighting qualities, gained little for Prussia.

Frederick's successor was his son, Frederick William I, who resolved that the Prussian army should be greatly increased and, what was just as important, maintained entirely without foreign subsidies. This aim he pursued with a single-mindedness akin to mania. Indeed he had a passionate love for anything to do with the army, and said himself, 'I find pleasure in nothing in this world except in a strong army.' This was only a very slight exaggeration. He was also fond of food, beer, wine, and vulgar guard-room clowning. He spent most evenings at what was called the *Tabaks-Kollegium* (Tobacco Parliament); there in a barely furnished room he gathered several guests, mostly his chief advisers, high officers, and occasionally distinguished foreigners, and provided every guest with a pitcher of beer, pipes, and plenty of rough tobacco. The conversation, which went on for hours, was often about government business, but the favourite topics were the army or hunting. (The King had a passionate love of hunting; he slaughtered partridges, pheasants, hares, and wild boars by the thousand.) At these festive meetings the King was known on occasion to smoke as many as thirty pipefuls of tobacco; indeed, too much tobacco, food, and drink, and too much hard work, wore him out while he was still quite a young man. He enjoyed drilling his soldiers personally, hence his nickname 'The Sergeant King'. He made himself something of a laughing-stock in Europe by his passion for very big soldiers, a passion which he indulged by creating a special regiment of giants at Potsdam. They numbered over 3,000, and the King would go to any lengths to secure tall recruits; his agents scoured Europe with bribes and when those failed they kidnapped large young men, even on one occasion grabbing a huge monk out of a monastery in Rome. Other countries resented these man-hunts, and the Dutch executed some of Frederick William's agents. The more astute foreign authorities, however, gave him big recruits as gifts, for which his gratitude was touching—'He who sends them to me can lead me wherever he will', he once remarked, and such potentates as Peter the Great sent them regularly, knowing they would get diplomatic favours in return. (Such a gift from the Emperor persuaded Frederick William to desert the Hanover Alliance and to join the Austrian side at the Treaty of Wusterhausen in 1726.) Once when the Sergeant King was ill he got about two hundred of them to march through his bedroom, and the sight of his 'children', 'my blue boys', as he called them, did him more good than any tonic from the doctors.

This very curious King did find pleasure in some cultural things like music and painting, but had no use for learning other than the strictly practical; he distrusted science and called philosophy 'hot air'. He had good qualities also. He remained faithful to his wife and was sincerely religious (he was a Calvinist) and at the same time tolerant. He loved his people and wanted them to love him, but not many did because of his uncontrollable bad temper, which might lead him to thrash anyone, from the Crown Prince downwards, with a thick stick which he always carried. From the viewpoint of Prussian greatness his chief virtue was his complete devotion to the task of making his country strong. He rose at five in the morning and worked like a galley-slave, regarding himself as responsible not only to God for the way in which he discharged his duties, but also to the State which he looked on as a sort of idealized entity of which he was 'only the first servant', 'commander-in-chief and minister of war for the King of Prussia', as he described himself.

This boorish and bizarre little man (he was five feet five inches tall, but ended by weighing twenty-one stone) set about the business of being 'the King of Prussia's commander-in-chief' with a will, aided by his trusted colleague, Leopold of Anhalt-Dessau, affectionately called by the nickname of 'Old Dessauer'. The army was increased from 40,000 men at his accession in 1713 to the prodigious figure of 83,000 by the time of his death in 1740. He raised its quality in about equal proportion, by endless drilling which made it the best army in Europe, having a rapidity of fire which made a Prussian infantry battalion into a 'walking battery'. He provided it with infantry regulations which covered every situation and every need years before anything comparable existed in any other army in Europe; the uniforms were standardized too. His efforts at improving the cavalry were not so successful, because he favoured large horses carrying large men, which were not so manœuvrable nor so tireless as smaller ones.

Two questions at once demand an answer. Where did he get the men, and where the money? For Prussia was a thinly populated and poor State.

Various measures solved the man-power problem. One was recruiting in other countries; about a third of the army was made up of foreigners. As for the King's own subjects, they had never had the legal obligation to serve in the regular army, but a decree of the King in 1713, which abolished the local militia organizations (they were next to useless because they were for local defence only) and which said that anyone leaving the country to escape military service would be treated as a deserter, created the principle of universal obligation to military service, at least by implication. But it did not become practice until the decrees of 1732–3. By these, every regiment in the army was allotted its own recruiting district or 'canton', consisting of about 5,000 house-holds. All the young males of the district had their names on a register, and, when the number of men in the regiment could not be kept at the right figure by voluntary enlistment, men were taken from the lists. This by no means meant universal conscription, for all skilled workers in industry, in fact practically all but peasants, were declared exempt, and even the peasants called to the colours were given very long leaves, often for all the year except the drill period of April and May, so that they could go home to help with the harvest and other work. In effect, then, the huge Prussian army could be regarded in peace-time as consisting in the main of a highly trained reserve.

This 'canton system' as it was called provided enough peasant lads to fill the ranks, but it was a more difficult matter to find suitable officers to lead them. Frederick William's solution was brilliant and forceful. He determined to use the nobles for this purpose, since they seemed the natural leaders of the peasants. At first many of them were extremely reluctant, and refused to obey. He drew up lists of all young noblemen aged between twelve and eighteen, and endeavoured to conscript from these lists as many as necessary for the cadet corps in Berlin, and when they still offered resistance, as many did, particularly in East Prussia, Frederick sent police and soldiers and rounded up his future officers in gangs and marched them to Berlin. However, he was not so foolish as to rely purely on compulsion. His officers were given the most privileged position in society, a better education than many of them could afford, and the distinction that came from rubbing shoulders with their King on terms of equality, while their profession was flattered as being the only one for a man of spirit and honour. Gradually this attitude won the nobles over, and they ended by regarding the army as the finest of all professions for their sons. Frederick had had to begin by force and threats (a famous remark of his was, 'I will ruin the authority of the Junkers and stabilize the sovereignty like a rock of bronze'), but he finished with small need to employ either bayonets or bluster to drive them into the army.

There still remained the crushing, the almost unendurable, cost of keeping such a huge force. Frederick William began to tackle this as soon as he had given his father a good funeral. The expenses of the court, enormous under his predecessor, were reduced immediately to the barest essentials. Hordes of decorative but unproductive court functionaries were thrown out, some of them being thrown into the army instead, like the twenty-six trumpeters that his father had kept for State ceremonial. The salaries of the remainder were reduced. Frederick William himself set the example of a merciless economy-drive by wearing, when at his desk, linen cuffs over the sleeves of his uniform so as to make it last longer, and by a constant inquiry into any expenditure, however petty; he went so far as to ask his wife the price of eggs consumed at the royal table, and was annoyed when that lady, who had more grandiose ideas, told him she did not know.

Such cheese-paring, of course, does not support an army. To do that, Frederick William reformed the entire administration of the country, making what had been a haphazard jumble into a despotic State in which he controlled the most efficient bureaucracy in Europe.

At the time of his accession the revenues came from three main sources. First, there were the royal domains, which were very extensive (about a third of all the peasants in the country lived on them). These were divided into large estates, each under a royal official called a *Beamte* (Crown Bailiff). Before Frederick William's time the farms on them had been let out on very long leases, but he let out each estate entire to the *Beamte*, who paid him a fixed sum for it, on a six-year lease; the *Beamte* then got what he could out of the farmers and so had an interest in seeing they were efficient; he evicted inefficient ones, and also collected feudal dues and profits from the Crown's mill and brewery monopolies, besides administering justice. The King thus got far more money than previously. To supervise the Crown Bailiffs every province had a Chamber (*Amtskammer*) of royal officials, and these provincial Chambers were themselves supervised by the General Finance Directory in Berlin.

The second source of revenue was the 'Contribution' levied in the countryside. This was a complicated mixture of a property and an income tax, and had been created to support the army. It bore very hardly on the peasants, but the nobles, except in East Prussia, did not have to pay it, and Frederick William was unable to alter the assessment except in a few details, for he could not risk offending the nobles too much as he needed them for administration as well as to officer his army. At first the Contribution had been collected by the officials of the local provincial estates, but these had been ousted by royal officials called Rural Commissioners (*Landräte*), each one in charge of a district, and each directing and supervising the peasants in many ways besides actually collecting the tax. Of course they did not exist on the royal domains, for the tax was not collected there, as the King's income from there came only from the Crown Bailiffs. The Rural Commissioners in each province were supervised by a War Commissariat which was in turn responsible to the General War Commissariat in Berlin.

The third source of revenue was the Excise. This was first introduced by the Great Elector as a system of taxation for the towns, which had previously paid the Contribution but which could obviously afford heavier taxes than the countryside. It comprised a small ground, occupation, and poll tax, and also, and by far the more important part, a tax on most commodities. It was collected by Local Commissaries (*Steuerräte*), whose functions, however, went far beyond that as to a great extent they directed the economic activities of the towns, besides co-operating with the garrison commanders. They were hampered by the old municipal officials, who were too eager to escape royal control, so Frederick William gradually abolished the independent rights of the towns, together with the officials who had sought to preserve them, and put in their place three Burgomasters in every town, assisted by varying numbers of Councillors. All of them were paid and appointed by the Crown, and the Local Commissary supervised them all for the King, who thus had the entire system of local government under his thumb. The Local Commissaries, like the Rural Commissioners, were in turn supervised by the provincial War Commissariat and of course the latter were controlled in this aspect too by the General War Commissariat in the capital.

All this was very cumbersome and did not work very well. The General Finance Directory (*Generalfinanzdirektorium*), and its subordinates the Chambers (*Amtskammern*) and Crown Bailiffs (*Beamten*) supervising the domain lands, frequently clashed with the General War Commissariat (*Oberkriegskommissariat*), and its subordinate War Commissariats and their Rural Commissioners (in the countryside other than the domains) and Local Commissaries (in the towns). (Frederick William said that over a thousand cases of such clashes were personally known to him.) So in January 1723 the King introduced a sweeping reform. In effect this was a fusion of control at two levels. At the top, the two chief bodies, the General Finance Directory and the General War Commissariat, were merged into one supreme body, the *Ober-Finanz, Kriegs, und Domänen-Direktorium*, known more usually by the briefer title of the General Directory. At the provincial level, the War Commissariats and the Chambers were also merged into single War and Domains Chambers, which supervised the local officials: the Rural

Commissioners, the Local Commissaries, and the Crown Bailiffs, all now fused into one more or less harmonious service.

Two points emerge out of all this. One is that the General Directory had thus complete control over the entire administration of the country, except justice, education and religious affairs, and its various subordinate Chambers and officials swept aside all traces of local independence. The other point is that the King himself appointed and controlled, very closely, the General Directory itself. Prussian despotism therefore reached its height in his reign. The close supervision of the whole country was too much of a task for the four members of the General Directory so it ended by being composed of the four chief ministers assisted by Privy Councillors reponsible for finance. At first there were three or four such assistants, but the number eventually rose to about twenty.

So much for all this machinery of government. It would have been of little use to create such a system, however, if the men who belonged to it were idle, dishonest, or inefficient. Frederick William worked like a terrible tornado to prevent any such thing. He supervised closely and constantly, making frequent journeys in the provinces to satisfy himself that all was well. The discipline exercised over his officials was just as stern as that over the army, and the civil servants, like the soldiers, were expected to give the same blind obedience to orders, and were reminded of this by the King—'You must serve your master body and soul', 'There must be subordination; that is the most important thing in the entire service', were typical remarks of his, backed up by the ever-present cane, by bloodcurdling threats ('I will hang and roast and treat them like rebels') and by fines, imprisonment, and even by hanging. The King's own supervision of his officials was backed by the efforts of a separate body of officials called the *Fiskalate*, and furthermore the officials worked the better because they were made responsible for the errors of their subordinates. As to the quality of the civil servants, the King usually insisted on high standards of education, though he gave preference to old soldiers or to anyone offering him a big enough bribe. The Prussian bureaucracy was the most hardworking, honest, and efficient in Europe, though most of its members could hardly have had much initiative. This was the body, however, whose diligence resulted in the annual collection of taxes amounting to seven million *thalers*. Of this, no less than five million were spent on the army, but the King thus had this huge army and kept it without reliance on foreign subsidies; more, he even managed to save for emergencies no less than eight million *thalers*, which were packed in cases and kept in the cellars of the palace.

Getting all that money out of the taxpayers was not just a matter of having an efficient civil service; the taxpayers had to earn the money in the first place. To increase the taxable wealth of the country therefore became one of the Sergeant King's chief preoccupations. His policy was mercantilist in the double sense that it was in part aimed at bringing all the economic activity under government control and in part aimed at increasing the wealth of the country as a result of governmental measures; it was a system of power as well as of economics.

As for government control, that was achieved by two sorts of measure, the one sort intended to make people work harder, and the other consisting of administrative changes. Greater effort was stimulated by the King's own tireless energy, by exhortation expressed in the oft-repeated 'Ein Plus machen' ('Make more'), and by his constant inspections everywhere, cane in hand. 'Whoever has money,' he said, 'gains the respect and admiration of the world,' and he saw to it that there were no idlers. Beggars were pushed into workhouses or the army; gipsies, who all in his opinion contributed nothing to the nation's wealth, were expelled; everyone had to work—even the market women had to knit or sew while waiting for customers instead of 'sitting with open mouths' (Edict of 1723). The second measure was chiefly that, as we have already seen, economic administration passed from local authorities entirely to the royal agents, the Local Commissaries and the Rural Commissioners. In addition the Edict of January 1723 and the *Reichspatent* of 1731 (the latter being a law which he persuaded the Imperial Diet to pass as applicable to all the Empire) gave him the right to bring the old guilds completely under royal control. The result was that they were left without a shred of authority while the workmen (journeymen) were placed under even closer governmental control than were the masters, an important point since they had been the cause of a lot of trouble.

Government control over economic life being thus established, Frederick William used it to further industries and agriculture which he regarded as the chief source of a country's wealth. (He placed less reliance on trade, but did not neglect it.)

The woollen industry received most of his attention. He encouraged it by countless edicts, among them the regulation that the army had to be dressed in cloth of home manufacture, by dozens of regulations governing the price, qualities, and measures, by forbidding the export of raw wool from most of his provinces, by prohibitions on the use of foreign luxury cloth such as calicoes and silk, and by heavy customs duties on imported woollen cloth. He also set up a great centre for the manufacture of woollens, the Berlin *Lagerhaus* (1714). The results of all this was certainly impressive; for instance, the amount of raw wool used in Berlin for manufacturing purposes increased from 34,969 stones in 1720 to 81,955 stones in 1735. The leather industry was nursed too by edicts which forbade the wearing of wooden shoes, by heavy duties on imported leather, and by a prohibition on the importation of foreign shoes. Heavy duties on imported linens also helped the native linen industry. The King tried also, and with considerable success, to create new industries by encouraging skilled craftsmen and manufacturers to come from foreign countries and settle in Prussia. Thousands, lured by offers of financial assistance, immunity from military service, and various other inducements, did so.

As for agriculture, the King encouraged this principally by inducing immigration on terms similar to those offered to industrial workers—free agricultural implements, houses, and cattle being the bait in this case. Here too the King was strikingly successful, for example in East Prussia, which had become an almost uninhabited desert after the very severe plague of the years 1708–11, and of which Frederick the Great said a few years later 'the country is more prosperous and fertile than ever'. One reform of the greatest importance, however, was defeated by the King's own bureaucracy. In 1706 his predecessor had abolished *Leibeigenschaft* (strict personal serfdom) in eastern Pomerania, but the civil servants, who were largely drawn from the Junkers (landowning aristocracy) took no notice of the order. Frederick William in 1718, 1719, and 1727 tried to carry out the reform, but failed completely. Neither did he succeed in an attempt to stop the eviction of serfs by their masters which, he said, 'desolated the farms and depopulated the country'. The truth is that his despotism had to be based on the support of the Junkers who were indispensable as army officers and as civil servants. Despotism, after all, cannot exist in a vacuum: it must rest on support of some sort. The only alternative would have been for the Prussian rulers to base themselves on the support of the middle classes, but these were not numerous in their eastern provinces at least, and in any case the whole system was created for the sake of a big army, for which the Junkers were thought to provide the only possible supply of officer-material, the middle classes being regarded by the kings as deficient in honour and courage: Frederick the Great referred to them as 'ces gens dont la conduite ou la naissance ne répondait point au métier de gens d'honneur'.

The Sergeant King had thus created a large and magnificent army, supplied by the labours of a thriving country administered by a royal bureaucracy. He was the creator of Prussian militarism and of Prussian despotism, with the Junkers as the chief support of both. One central feature of that despotism evidently was that it entailed an excessive amount of work for the King himself, with the corollary that it killed initiative in the officials. The system revolved around his person and could only function at all so long as he was prepared to shoulder a colossal burden.

This is the chief reason for his notorious treatment of his son, the Crown Prince Frederick. The latter was a terrible disappointment, for instead of showing enthusiasm for the army, he very soon displayed a marked preference for music (he played the flute) and poetry. The Prince spoke only French, for he regarded German as fit only for un-cultured boors, whereas his father insisted on speaking German. (Actually it was a unique mixture of German, Latin, French, and English; his edicts had to be translated by his secretaries so as to make them intelligible to his subjects.) Frederick William, whose only idea of making people love him was to cane them, spared not the rod, and the two became totally estranged. The climax was reached when the Prince tried to run away; he was caught and with a friend tried by court martial for desertion. The friend was executed before the Prince's eyes, but the officers of the court refused to sentence the heir to the throne. However, the Prince realized that further overt resistance to his father's wishes was useless, and he applied himself thereafter to learning the routine of a Prussian king's job. He began no doubt hypocritically but ended with a genuine love and respect for the work and for his father, a love which was returned by the delighted King in good measure. Frederick William in fact saw in his son more than a worthy successor: his son was to be his avenger too.

For the odd thing about the creator of the best army in Europe was his total failure in diplomacy. A loyal German, he for the most part based his foreign policy on loyalty to Germany's Emperor, in the hope, indeed, that Charles VI would help him in return to obtain his cherished ambition, which was to secure Jülich and Berg. But the Emperor duped him completely (nor did Frederick William get better luck when finally, disillusioned, he went cap in hand to the French). One day the humiliated Sergeant King pointed to his son and exclaimed, 'Here is one who will avenge me.'

Few in Europe, at the death of Frederick William in 1740, imagined that the son, now Frederick II, would do any such thing. The general impression was that Prussia was strained to breaking-point by its efforts to maintain its huge army and that the lover of music and poetry, who moreover wrote poetry himself, and was surrounded by French wits, who had become the friend of Voltaire and a tremendous admirer of the French Enlightenment, would speedily reduce the army and keep a brilliant court. This impression was heightened by a book called *Anti-Machiavel* which Frederick had himself written, a book in which the young man (he was twenty-eight in 1740) condemned unjust wars and announced his intention of taking the Emperor Marcus Aurelius as his model. They had not seen the Sergeant King, on his death-bed, tortured by pain, throw his arms about his son, nor heard him say, as they were clasped in each other's arms, 'Oh, God, I die content, since I have so worthy a son and successor.'

The shock was all the greater then, when after the cynical diplomatic moves we have already mentioned, on 6 December 1740, the disciple of Marcus Aurelius placed himself at the head of the army his father had laboured so hard to create, and invaded the Austrian province of Silesia, without a shadow of excuse, the reasons he later gave being that he wanted to get himself talked about and that he wanted Silesia.

At first sight it seemed an easy matter, for Maria Theresa had an empty treasury and a weak army. She herself was young and inexperienced, and her ministers old and incompetent. Worse, the loyalty of many of her subjects, particularly the Hungarian nobility, appeared more than suspect. Frederick in fact expected a walk-over, and after his easy entry into Silesia offered to pay her a sum of money in return for the province to help her to defend the remainder of her possessions, and to vote for her husband, Francis, at the Imperial election. To his surprise she refused, although it would be some months before she could put even a small army in the field against him. However, she had hopes of help from England, and calculated that a quick success might deter other likely aggressors.

(c) *THE WAR OF THE AUSTRIAN SUCCESSION, 1740-8*

Maria Theresa's decision to fight in no way perturbed Frederick, for he knew that his own attack would be the signal for others to join in. Charles Albert of Bavaria wanted the Imperial Crown for himself and the Habsburg dominions, or at least some of them, for his wife, daughter of the Emperor Joseph. His army and treasury were in an even worse state than Maria Theresa's, but he counted on French help. This, Fleury was not very willing to give, but he was losing his control, being now aged eighty-six, over the direction of French policy, a control

which increasingly fell into the hands of the anti-Austrian faction led
by the Comte de Belle-Isle. Fleury had to yield to them. The result was
that France made treaties with Prussia and Bavaria in December 1740;

The WAR of the
AUSTRIAN
SUCCESSION
1740–48
Austrian Dominions..
Prussia.........

France did not offer much help by these arrangements, but further
agreements in the next month committed France to support of the
Bavarian claim by force of arms, and by the summer Belle-Isle had
built up a complete system of alliances embracing also Saxony, Spain,

and Sweden (this last to provide a diversion against the Russians, who were still the allies of Austria).

It seemed for a while as if the brave Maria Theresa's domains would be torn to shreds. Frederick on 5 April 1741 beat the army she sent against him at Mollwitz (the Austrian cavalry beat his, and, fearing the day lost, he fled, only to learn that the Prussian infantry was more than a match for the Austrian cavalry and infantry together; he as hastily returned to the scene and never again behaved other than bravely and brilliantly in countless battles). The Franco-Bavarian forces captured Linz and all of Upper Austria, Charles Albert was crowned as Archduke of Austria, while their forces also invaded Bohemia and Westphalia. Maria Theresa's answer was to win over the semi-rebellious Hungarians to her side and then to conclude an armistice with Frederick at Klein Schnellendorf in October, so as to concentrate against the French and Bavarians. She had little luck at first, for the French captured Prague on 25 November 1741, and Charles Albert was elected Emperor on 24 January 1742.

Her plight was indeed desperate, but at this point the English came to her help. They had, after all, signed the Pragmatic Sanction, and public sympathy for the young queen was considerable, but the government thought it could hardly afford to let its chief continental ally be overwhelmed by France. Besides, nothing very brilliant had been achieved against the Spaniards and some of the government feared French intervention in the War of Jenkins's Ear; in that event it would be necessary to contain the French in Europe; as Hardwicke put it, 'We must henceforth fight for America in Europe' (a remark that considerably pre-dates the famous one of Pitt to the same effect). Walpole was not in favour of a continental war, but he was furiously attacked and resigned in February 1742, the most prominent man in the English government being thereafter Carteret. Before the fall of Walpole, Carteret had in June 1741 remade the alliance with Austria, and formed an army called the Pragmatic army, consisting of Hessians, Hanoverians, and English.

Evidently the English policy had more of calculation than of chivalry in it, for the English statesmen from the first tried to get Maria Theresa to buy off Frederick by ceding Silesia to him so that she could fight the French for them. English persuasion, and another defeat at the hands of the Prussians, induced her to cede Silesia to Frederick by the Treaty of Berlin on 28 August, and this ended the First Silesian War.

The removal of Maria Theresa's most formidable opponent brought with it a distinct improvement in her position. Saxony deserted the

French, with the result that the latter had to evacuate Bohemia in December 1742, and the Austrian troops overran Bavaria. In the meantime Carteret signed a convention with Prussia at Westminster (November): he was aiming at a great alliance against the French, and was helped in this by an English victory at Dettingen over a French army in June 1743. His next move was to detach Charles Albert of Bavaria (now the Emperor Charles VII) at the Treaty of Hanau; the Austrians were to evacuate Bavaria, while the Emperor recognized Maria Theresa's rights in Austria, Bohemia, and Hungary. The lively Carteret followed this by a similar deal with Sardinia (Treaty of Worms, September 1743), at the expense this time of ceding Milan, and he also got a promise of help from the Dutch. The same year saw also the collapse of France's Swedish allies, for they were hopelessly beaten by the Russians.

Carteret's diplomacy was brilliant but precarious. The Austrians were disgusted by the way the English were getting them to buy off one foe after another with Austrian territory, and in particular Silesia, simply so that Austria would be the more free to fight England's battle for her against France. As far as Austria was concerned, these over-clever arrangements at Berlin, Hanau, and Worms were the real roots of that dissatisfaction with the English alliance which was to be one of the causes of her eventual rupture with England and of her alliance with France. Further, Frederick of Prussia feared that the English would restore Silesia to Austria as soon as they had polished off the French, so he decided that a French defeat was something he could not afford.

Not that a French collapse seemed so very likely. Fleury had died in January 1743, and Louis XV decided to pursue a more vigorous policy. However, he found the effort of directing affairs a bit too much for him, so he tended to let his ministers carry on while he supervised them by personal agents of his own. In effect this produced a private royal policy as well as a ministerial one. (It is often called 'the King's secret', a word much in use in reference to eighteenth-century diplomacy to describe dynastic policies, such as the 'secret' of the Regent Orleans who before Louis had made an alliance with the English for his personal benefit, or the 'secret' of Elizabeth Farnese's Italian policy, which was using Spanish power for her family ambitions. As a word to signify double-dealing under a respectable, in those cases patriotic, disguise, it could even be applied to the English as well, their 'secret' being smuggling into the Spanish Empire under the shelter of a respectable treaty.) At all events, Louis XV's efforts produced horrible confusion in French policy, for though it was now decided to fight the war with more energy, nobody in France was quite sure in what theatre of war the energy was to be displayed, nor could anyone think of a sensible reason for displaying it at all.

It was finally decided to attack in three separate places. Another alliance was concluded with Spain at Fontainebleau on 28 October 1743, by which an attack was to be made on Sardinia, Naples was to be secured for one of Elizabeth Farnese's sons and a part of Lombardy for the other, and the French were to help to recapture Gibraltar. The second plan was an invasion of England in support of the Stuart rising to be undertaken by the young Prince Charles Edward. And last, it was decided to invade the Netherlands, for no very good reason except that victories seemed probable there. The Italian venture did not prosper and the fleet meant for the attack on England was dispersed by a storm, but the French commander, Marshal Saxe, made some headway in the Netherlands, which worried Maria Theresa not one jot, for instead of sending troops to defend her possessions there, she ordered a big assault in Alsace, and the Austrians drove the French there back to Strasburg. This so alarmed Frederick II of Prussia that he concluded alliances with Bavaria and the Palatinate in May and with the French in June 1744, and immediately invaded Bohemia, thus starting the Second Silesian War (so called because his main object was to prevent the Austrians from becoming strong enough to take Silesia from him). By September he had captured Prague, and this forced the Austrians to withdraw their troops from the Rhine, so that the chance of a great defeat of France, if it had ever existed, now vanished.

This was a disappointment to the English, many of whose statesmen blamed Carteret for the collapse of his schemes, and he was pushed out of power, his place being taken by the Duke of Newcastle and his brother, Henry Pelham. Shortly before this the direction of French foreign policy had been entrusted (18 November 1743) to the Marquis d'Argenson, who had an all-embracing but secret plan for securing the tranquillity of Europe which involved action against Austria, Russia, England, and Spain. The inclusion of the Spanish allies in the list of opponents to be quelled, as being centres of trouble, was patently ridiculous in the middle of a great war in which Spanish help was necessary to France, and the muddle drifted into utter chaos when on top of this Louis XV privately pursued a wholly different policy. Fresh confusion was added to this war, which has been described as an historian's nightmare, when the Emperor Charles VII died (20 January 1745). D'Argenson failed to prevent the election of Maria Theresa's husband, Francis, in September, but could console himself with an utterly pointless victory over the English at the Battle of Fontenoy (in the Netherlands) in the previous June, and he went gaily on with his scheme for using Sardinia to turn his Spanish allies out of Italy.

The English for their part were trying to push Maria Theresa into Italy to fight the French there for them, but she still persisted in directing her main energies against the Prussians. Her armies were smashed by Frederick at the Battle of Hohenfriedberg in June and by Leopold of Anhalt-Dessau at Kesseldorf in December, and Frederick invaded Saxony. Meanwhile Perfidious Albion had signed a convention with him at Hanover in July; the English actually guaranteed him in the possession of Silesia. Austria therefore gave up the task of recovering Silesia as hopeless, and signed the Treaty of Dresden with Frederick, ceding him that province, on 25 December 1745, thus ending the Second Silesian War. This necessity hurt Maria Theresa bitterly, but it quite pleased the English, who imagined she would be free to attack France; instead she began to negotiate with that Power. At the same moment Charles Emmanuel of Sardinia, who had been all the time revealing d'Argenson's plans to the English (who were thus better informed about his intentions than anyone in Paris was, for he had kept the whole business secret there), threw off the mask and began an offensive in Italy as the ally of Austria. The whole scheme then leaked out and the fury against the Marquis both in Madrid and at the court of Louis XV was considerable, but the King did not dismiss his minister, who had already cost him the defection of his ally Prussia, the defection of Sardinia, the loss of Milan, a threat to Naples, accusations of treachery from Spain, and the loss of Cape Breton and Louisburg to the English. D'Argenson in exchange for all this could only point to the capture of Brussels by the French, so he decided on peace, on the basis of a return to the *status quo* for England, France, and Spain, recognition of the Pragmatic Sanction and of the Emperor Francis, and some territory for France in the Netherlands, and in May 1746 suggestions along these lines were sent to London.

At first the Duke of Newcastle was in no hurry to end the war on these or any other terms. He was counting on more English successes first, but did not get any, except that a French attempt to recapture Louisburg was repulsed. On the other hand, the French took Madras in India (September 1746), defeated an Austro-Sardinian invasion of the Riviera, and in the campaign of 1746 Marshal Saxe captured most of the Austrian Netherlands. On 17 April 1747 the French declared war on Holland, which seemed at the mercy of the brilliant Saxe. In spite of the revolution which promptly gave power to William IV of Orange, Holland was unable to defend herself, and when the English Duke of Cumberland tried to assist he was heavily defeated by Saxe at the Battle of Laufeldt (2 July 1747). The French capture of Bergen-op-Zoom on 16 September made Holland's position hopeless. King Louis XV, as well as his clever and humane Marshal, was sick of the war, and these defeats convinced the English that it had better be ended. The result was the Treaty (or Treaties) of Aix-la-Chapelle, signed on 18 October between England, Holland, and France, with Spain, Austria, and Sardinia adhering on 20 October, 8 November, and 20 November 1748 respectively.

At first sight the war ended without victors or vanquished, for the *status quo* was restored between France and England by the mutual exchange of colonial conquests (Madras for Louisburg) and between England and Spain, while the French gave up their conquests in the Netherlands, Savoy, and Nice. Maria gave a part of Milan to the second son of Elizabeth Farnese, Don Philip, and Sardinia got a small portion of Lombardy, but Maria Theresa was confirmed in the possession of the remainder of the Habsburg dominions, except, of course, Silesia.

The French after so many victories had good reason to be dissatisfied with these mediocre results, and 'bête comme la Paix' soon became a catch-phrase in Paris. The real gainers were Prussia and Russia; the former became evidently a first-rate Power at one bound, while Russia, who had defeated Sweden during the war and conquered Finland, only returning it in exchange for the acceptance of a Russian nominee to the Swedish throne, was clearly one of the arbiters of Eastern Europe too. So much had both these Powers obviously grown that it was clear that the future of all of Europe would henceforth be greatly affected by friendliness or hostility between them.

The Peace was quite as unstable as it was 'bête'. For nobody believed for a minute that any number of treaties or guarantees would prevent the Austrians from trying to recover Silesia as soon as a favourable chance presented itself, while hostilities between England and France overseas went on much as before.

12 · The Colonial Rivalry between England and France until 1756; the Diplomatic Revolution 1748–57, and the outbreak of the Seven Years War

(a) COLONIAL RIVALRY BETWEEN ENGLAND AND FRANCE

The French and English governments until nearly the middle of the eighteenth century usually preferred to try to ignore the fact that their subjects frequently clashed on the high seas and in the lands beyond them. However, rivalry in Central and Northern America and in India ended by involving the home governments in full-scale war.

In the Caribbean that rivalry was of two sorts. In the first place they competed for trade with Spanish possessions. A great deal of golden glamour enveloped the Spanish trade, which was not nearly as lucrative as most people thought, for the inhabitants of the Spanish Empire were not particularly wealthy, and the Spanish government did its utmost to prevent foreign merchants from trading with them. The English South Sea Company whined repeatedly about the meagreness of its profits from the slave concession which the negotiators of the Treaty of Utrecht had been so anxious to obtain, though the Company flatly refused to support its grumbles by producing any accounts, possibly because it was supposed to pay a percentage of the profits to the King of Spain. As for the permission to send one ship a year to trade with South America, it is true that the Company sold the cargo and then filled the ship up again with a fresh cargo under cover of darkness, but this was a trifling matter, for in the whole history of the concession the annual ship only sailed eight times. Smuggling was far more important, and this, backed up by the English government, led to the outbreak of the War of Jenkins's Ear with Spain in 1739. This could very easily have led to a war with France as well, especially if the English had made any significant conquests at the expense of Spain and thus altered the balance of influence in the Caribbean to France's disadvantage. As it turned out, the English failed to achieve anything very notable, while the French fleet under d'Antin, sent out there by a reluctant and pacific Fleury, accomplished nothing either, and after running out of supplies it had to go home.

War broke out between the English and the French in the West Indies for a different reason. The second sort of rivalry was that between each other's West Indian islands. They were very valuable because they produced very large quantities of sugar, besides smaller amounts of cotton, ginger, indigo, and coffee. In this the French enjoyed a great advantage, as their islands, particularly Martinique and Guadeloupe, were bigger and had better soil than the English ones, and the French therefore produced sugar more cheaply than the English planters could. The result was that the French were capturing not only the European market but also the English colonial market in North America. In spite of the Molasses Act of 1733, which tried to protect the English planters, the settlers in North America continued to trade with the French. So war broke out between the English and French in 1744 in the West Indies; but, as both sides were heavily engaged in fighting each other in Europe, neither could spare large forces for use in the Caribbean. The English war aim was that of the English planters, to cripple the trade of the French islands by blockade and similar measures, not to conquer the islands themselves, for these would, if conquered, be inside the English free trade area and could ruin the original English islands all the more easily. There was little fighting, and the Treaty of Aix-la-Chapelle in 1748 left things much as before: no territories changed hands, but four disputed islands (Dominica, St Lucia, St Vincent, and Tobago) were declared 'neutral', and both sides agreed to evacuate them. However, French settlers continued to drift into them, much to the annoyance of the English, and the French islands increased their share of the sugar trade and of the trade with Spanish dominions at the expense of the English. So causes of future conflict remained in plenty.

While French commercial competition was cutting the throats of the English in the West Indies, French pressure was becoming intolerable on the North American mainland, where both countries had colonies. French settlements were concentrated in the south around the Mississippi delta, and in the north in Canada, from the mouth of the St Lawrence to the Great Lakes; while the English colonies, after the acquisition of the French colony of Acadia in 1713 and the founding of Georgia in 1731, covered the eastern seaboard as far as the boundaries of the Spanish colony of Florida. In any conflict the initial advantage lay with the French, for they were under capable and unified control, whereas the English colonies could not be induced to take concerted action against a common enemy. But in the long run the French were at a hopeless disadvantage. They were outnumbered, the English settlers numbering about one and a half millions against their fifty or sixty thousands, and since their chief economic activity was the fur trade they depended on the mother country, far more than did the English settlers, who extensively cultivated the soil, for supplies of weapons, manufactures, and even provisions. The French colonies depended entirely on command of the sea route between themselves and France, and if, as seemed more than likely, this were lost in the course of a great war between the two home countries, then New France in America would be extinguished.

In spite of this obvious risk, or perhaps because of it, the French in the early part of the eighteenth century embarked on a policy of expansion. In the far south they founded New Orleans in 1718. This colony proved very difficult to develop, but it was useful for trade with the Indians of the Gulf hinterland. This led to clashes with hunters from the Carolinas, and an obscure war developed there, a war to which the English government contributed by building a fort on the River Altamaha in 1721. However, in this huge territory stretching from the Lower Mississippi to the southern Appalachians, distances were too formidable, the terrain too difficult, and the opponents too few, for a big conflict. Farther north, in the Illinois country lying between the Rivers Mississippi, Wabash, and Ohio, French expansionism led to a more serious situation. They already had some fortified posts in this area, and these were successively added to by the building of fortified trading posts—Forts Chartres, Orleans, and Vincennes—in

1718, 1720, and 1723 respectively. These guarded villages which came
to be populated (by about 1750) by approximately 1,000 Frenchmen
and their Indian wives, who busied themselves not only with the fur
trade but also with growing corn, which they could supply in case of
need to French forces operating in the Ohio Valley and to their forts
on the Great Lakes. The region thus became the key to French power
in the interior, but the French there soon clashed with English traders
from Pennsylvania and the Carolinas. Their goods, of excellent quality,
and cheaper than French goods, proved acceptable to the Iroquois
Indians of the region, but the latter, while appreciating the goods,
became concerned about increasing English penetration and soon
began to look to the French for help to drive the English away. Along
the Great Lakes, too, French expansion indicated a likely clash, for the
French in that area tried their best to consolidate their trading position.
In 1719 they built a trading post on the River Niagara, to which their
opponents (mainly of Dutch origin in this case) replied by building
Fort Oswego, whereupon both sides turned their forts into strong
stone-built affairs. Conflict here was, however, delayed for two reasons.
One was that the Indian Confederation of Six Nations did not want
war to disrupt their trading, and used their power to try to keep the
peace. The other reason was that most of the English colonists did not
want war either; for instance, the majority in the New York Assembly
favoured a policy of neutrality. The remaining area where the French
were preparing for trouble was at the entrance to the St Lawrence,
where they had built the great fortress of Louisburg on Cape Breton
Island.

The home governments were reluctant to commit large forces to a
war in North America during the War of the Austrian Succession
(1740–8), and this fact, together with what has just been said about the
difficulties of the terrain in the south, and the attitude of the Indians
and of the English farther north, meant that no important military
operations occurred in that time, with one exception. The Governor
of Massachusetts, William Shirley, was alarmed at the threat made by
the French to the English fisheries, trade, and expanding frontier. He
persuaded his Legislature to agree to a wild-cat scheme to attack
Louisburg (they assented by a majority of one vote) and he dispatched
a force of 3,000 New Englanders (Connecticut, Maine, and Rhode
Island helped) against the fortress in 1745. A squadron of the Royal
Navy was detached from the West Indies to assist, and the expedition
took the defence completely by surprise and captured the fort. This
dazzling success was thrown away at the Peace of Aix-la-Chapelle

three years later, when Louisburg was returned to the French in exchange for Madras in India. This might seem foolish, for if the English had held it the position of the French in America would have been next to hopeless, but, among other reasons for this decision, the English government did not want the bother of trying to assimilate French subjects, which was already a problem in Acadia (Nova Scotia).

The Peace of Aix-la-Chapelle in 1748 was no peace for America, where both sides got to grips with far more determination than ever before. It was obvious that control of the St Lawrence and of the headwaters of the Ohio was vital. The French promptly rebuilt Louisburg and built Fort Beauséjour on the neck of Acadia itself so as to tighten their grip on the entrance to the St Lawrence. The answer came at once: the English forcibly evicted the French inhabitants of Acadia and founded the port of Halifax. The Ohio region saw still more vigorous measures by both sides. English traders were penetrating more and more into this region; they had a trading post as far west as Picawillany, on the River Miami. The French determined to drive them away, not an easy task as the Indians there wanted English goods. In 1749 the French Governor-General, La Gallissonière, sent an expedition as far as the junction of the Rivers Ohio and Monongahela to lay claim to the region, a move which had become urgently necessary because the English were appearing not only as traders but also in the guise of land-speculators, backed up by wealthy magnates on the eastern seaboard. So in 1752 a French-led force of Chipewa and Ottowa Indians destroyed Picawillany and drove the English traders off. In the next year the new French Governor Duquesne put up three forts at Presqu'ile, Le Bœuf, and Venango. These pointed in a straight line at the forks of the Ohio, and so the French, having smashed the English forward position at Picawillany, now clearly intended to prevent any more English westward penetration by cutting the westward routes near to their origin. On hearing of this move, the Governor of Virginia, Dinwiddie, sent George Washington with a small force to demand the withdrawal of the French from Fort Le Bœuf. This was naturally refused, so, to prevent any further extension of the French flanking movement, he put up a small fort at the forks of the Ohio, but was promptly expelled from it by the French, who built a much stronger fort there, Fort Duquesne. In 1754 Washington tried to capture this fort, but, after beating some French troops at Great Meadows, was himself totally overwhelmed at the improvised Fort Necessity and captured (July).

This meant the outbreak of a real war between the Virginians and the French. It was at first confined to them, as the other English colonies would not help: the Carolinas had no troops to spare and the Pennsylvanians concealed their reluctance to pay war taxes behind a self-righteous pacifism. It was thus only from the English government that the Virginians could expect help. The government had been at first inclined to follow a purely mercantile policy, and to think that large sums of money spent on military operations would hardly bring in a commensurate cash return. But it now altered its mind. Trade with the American colonies was now so great that it seemed sensible to protect it even at great cost, nor was the government unaware that it could not honourably abandon the defence of so many British subjects.

The government in November 1754, therefore, while not desiring a full war with France, decided that the French in America must at least be driven back to the positions they held in 1714, and sent an expedition under General Braddock to capture Forts Duquesne, Niagara, Crown Point, and Beauséjour. Four months later, when Braddock was disembarking in America, the government's attitude hardened and a fleet of seventeen battleships under Admiral Boscawen was sent to Halifax so as to cut the French communications with the mother country and to capture all the French warships that it could. Braddock's expedition was a total fiasco. His force of 1,400 Regulars and 600 Colonials was ambushed in the forests near the River Monongahela and lost 863 killed and wounded, Braddock himself being among the slain (1755). Boscawen met with no defeat, but only got a small and useless victory—he encountered a French squadron in June 1755, under Du Bois de la Motte, which was on its way to reinforce the French in America. In spite of the fact that the French were taken unawares, for they thought they were at peace with England (the Captain of the *Alcide* asked the Captain of the English battleship *Dunkirk* through his megaphone if they were at peace or war, and got the answering bellow of, 'At peace, at peace; fire!'—the last word being addressed to the English gunners), the French all got away except for two ships, the unfortunate *Alcide* and the *Lys*.

By this time the Duke of Newcastle had decided that his diplomacy in Europe was a failure and that his best chance of dealing with the French was to knock them out before a war was declared. So he ordered the Portsmouth fleet under Admiral Hawke to put to sea and seize every French ship they could find. In November 1755 this vast piratical enterprise took 300 French merchant ships, but as a knock-out blow it was a failure, for the French battle fleet remained intact. In the next month the Duke received and rejected a French demand for the return of the ships, and in January 1756 the two countries were at war.

Rivalry between England and France in India did not directly help to cause the Seven Years War, but it did nothing to sweeten relations. In that country the English had many trading posts, run by the East India Company, of which the most important were Bombay, Madras, Calcutta, and a post on the Hugli. The trade was very valuable, the turnover being more than a million pounds. Other European nations had trading posts in the country too, but the most dangerous rivals were the French, whose *Compagnie des Indes Orientales*, founded by Colbert in 1664, had posts at Pondicherry and Chandernagore. India itself was dominated by the great Mogul Empire, but this Muslim Empire, whose capital was at Delhi, was on its last legs and a ring of semi-independent principalities had sprung up around the decaying centre, while the Hindu Marathas, who had begun as guerrillas fighting against the Empire, with their centre in the Deccan, were ravaging far and wide.

There were accordingly plenty of troubled waters for the English and French to fish in if they had been so minded, but they were hopelessly outnumbered by the millions of native inhabitants and were there for trade, not intrigue or fighting. The French Governor-General Dupleix was therefore embarrassed by the outbreak of the War of the Austrian Succession in Europe in 1740, and suggested local neutrality to the English in India. They refused because they could not answer for their home government, and the result was the outbreak in 1744 of the First Carnatic War. The English fleet threatened Pondicherry, and as there were no French warships in Indian waters, Dupleix asked Anwar-ud-din, Nawab of the Carnatic, and the Governor of the French island of Mauritius, Labourdonnais, for help. Nothing came from the former, but the latter arrived with eight warships and 1,200 troops in June 1746, forced the English squadron to retire, and in September blockaded Madras while Dupleix laid siege to it. The English also had asked the Nawab for help. He gave it, but on his arrival at Madras found that the French had captured it on 10 September, and the small French garrison sallied out and put his huge army to flight. The French fleet had to return to Mauritius because of a storm, and while Dupleix, nothing daunted, laid siege to the English Fort St David, a large English fleet appeared from England under Boscawen. Dupleix failed to take Fort St David, and the English besieged Pondicherry. Before they could take it the news arrived of the Peace of Aix-la-Chapelle in 1748, which returned Madras to the English in exchange for Louisburg in America.

Dupleix was not responsible for the First Carnatic War, but he certainly caused the Second. He conceived the idea that he could ruin the English in India, although he must have been aware that sea-power, in which France was inferior to England, would almost certainly play the decisive role. He did not realize that the English resources in India were greatly superior to those at his disposal, and imagined he could carry out expensive schemes of conquest without financial help from France (he never asked for any). Rather did he pin his hopes on using his troops to put pressure on Indian potentates whom he could then turn against the English; although there was no reason why the English should not play at that game also. Opinions vary about Dupleix; perhaps it is not too harsh to say that he was an able but over-optimistic man who took on a bigger opponent needlessly—or, putting it bluntly, a fool.

In 1749 he allied with a claimant to the throne of the Carnatic, Chanda Sahib, and defeated and killed the ruling Nawab. Chanda Sahib became the new Nawab, thus giving Dupleix great authority in the Carnatic. In the following year he practically gained control over the Deccan, where an army of his under the command of the Marquis de Bussy held sway. Not liking the imminent prospect of ruin, the English Governor of Madras, Thomas Saunders, put Mohammed Ali, a relation of the late Nawab, into the citadel of Trichinopoly, which dominated the great plain of the Carnatic, whereupon Dupleix sent an army to take it. To relieve the pressure, a tiny English force under Robert Clive seized Arcot, the capital of the Carnatic, in 1751, and successfully defended it for fifty-three days. Clive won two more battles against the French in the same year, and in the next he and Stringer Lawrence captured the French commander. So Dupleix, largely because of his folly in allowing Bussy's army to remain winning useless victories in the Deccan, lost control over the Carnatic, at which point the French government, tired of him and his expensive failures, recalled him (1753). His successor negotiated a peace with the English, but it was never ratified because of the outbreak of the Seven Years War.

(b) THE DIPLOMATIC REVOLUTION AND THE OUT-BREAK OF THE SEVEN YEARS WAR

From the foregoing account it can be seen that the English government was becoming more and more preoccupied with colonial expansion, and was aware that a great colonial war with France was brewing. In such a war England counted on her old ally, Austria, to defend the all-important Netherlands from France and at least to assist in the defence of Hanover. France, they hoped, would be tied down in Europe, while they could devote their chief energies to colonial and maritime victories. Hitherto Austria had been obliged to fall in with England's notions of where and how wars against France should be fought because England provided the money without which Austria could not fight a major war at all.

That was a highly displeasing state of affairs for the Austrians, who had been incensed by English behaviour in the War of the Austrian Succession, when the English had used their money-power in their attempt to make Austria give Silesia to Frederick II of Prussia, and fight France, for England's benefit, instead. England, then, by 1748 had lost most of her attraction for Maria Theresa, whose chief ambition was to recover Silesia from Frederick. In her eyes Frederick had replaced France as the chief enemy. As for the Netherlands she cared little, and for Hanover nothing. To escape from dependence on England's money, to create an army good enough to have some hope against the Prussians, and to find an ally more fitted to help her to recover Silesia, therefore, became for her the object of a twofold programme.

The first problem was one of internal reform. Assisted by the minister Haugwitz, she raised the strength of the army to 140,000 men, gave it a good artillery, and made it copy Prussian tactics and drill. A Military Academy was founded at Wiener Neustadt, regular camps were established, and the conditions for officers and men improved. The underlying weakness had been lack of money, but any fiscal reforms would involve a fundamental reform of the entire system of administration throughout her dominions. She knew perfectly well that the separate provinces of her Empire would defend their considerable local autonomy, and her reforms did not touch most of them. They were confined to the Austrian and Bohemian lands and to a certain extent to Lombardy (where she made the Church pay a property tax). She swept away the financial machinery used by her father and reinstated the *Hofkammer* to deal with the national finances, and then put the affairs of the Imperial House into the hands of a new office, the *Geheime Haus- Hof- und Staatskanzlei* (Privy Family, Court, and State Chancellery). She also got the Estates to promise to vote taxes for a period of ten years in advance, a property tax which was to be extended to cover noble land also, in exchange for a promise that no further demands would be made on them for the upkeep of the army. That at least ensured that the army would have some money to support it for a useful period, but even then the amount was not enough. As for the further administrative reforms that were necessary, most of them we can post-pone examining because it was many years before they could be put into practice. However, she did at least make a start in Austria and Bohemia by abolishing the court chanceries which had been clumsily dealing with judicial and political concerns. She replaced them by two new bodies, namely the Supreme Judicature (*Oberste Justizstelle*) as a court of appeal, and the *Direktorium in Internis* which dealt with all administration except foreign affairs (under the *Haus- Hof- und Staats-kanzlei*) and defence (under the *Hofkriegsrat*). All these efforts at least enabled her to fight a big war, but as it turned out neither the army nor the administrative reforms went far enough.

The other part of her programme, suggested to her by the brilliant diplomatist Kaunitz, was nothing less than an attempt to throw over the English alliance and to replace it by one with the secular enemy, France, whose huge army would be far more useful in the recovery of Silesia than the mob of mercenaries usually paid for by England. It is true that Austria already had the Russians as allies, and this old alliance had been reaffirmed by the treaty of 1746. But to make certain of success in what would amount to a plan to wipe out Prussia the French army was necessary, the more so as Russia of late had not seemed too reliable.

Accordingly Kaunitz visited France in 1750–2. In spite of his skill he made little headway there, for France wanted peace and Louis XV wished rather to restore French influence in Central and Eastern Europe, more particularly in Poland and among the German princes. This was the traditional French policy of containing the Habsburgs, so naturally Kaunitz failed. He returned home and waited.

In the end, of course, the English would come to him for a renewal of the old alliance against France, and this they did. Negotiations were opened between England and Austria in March 1755. They dragged, because the former was not prepared to make concessions about getting back Silesia, while for their part the Austrians were not wildly enthu-siastic about defending the Netherlands or Hanover. More progress was made with a scheme, ostensibly the work of Saxony, whose object was to attack Prussia with a coalition of Saxony, Austria, Russia, Hanover, Brunswick, Bavaria, and some of the smaller German States, but when the British Cabinet heard in June that this was to be financed with English money it exploded with rage and dropped all the negotia-tions, leaving of the wreck only a subsidy treaty with Hesse (and one with Russia which was eventually completed in September 1755).

This meant the collapse of the old Anglo-Austrian alliance, so, in a panic about England's likely plight with no allies, the Duke of Newcastle ordered an approach to Prussia in July. At first this met with little success, but after obtaining the subsidy treaty with Russia on 30 September the English found Frederick more ready to listen. He was horrified at the notion of 55,000 Russian troops in English pay roaming around Germany, and, for all he could foresee, acting against him in concert with the Austrians. So he signed the Convention of Westminster on 16 January 1756, by which England and Prussia guaranteed each other's possessions and agreed to prevent the invasion of Germany by foreign armies. It also stipulated that Frederick would not have to fight for the defence of the Netherlands. Frederick's own calculation was that if he were going to get English money, then England would hardly be foolish enough to give any to his Austrian and Russian enemies as well, and without that money they might not be able to fight him. Of course he was still the ally of France, but it must be remembered that at that instant France was not yet allied to Austria, so that an isolated France engaged in a colonial war against England would be highly unlikely to take much action on the continent of Europe except perhaps in the Netherlands—and the Convention of Westminster exempted him from any obligation to fight there himself. Frederick therefore congratulated himself on having removed the night-mare of a possible Anglo-Austro-Russian attack against him, an attack in which his French ally, who would presumably be fully occupied in a colonial struggle with the English, would be of little help to him. He saw no reason why he could not still remain on friendly terms with the French, since in a Franco-English war he would be nowhere near the scene of the conflict, and could maintain neutrality in it. As for Newcastle and George II of England, they seem to have been under the impression that their agreement with Prussia was quite compatible with the subsidy treaty with the Russians, and even with a possible alliance with the Austrians, which proves both of them political innocents. At all events, Frederick and Newcastle were in for a nasty surprise.

Kaunitz had not the faintest intention of making any agreement with Newcastle, and early in September 1755 he ordered the Austrian Ambassador in Paris, Starhemberg, to try negotiations with Louis XV once more. Starhemberg decided it was best to begin such a delicate matter by first approaching the King's all-powerful mistress, the Marquise de Pompadour. She relied for advice on an old friend, the Abbé Bernis. Both have been blamed since for having been outwitted by Starhemberg, but in reality all the decisions were the King's. Louis had been as little charmed by Frederick's behaviour in the War of the Austrian Succession as Maria Theresa had been with England's, and he resented being regarded as an equal partner of the 'Margrave of Brandenburg' even more than he disliked the latter's cynical brand of Protestantism, while alliance with Austria would seem to free France from any danger on the Continent. Starhemberg suggested that France should get most of the Netherlands as a patrimony for the King's son-in-law,[1] to be exchanged for his Italian duchies, while France itself could have Ostend and Nieuport. This pleased Louis XV, but he and his advisers were still reluctant to commit themselves, and the negotiations were getting nowhere. The King and his ministers were somewhat shaken by Starhemberg's assertion that Frederick was secretly negotiating with the English, so Louis, in order to see just what his precious ally's intentions were, sent the Duke of Nivernais on a special mission to Berlin. The Duke was a handsome, charming, and highly cultivated man, and Frederick thoroughly enjoyed his company, but the party was spoilt when the news of the Anglo-Prussian Convention of Westminster came out. The King of France, furious at the conduct of his ally while he himself was on the eve of a great war with England, thought that Frederick had made him the laughing-stock of Europe, and refused to renew his treaty of alliance with Prussia, although he might still have done so had Frederick adopted a more humble attitude.

This was Austria's chance to push her schemes which the French had more or less rejected in the previous autumn, and in March 1756 the Austrians tried again. Their great aim was to persuade France to take a big part in a war against Prussia, but the French were still dubious and the Austrians had to be content with drawing them in gradually. At last on 1 May 1756 the French signed with the Austrians the First Treaty of Versailles. This provided for the neutrality of Austria in a Franco-English war, and Louis promised not to attack the Netherlands or any other possession of Maria Theresa. Secondly, it provided a defensive alliance: if any of the European possessions of either Power were attacked by anyone then they would render each other assistance in the shape of money or 24,000 men, but Austria was still exempted from the need to help France against England.

All this was going to be a nasty shock for Frederick, although the alliance was still only defensive. (A diplomatist of Kaunitz's ability can always make the other side appear the aggressor.) Still more ominous

---

[1] The Infant Philip, Duke of Parma, married to Louis XV's eldest daughter.

was the effect of his Convention of Westminster on the Russians. To the latter the value of England as an ally at once seemed to be precisely zero, for the Russians had concluded their own subsidy treaty with England in order to attack Prussia. This made it relatively easy for Kaunitz to persuade the Russians in April 1756 to agree to join in an attack on Prussia with a force of 80,000 men.

Austria still needed to get French help as well as Russian to make certain of success against Frederick, and this the French, who had signed the Treaty of Versailles in order to keep the peace in Europe, not to build up a mighty Austria on the wreck of Prussia, refused to give. A Russian attempt to persuade the French to join in met with a rude refusal.

It was Frederick himself who finally pushed the French into falling in with Kaunitz's schemes. In the summer of 1756 he became convinced that war was inevitable, and with so many huge enemies gathering around him he decided that he must strike soon, hard, and fast, before the enemy could concentrate. On 29 August 1756 his army invaded Saxony; his intention was to capture the resources of that State and then administer a quick knock-out blow to the Austrians before anybody could help them. He had thus walked straight into the trap prepared for him by Kaunitz. He did indeed capture the Saxon army, but it took him six weeks longer than he had calculated; he missed whatever chance there had been of smashing Austria; and instead hastened the completion of the great coalition against himself. The French at last in May 1757 agreed to the Second Treaty of Versailles, the 'offensive' treaty, by which they were to give enormous subsidies to Austria, Russia, and Sweden, but even before the end of 1756 Kaunitz was able to gain their help under the defensive one.

Frederick's doom therefore appeared inevitable. He certainly brought it on himself by his treatment of France in signing the Convention of Westminster and by his attack on Saxony, which levered the French into the war against him, an attack without which there might well have been no war at all. As for the French, their own miscalculations were just as serious, for Louis undertook a great war against Prussia on the assumption that the latter could not stand more than one campaign against so many foes. That turned out to be wildly wrong, so France had to fight a big colonial and maritime war with England under the hopeless handicap of a big land war against Prussia as well. On the wider view, it might be thought that at least the French had got something that Louis XIV in his last years, as well as Cardinal Fleury, had wanted—an alliance with Austria, and through it a domination of the Continent which would elbow out English influence. That might have been a good idea at one time, but it was no longer, for Prussia was a stronger Power than Austria, and the calculation took no notice of the power of Russia in Eastern Europe. The Austrian alliance came too late, and brought France nothing but disaster.

13 · The Seven Years War, 1756–63

(a) *THE WAR IN EUROPE*

The Seven Years War was a double conflict. The European war was an attempt by a coalition, inspired by Kaunitz and consisting of Austria, Russia, Sweden, and France, to destroy the upstart State of Prussia. The other war was a colonial one fought between England and France in the Americas and India.

Frederick II of Prussia, whose exploits in this war won for him the title by which he is always known, Frederick the Great, certainly behaved rashly in provoking the European war by his invasion of Saxony. The population of Prussia was probably less than a sixth of the French and a quarter of the Austrian, while the allies disposed between them of at least five or six times as many soldiers. Prussia should therefore have been erased from the map. She was not, and this seeming miracle was caused by dissension and lack of cohesion among the allies, by the advantage given to Frederick in that he was working on interior lines against enemies whose supply problems became more serious with every mile they advanced, and by his own military genius. To that must be added some freakish good luck.

Frederick's chief virtues as a general were his audacious spirit (Napoleon afterwards said of him, 'He carried out things I never dared to do') and his readiness to learn from his mistakes. For instance, in his earlier campaigns he relied more on the bayonet than on fire-power, but found this was a mistake, and he afterwards did his best to increase the power of the musket and of the cannon in his battles, particularly the latter, for he created the first horse-artillery in Europe, and used as many cannon as possible, including some very heavy ones. He was also a brilliant tactician, making use of the superior speed with which his army could deploy. Once the enemy had drawn up in line of battle they usually found it very difficult to alter their formation and position very quickly, so Frederick, whose own army had been drilled to perfection, attacked heavily with superior numbers against only one wing of the enemy while refusing combat with the others. If this local superiority led to the crushing of that enemy wing, he could take the remainder of the enemy army in flank before they could properly redeploy. That was the rough idea of his famous 'Oblique Order', but Frederick was not a slave to it.

Before invading Saxony, he left a force of 11,000 men to keep an eye on the Swedes, another of 26,000 to watch the Russians, and a third of 37,000 to defend Silesia. He himself dashed into Saxony with an army of 70,000, took Dresden on 10 September, and defeated an Austrian army at Lobositz. Winter put a stop to the campaign, but later he advanced on Prague and again defeated an Austrian army. This invasion of Bohemia, however, ended in failure, for on 18 June 1757 he recklessly attacked an Austrian army under Marshal Daun which was nearly twice as numerous as his own at Kolin. He tried the famous oblique attack, but the enemy had plenty of leisure to see what he was up to, and reformed in plenty of time so that he was committed to a big frontal attack which ended in disaster and a loss of 13,000 men. That meant the evacuation of Bohemia, but it also meant that Frederick drew the correct conclusion from this bitter lesson; namely, that his oblique attack could only succeed against an intelligent opponent if his own movements could be concealed from the enemy up to the last minute.

Frederick's defeat also greatly encouraged his enemies, who now determined on concerted action to overwhelm him. Their plan was: Prince Joseph of Saxe-Hildburghausen at the head of the Reich army of 33,000 was to join the 30,000 French under Marshal Soubise and to reconquer Saxony; a huge French army of 100,000 men under Marshal d'Estrées was to wipe out the English and German army commanded by the Duke of Cumberland in Hanover; a Russian army was to invade Prussia, and a Swedish one to invade Pomerania; and 100,000 Austrians

DENMARK

SWEDISH
POMERAN

OLDENBURG

Hamburg

Klosterzeven

Bremen

HANOVER

BRANDE

Hanover

Minden

Hastenbeck

Elbe

UNITED
NETHERLANDS

CLEVE

MARK

Warburg

Weser

Rossbach

AUSTRIAN
NETHERLANDS

Crefeld

Rhine

The SEVEN YEARS WAR
in EUROPE
1756 – 63
Boundary of Empire in 1756 ---- ▬▬▬▬
Brandenburg-Prussia in 1756 --- ⋯⋯⋯

0   1   200 mls.

Landsh

BAVARIA

S

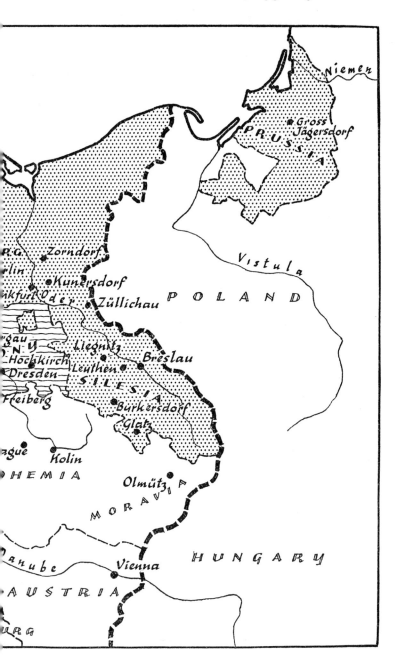

under Prince Charles of Lorraine and Marshal Daun were to wipe out the remains of Frederick's Kolin army.

Frederick was thus in a position which quickly degenerated from bad to hopeless. The Russians penetrated into Prussia, where they committed appalling barbarities at the expense of the civilian population, while the French under d'Estrées defeated Cumberland on 26 July at Hastenback. This victory did the French commander no good personally, because he had fallen out with the banker, Parîs-Duverney, who was as usual supplying the army, and the latter used his influence with Louis XV and Madame de Pompadour to have d'Estrées sacked. He was replaced by the worthless Duke of Richelieu, whose conception of the duties of a commander of a French army did not go much beyond feathering his own nest by exactions, plunder, and the taking of enormous bribes from Frederick the Great in exchange for inactivity. Richelieu concluded with the defeated Cumberland the notorious Convention of Klosterzeven, which neither commander had authority to do, by which the Anglo-Hanoverian army had to break up and its soldiers return to their respective countries (8 September). This should have meant that Richelieu's army was freed for service against Frederick directly, but it made no attempt to join Soubise's army and continued plundering. This was more helpful to Frederick than to the allies, but the virtual uselessness of Richelieu's army still left him in terrible difficulties. The Russians meanwhile had opened the road to Berlin by defeating the Prussian General Lehwaldt on 30 August at Gross Jägersdorf, though they retired again chiefly because of supply difficulties, while the Austrians, who had by then reconquered most of Silesia, entered Berlin on 16 October; they too retired, however, after levying a tax on the inhabitants.

Frederick decided to leave the Duke of Bevern with a small force to do what he could against this Austrian army under Prince Charles, while he himself advanced against Soubise and Saxe-Hildburghausen. He brought these to book at Rossbach on 5 November. The combined army tried to take Frederick in flank, but he completely outmanœuvred it by moving his army behind a low ridge, from which it emerged to attack across the head of the advancing French columns. These had no time to re-form and were flung into disorder and overwhelmed. The remainder were caught up in the confusion and, unable to deploy, were mown down by musket, and especially by artillery, fire. The retreat became a rout, and the French army fled, a panic-stricken rabble, losing 3,000 killed and 5,000 prisoners, including eight generals, against Frederick's losses of 165 killed and 376 wounded. No other battle in the entire war produced so great an impression. The French army was the object of derision by friends and foes, and England went wild with delight.

Great as was the victory, it was only the first instalment. For Frederick next tackled the Austrians under Prince Charles and Marshal Daun, whose army had defeated Bevern at Breslau on 22 November. Frederick's army marched over 170 miles in a fortnight and met the Austrians at Leuthen on 5 December. This battle was a classic example of Frederick's methods at their best, for he first advanced towards the enemy right, which made them heavily reinforce that wing, but then behind the cover of rising ground the Prussian columns wheeled as if on a parade ground and suddenly reappeared in overwhelming force against the enemy's left wing, which was broken to fragments. Some of it recoiled into the village of Leuthen, but the Austrians reinforced that little place so thoroughly that the overcrowding was worse than it had been in Blenheim fifty-three years earlier, and the garrison had to endure a torrent of shot from the Prussian batteries. The village was taken and an Austrian attack on it broken by the terrible Prussian artillery. An attempt by the Austrian right-wing cavalry to take the Prussian infantry in flank was smashed by the cavalry of General Driesen, who then wheeled to his right and charged the Austrian infantry in the rear while General Wedel attacked them from near Leuthen. The Austrians broke and fled, with Frederick in hot pursuit, capturing more than 2,000 prisoners and taking Dresden on 19 December, its garrison of 17,000 men being all captured.

The two Battles of Rossbach and Leuthen probably did more to save Prussia from extinction than anything else, and furthermore gave the Prussians a conviction of their superiority which was ever after a source of immense inspiration to them. They also delighted the English, whose Parliament cheerfully voted an increase in the subsidy to Frederick (the grant of £164,000 was raised to £670,000 a year).

The campaigns of the remainder of the war followed much the same pattern as those of the year 1757, with the Prussian army marching desperately back and forth fighting one enemy after another, but although helped by the fact that the enemies' problems of supply made it difficult to overrun Prussia completely, the Prussian army found it increasingly difficult to replace its losses in skilled officers and N.C.O.s, and correspondingly harder to stop the country from going under. They were helped by the formation of an army paid for by the British and placed under the command of Ferdinand of Brunswick, who managed to hold up the French, so leaving Frederick to deal with only the Russians and Austrians.

Even that was too much. Frederick in 1758 cleared Silesia of the Austrians, but had to give up an attack on the town of Olmütz in Moravia because he was now too far from bases of supply. In the meantime the Russians and the Swedes invaded Pomerania, so Frederick's weary troops had once more to march to stop them. They met at the Battle of Zorndorf on 25 August, and though Frederick's army was victorious it was only at the cost of crippling losses. For the army there was no rest, because it had once more to turn back to meet another Austrian invasion of Silesia. A battle at Hochkirch duly followed on 14 October, in which the Austrians were victorious, but they failed to follow up their victory. There was at the same time the consolation of successes obtained by Ferdinand of Brunswick against the French. Ferdinand captured Minden, drove the French back over the Rhine, won another victory at Crefeld on 23 June, and although he lost a battle at Sonderhausen on 23 July against the French Duke of Broglie (Richelieu had been shelved), he managed to hold Hanover and Westphalia. By that time Bernis, the French minister in charge of foreign affairs, had grown so despondent that he was replaced by a far better man, a protégé of Madame de Pompadour, the Duke of Choiseul (1758—Choiseul received his dukedom at the same time; he was until then the Count of Stainville). This appointment was later to result in a lessening of the pressure on Frederick, which was just as well, for the year 1759 was a bad one for him.

The Austrians simply waited for Frederick to attack as usual, but the Russians under General Saltykov once more invaded Brandenburg, and after beating the Prussian general, Wedel, at Züllichau on 23 July, captured Frankfurt-an-der-Oder. Frederick was unable to prevent a small Austrian force from joining the Russians, but nevertheless attacked the combined armies at Kunersdorf on 12 August. His attacks failed completely and the Prussian army was almost wiped out of existence. The Russians could probably have finished the war and Prussia if they had wished, but instead, intensely suspicious of the Austrians, they retired. Even so, the position was desperate, for the Austrians took Dresden on 14 September, and on 21 November captured, at Naxen, a Prussian army sent against them.

The picture in the west, however, after the gloomy news of the defeat of Ferdinand of Brunswick by Broglie at Bergen on 13 April, and the subsequent capture of Minden, was much more cheering after the rout of the French by Ferdinand at the Battle of Minden on 1 August. Before that Choiseul had decided that the true interests of France were not being well served by expensive and generally calamitous attempts to fight the Prussians merely to win back Silesia for the Austrians, nor by spending enormous sums of money in subsidies to his allies. So after drastically reducing his military and financial help to the Austrians by the Third Treaty of Versailles in March 1759, Choiseul turned instead to a project for the invasion of England. This ended in utter disaster, for one French fleet was heavily defeated by Boscawen at Lagos in August and a second obliterated by Admiral Hawke at Quiberon Bay in November.

In spite of these successes of the English, Prussia was at her last gasp. Frederick managed to scrape together a force of 100,000 men for the campaign of 1760, but was heavily outnumbered by the Russians and Austrians. The latter again invaded Silesia and an army under Loudoun defeated a Prussian army under Fouquet at Landshut on 23 June, and occupied Glatz. They were joined by another Austrian army under Daun and a Russian one under Czernitcheff, and the united force attacked Frederick at Liegnitz on 15 August. Although his army of 30,000 men was outnumbered by three to one, Frederick gained the victory. While he was thus occupied, however, the Russians had sent yet another army into Brandenburg, which once more occupied Berlin for a few days in October before once again withdrawing. The Austrians also were able again to keep their hold on most of Saxony, including Dresden, in spite of Frederick's defeat of Daun at the Battle of Torgau on 3 November. Frederick was at least able by a victory against the French at Warburg to save Westphalia and Hanover from being completely overrun, but in the following year (1761) the Austrians still occupied most of Silesia and Saxony, and, although Ferdinand of Brunswick was defeated by Broglie at Gruneburg on 21 March, and the French were held up by Ferdinand's victory at Villinghausen (15 July), the situation in the east remained beyond hope, for there were simply no resources to meet any attack that the Russians should care to make.

But fortune at last favoured the brave, and without it Frederick must have succumbed, for although the appearance was of a strategic stalemate, with an annual invasion of his territories monotonously repulsed, Frederick's resources of man-power were reaching vanishing-point. The last days of 1761 saw a cruel blow for him in the resignation of the great English minister Pitt, which was soon to be followed by a slackening of

English help. Then in January 1762 came the miracle. The Tsaritsa Elizabeth of Russia died. She had been the most inveterate enemy of Prussia, partly because Frederick had personally insulted her, but also because she feared the growing power of Prussia, which she was determined to remove as a source of possible danger to Russia. With her death came a dramatic, not to say ridiculous, change in the situation. Her nephew, who followed her as the Tsar Peter III, was an unbalanced person who loathed Austria and France and worshipped Frederick, regarding him as the world's greatest hero. He at once made Russian policy do an about-turn by hastening to make a give-away peace with the delighted Frederick on 5 May. Russia restored all her conquests, merely asking for Prussian help in a war which the Tsar proposed to wage against Denmark. He had a good claim to its throne, and his desire to attack Denmark accounts for his exit from the war with Frederick as much as does his admiration for the latter. Nor was this the end of Frederick's good fortune, for the Russians persuaded the Swedes to make peace with Prussia on 22 May, while on 16 June they even supported him with troops.

In these peculiar circumstances Frederick was soon able to deal with the Austrians. Silesia was retaken after the defeat of Daun at Burkersdorf on 21 July, and Frederick's brother, Prince Henry, beat them also in Saxony at the Battle of Freiberg. Russian help ceased with the assassination of the Tsar Peter in July, but his successor, Catherine II (Catherine the Great), while not maintaining the alliance with Frederick, had no desire to fight him. The Austrians had to admit that their attempt to crush Frederick and to recover Silesia was now out of the question, and so there were few further obstacles to the making of peace.

(b) THE WAR IN THE AMERICAS AND INDIA

The Seven Years War saw much heavier fighting in the Caribbean and North America than had taken place in the period up to 1756. English policy in the former area altered somewhat too, for the English aim became increasingly to conquer the French islands rather than merely to ruin their trade—a trade whose competition was becoming ever more disastrous to the English.

At first it almost seemed as if the initiative might lie with the French, for the English direction of the war until the advent to power of

William Pitt was quite exceptionally feeble. The French produced a co-ordinated plan involving the use of three fleets in 1757: one in the West Indies, another to help in the defence of Canada, and a third to operate off North Africa, but nothing much came of it. The fleet in the West Indies soon had to go off to assist in the defence of Canada, and after that the English had it nearly all their own way in the West Indies. Obviously the best way of throttling the French in the Caribbean, and in Canada, was to blockade the French fleets in French harbours; this was done, but some line-of-battle ships occasionally slipped out, although they were never able to achieve much, and from 1757 on the French were on the defensive.

Their defence was unsuccessful. Late in 1758 the English took Goree in West Africa, and the loss of this slaving station was a disaster to the French sugar islands in the Caribbean. The next blow was the capture of Guadeloupe by the English, although it was soon difficult to tell which side was affected worse by this, as the English gave the French on the island amazingly generous terms of surrender which permitted them to trade freely with English North America as well as with London, and their output caused a big drop in the price of sugar on the English markets, to the chagrin of the planters of the English sugar islands. Pressure on the French islands eased during the latter part of 1759 and in 1760 because Pitt was concentrating his forces against the French in Canada, but the war in the Caribbean flared up again in 1761 and 1762. The French were helped by the Spaniards, who had become exasperated by the arrogant way in which English warships exercised their rights of search, and who in any case could foresee a total obliteration of French power in the Caribbean which would leave Spain to tackle the English unaided in that area. The Spaniards therefore signed another Family Compact with the French in 1761, not so much because they were anxious to fight and thus go down with the French in common ruin, but because they hoped to strengthen the French in the peace negotiations then being held. However, they promised to join in the fighting if there were no peace by May 1762, and were all the more dismayed when the English proved more difficult, not less, to deal with as a result of this treaty, and instead anticipated matters by declaring war on Spain in January 1762. The French did indeed make an effort in the West Indies and dispatched a fleet there, but it arrived too late to prevent the capture of Martinique by the English fleet under Rodney (the island was accorded the same generous surrender terms as Guadeloupe had had). So far from being able to retake Martinique, the French fleet was blockaded at Saint Domingue while the English went on to make an almost clean sweep of the remaining French islands, Dominica, Tobago, St Lucia, St Vincent, and Grenada falling in rapid succession. As for the Spaniards, they lost Havana in August 1762. Soon afterwards Manila went the same way, and by that time they were ready to give in altogether.

The war in North America opened well for the French, but ended in a disaster no less comprehensive than that in the West Indies. The Marquis of Montcalm was sent out to take command of the French forces, and a month before he sailed the English had sent out a prize pair of incompetents in the persons of Lord Loudon and General Abercrombie. Loudon spent his time contemplating, and then abandoning, projects for attacking Ticonderoga and Louisburg, while the French captured Forts Oswego and William Henry; the news in the Mediterranean was just as bad for the English because the French took Minorca, a feat to which the English could find no better reply than to shoot Admiral Byng for failing to save the island.

Those were, however, virtually the last important French successes. In 1757 the direction of the war was taken over in England by the brilliant and energetic William Pitt, who, assisted by Marshal Ligonier, soon made plans for winning the war and took care to find the right military and naval commanders to carry them out. His aim from the first was to prevent the French from being able to reinforce their overseas possessions, and this he achieved partly by giving greatly increased help to Frederick the Great, partly by distracting raids on the French coasts, but chiefly by adding enormously to the navy. The navy was thus able to blockade as well as outnumber the French fleet. Consequently the defeat of the French overseas was simply a matter of sending out enough troops to overwhelm the French, who could not be reinforced.

Pitt needed no particular insight to realize that Loudon was not the man to conquer Canada, so he replaced him by Abercrombie, whom he would have done well to sack too, and also sent out a far better man, General Amherst. The plan for 1758 was to take from the French the three pivots of their power in America, which were Louisburg, Fort Ticonderoga (on Lake Champlain), and Fort Duquesne. Louisburg's defences had been considerably strengthened, and its garrison of 3,000 troops were helped by twelve ships of the line. Amherst was able to take it in July, however, because his forces, supported by twenty-two line-of-battle ships, outnumbered the French. The gateway to the St

Lawrence was thus open to attack, but Admiral Boscawen did not think it a very safe enterprise to attack Quebec so late in the season, so nothing further was done that year. The attack on Fort Ticonderoga was entrusted to General Abercrombie. This was a flanking attack on the St Lawrence through which it was hoped to launch another attack on Quebec and afterwards Montreal. Pitt was rightly dubious of Abercrombie's abilities, so he gave him a very competent second-in-command, Lord Howe, and a more than adequate force of 6,350 Regulars and 9,000 Provincials. Even this insurance was not enough to obtain success, and in any case Abercrombie's scanty store of self-confidence evaporated when Howe was killed while reconnoitring on the shores of Lake George. Eventually Abercrombie arrived at Fort Ticonderoga, but instead of blasting it into surrender with his artillery, which he could have done with ease, ordered frontal attacks by the infantry. Seven such attacks were repulsed with losses numbering over 2,000, and when at last the retreat was sounded the troops rushed back to their boats in wild panic. The attack on Fort Duquesne was led by General Forbes, who was in poor health but did not lack determination. His force of 1,500 Regulars and 4,800 Provincials was too much for the French defenders, who burnt the fort and evacuated it, leaving Forbes to occupy it on 25 November. That at least meant that Canada lay open to an attack in the next year, and it duly came.

This was made on an even wider front. The arrangement was that General Wolfe, supported by a powerful fleet, was to move up the St Lawrence and take Quebec, another army under Amherst was to take Ticonderoga and continue from there to Montreal, while a third army under General Prideaux was to advance up the River Mohawk, clear Lake Ontario, take Fort Niagara, and so open the trade route to Lake Erie and the west. Helped by the fleet, without which the expedition could not have ascended the St Lawrence, Wolfe captured Quebec in September; he skilfully carried out a plan suggested by his subordinate generals, scaled the Heights of Abraham, and in a battle in front of Quebec annihilated the garrison which sallied forth to attack him. Both he and Montcalm were killed in this battle, and the English force was henceforth commanded by General Murray. The second force under Amherst took Forts Ticonderoga and Crown Point but could not advance farther before the winter, which also prevented Prideaux from farther advance after his capture of Niagara. There were still strong French forces at Montreal, but the shattering of the French fleets at the Battles of Lagos and Quiberon Bay and the dispersal of a French convoy meant the isolation of Canada, and in spite of a French counter-attack against Quebec the English were able to resume their inexorable forward movements in 1760. They converged on Montreal from three directions: Murray from Quebec, Haviland from Lake Champlain, and Amherst from Lake Ontario, and after some initial difficulties the campaign concluded, and with it the fighting in North America when Montreal was taken on 8 September.

The English triumph in India was no less complete. The truce there which had followed the failure of Dupleix's schemes had not extended to the Deccan, so that Bussy continued to dominate that State. The English toyed with the idea of exerting themselves to push him out of it, but instead had to divert their forces to Bengal.

The Nawab of Bengal, Siraj-ud-daulah, was a pleasure-loving youth of twenty who succeeded to the throne in April 1756 and promptly fell foul of the English at Calcutta. The English had fortified it without permission and refused to obey an order to remove some of the walls. The Nawab set out with a large force to deal with the tiny garrison, which consisted of only 264 soldiers. The English governor, Drake, hastily fled with most of the English, but left some behind. These were soon forced to capitulate (20 June 1756) and 146 of them were put that night in the notorious Black Hole of Calcutta, where 123 out of 146 failed to survive the night. At least, that is the story, although the evidence for the gruesome details is not good, and in any case the Nawab was not directly responsible for whatever it was that happened. Clive was sent with a small force to avenge the outrage. He captured Calcutta and signed a treaty with the Nawab which reconfirmed all the English privileges there. However, the Nawab intrigued with the French, and Clive, whose own behaviour throughout was just as dishonest, finally brought him to book at the Battle of Plassey on 23 June 1757, gaining an easy and almost bloodless victory (his losses amounted to eighteen killed and a few dozen wounded) over the Nawab's huge but treacherous and chicken-hearted army. One of the Nawab's generals, who had agreed to desert his master in the middle of the battle, was made Nawab in place of Siraj-ud-daulah. In effect, of course, the English became the masters of Bengal, and after the collapse of French power in Bengal, which was assured by Clive's capture of their post at Chandernagore, its resources were soon turned against the French elsewhere.

The new French general, Lally, was an able commander but could not hope to succeed against superior English naval forces and all that

that meant in isolation for himself and reinforcements for his enemies. He captured Fort St David, but the French fleet was smashed by

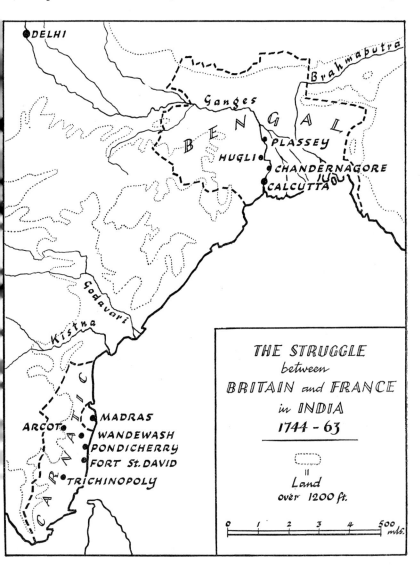

DELHI

Brahmaputra

Ganges

BENGAL

PLASSEY

HUGLI

CHANDERNAGORE

CALCUTTA

Godavari

Kistna

CARNATIC

THE STRUGGLE
between
BRITAIN and FRANCE
in INDIA
1744 - 63

Land
over 1200 ft.

ARCOT

MADRAS

WANDEWASH

PONDICHERRY

FORT St. DAVID

TRICHINOPOLY

0   1   2   3   4   500
mls.

Admiral Pocock, and soon after that more English troops arrived. Consequently Lally failed to take Madras and was decisively beaten by Sir Eyre Coote at Wandewash on 22 January 1760, and a year later

Pondicherry was captured by the English, which meant the end of French resistance in the Carnatic.

(c) *THE PEACE OF PARIS*

The Seven Years War thus ended with the failure of the allies to overthrow Frederick the Great and with total English victory in the colonial war. By the Treaty of Hubertusburg on 15 February 1763 the *status quo* was restored, with the retention of Silesia by Frederick. At the Treaty of Paris, 10 February 1763, the English atoned in some measure for their treacherous desertion of Frederick by giving up some of their colonial conquests to save him from loss of territory, although the generosity of the English was also motivated by war-weariness and a wholly mistaken notion that they might conciliate their former enemies by not imposing too hard a peace. England took Canada and all of North America east of the Mississippi, gaining Florida in exchange for Cuba, which was restored to Spain. England kept Grenada and the neutral islands, but restored Martinique, Guadeloupe, and St Lucia as well as the trading stations in West Africa, and on top of that the French were even allowed to keep fishing rights off Newfoundland (which caused disputes only finally settled in 1904). The English took back Minorca, but left the French in possession of five towns in India, which, however, could not be fortified, so leaving England as the Power of the future in India.

The Seven Years War had thus confirmed Prussia as a Great Power, though she failed to gain Saxony, and her dominions were in a state of ruin. France was likewise ruined and discredited, while the English victory was to some extent illusive, as French power could still be a menace in the West Indies. As for North America, the usual opinion was, and is, that it was a mistake to take Canada, as the danger from the French had been a powerful reason for the continuance of the loyalty of the American Colonies to the English Crown; the Americans needed English troops for their defence. As Vergennes said as early as 1763, 'Delivered from a neighbour whom they always feared, your other colonies will soon discover that they stand no longer in need of your protection.' He prophesied that the Americans would seek their independence. He was quite right, and in that they were to be helped by the French, who were burning for revenge. England's victory was more useful in India.

The heavy cost of the war made some of the European Powers the more ready to listen to the advice of the *philosophes* in the ordering of their internal affairs, as that advice aimed at improving the efficiency (and thus the power) of States. Before considering such efforts at internal reforms as were carried out by many of the States after 1763, it is appropriate to look at the ideas of the *philosophes* which were their alleged inspiration.

14 · 'The Enlightenment': the *Philosophe* Movement in the Eighteenth Century

In a previous chapter a sketch was made of the early *philosophe* movement at the end of the seventeenth century. At that time, inspired by science and several other factors, a whole host of writers and thinkers showed a strong critical tendency, and the chief target of their criticism was religion. Sometimes the attack was made obliquely in the form of travel books in which European institutions were tacitly or openly contrasted to their detriment with those of real or imaginary lands; more often, as in the works of men like Bayle or Toland, the attack was directed openly against Christianity. Nor was the attack purely destructive. While the City of God was to be torn down, it would be replaced by a secular society. Revelation was to be overthrown by Reason, which would guide Man to a life of harmony and happiness on this earth, and this happiness would grow ever greater, so ran the prevailing optimism, because science would give Man ever greater control over his material surroundings, that is, he could apply scientific knowledge to the problems of producing goods. That itself was an agreeable prospect, to say the least. Still more intoxicating was the prospect that seemed to be opened up by Locke's theory of knowledge, as set out in his *Essay Concerning Human Understanding*, the prospect, that is, of far greater control over Man himself. Locke seemed to have made more than a start at the work of mapping the human intellect, and from that it did not appear to be too far a cry to reduce human psychology to a science as precise and clear, and as accurate, as the scientific laws of Locke's great source of inspiration, Newton. Hence could be found laws of human life, laws of morals, politics, education, justice, economics, and so on, which could make the perfect society and bring about the perfectibility of Man.

This trend of thought, the *philosophe* movement, also called the 'Enlightenment', was to become, aided by further progress in scientific knowledge, far more powerful in the eighteenth century than it had been in the latter half of the seventeenth. The ideas were spread by a few very great writers and a much larger number of lesser ones, and the diffusion of their notions was helped in France at least by the protection they received from a few very powerful individuals such as Madame de Pompadour, by the fashionable *salons* of ladies of rank, and by an increasing number of scientific societies. The influence of the writers (it is usual to refer to them as the *philosophes*, for since scarcely one of them was a philosopher in any ordinary sense of that word, it is better to leave it in its French form as meaning writers spreading notions inspired by science) was enormous in the political field. A note of caution should, however, be sounded; it would be false to claim that influence as being paramount in politics, and downright ridiculous to suppose that the eighteenth century saw Europe filled with cool, sceptical devotees of Reason, devoid of passion and of faith.

This is not intended as a history of science, so one or two brief examples will suffice to serve as a bare indication of some of the progress of science in the eighteenth century. The Frenchman Georges-Louis Leclerc de Buffon gained a reputation hardly second to Newton's (Catherine the Great said that he had made the second step forward, whereas Newton had made the first) by his publication of his *Histoire Naturelle* in 1749. His step was in a somewhat different direction, though, for he proclaimed his opinion that mathematics were too abstract and suffered from being all drawn from propositions of our own devising ('There is therefore nothing in that science but what we ourselves have put there'), and he instead preferred a pure empiricist observation of external facts, which give us 'concrete proof'. If he was aiming at Newton, such a statement seems like a travesty of the great Englishman's work, for Newton looked at plenty of facts and then reasoned about them mathematically, but Buffon's attitude must have been a comfort to many who were eager to learn some science but who found mathematics too difficult. Buffon overdid the collecting of facts, and over-ambitiously tried to grasp the whole of Nature in one great system. But he proved vastly stimulating. He classified plants and animals, and, tireless in his endeavour to provide a complete description of the whole natural world, went on to the physical environment of the animal kingdom, at the centre of which is Man; rivers, seas, marshes, volcanoes, and the rocks beneath us all came under his survey. It was really too much, but at least he is interesting as adumbrating the idea of evolution. To his contemporaries he seemed the personification of the spirit of science, and he became the most honoured man in Europe; people wrote poetry to him and raised up statues in his honour.

He was also paid the flattery of imitation, although of course he was not the sole creator of the contemporary mania for exploring the marvels of nature. The great work of Linnaeus, *Systema naturae*, a work which made huge strides forward in the classification of plants, appeared in 1735. Maupertius's house was a positive menagerie; Abraham Trembley cut up aquatic plants; and Réaumur went one better by cutting up worms, while Spallanzani gave the same treatment to snails; their astonishment at what they observed about the life of these creatures was equalled by that of Charles Bonnet when contemplating the green fly. Some of this work embodied a true application of the scientific method, especially important being the stress on classification. Valuable work was also done in horticulture, for instance in investigating pollination and hybridization. Chemistry, however, still remained in the doldrums until the publication of Lavoisier's *Traité élémentaire de chimie* in 1789. Before then the most interesting theory of the German, Stahl, concerning combustion, postulating an inflammable principle which he called 'phlogiston', turned out to be valueless; but the Scottish chemist, Joseph Black, made a useful advance with his discovery of 'fixed air'[1] in 1735. Medical knowledge made little progress, but more accurate scientific instruments kept on appearing. There was little harm to religion in most of this, apart from the fact that an interest in science took the place of an interest in religion for many people. The case was very different with geological discoveries (in which Buffon played a big part) because the ages of rocks made it impossible to take literally the date of the Creation worked out from the Book of Genesis, and this resulted in furious controversy.

So much (or rather so little) for the progress of science in the eighteenth century. It continued to play an increasingly important part in

---

[1] This really means gases fixed in substances as solids; it was an important advance because until then no gases had been clearly described as distinct in species from common air.

that European mental revolution whose origins have been discussed in Chapter 6, and which gathered force as the eighteenth century grew older. It is impossible to say with any sort of certitude whether science exercised the chief influence in that revolution before about 1730, but after that, when Newtonian science and Lockian philosophy crossed the Channel into France, it almost certainly did.

The most important writings of that revolution appeared after 1730, so a glance at some which appeared before that date can be brief.

The briefer the glance at the work of the Curé Meslier, who took good care that it did not appear during his lifetime (he died in 1727), the better. His *Testament* seemed to contain startling blasphemies; he raved at religion and at God Himself. But in reality he was, in the name of the God of the New Testament, protesting at social wrongs. More worthy of note, and certainly infinitely more influential, were the writings, chief among which were the *Lettres juives* ('Jewish Letters') and *Philosophie de bon sens*, of the Marquis d'Argens (1704–71). He was not a great writer, but his books were very popular. The title of the latter-named one gives the key to his attitude: he preached a common-sense philosophy which had no use for metaphysical speculations. Despising prayers as useless, he thought that good and useful action was preferable, and he particularly disliked monks, fanaticism, and intolerance. He was not an atheist, and believed in God and the immortality of the soul, though he was not too much concerned about either, his chief aim being the attainment of a somewhat placid and unexciting happiness. Neither did he concern himself much with politics, though he expressed a vague preference for a benevolent despotism. Hardly in the same anti-religious vein, but expressing rather a critical spirit just as typical of the times, were two other famous works. One was by the misanthropic Jonathan Swift; his *Gulliver's Travels* (1726) is a sour attack not only on institutions but on the whole human race. The other was Gay's *The Beggar's Opera* (1728), aimed (indirectly) at governments and the upper classes generally.

The times saw also no lessening of the spate of works ostensibly dealing with far-off climes and with Utopias; the Wise Chinese, Turks, and Hurons jostled each other for a share of public attention; needless to say, these, as well as the only slightly more imaginary 'Agoians' and 'Philadelphoi', not to speak of the denizens of the 'Island of Women Warriors', were trotted out to criticize everything in Europe. The most famous of these books gave the palm for wisdom to the Persians. This was the *Lettres Persanes*, written by Charles de Secondat, Baron de Montesquieu (1689–1755), and it appeared in 1721. He was a member of the legal nobility, and was later to win enduring fame with his *L'Esprit des Lois*. In the meantime, his *Persian Letters* brought him notice enough. They poured scorn on miracles, superstition, intolerance, and the authority of the Pope, all of which were subjected to a scrutiny in the light of Reason, and all of which were condemned. When touching political matters, however, Montesquieu was less audacious; he attacked upstarts, intriguers, financiers (Law's schemes had just collapsed), and shady gentry of that sort, but made only scanty references to the origin of societies, the rights of Man, forms of government, and so on, although he was to return to these themes in 1748. The chief importance of the *Persian Letters* is, then, that they dealt very roughly with obedience and tradition.

The *philosophe* movement became more important, bolder, and more influenced by science than ever before in the 1730s, and found writers of greater stature to champion it.

Until about 1730 the scientific system to which the French gave their allegiance was that of Descartes. But many were beginning to wonder if Newton's system was not to be preferred to Descartes's vortices. The balance was decisively tipped in favour of Newton by two, or rather three, works. The first was the *Discours sur la figure des astres*, published in 1732, and written by Maupertius. The others were far more influential, and came from a pen that was to produce fifteen million words, the pen of Voltaire (1694–1778).

Voltaire had been obliged to leave France after a quarrel in which he was greatly wronged by a member of the nobility, and he landed in England in May 1726. It is often said that the Age of Reason may be dated from that moment, for though, as we have seen, the new mental outlook was born in the seventeenth century, its influence was still nothing like so wide as it became in the eighteenth. It owed its diffusion more to Voltaire than to any other single writer. He was the perfect popularizer, with a beautifully clear style and a merciless wit which assured him a huge public. Voltaire was enraptured by everything he found in England (with the exception of the climate). He was given the complete *entrée* to polite society, and he found to his delight that the aristocracy was useful and that the middle classes were flourishing and often cultured as well; better still, he found a degree of civil liberty which was totally lacking in France, which nevertheless did not lead to confusion and inefficiency; and, best of all, a toleration in religion which, contrary to the view then general on the Continent, did not lead to the abandonment of morality. Last, he found the science of Newton and the philosophy of John Locke, which together provided an irrefutable basis for toleration and liberty.

He went home after a very happy stay in England, and his *Lettres philosophiques* appeared in 1734 (the English version, *Letters on the English*, had been published in the previous year). His picture of England came as a revelation to a wide public in France, but the work was also an attack on Descartes and a defence of the science of Newton. Voltaire clinched the argument as far as most Frenchmen were concerned with his next work on this theme, *Éléments de la philosophie de Newton*, which was published in 1738. After that Newton and Locke enjoyed an enormous popularity in France, and it was not long before many French writers were trying to draw what they thought were the logical conclusions of the thought of those two masters—to find, that is, the rules for perfection in social matters, in politics, in law, the administration of justice, education, and economics.

Voltaire was far from being merely a popularizer of Locke and Newton, brilliant though he was in that role. He took Reason as his guide, and soon all Europe knew, from the pen of one of the finest writers of a country which has produced so many literary geniuses, where Reason led one of the clearest heads of the century. He was an important writer from about 1730 onwards, but it took him some years before he became *le roi Voltaire*, king of the world of letters, and in his earlier works he did not risk offending religious susceptibilities too much and his language was restrained. Nevertheless Reason led him to Deism. In *Letters on the English* he hints that all religions have some value, but he dislikes mystical fervours, casts doubts on miracles, and as against the theologians comes down in favour of those who observe and experiment, of Bacon, Locke, and Newton. Inspired by Locke, he vigorously preached toleration and attacked fanaticism in works like the *Henriade* (a eulogy of King Henry IV of France, who had issued the tolerant Edict of Nantes in 1598), and *Mahomet*; and substituted for an intolerant religion and a belief in Providentialism his own emphasis on a human morality and human responsibility, and he derided the teleology of such writers as Pluche, for whom God's care over the human race included tides created to help shipping. He preached therefore a lay morality which saw no harm in the pursuit of happiness and in which virtue consisted of helping one's fellow-men.

After about 1748 Voltaire's attacks on the Church became far more violent. In his *Essai sur les mœurs et l'esprit des nations* he appeared as a deadly enemy of intolerance, which he thought the biggest cause of war and suffering. He lost his optimism with the great earthquake disaster at Lisbon, but in his *Le désastre de Lisbonne* and *La loi naturelle* he kept up his hostility to providential, and his belief in natural, religion, if in *Candide* he demolished with sad but amusing irony the case for optimism. The Catholic Church became for him the 'infamous thing' to be crushed; *écrasez l'infâme* became his watchword. 'Like Cato,' he wrote, 'I always end my harangue by saying *Delenda est Carthago.*' But he gave up his search for universal truths and universal remedies for universal ills. In his later years he tirelessly poured forth his intelligence and his money to try to reduce if only in small measure the frightful total of human misery, more especially by defending the victims of religious cruelty. He championed victims of the Church and of a barbaric system of justice, such as the Chevalier de la Barre, who was beheaded for sacrilege in 1766, and the Protestant Calas, who was condemned to be broken on the wheel because of an unproved accusation that he had killed his son so as to prevent him from becoming a Catholic (1762). Voltaire thus preached equality before the law, civil liberty and freedom of discussion, and bitterly attacked the use of torture in judicial proceedings; in this he was influenced by the book *Dei delitti e delle pene* (1764) (*Concerning crime and punishment*) by the famous Italian, Beccaria (1738–94), a book which had immense influence, as well as by the spirit of toleration taught by Locke.

Voltaire thus exposed, in a manner that proved deadly to them, two of the biggest flaws in the Old Régime—religious intolerance and barbaric justice. He was the most important propagandist of the age in preaching toleration and a humane legal system, and also the use of Reason as a guide to all human affairs. He was the most important propagandist of the science of Newton and the philosophy of Locke. But it might well be asked how he applied all this to politics. The somewhat disappointing truth is that he said very little about politics. He was certainly no democrat, as he often referred to the ordinary people as 'la canaille' (rabble), and his preference as regards forms of government was for a benevolent despotism strong enough to carry out reforms. He did not even attack feudal dues; indeed he owned some himself. More than that; he had a flat in the royal palace at Versailles (thanks to the influence of his friend, Madame de Pompadour), and his strong wish to shine at court was frustrated only by his own lack of tact. He is often regarded as a precurser of the French Revolution, but this view is only correct inasmuch as his work had certain subversive tendencies, of which the chief victims were two very old institutions, the Church and the *parlements* (the latter because of their corrupt and barbaric judicial methods), but of course an attack on the Church would not help rulers who sheltered behind theories of Divine Right.

If Voltaire's writings had little direct political influence, very different was the chief work of Montesquieu. After the success of his *Lettres persanes* Montesquieu spent years composing his masterpiece, *L'Esprit des Lois* ('The Spirit of the Laws') which was published in 1748. This might well be regarded as one of the most important books ever written, for it not only had an immense influence in France but has also greatly influenced many of the States' constitutions of the U.S.A. (a notable exception being the Constitution of Pennsylvania); and the American Federal Constitution, under which is now governed the strongest and richest country on earth, was directly inspired by it. The influences on Montesquieu himself were twofold: a very wide reading of history, and the English constitution of the day as studied by him in a personal visit to England, and still more as understood by him after reading Locke. It was a great treatise on social science, an attempt to apply Locke's philosophy to legal and political problems.

The book is remarkable for two things. The first is that it says that laws are not in themselves absolutely just or unjust, but are good if they succeed and evil if they fail, and furthermore their appropriateness depends on local conditions, on climate, geography, and local customs. In this Montesquieu was far more profound than most of the *philosophes*, who hoped for simple Newtonian laws in social matters, applicable to all places and all times. What is significant about this point too is that Montesquieu is sanctioning the divorce between Natural Law and God's Law. The other remarkable thing about the book is that Montesquieu, anxious to find a constitution which would protect the scientific right to investigate, which would secure, that is, personal liberty in the Lockian sense of freedom from restraint, advocated, as the best way to preserve liberty, a constitution of which the outstanding characteristic was the separation of the three branches of government, the separation of the powers of the legislature, executive, and judiciary. That, then, was his method of securing political liberty, a method by which the three branches of government would divide power and none be powerful enough to tyrannize over the others, but in which each of the three parts would be strong enough to maintain itself against the others, 'le pouvoir arrête le pouvoir'. In that state of affairs the liberty of the individual would be preserved.

His practical proposals concerning this are briefly as follows. The executive power was to be in the hands of a king, who would, however, have a limited legislative power himself, that is, he could veto laws suggested by the legislative body, for 'if the executive power has not the right of checking the enterprises of the legislative body that body will become despotic for it can give itself all the power it needs to annihilate all other powers' (that is, without the right of veto the executive could be voted out of existence by the legislature). On the other hand, the legislature was to be given powers to check an over-strong executive by the right to supervise and, if needs be, punish, the ministers, and also by having the sole right to vote taxes—if it did not have this latter right especially, the executive would become too strong, for, says Montesquieu, the voting of taxes is the most important part of a legislature's functions; the most important laws are fiscal laws. As for the judiciary, their powers, too, could become too great, for they could end up by effectually nullifying every act of both the executive and the legislature, so he favoured checking this danger by not giving judicial power to a permanent body of men but to people drawn from the people 'for as long as necessity requires'; that is, by election. Further significant recommendations are that the legislative body should be divided into an Upper and a Lower House, the point of which is still further to protect the liberty of the individual, and, more important, to give the distinguished class in a nation political power in proportion to their real power, as 'there is always in a State [a class] . . . distinguished by birth, riches and honour who will have no interest in defending it if they are sunk into the common will'. So members of the Upper House would have the right to be tried by their own assembly to protect them from popular malice, and, he adds, they are the obvious ones to conduct the trial of a minister encroaching on the powers of the legislature as the Lower House, being the injured party, can only act as the accuser.

As further safeguards of liberty he also recommended habeas corpus and trial by jury.

It is usual to advance two famous criticisms of Montesquieu's great work. One is that he was not really so genuinely concerned about liberty as about the selfish interests of his own class. He, as President of the *parlement* of Bordeaux, was an important member of the Nobility of the Robe, and was thus in effect attacking the monarchy in the interests of that class—his recommendations would if carried out, have much increased the strength of his class *vis-à-vis* the king, but on the other hand he was not interested in anybody else's liberty for he certainly defended feudal rights. Much of the book was perhaps written as a refutation of a book by the Abbé Dubos (*Histoire critique de l'établissement de la monarchie française*, 1734, a defence of the king's absolute power). All one can say about that criticism is that few writers can preserve a total detachment from their own interests, and in any case nobody, even if it had been suggested, could realistically claim that France was fit for democracy in 1748.

The second criticism stems from the fact that Montesquieu's notions of the separation of powers were copied from the English Constitution of the time, and it is often said that, because of the growth of the Cabinet system, the separation of powers no longer existed in England; he was thus basing his system not on proved observed facts, as he thought, but on a myth. As to that, two observations will suffice. In the first place, Montesquieu did not claim that English liberty even existed, but that 'it is established by her laws, and I do not search beyond that'; in other words, he was only claiming to be describing the forms of the constitution, not the actual practice, and his description is not therefore so far wrong. In the second place, it is more than dubious that the separation of powers had nearly disappeared in the England of his day. The King was in fact very much the head of the executive, and the existence of the British Cabinet of the time no more disproved the separation of powers than that of the American Cabinet does now. Members of Parliament in the eighteenth century for the most part, on the other hand, had nothing to fear from the executive, which was why the only way the executive could get anything done was to bribe them, and even that did not work always, as Walpole's various surrenders to parliamentary pressure show. The truth is that the first time the Prime Minister of England owed his position not in the least to the monarch but to a parliamentary majority which he could genuinely control, so ending the separation of powers, was in the 1840s, and the Prime Minister in question was Sir Robert Peel. Montesquieu was therefore a better observer of the British Constitution than some of his later critics.

If there can be disagreement about Montesquieu's accuracy as an observer, there can surely be none about the importance of his work. He set the fashion for political discussion in France; people had hitherto for the most part prudently refrained from discussing politics, and his book was terribly damaging to the Old Régime which postulated an absolute monarchy as coming from the will of God. His hatred of despotism and clericalism, his demand for toleration and for the reform of taxation and of the system of justice, based as they seemed to be on science and the irrefutable Locke, were eagerly taken up by the other *philosophes* and by a wide public. Many of his notions were actually embodied in the French Constitution of 1791. The trouble was that they were also seized on by the French *parlements*, who used them against the monarchy purely for their own selfish ends. The fathers of the American Constitution borrowed from him the idea of a written constitution based on a law of nature and on the separation of powers. If 'President' is substituted for 'King' the debt of the American Constitution to Montesquieu becomes obvious, and that difference is one of name, for the powers of a modern President of the U.S.A. approximate to the powers of George III; he has been called a 'fossilized George III' because his powers have not shrunk as have the powers of English kings. In its most central features, then, the American Constitution is a fair copy of the British Constitution of the eighteenth century as seen through the eyes of Montesquieu.

After 1748 the number of writings preaching the new moral, political, educational, and economic doctrines derivable from Locke greatly increased. Indeed, the same year that saw the publication of Montesquieu's *L'Esprit des Lois* saw the appearance of another well-read book, *Les Mœurs*. Its author was not a great writer, but he was very popular at the time—among his readers, that is, for François-Vincent Toussaint was the first of the *philosophes* who was forced to flee from the country. His book is an exposition of that humanitarian and lay morality so dear to all the *philosophes*, and refuses any credit to authority or to faith, its author expressing faith only in Reason. Virtue is obedience to the dictates of Reason ('Qu'est-ce que la vertue? C'est la fidélité constante à remplir les obligations que la raison nous dicte.'). Man, he says, seeks happiness, and can only find it in the satisfaction of his passions (an echo of Locke's praise of the passions as being the driving-force of action), and passions are not evil, but 'good, useful, and necessary'. Toussaint's praise of the passions did not mean that he was in favour of wild passionate outbursts, for, he said, happiness is only attainable if one showed moderation and humanity, one must think of others: 'To love men and to treat them with goodness, considering them only in their simple condition of men, and not for the love of God, that is true humanity.' That is, one should be good to others because one owes it to their humanity and not because charitable behaviour is ordered by the Scriptures. This is the new religion of Fraternity.

Locke's ideas were next given further popularity by a work written by Étienne Bonnot de Condillac (1715–80). Condillac was a priest who did more to upset belief in the Christian doctrine of Original Sin than any other man in eighteenth-century France. Locke had said that all knowledge was derived from the senses. Condillac in his *Traité des sensations* (1754) pushed this notion further, and set out to show that even the power of reflection itself was nothing but transformed sensation. This was a genuine revolution in human thought which had momentous consequences. It followed that men were born neither good nor bad, but simply neutral, blank sheets whose character was built up solely by experience. Hence the divine gift of Grace meant nothing, while human methods of education were everything. To improve people, it would merely be necessary to improve their environment, and thus the perfectibility of Man seemed to be around the corner; this meant, naturally, that men could now feel a far bigger sense of mastery over their destinies than had ever appeared possible before; and with this feeling was born a new sort of optimism and a new sort of belief in progress. Condillac seemed to have proved scientifically and beyond doubt that Reason and Science could make perfect men in a perfect society.

This was thus a positive creed, something positive to be added to the rather negative scepticism of writers like Bayle, and it was chiefly this, and further deductions made from it, that distinguished the eighteenth-century *philosophes* from their seventeenth-century forerunners. One evident deduction was of course that the doctrines of the Church were only the result of fallible and accidental experience, and this meant yet another blow to religion. It was also an argument in favour of equality, since one blank sheet equals any other blank sheet. The same argument could lead just as well to democracy, for Man can be made not only equal to any of his fellows, but also perfect. The belief in progress led also to a disdain for old institutions like the Church and the monarchy which depended on tradition and authority, for if we are going to keep on getting better it is no virtue in any institution to be old, and this led eventually to a contempt for history as well. Later in the century this helped to turn many from their admiration for the old English Constitution (which Sieyès called a 'Monument of Gothic Superstition'). Condillac's book became the favourite bedside reading of the other *philosophes*. (It should hardly be necessary to point out here that belief in progress, democracy, equality, or anything else, cannot be upheld by quoting Condillac, unless one chooses to ignore the whole of the more recently developed science of Biology, which *inter alia* points out the importance of hereditary factors.)

Two writers were quick to seize on and to develop the ideas of Condillac. The first was Claude-Adrien Helvétius (1715–71), whose most important book, *De l'Esprit*, appeared in 1758. He stressed the point that at birth a person's mind is simply a *tabula rasa* (a smoothed or blank tablet), and his character is built up by education (by which Helvétius meant all his experience as well as schooling). In Man, he said, there was only one constituent, that is, sensitive matter, which is exactly the same in quality in everyone, but which is made different by different experiences, and which disappears at death. The matter is sensitive only to sensations of pleasure and pain, with the result that men can only be led by the prospect of reward or punishment. Thus self-interest, more or less enlightened, is the single key to any moral system, and it followed that goodness could only be whatever led to happiness, the greater the number being made happy the better. So sound virtue was whatever led to the greatest happiness of the greatest number (a notion later taken up and developed by the English Radicals, of whom the most famous was Bentham).

Helvétius is thus saying that he has found a single, scientific, Newtonian law for human psychology, on which wonderful things could be built. By merely improving education, it would be possible to carry on indefinitely with the improvement of men; there were no fools and no geniuses at birth, simply the same matter, which could be affected in any way by changing its experiences and environment. Secondly, he has now provided law-makers with the key they need, which is to provide the right pains and rewards; so a perfect system of laws becomes possible, and since the laws under which we live are a very important part of our environment, to provide the right laws is itself a big step towards the provision of the right education, in the wide sense, and so towards perfecting Man. 'It is certain,' he said, 'that great men, who now appear by chance, will in the future be produced by the legislature; by really good education they can be infinitely multiplied.' He did not take these notions far into the field of practical politics, however, and even then did not carry the obvious democratic implications of his doctrines to their logical limits, for he was not in favour of granting the vote to the poor and the ignorant, who in actual fact have not had the good fortune to have had the sort of upbringing that he had in mind, and could not be expected to consider wisely. Much more surprising, he also argued that men need a religion, and he favoured the Christianity of the Gospels.

The same basic belief in materialism, that is, that we are made out of sensitive matter, was used by Paul-Henri, Baron d'Holbach (1723–89), in a way that appalled even most of his *philosophe* colleagues, and his book, *Le vrai sens du Système de la Nature*, which appeared in 1770, brought its author considerable notoriety. Holbach made the most violent attack on Christianity, which he denounced as 'un tissu d'absurdités, de dogmes insensés, de cérémonies puériles'. All religions he held to be false, for in the world there only exists matter endowed with feeling; sensations felt by matter create what is called thought, which he equated with the soul, so when the body comes to an end so must the soul likewise, and therefore all religions that teach of immortality, or even of God, are 'lies'. From this one might be tempted to suppose that it would be a waste of time to teach any moral system, but Holbach contradicts himself; few men, he thought, are ruled by Reason, and the majority needed to be led by some sort of moral system, and even by some sort of religion. So the State would have to manufacture a religion for them. It would not resemble other religions, though, for it would teach self-evident truths designed only for the happiness of mankind.

Holbach's views on politics were much more violent than his ideas about religion, and kings and all institutions he denounced with even less respect than he showed to Christianity. Following, and going further than Locke, he held that all government is the fruit of a pact made between rulers and ruled, so that 'society always remains mistress of sovereignty, the power of the monarch remains always subordinate to that of the representatives of the people, and these representatives depend always on the will of their constituents'. He thus grants the right of revolt in a much more sweeping way than Locke did, but again in practice he had doubts about the suitability of democracy except in very small communities at certain places and in certain times. His preference in a very large country like France in the circumstances of the eighteenth century was for a benevolent despotism (he later addressed Louis XVI as 'a just and humane monarch, the father of his people'), so one must be left to suppose that he was aiming more against the dominance of the Catholic Church than against political despotism in France, and what he wanted was perfect liberty for a cultural *élite* while a kindly king ruled the masses for their own good.

Of all the so-called *philosophes* in France, the two who came nearest to deserving the title of 'philosopher' in the proper meaning of the word were Condillac, about whom something has already been said, and Denis Diderot (1713–84). Diderot was not only one of the chief *philosophes* in his capacity of editor of their great joint work, the *Encyclopédie*, but a considerable scientist in his own right who foreshadowed the theory of evolution. However, nothing of his purely scientific work mattered at the time; his contemporary influence was that of a prophet of the lay and humanitarian morality and as an enemy of fanaticism and superstition. He taught that man is naturally good and that only an evil religion has made us believe otherwise. But, he said, we cannot be happy if we are selfish because that leads to strife, and besides we have a natural need of affection which others will not give us unless we treat them properly. He was thus one of the architects of the new religion of virtue. Not all the *philosophes* reached his moral heights in this respect; for instance, Morelly taught that it was good to seek happiness but also to obey one's passions. He thus carried Locke's high opinion of the passions as the mainspring of action to a point that would have embarrassed Locke himself, and made remarks like: 'To enjoy oneself is to honour God, so let us enjoy ourselves; He orders it!' So morality became 'the science of social good', but since it was a tall order to bring happiness to all mankind at once, the humanitarian morality became narrowed to concern for the French 'citizen'—an entity whose existence had been unsuspected in the reign of Louis XIV.

Emphasis on the passions was made by a far more important writer, Jean-Jacques Rousseau (1712–78), and that to such an extent that it becomes difficult to class him as belonging to the *philosophe* movement at all. He came of poor parents and lived the life of a vagabond, with brief and usually unsuccessful attempts to earn an honest living, and was often fortunate to find some kind woman to befriend him. His life story is contained in one of the frankest autobiographies ever written (his *Confessions*), and it does nothing much to induce admiration in the reader; he was a liar, a bad and faithless friend, not above occasional theft, and he abandoned all his children in their infancy. He was, however, very proud that his heart was a warm one; it may have been, and he was certainly abnormally sensitive.

He was indeed different from the other *philosophes*. They taught the great value of the intellect and of science in bringing about happiness and material progress; Rousseau admitted this was very likely, but he hated civilization and material progress, which he regarded as corrupters of mankind. To him, natural Man was only happy in an original savage, utterly simple, and nomadic life; even the growing of wheat had brought nothing but misery. In the natural state, however, Man was not only happy and contented, but good. Most of the *philosophes* could agree with that last adjective, but Voltaire at least had his doubts about the argument, for he told Rousseau after reading the latter's *Discourse on Inequality* (1755), 'One longs, in reading your book, to walk on all fours, but as I have lost that habit for more than sixty years I feel unhappily the impossibility of resuming it.' Rousseau realized quite well that one could not destroy civilization, but he taught that one could at least love one's fellow-men. He was the apostle of the emotions, and his novel, *La Nouvelle Héloïse*, which appeared in 1760, took society by storm. At that time plenty of people were becoming a little bored with Reason, and many more thoroughly enjoyed his romantic treatment of love; in his 'sensibility' (to use the eighteenth-century word for response to the emotions), and in his appeal to the heart, he filled a huge gap which the other *philosophes* had left, although it should be said that they too knew that Reason could only mean much to a small number and that the majority needed a moral and emotional 'education' rather than pure Reason. Therefore they did not for the most part regard his work with hostility, but more as something complementary to their own, which is another reason for regarding him as a *philosophe*. This appeal to the emotions, which was so immensely popular, had two main results. One, with which we are not greatly concerned here, is that it provided one of the chief impulses causing the Romantic Movement in literature. The other was that it was in great measure thanks to Rousseau that everyone became aware of what so many of the other *philosophes* had said less effectively, that is, that Man is not naturally wicked, only miserable, that Man needed pity and love, and that social and political reforms needed to be based on a feeling of Fraternity.

The same sentimental attitude was applied by Rousseau in an equally successful book to problems of education and religion. His *Émile* (1762) is a very long account of his notions about education, and it puts forward the view that children, being naturally good, should be brought up with kindness and in an atmosphere of freedom; and in this his influence has been wide and beneficial to the present day. His views on religion were expressed in an interlude in the fourth book of *Émile*, an interlude which he called 'The confession of faith of a Savoyard Vicar.' Rousseau believed profoundly in God, but his reasons for doing so were based entirely on the heart—not the head, as had until his time been usual in everyone with the least intellectual pretensions. His chief reason was in the beauty of the Creation, and in what he called the voice of Nature in its promptings to his heart. This has been popular ever since his time, but it is unsatisfactory to the extent that there is no way whatsoever of proving that the promptings of the heart correspond to anything about God.

In his other great work, *Du contrat social*, which appeared in the same year as *Émile*, Rousseau showed himself just as concerned about liberty as were all the other *philosophes*. The book, however, had practically no influence before the French Revolution, or indeed before about 1793;

it was very little read and was regarded by Rousseau himself as merely a fragment of a much bigger work (which he never wrote). But it became the Bible of the Jacobins in the French Revolution, and its influence since then has been so enormous that a few words about it may be said here.

The book was a valiant attempt to square the circle, for Rousseau passionately believed in two incompatibles. The first was liberty, which to him was of absolute importance, not to be diminished in any way. He held that Man is not Man at all unless he is utterly free; slavery, he said, is contrary to Nature, to renounce liberty is to give up being a man at all. The second was the absolute value of some sort of social order, based on the sacred laws of Nature, and since rules and order mean we have to obey, that means an infringement of the equally important liberty. He was therefore determined to reconcile the two. That is what he meant in his famous opening statement that Man is born free but is everywhere in chains, hates living under the rules of society; and he sets out to find rules which shall yet leave us as free as if they did not exist.

He thought he had succeeded. The solution lay in a social pact or contract, to which everyone should adhere. By this, everyone, without exception, surrendered all his rights to the community, what he called the total alienation of each associate, together with all his rights, to the whole community. The argument then is that each man, in giving himself to all, gives himself to nobody, and the conditions being the same for everybody, nobody has any interest in making them burdensome for others. This is to say that if all agree to obey the laws everyone will still be free because the laws are all of their own making, and since they will have to be obeyed by everyone, nobody will want to make unpleasant laws as the maker of such laws would have to obey them himself. Society will thus be ruled by what he called the 'General Will'. This is a rather more obscure notion, but is the essence of the social contract then made (everything else not being important). He explains the General Will as the sum total of everyone's public-spirited desires, which he carefully separates from their private and purely selfish desires. If that means anything at all, it is something as follows: if, say, ten people all have a public-spirited desire that will be their General Will, while any selfish desires they might have form no part of the General Will. From this it follows that if only, say, two of them have a public-spirited desire and the other eight have only selfish desires, then the General Will of the whole of such a little community is to be found only in the two persons and not at all in the other eight. From this it follows that in a State composed of a majority of selfish persons the General Will is not the will of the selfish majority but of the public-spirited minority. So anyone refusing to obey the General Will must be forced to obey it—shall be 'forced to be free'. That follows, because one can only be free under the social contract, of which the essence is the General Will.

All this might sound like an argument in favour of democracy, and so perhaps it is. But it is also the basis for a totalitarian dictatorship, for the State will not in Rousseau's system allow any association of men other than the original contract, that is, in effect, that things like trade unions, churches, or political parties, or even organizations like the Boy Scouts will all be forbidden because they are the embodiment of sectional desires—forbidden, that is, unless they all are controlled by the State. That is the totalitarian side of it. As for dictators, nothing is easier than for them to proclaim that they and they alone embody the General Will, everybody else only having selfish, unpatriotic, or non-public-spirited desires. They can claim this, and still of course call it a democracy; what could be more democratic than the General Will? It thus made possible the mystic association of the dictator with all his people without troubling about such matters as a ballot-box (they have 'elections' in dictatorships sometimes, but the voters daring to vote the wrong way find themselves 'forced to be free'). This frightful idea was the basis of the dictatorship of Robespierre in the French Revolution, and was in part the basis of the dictatorships in Russia under Stalin and in Germany under Hitler, not to speak of the Italy of Mussolini. It also appears to be what the Russians still mean when they talk about democracy; no wonder people in the West, who get their own notions of liberty from Locke and from Montesquieu, and of democracy from such things as the present American Constitution, find it confusing.

To be fair to Rousseau, it should be pointed out that he would almost certainly, as the prophet of love, sentiment, and fraternity, have been horrified by twentieth-century dictatorships. His work has in fact been used to support all sorts of widely differing political opinions. Believers in modern democratic systems, however, are not justified in supporting their views by quoting him, for he believed only in direct democracy, that is, in every citizen directly voting for each single law, and said that 'every law the people has not ratified in person is null and void—in fact is not a law'. He thought representative government an absurdity, and for that reason held that democracy is only possible in a very small State.

While the fields of morals, religion, laws, and politics were being scrutinized by the *philosophes*, who produced from their examination of these by the light of Science and Reason, a belief in Deism, in natural and humanitarian morality, in equality before just and humane laws, in religious toleration, in progress, in the perfectibility of Man by education, in liberty and fraternity, and even, although they mostly thought reforms could best be carried out by a benevolent despot, in some sharing of the political control of the State by at least some sections of the community, another group of *philosophes* was busy subjecting economic life to the same scientific scrutiny. This was the group who came to be called the 'Physiocrats'.

There had already, as a result of the high and unfair taxation, of the mercantilist restrictions, and of the sheer misery brought by endless wars, been a considerable amount of criticism directed at the way in which the economic life of France was run. For instance, Marshal Vauban had suggested a fairer system of taxes; while at the same time soore original thinkers such as Boisguillebert (who died in 1714) showed more signs of early physiocratic tendencies—Boisguillebert thought that just as there were laws in the physical world, so there must be in the economic, and that goods should be kept circulating briskly in a healthy society just as water should not be left stagnant. There would therefore in any case have been considerable criticism of the economic conditions prevailing under the Old Régime, but thanks to science that criticism took what the critics, at least, imagined was a scientific turn.

In 1755 Cantillon's *Essai du Commerce* did for economics what Voltaire's *Letters on the English* had done for 'philosophy'; that is, it summarized English, and in particular Locke's, views on property and economic liberty and presented them to the French public. Other writers concerned themselves with demanding liberty to sell corn in any part of France (it was only permissible to sell it locally, in case local famines might result). However, it was after the publication of Montesquieu's *L'Esprit des Lois* in 1748 that there came a great outburst of economic discussion, and by 1760 a distinct group of Physiocrats was formed.

These deliberately applied the scientific view that there must also be a natural order in economics, that the world of production and distribution of goods must obey strict laws. These laws would, moreover, be even more easy to discover than those of Newton had been, for, as Mercier, one of the Physiocrats, argued, we are perfectly simple creatures who obey the call of pleasure and avoid pain, and this simple tendency would lead us to happiness, and, being capable of reflection, we can see easily that it is not in our interest to harm others. Now the laws of economics are just as simple, since they refer to our physical wants, and once these elementary laws have been deduced from a study of the facts or even after a look at ourselves (Man had only 'to examine himself, to find within him an articulate conception of these laws') the rest is simple arithmetic. The amount of taxation, for example, that the sovereign should demand, can be discovered by 'addition and subtraction'. All you needed 'to become a good politician', said another of the Physiocrats, was 'that amount of capacity and patience which a child who is good at arithmetic employs'.

It was really all too easy, and they found it just as easy to work out the laws from these simple premisses. The most obvious teaching of the Natural Law was that men were dependent on each other. So in a natural society the sensible thing was for men to exchange with each other goods they could best produce, or had least use for; and because some were rich in one thing, and some in another, all would gain. Hence as a result of each man following his own self-interest, a natural harmony would be established by men. (This is a sort of providential attitude towards economic life, for a 'hidden hand' guided seemingly selfish chaos into a natural harmony.) Since men worked best when they worked for their own private gain, the first duty of the State was to remove completely any restrictions whatsoever. There must be complete freedom: freedom of contract, freedom of trade without hampering restrictions or customs duties, and freedom to follow one's best abilities, that is, freedom to follow any career, and equality of opportunity. Only thus could the natural harmony come about. The leader of the Physiocrats, Quesnay (1694–1774), was a doctor (personal physician of Madame de Pompadour), and to him freedom in economics seemed just as vitally necessary to economic health as the free circulation of the blood was to physical health. He produced the famous *Tableau Économique*. Once, when asked by King Louis XV what he would do if he were king, Quesnay is said to have replied 'Nothing', and when the King asked who then would rule, Quesnay said 'The Laws'. He was not the one who coined the famous motto of the Physiocrats, however. The honour of having expressed it as *Laissez-faire, laissez-passer* (i.e. leave things alone) is said to belong to a less well-known Physiocrat, Gournay.

As could be expected in a great agricultural land like France, especially whenever wars produced famines, the Physiocrats regarded land as the chief source of wealth. This led them to attack feudalism because it was inefficient and interfered with personal liberty, and they took a great interest in agricultural improvements. They were also in favour of a single tax on land as interfering, as they thought, less with liberty. Their high opinion of the value of land even led them to attacking other sources of wealth, such as industry, and the towns which sheltered industry. The Marquis de Mirabeau referred scornfully to 'the voracious fraudulent peoples of towns', and this attitude helped to foster a sort of 'back to the land' fashion, so much so that it helped to popularize the 'simple life' creed of Rousseau.

It might be expected that, with all their emphasis on liberty and equality of opportunity, the Physiocrats would also favour some sort of democracy with the same fervour that Rousseau had done. Nothing of the sort was ever in their minds. To them it seemed that the natural order had been perverted and undermined for centuries by thousands of artificial rules and regulations, and had been strangled by vested interests. Suddenly to restore *laissez-faire* would not therefore be a very practical policy. The great task of destroying vested interests and out-of-date institutions must therefore be performed by the State. To carry this out a strong government would first be needed, and in the view of the Physiocrats only a despot could do it. Therefore they detested the idea of democracy, and even distrusted such a division of a despot's power as would be involved in Montesquieu's notions of the separation of the three parts of the constitution.

The Physiocrats collaborated fully with the other *philosophes* in their great joint work, the *Encylopédie*. The *Encyclopédie* was a huge work whose seventeen volumes appeared between 1751 and 1765, edited by Diderot and by Jean le Rond d'Alembert (1717–83). There was nothing new in the idea of making an encyclopaedia which should furnish useful information on a wide variety of topics; Bayle had already pointed the way in France, while several others already existed elsewhere; for instance, *Chambers's* first appeared in 1728. Indeed the great French work borrowed freely from that and other works, as the prospectus published in 1750 admitted. Apart from such borrowings, a great number of the articles came from the pen of Diderot himself, and others from all the other leading *philosophes*, particularly Voltaire, d'Alembert, Montesquieu, Helvétius, Holbach, Rousseau, Buffon, and Quesnay.

The aim of the compilers was to present an account of the most useful information available on every conceivable topic from physics to gardening, from medicine to grammar, from crafts to mathematics, and to explain to the reader the relationship of one science to another, as well as to express their own basic philosophy. Hence it was to be a 'reasoned dictionary', and in the *Discours préliminaire* d'Alembert sets out these aims; not surprisingly, it contains praise for Newton and Locke ('On peut dire qu'il [Locke] créa la métaphysique à peu près comme Newton avait créé la physique'—he is referring to the former's theory of knowledge).

The *Encyclopédie* proclaims very strongly that the destiny of humanity is not to turn to Heaven but to find happiness on this earth, thanks to Reason, and some hint about how to obtain it is conveyed perhaps by the hundreds of diagrams of agricultural machinery. It attacks authority and any obstacle to free inquiry. The attack on religion had to be handled cautiously because of the censorship, but the authors got round this difficulty by writing in an orthodox way on dangerous topics, but then referring the reader to other and less cautious articles which the censor was unlikely to bother to look at. Another trick was to pretend an exaggerated respect for religious mysteries and thus ridicule them. But the writers did speak out in some articles such as in the article on 'Persécuter', while the article on 'Priests' accuses that body of having caused the shedding of 'seas of blood' and of having gained a great position thanks to 'the ignorance of peoples and the weakness of sovereigns'.

As for sovereigns themselves, the *philosophes* were still more cautious, and in any case as we have already seen they were for the most part in favour of an enlightened despotism. Even so, some of the articles contained criticism, though the same sort of devices that concealed their religious attacks were used. For example, the article on 'Gabelle' has no criticism of that tax, but the article on 'Sel' (salt) calls the tax on salt a *fléau* (scourge), and says that apart from the even more arbitrary *taille* it is 'the most deadly that could be imagined'. The article on 'Liberté' also is quite bold and the article on 'Autorité politique' says that 'no man has received from nature the right to command others'.

Generally, then, the *Encyclopédie* was more open in its religious attacks, and more concerned to preach progress through science, than to attack political institutions, and in this it had an enormous influence, in spite of the fact that it was officially suppressed in 1759. That did not make a lot of difference, because subscribers were allowed to keep their copies. Besides, some very important people indeed were at least partly in sympathy with it. The censor himself, Malesherbes, was in favour of many of the *Encyclopédie*'s teachings, and kept the type of the volumes hidden in his own house so that it should come to no harm. Madame de Pompadour, the King's all-powerful mistress, was very fond of Quesnay, who was her own doctor, had a very sincere affection and respect for Voltaire, and also liked Buffon the naturalist because she was very fond of pet animals (so was the King, who also liked Buffon). On one occasion, after a little supper party at the Trianon, Madame de Pompadour actually induced Louis XV to read some of the *Encyclopédie*; he and his male guests looked up the article on gunpowder while she happily consulted it about face-powder. As well as this powerful protection, the *philosophes* gained from the divisions within the Church, which was being rent by controversy between Jesuits and Jansenists. Last of all, they were actually employed by the government to write articles in defence of Machault's new taxes, and hence became so powerful that they were able to get the government to suppress books unfavourable to *philosophe* doctrines. (This happened to a work by Fréron.) Towards the end of the reign of Louis XV the *philosophes* could say practically anything they pleased, while the lack of government control only meant that to ban a work was the surest way to get it a large sale.

While the *philosophes* had such powerful protection they also enjoyed the support of fashionable society. The *salons* of such influential ladies as Mme du Deffand, Mme de Lambert, and Mme de Tencin, to which the polite world crowded to hear good conversation, were a great medium for the dissemination of the ideas of the *philosophes*. So were numerous literary periodicals such as the *Nouvelles Littéraires* founded by Desfontaines in 1721. Much the same work was also done by the English Royal Society and the French *Académie des Sciences*, both of which were founded in the seventeenth century.

From France the ideas of the *philosophes* quickly spread to other countries, and by much the same means. Voltaire himself had a long and intimate, if not always harmonious, friendship with Frederick the Great, and Diderot became the adviser to Catherine the Great of Russia. Holland became a centre through which the new ideas were spread throughout Europe, Leclerc's *Gazette de Hollande* being particularly influential in this respect. Other countries too founded learned and scientific societies (Berlin in 1701, St Petersburg in 1724, Uppsala in 1710, Stockholm in 1739, and Copenhagen in 1743) and new universities which had the same sort of inspiration, such as at Göttingen (1734) and Moscow (1755). Germany in particular was influenced by the Enlightenment, and in that country the *Aufklärung* was spread by men like Christian Wolff, who taught at the University of Halle, by Professor G. F. Lamprecht of the same University, as well as writers like Martini and Sonnenfels. The German *Aufklärung*, however, became more purely literary than its French counterpart of the Enlightenment, and the earlier work of the greatest of all German writers, Goethe (1749–1832), such as *The Sorrows of Young Werther* which appeared in 1774, owes its sentimentality more to Rousseau than to the author of *Candide*.

It would of course be wrong to think of the eighteenth century as being the 'Age of Reason' if by that is meant a time when Reason predominated. It would be nearer the truth to call it the Age of Reason in the more restricted sense of the time when Reason, in the *philosophes'* use of the word, first played a powerful part. But it was also the time of the Pietists in Germany, led by Zinzendorf, who influenced the founder of the Methodist Movement in England; of the apocalyptic philosophy of Swedenborg; and, in America, of the mystical Calvinism of Jonathan Edwards. None of these was anything but utterly different from, or hostile to, Reason, and their followers were more numerous; Reason never touched the masses at all, and as for the literate, far more devotional and religious books than ones expounding the new Enlightenment appeared. The century also saw the great popularity of opera and of the sentimental novels of people like Richardson, neither of which have anything very reasonable about them, while to descend to the bottom of the scale, it was also a time when half the inhabitants of England were drinking far too much. Even the leading *philosophes* themselves were, naturally, not merely cold-blooded creatures with large brains and no heart. Their very 'philosophy' was in reality a new religion which they preached with all the fervour of revivalists; Voltaire died describing himself, and with some justice in view of his pity for suffering, as 'a good Christian'; while as for their private lives most of the *philosophes* lived with mistresses, and Voltaire managed to fall head over heels in love with his niece as well.

Yet it would be even more wrong to suppose that the influence of the *philosophes* was not great. True, their doctrines of a New Man in a new society; of a Man no longer enslaved by superstition, by cruel laws, and by senseless restrictions imposed by irrational and unfair economic and political systems; a Man, that is, who would be free to pursue his happiness, bound to his fellows by love and fraternity; who would be made perfect by an enlightened education; who would enjoy religious toleration and freedom from irksome restraints whether political or economic; and who would enjoy, too, equality of opportunity and a career depending on his talents, not his birth; and who, finally, would have some say in his own political fortunes—these doctrines, this glorious vision of a new world, meant nothing as yet to the masses. On the other hand, the masses in those days still had little or no importance. In most countries the chief or even sole political reality was still the monarch, and on most kings the influence of the *philosophes* was considerable; the eighteenth century was also the 'Age of the Enlightened Despots'. It was also to become the age of the American and French Revolutions.

15 · The Reforms of the 'Enlightened Despots'. (1) In Prussia, the Habsburg Dominions, and the lesser German States

The peace settlement of 1763 seemed to statesmen in many parts of Europe to be a precarious affair. France and Spain certainly wanted revenge for their recent heavy defeats by the English, and it was to be presumed that Austria would make yet another attempt to recover Silesia should anything like a good chance present itself. That is to name only the most obvious sources of trouble; there were plenty more. Meanwhile, most of the late combatants found their countries financially ruined, or, as in the case of Prussia, largely devastated. To build up their economic and military resources was a matter of considerable urgency. For this purpose many of the rulers adopted a number of the reforms suggested by the *philosophes* and the Physiocrats, because those reforms seemed likely to bring much greater efficiency and greater wealth, and could therefore increase the military power of the State. The reforms could only be put into effect by the monarchs themselves, so this period of great monarchical activity which followed the Peace of Paris is often called the era of the Enlightened Despots, because the reforms were supposed to be inspired by the teaching of the 'Enlightenment'.

Put like that, it seems justifiable to repeat the oft-stated view that the monarchs concerned acted not at all through admiration for the 'Reason' of the *philosophes*, but in obedience to power politics; *raison d'État*, not *la raison*, was their inspiration. There is a good deal of truth in it. They certainly did not adopt indiscriminately all the doctrines of the *philosophes*. They could also see clearly enough that the *philosophes* enjoyed immense international prestige, so that to pose as disciples of the latter would add greatly to the prestige of the monarchs themselves and facilitate acceptance of their reforming measures. Still, it would be wrong to regard the monarchs as wholly hypocritical. To some extent they all genuinely admired the teachings of the *philosophes* as being good in themselves. An examination of the workings of enlightened despotism in the various countries will throw some light on the extent of the influence of the *philosophes* as well as on the nature and importance of the work itself.

(a) IN PRUSSIA

Frederick the Great, King of Prussia from 1740 to 1786, had more need to work at reconstruction than had any other ruler because his country suffered most by the war. He himself said that it had lost half a million of its inhabitants, while most of the survivors 'had nothing left except the miserable rags which covered their nakedness'. In the eastern provinces, particularly, the devastation was enormous; in Pomerania hundreds of houses had been destroyed as well as thousands of sheep; in the Electoral Mark the losses in sheep, horses, and cattle totalled tens of thousands, and the losses in Silesia were even worse. Almost as bad as the material damage was the moral collapse resulting from years of anarchy and confusion. Frederick began the work of restoration the same day that he returned from the war.

The exact extent to which he was influenced by the *philosophes* in that work is very hard to determine. He had a genuine admiration for many of them (he gave a pension to d'Alembert because 'he has a beautiful nature and is also sublimely gifted', and his admiration for Voltaire was certainly genuine). But he also sneered at the French *philosophes* because he thought some of their notions unrealistic; he said he could only find in their 'flood of writings' 'a small number of good things'. As for the German exponents of the *Aufklärung*, he found less than that in their notions, and would not allow them even literary ability—in a letter to

Schiller in 1780 he called German literature a 'flood of verbiage', and
the works of Goethe, Lessing, Klopstock, and Herder are contemptuously dismissed with the cold remark that 'up to this time literature
had not flourished on our soil'. The writers of the *Aufklärung* were
preaching not only the supremacy of reason and the need for an
enlightened despot, but also a German patriotism inspired by admiration of Frederick's epic deeds in the Seven Years War. His low opinion
was based mainly on literary considerations, but it is certain that the
writers had no sort of political influence on him. It should perhaps be
added in defence of their merits that Frederick's literary judgement
would not win universal approbation nowadays; he described Shake-
speare's works as 'abominable plays, absurd farces fit only for the
savages of Canada'. The French *philosophes* managed to preserve their
admiration for Frederick, although it must have been rather a strain.
Frederick was in fact somewhat of an enigmatic character, capable of
saying that he was 'an enthusiastic follower of Newton and Locke' and
also that he would throw away Voltaire like 'a squeezed orange' when
the latter had ceased to be useful.

In his own writings, starting with the *Anti-Machiavel*, he sets out his
own attitude to his duties. He denounced war, though not defensive, or
even preventive, wars, for although his own military record would
hardly lead one to guess it, he did not much like wars, and says that the
first duty of a sovereign is to provide justice, and that the king is but
'the first servant of his people'. In later works, such as *L'histoire de mon
temps* and the more famous *Testament Politique* (1752), he says that his
first duty is to assure the happiness of his people, but this is to be done
by acting as a despot, and his opinion of his subjects was that they were
'an imbecile people'. He had nothing of the high hopes for man's destiny
that so inspired the *philosophes*; his enlightenment, such as it was, was
mixed with a very large dose of cynicism. Nor should it be forgotten
that he owed a great deal more to his royal predecessors than to the
philosophes, as an examination of his reforms will indicate.

Frederick's gigantic task was helped from the outset by two things
which had escaped destruction. One was the machinery of government
that his father had done so much to perfect, the other was a full
treasury, because he had paid for most of the war with English subsidies. He made no change of any importance in the system of government, and the General Directory continued to supervise the same
subordinate bodies (see Chapter 11). He did not allow the General
Directory any authority over the newly acquired provinces (Silesia, and

later, Prussian Poland), but placed over each a minister responsible directly to himself. For the rest, he worked as hard as his father had done to make the same machine work, allowing none of his ministers and civil servants any initiative at all. 'The State', he remarked, 'does not belong to the ministers', and, 'Newton would not have made his discoveries in collaboration with Descartes'. Thus the despotism of Frederick II was even more complete than that of Frederick William. As for the full treasury, that was useful for his work of economic reconstruction.

If in this work he acted despotically ('it is my responsibility to ensure bread for my subjects'), he was at least benevolent too, for the money came chiefly from his own pocket. He took from the Physiocrats, so it is said, the idea of the prime importance of cultivating the soil, but there was nothing peculiar to them in that, and in his determination to drain marshes and restore a working peasantry to empty places he was also following his father as well as obvious necessity. At all events, he brought large areas of marshy land into cultivation by drainage, especially in the Oder region, and improved the sandy soil of Brandenburg by irrigation. He also gave peasants large sums of money to restock their farms and rebuild their dwellings. He did what he could to induce immigrant labour to settle in Prussia, but with only modest success as there were no longer the large numbers of religious refugees there had been in the time of the Great Elector; but he still got many Germans, chiefly from Mecklemburg, to repopulate parts of his dominions.

Frederick did a great deal for industry, too. He created a special Ministry of Commerce and Manufactures (which was supervised by the General Directory) and carried on the work of his predecessors, with the addition of encouraging luxury manufactures, particularly silk and velvet, established at Crefeld, Magdeburg, and Halle. These made surprising progress, for the Prussian production of silk rose from nothing to an amount equal to half the output of the great French centre of Lyons. He helped these infant industries, as well as the longer-established wool industry, by a rigid mercantile policy of protection, and in this he certainly ignored the teachings of the Physiocrats. Other new industries of lesser importance were cotton, cutlery, and porcelain, but they had a hard struggle against foreign competition. These efforts were helped not only by State aid and tariffs, but also by a bank established at Berlin in 1765, which made loans to new enterprises at low rates of interest—the capital was again Frederick's own. The results as a whole were good, for Prussian industrial production towards the end of his reign was worth the considerable sum of thirty million *thalers* a year.

In order to sell all these products Frederick adopted a completely mercantilist policy, and aimed at a favourable balance of trade by all the usual methods known to mercantilists. There was therefore absolutely no trace of that economic liberty so dear to the Physiocrats in his measures to help commerce. He helped trade by building canals, of which the most famous was the Bromberg Canal joining the Oder and the Vistula; he hoped by this to ruin the trade of Danzig in favour of his own port of Elbing (1773). He also tried to divert trade from Hamburg to Stettin, and had a tariff war with Saxony. The converse of that was a trade treaty with France (which lapsed in 1756) and one with the United States of America in 1785. He felt the widespread lure of the East, and responded to it by founding an East India Company in 1764 as well as a company for trade with the Near East. Last, he assisted Prussian shipbuilding, and the Prussian mercantile marine by the time of his death boasted the not inconsiderable number of 1,200 ships. The results were impressive, for the trade of Prussia was worth fifteen million *thalers* in exports and twelve million in imports.

Some of this found its way back into his treasury again in the form of taxes. He made no great changes in the financial system, merely carrying on that of his father and with even greater parsimony, if that can be imagined. His well-drilled bureaucrats managed to raise some eighteen million *thalers* in the year 1786, compared with seven million in 1740. This, of course, was due to the rise in the numbers as well as the wealth of his subjects, for, thanks chiefly to the acquisition of Silesia, these numbered about 5,700,000 in 1786 compared with 2,200,000 in 1740. The increase in State revenues owed something as well to the reorganization of the indirect taxes by French experts whom Frederick called to his aid, chief among them being Helvétius and de Launay. Frederick was able to spend thirteen millions a year on the upkeep of the army (nearly twice as much as his father's entire income) and yet manage to save the huge treasure of fifty-five million *thalers* by the end of his reign.

For the point of all these schemes for enriching his country was mainly to keep the army, an aim which had nothing enlightened about it, but which was necessary; after his Silesian adventures he had to be *toujours en vedette*, always on the watch. The huge army of 80,000 which he had inherited from his father suffered terrible losses during the Seven Years War, and Frederick, far from resting content with restoring it to this figure, went on adding to it until it reached the prodigious total of 180,000 men, supplied with new muskets and supported by

868 cannon (with an equal number in reserve), and 60,000 horses. He also built several new fortresses. But by other measures he sowed the seeds of its ultimate ruin, and the fact that the army of Prussia's greatest hero was to be smashed with humiliating ease by Napoleon in 1806 at Jena was due in no small measure to the victor of Leuthen. For he fatally weakened the quality of its personnel. During the Seven Years War he had been obliged to make use of non-noble officers, who had given fine service, but once the war was over he hastened to rid it of this, to him, objectionable material. He was convinced that only nobles could make reliable officers, so he ejected most of the *bourgeois* officers (a process continued after his death, so that by the time of the Battle of Jena there were only 695 non-noble officers in the entire army, out of a total of over 7,000 officers, and most of those were in the artillery and subsidiary branches of the service). The noble class in Prussia was simply not numerous enough to supply the officers needed, so foreigners were enlisted, often of very dubious quality. Frederick did much the same thing to the lower ranks, though for different motives. He watered down his father's cantonal system to a dangerous degree because he preferred to see his own peasants creating wealth by working on the land. He did not think that native conscripts should ever be more than three per cent of the male population, so he ended with a majority of foreign mercenaries. His army though large was deteriorating badly in quality, the more so as the troops were given excessive leave and the officers no education. It is not too much to say that the Prussian army degenerated into a poorly-trained and faint-spirited force led by brainless officers; no wonder Napoleon smashed it without difficulty.

Not that Frederick was indifferent to education in general, although he had not a trace of the *philosophes'* hopes of a race made perfect by education. On one occasion, after listening to some optimistic talk along those lines by his Inspector of Education, Sulzer, Frederick, who still believed in Original Sin, said, 'Ah, my dear Sulzer, you don't know this damned race!' Nevertheless, he did carry out some educational reforms. He ordered, by the *règlement* of 1763, that there should be compulsory education for all children between the ages of five and thirteen. This is a wonderful step if compared with, say, England, which had to wait more than another century for universal education, but the spirit behind it was not very enlightened. Frederick was quite irreligious himself, but he wanted religion taught so that his subjects would learn obedience; in fact, the words of the *règlement* specified 'religion and other useful things'. Chief among these utilities was the cultivation of

mulberry trees for the silk industries (paragraph 14). Frederick's conception of education for the masses did not go much beyond the Ten
Commandments and messing about with silk-worms. Even that incon-
gruous syllabus failed to reach all his subjects, for education was not
free, and many parents could not afford the modest fees, while there
remained a lack of teachers which Frederick did not make good,
although he persuaded some to come from Saxony. This reform was
therefore a failure, but rather more success attended his efforts to
improve secondary education; alongside the *Gymnasien*, teaching classics,
he reformed the *Realschulen*, which taught modern subjects such as
botany, mechanics, and commerce. In 1788 a sort of ministry of education was established (*Oberschulkollegium*) and a standard examination
(the *Abitur*) of about university entrance level.

Frederick displayed no more enlightenment in justice than in education, for beyond attempts to speed up its administration, he did little
except to commission the great jurist, Cocceji, to establish a single
judicial system for the whole of his dominions, to improve the quality
of lawyers and judges, and to codify the laws. All of this was done in his
lifetime, but the codification was not complete until 1795. Some of it
was useful; for instance, the judges and lawyers had to pass examinations
and even the seigneurial judges had to serve a sort of apprenticeship.
But the motive was national efficiency, not abstract enlightenment,
and the rule of law was not, strictly speaking, established in Prussia
for Frederick arbitrarily interfered with the judgements of the
courts.

Lastly, he might be said to have displayed something of the enlightened outlook in his attitude to the Press and to religion, for he was
certainly remarkably tolerant in permitting libels about himself to
circulate, and he gave complete religious toleration (even to the Jesuits
after they had been elsewhere suppressed). He also tried to abolish
serfdom, but without success, though he did manage to mitigate its
harshness. The Press, although in practice permitted a fair degree of
liberty, remained subject to censorship, while religious toleration was
a military and economic necessity to a State that hoped to attract
foreign immigrants (besides, it had been practised by his predecessors);
and as for serfdom, he really did a deal with the nobles, allowing them
privileges over their serfs and the best administrative and military posts
in exchange for their help. To conclude, therefore, Prussia remained
under Frederick a despotic State run for the benefit of the army and the
nobles, with enough enlightened window-dressing to allow us to class
its ruler as an 'enlightened' despot.

(b) IN THE HABSBURG DOMINIONS

There is not the slightest doubt that motives of 'enlightenment' were far stronger in the Austrian dominions, especially in the reign of Joseph II. Joseph, on the death of his father in 1763, was made co-ruler with his mother, Maria Theresa, and these two worked in partnership until her death in 1780. Their methods differed chiefly in that Joseph was more reckless in his desire to push through as many reforms as possible in the shortest possible time, whereas his mother was less impetuous, but their aims did not differ seriously.

The need for reforms was even more urgent than in the Prussian dominions for the possessions of the Habsburg family were more loosely knit and the jumble of States which comprised them had suffered three terrible blows in the mid eighteenth century—the loss of Silesia, the election of a non-Habsburg (the Elector of Bavaria) to the dignity of Emperor, and finally the invasion of Bohemia by Frederick. It was quite clear that, in their existing state of disorganization, the Habsburg possessions would not be able to weather another such storm, and large-scale reforms were thus a matter of life or death. If it was therefore the Prussian menace that made reform necessary, the reforms themselves were animated to a surprising degree by the spirit of the Enlightenment. But reform was to be carried out by the monarch as despot; there was no idea of liberalism.

Maria Theresa had already effected a few reforms in the organization of the central government immediately after the War of the Austrian Succession (see Chapter 12). The trouble remained that the central government did not have the power to interfere much in the internal government of the various States which made up the Habsburg Empire. A glaring example of this was in Hungary, where twenty million *gulden* were raised in taxation but only three and a half million reached Vienna, and that by way of a voluntary grant. So diverse were the various administrative systems in the various States that the reforms of Maria Theresa and Joseph cannot even be studied as a whole because the local conditions varied so much, although of course the overall aim of obtaining more central control and the pushing through of various reforms applied to all the States.

Neither Maria Theresa nor her son was able to accomplish much in Hungary. The reason for that lies far back in Hungarian history. In the year 1000 Stephen, head of a warrior-herdsmen community, had himself made king, but the warriors allowed this only in exchange for complete control over their serfs and for immunity from taxation, giving the new King military support in return. The warriors became the nobility and although by the eighteenth century they numbered only about a twentieth of the population the arrangement continued unchanged in essence, and the nobility took entire charge of government in their own local subdivisions, or counties. They were responsible to local Diets, which, however, meant little as they elected the members of the Diets from among their own ranks, while they also filled the central Diet. Charles VI had simply accepted this position and allowed the nobles to keep all their power and fiscal immunities in exchange for their promise of continued military help and their recognition of the Pragmatic Sanction. So the Hungarian nation, by which is meant the great nobles (magnates) who filled the Upper House of the Diet and the lesser ones who were represented in the Lower House, was able to retain all its independent rights and liberties.

The monarch was by no means helpless, however, and Maria Theresa used her powers with great skill—she could create new nobles devoted to herself, make Church appointments and she had rights of interfering with noble law courts. She called the Diet very rarely, crowning her work by appointing a lieutenant-governor of her own as head of the government in place of the Hungarian Count Palatine. She then felt secure enough to give some measure of liberty to the serfs, or at least to lighten their burdens. Joseph did not imitate her caution, and declared all the serfs free in his great Edict of 1781. This gave the serfs their land, but left them subject to the justice of their lords. It was a triumph for the Enlightenment, but Joseph's motive was mixed. He was certainly a genuine devotee of Reason and 'common sense'; when he visited France in 1777 he showed a marked preference for conversation with Turgot and other Physiocrats. But he also wanted the peasants to be more directly under his control instead of under that of their lords, and by freeing them from nearly all feudal dues and services and making them free proprietors he hoped to be able to tax them for himself. He did in fact prove this by his other great innovation—the single land tax, the pet idea of the Physiocrats. Unfortunately the peasants thought they had been tricked, while of course the nobles were furious. One peasant revolt was suppressed, but when Joseph's foreign policy ended in disaster in 1789-90, a general revolt broke out in which the nobles joined, and in 1790 he had to give up his reforms in Hungary.

Both Maria Theresa and Joseph were able to do more in their hereditary States. These included the States of predominantly German population—Austria, Styria, Carinthia, the Tyrol—as well as the non-German States of Bohemia, Moravia, part of Silesia, Belgium, and Lombardy, but it will be convenient to treat the last two separately.

The aim was to centralize all of them under the authority of the monarch as a preliminary to carrying out vast reforms of various sorts. The chief weakness of the monarch was that each province had its own Diet, consisting of four 'Estates', clergy, greater nobles, lesser nobles, and representatives of the towns (except the Tyrol, which had a peasants' Estate instead of the towns'). These not only controlled taxation, voting to the central government as much or as little as they pleased, but they and the whole noble classes in general stood between the Crown and the mass of the population. Maria Theresa began with Bohemia, whose separate Chancellery she abolished, placing the country under the control of the Privy Chancellery at Vienna; and she then did likewise for all the hereditary German States. Subject to supervision from Vienna, local administration was run by a council in each State, made up entirely of paid civil servants. Below the council the States were divided into 'circles', at the head of which was another paid civil servant, a *Hauptmann* or *intendant*, who also supervised administration in the towns. Joseph created no new administrative machinery but tried to work that of his mother more effectively so as to unify all real control under himself, to make his dominions one nation instead of a collection of separate States having only common allegiance to the Crown as their link. He called the various *Stände* (Diets) very rarely, and took the revolutionary step of sweeping away all the boundaries between the various provinces. He also tried to Germanize them all by insisting on the use of the German language. All was to be run by his own German-speaking civil servants, whose quality he tried to improve, with only moderate success, by making them have a university education and a respectable private life. He also improved the police. He himself directed everything from Vienna; usually he ignored the Council of State and governed with eight secretaries, of whom only two were nobles. There were plenty of nobles in Austria anxious to work as civil servants, because on most noble estates everything went to the eldest son, thus leaving many younger sons unprovided for. Unfortunately, they were rarely efficient, and Joseph imported foreigners and promoted many men from the middle class, thus creating a body faithful to his policies.

Having thus arranged the machinery of government, Maria and Joseph made a series of reforms whose effect was to revolutionize the entire life of their dominions. Of these the most striking was the liberation of the serfs. Most of the peasants, except in the Tyrol whose peasants lived in almost democratic communities, were serfs bound to the land and obliged to pay numerous feudal dues and to give their labour to their lords. Maria limited this forced labour to 100 days a year (which gives some idea of the extent of the peasants' burdens), by her Patent of 1775; in this she was influenced by Raab, a Physiocrat. She also liberated the serfs on the royal domains, hoping that the nobles would imitate her. Her motive was enlightened, but she also hoped that the lords' serfs, once free, would be able to pay taxes to her. Further than that she dared not go, even when none of the nobles showed the faintest intention of freeing any serfs. Joseph had none of her fears, though he was far more than his mother influenced by the teachings of the Physiocrats. His Edict of 1781 virtually freed all the serfs, although they were still subject to their lords' law courts and had to pay a reduced number of feudal dues. The next step was to introduce the Physiocratic land tax, which all had to pay, whether peasant or noble (1789)—the peasants had to pay twelve and a half per cent of their income to the government and seventeen and a half per cent to their lords. Joseph showed how sincere was his care for his subjects' rights and dignity by appointing special State advocates who looked after the peasants' legal rights, so it would be wrong to suppose that these fine measures were occasioned merely by a wish to get taxes out of the peasants for himself.

Both monarchs did as much as possible to further trade and industry, and, while Maria's notions did not go beyond ordinary mercantilism, Joseph mixed his own mercantilist ideas with a dose of Physiocratic freedom. Maria discouraged imports of luxuries and of wine, butter, and cheese, as well as of metal objects, at the same time prohibiting the export of raw materials. This was just the usual mercantilist policy of creating a favourable balance of trade. Joseph, in this respect too, went much further by his protective tariffs of 1784 and 1788, which virtually stopped luxury imports altogether. He also freed trade within his dominions, improved roads and the postal services, tried to develop the port of Trieste, and made a treaty of commerce with Russia in 1784. All this was normal mercantilist practice, but in July 1782 he carried out a purely Physiocratic reform by attacking the monopoly of the guilds; henceforth anyone could open any factory or follow any trade he wished; this was complete freedom of competition.

The reforms so far mentioned did not earn Joseph the gratitude of the nobles, peasants, guilds, nor of the subject provinces, but they resulted in a greatly increased revenue—for the government, heavily in debt and having an annual income of only twenty million florins in 1740, was finding, and spending, eighty-five millions every year by 1786. Though a lot of that went on the army, even in that sphere Joseph tried to follow enlightened opinion at least in so far as to create a national army. In that he was only able to make some sort of start by garrisoning troops in parts of the Empire remote from their own homes, so as to create more national feeling among them. For the rest, he cleansed the ranks of criminals and looked after the food and conditions of the men far better. His mother had increased the size of the army and under Joseph it was raised to over 200,000 men. The quality was still doubtful in spite of Joseph's attempts, and the artillery and engineers were supposed to be inferior to those of the French and Prussian armies. As for the generals, they preferred spending long holidays in Vienna to devoting themselves to their duties; as Joseph said, 'I can find no zeal nor energy among our generals.' Be that as it may, the Habsburg armies were improved in numbers and quality.

Most of the foregoing reforms were evidently caused as much by the need to improve the power of the government as by enlightened ideas, but in the remaining fields of justice, education, and religion Joseph at least showed himself a most glorious disciple of the *philosophes*.

Maria Theresa's notions of justice remained old-fashioned and severe, and her creation of the High Court of Justice in 1749 and her Penal Code of 1768 had something of efficiency but nothing of enlightenment about them. Joseph, on the contrary, was anxious to give all his subjects just and rational laws. In 1787 his new Code abolished primogeniture, established civil marriage, and under the influence of Joseph von Sonnenfels, who was himself a disciple of Beccaria, abolished torture and the death-penalty. Joseph also constructed a complete judicial system: he created State Tribunals of first instance in the towns and countryside, and a total of seven Courts of Appeal in the hereditary States (one in each), as well as a Supreme Court in Vienna. This was a wonderful and noble work, scarcely less admirable than his work for education.

Joseph established a complete system of primary education, directed by a ministry in Vienna which saw to it that district commissions had schools built. This education was compulsory, and it says something for Joseph that at least a third of the children of his dominions actually attended school—a prodigious achievement. He also improved the *Gymnasien* (secondary schools) by creating examinations and by leaving the teachers far more liberty of action, and this spirit of tolerance was extended to the universities, the University of Pavia, for instance, after its reorganization after 1771, becoming famous as a centre of scientific studies. Last, non-Catholics were admitted to the universities. Education was not only improved in a staggering way, but also taken out of the hands of the Jesuits after their suppression in 1773.

Both Maria Theresa and Joseph were determined to get religious matters more under their own control and less under that of Rome. In this they were helped by the attitude of many of the higher clergy, including Cardinal Herzau and several bishops. Maria published an Edict in 1767 which decreed that no Papal Bulls should be published in her territories without her consent. She also had leanings towards toleration, and in 1774 an Edict gave a measure of toleration to the Protestants of Hungary (she cancelled their obligation to assist at purely Catholic processions, and allowed them to bring up their children in their own faith). As usual, Joseph went much further. He practically took over complete control of the Church himself, tried to democratize it, fixed lower incomes for the bishops and clergy, and endeavoured to bring its whole attitude more into line with 'enlightened' opinion. He suppressed fifteen saints' days, urged the seminaries to teach a useful morality instead of theology, and prohibited dancing on week-days (he wanted his subjects to work), pilgrimages, and processions. He even prohibited graveyards around churches and family vaults, 'for all are equal in death', and to save wood and cloth ordered that the dead should be buried naked in sacks. He forbade his subjects to read superstitious books as they were 'incompatible with the purity of primitive religion'. All this caused offence, but not so much as his suppression of 359 monasteries and convents. He had hoped to profit from this last move as these institutions were very rich, but he did not at first make much because of the need to compensate their inmates, whom, however, he described as 'useless and consequently not agreeable to God'. So he closed some more rich ones. This did better as, for instance, the monasteries owned half the land of Carniola and three-eighths of that of Moravia. By the end of the reign half of them had been shut and the remainder placed under State control. Naturally the Pope did not like this, and visited Vienna in 1782; but he got no concessions from Joseph beyond the admission, in the Concordat of 1783, that from then on Joseph appointed bishops in Lombardy not by right but as a 'favour'. The greatest of his reforms was, however, the Toleration Edict, the famous *Toleranzedikt* of 13 September 1781. This was tantamount to a revolution. Toleration was granted to all except Jews and certain sects, although Jews could live unmolested in Vienna on payment of a tax, and Protestants (both Lutheran and Calvinist) and members of the Greek Orthodox Church could henceforward build their own churches, open schools, and enter any trade or profession. It was the supreme triumph of the Enlightenment in Austria; and not only Austria, because in the next year it was extended to Hungary, the Netherlands, and Lombardy.

Joseph's reforms were resented everywhere, but nowhere more than in the Netherlands. The Austrians had indeed only acquired the Netherlands as recently as the Treaty of Utrecht, and neither Charles VI nor Maria Theresa was particularly anxious to retain an area which was hedged about by a Dutch barrier of forts on the French border for defence against that country, and by commercial restrictions imposed on it by the English and Dutch. The Netherlands also had always enjoyed very considerable local self-rule, and the various Provincial Estates, composed of representatives of the nobles, clergy, and town corporations, really ran the country. The Imperial government was a lax affair. At its head was a Governor who did nothing, his role being played by a Minister Plenipotentiary appointed by the Emperor and assisted by two Councils (one for justice and one for finance) which did very little. Charles VI had interfered hardly at all and allowed the Provincial Estates to manage things. Maria Theresa showed her usual statesmanlike caution, not altering the form of government but quietly assuming a little more power. Joseph, knowing nothing about the country, its customs, and the pride of its inhabitants, quickly imposed all his stock reforms. Religious toleration was received quietly, for there were few Protestants to tolerate in that highly Catholic country, but his suppression of various religious Orders and his secularization of the Catholic seminaries caused more of a stir. The real trouble, however, was created by his political measures. He began by limiting the financial powers of the Estates, and, worse, he then ignored the old provincial boundaries and divided the country into nine 'circles' controlled each by an *intendant* (1 January 1787). Within a few days the Estates protested, the lead being taken by Brabant, the only one to have an ancient written constitution, and the opposition of the Estates was stiffened by that of the town corporations, even more jealous of their ancient rights. Led by a lawyer called Van der Noot, this opposition seemed so formidable that Joseph promised to examine their grievances, but he also sent to the Netherlands a tough soldier, D'Alton, to take charge of the troops, and a firmer Minister Plenipotentiary called Trautmannsdorf. They did not succeed in frightening anybody, and when a new Edict from Joseph in April 1787 said in effect that no concessions would be made the Estates refused to register it. Joseph's answer was to abolish all the constitutions, including that of Brabant. A revolt broke out at once, all the more dangerous because the guiding spirit was now another lawyer called Vonck, who wanted not just the preservation of the old rights but a constitutional monarchy. His followers easily defeated the feeble and small Austrian garrison in November 1789. Joseph then cancelled all his reforms, but it was too late. In December 1789 the Belgians declared themselves an independent republic.

The case of Lombardy was very different, for in that province the reforms of Joseph were a total success. The problem there was that the province was really governed almost entirely by members of a section of the nobility called the Patricians. They controlled all the magistracies, and therefore orders from the Council of Italy in Vienna were passed on to the Governor and his Grand Chancellery in Lombardy but never got any further, because the Patrician magistrates were able to decide everything—they formed 'an opaque and resistant body between sovereign and people'. Maria Theresa largely got round this by her reform of 1749. This created a body called the *Tribunale del Censo*, a fiscal body which soon had under it a whole organization of civil servants responsible for collecting taxes. These existed as a hierarchy with a chain of command from the highest to the lowest ranks. To some extent this by-passed the magistrates. Joseph completed their downfall. He was helped by the fact that a good deal of the teachings of the Enlightenment had already made a considerable impression in Lombardy quite independently of Joseph's own enthusiasm for them. He was helped too by the poverty of the younger sons of the nobility, who were anxious for reforms because they usually did not inherit any of the family money and had to fend for themselves. In any case the nobility lacked toughness and had not a spark of patriotism of any description. A Supreme Economic Council, established in 1765, had in a few years entirely taken all the powers of the local Senate into its own hands. In 1786 Joseph at one swoop abolished the Senate and all the magistracies, and their place was taken by a new Government Council (*Consiglio di Governo*) which worked through six departments, the staffs of which were entirely subordinate to it, while the city of Milan itself was placed under a political *intendant*. There was no resistance, and Joseph's successor, Leopold, got no trouble until the French invasion of Italy.

It was far otherwise in the remainder of the Habsburg dominions.

The example of revolt set by the Netherlands, already mentioned, was soon followed in Hungary and in the hereditary States. For Joseph had offended everybody except his own civil servants and had built his despotism merely on them, unlike Frederick the Great, who based himself firmly on the powerful support of the Prussian nobility. Joseph's nobles were nearly all infuriated by his measures depriving them of political rights and of their serfs, while the peasants were too ignorant to understand his work on their behalf and too conservative to appreciate any of the rest of it, while the feelings of the clergy were outraged by his religious reforms. The chance of all these disaffected subjects came with the total failure of Joseph's war with the Turks in 1788. There was uproar everywhere and at once, and in face of the revolt even the civil servants would do nothing to support their master. The Estates of Styria protested against taxes, those of Carniola refused to pay them, and they were joined by the peasants. That reaction was typical, and Joseph had to abandon nearly all his administrative reforms. The nobles again got the upper hand; they took over the administration of towns and countryside, levied taxes, and resumed control of the law courts and of taxation. Joseph himself said unhappily that he 'had failed in everything he had undertaken'.

The chief reason for all this was that he went too fast and based himself on the support of no strong section of the population. Yet although it is possible, as some do, to deride his efforts, it should not be forgotten that he was not the total failure that some writers portray him, for the most glorious part of his work, the bulk, that is, of his work in the reform of the law, in the Church, and in education survived him, as well as the reforms in Lombardy. It was his administrative reforms that perished—the enlightened part lived and the despotic part died. This was no great loss, for in revolting against a despotism, however benevolent, his peoples showed a correct instinct. Joseph tried to rule them all by himself, and showered his subjects in the ten years from 1780 to 1790 with more than 6,000 orders and decrees. He was fatally hurried and was too personally overburdened with detail which he should have left to subordinates; these faults of Joseph are at least as much to blame for his failure as any folly or selfishness on the part of his subjects. He was also aiming at a complete personal despotism. It is true it was a benevolent despotism, but his subjects showed a wise instinct in rejecting it. For what would happen if the man who gathered all that power into his own hands, from the best of motives, were to be followed by a despot who used it from the worst, by a despot without the benevolence?

(c) IN THE LESSER GERMAN STATES

The influence of the Enlightenment in the lesser German States varied from place to place, but is hardly worth describing at great length because none of the States concerned was of much importance. In general the type of monarch seemed very different in the second half of the eighteenth century from those who lived in the first half; at least, most of them stopped aping Louis XIV and showed a greater desire to put themselves at the service of their States and to try to raise the mental and moral level of their people. It is hard to say how much this new attitude owed to enlightened doctrines deriving from the *philosophes* and how much came from religious origins, for many of the German princes of the sixteenth century had shown similar impulses whose roots were fairly certainly religious. However, the influence of the *philosophes* is clear in the case of the Margrave Charles Frederick of Baden. He abolished serfdom and tried, after correspondence with leading Physiocrats, to impose the single land tax (without success). Charles Augustus of Weimar showed liberal impulses also, while some of the princes tried to improve agrarian conditions; for instance, by a new rotation of crops, and even to provide insurance schemes, all of which failed, for their subjects. But nobody except the Margrave of Baden tried to abolish serfdom or to reform the laws in any significant way. Some of the princes were anything but benevolent despots. The ruler of Hesse made a steady income by hiring out some of his subjects as soldiers for the English, and there was a strong reaction against religious toleration in Saxony and Hanover. Even in Prussia after the death of Frederick the Great there was opposition to enlightened ideas from members of weird organizations like the Rosicrucians.[1]

---

[1] A society devoted to alchemy, magic, and the occult, said to have been founded in 1484 by Christian Rosenkreuz. The date is uncertain, and Rosenkreuz himself may never have existed. According to some, the society is a revival of an Order which began in remote antiquity in Egypt. It still exists.

16 · The Reforms of the 'Enlightened Despots'. (2) In Russia, the Scandinavian States, Portugal, Spain, and Italy

(a) IN RUSSIA

There is quite a strong case for the view that the Enlightenment never really touched Russia at all. The reputed exponent of enlightenment in that country was the Empress Catherine II, who reigned from 1762 to 1796, and is usually called Catherine the Great. She made certain changes in the status of the nobility, in the administrative and legal systems, and in education, but it is quite another matter to declare that any of these changes had an enlightened purpose or result. Some sort of tentative verdict may be offered after a brief examination of these reforms. But one or two remarks about their author and the country she governed should be made first.

She was in origin an unimportant German princess who came to Russia at the age of fifteen to become the wife of the Tsar Peter III, whose eccentric rule lasted a very short time indeed—his performance in reversing Russian policy by allying with Frederick the Great was too much for anyone to stomach. Catherine conspired against him, helped by a lover of hers called Grigory Orlov and by some of the Guards. Peter was pushed out of the way and soon afterwards murdered (1762). At first Catherine's position was shaky, but she soon made herself a complete autocrat. She was a women of tremendous energy who read widely, who wrote prodigiously, and who loved even more prodigiously. She read the works of some of the French *philosophes*, particularly Montesquieu and Diderot, and also those of the English jurist Blackstone. She had a genuine regard for Diderot and became very friendly with him, inviting him to Russia for his advice, which was given in long and enthusiastic conversations. No doubt she thought highly of many of his notions, but to put any of them into practice in Russia was a gigantic task. The country was nearly all agricultural; in 1762 ninety per cent of the population were peasants, about three per cent lived in towns, and the remainder were nobles. (These figures are not reliable, for some experts put the number of nobles, including their families, at half a million out of a total population of about twenty-eight million.) Most of the peasants were serfs owned by the Crown, the Church, and the nobles, and their misery drove them into frequent revolts which were often dangerous, such as one in the Kalonga district which took six regiments to suppress. The worst revolt, however, was that of 1773-4. The original trouble came from the Cossacks, who revolted in 1772 because the government had abolished some of their autonomous institutions, but the peasants took advantage of it and joined them. For a year confusion was terrible, and at one time the rebels were expected to capture Moscow. They were defeated, but reforms of some sort seemed urgent.

Catherine actually busied herself more with the nobles. The origins of this class were various, but Peter the Great had succeeded in making all nobility dependent on service, either military or administrative, to the Crown. Service began at the age of fifteen and was for life, and Peter's Edict of 1722 divided all servants of the Crown into fourteen orders (or *tchin*), rising in two parallel ladders, civil and military, starting with registry clerks and sub-lieutenants, and ending with the Chancellor and field-marshals. The top eight ranks were given hereditary noble status and the remainder were nobles for life. The nobles were separated from the rest of the community by dress, law, habits, outlook, and even by language, for they generally preferred to speak German or French, and liked to live a life of astounding ostentation surrounded by hundreds of servants, if they could afford them (many could not), including their own private theologians, orchestras, actors, and even astronomers. They were in many ways very divided among themselves, and so it was not difficult for the monarch to behave as a complete autocrat. The nobles tried without success to keep their privileges and to dodge service. On the death of Peter II in 1730 they succeeded in part, and chose Anna, the niece of Peter I, as Empress, trying at the same time to tie her to concessions (the 'Articles') which would have made the Russian Crown elective. She managed to override them, giving them, however, a few concessions. Chief of these were the limitation of service to twenty-five years beginning at the age of twenty, the establishment of a cadet school so they could enter the army as officers instead of in the ranks, and a *Gymnasium* in Moscow for nobles only, so they would not have to go to the same school as common people. The weak Peter III abolished compulsory service altogether. This meant that they could now live on their estates far more than formerly (they had mainly lived in the capital) and some of them became rich by commercial enterprises of all sorts. The less fortunate majority were left behind in the pursuit of wealth in this way, and the continued subdivision of their estates by the process of sharing land among all male heirs saw more and more nobles reduced to near-poverty, some ending with little land and no serfs. Even the more fortunate failed generally to capture more than a small part of trade and industry from the merchant classes. That meant that, without service of the State or private means, some of the nobles were hard hit, and even the bigger ones were becoming relatively less important as compared with the merchants. A crisis of the whole noble class was approaching.

Catherine held a 'Commission' in 1763 to discuss reforms. There was a lot of enlightened talk, for the benefit of enlightened opinion, about easing the burdens of the peasants, but nothing was done about it. The question of compulsory service by the nobles was also raised, but no measures at all emerged from the Commission. More hopeful seemed one of her renowned projects, the great Commission of Reforms which she called for in 1767. Catherine had been reading Montesquieu and Beccaria, and her 'Instruction' to the Commission quoted those writers extensively. It is usual to suppose that her aim was, however, to cover herself with the authority of those enlightened writers the better to consolidate her own autocracy. At all events, the Commission, which consisted of 564 deputies (the nobles were outnumbered—there were 160 of them, 207 from the urban middle class and the rest were peasants), was supposed to create new laws, and there was fine talk of freedom of speech and equality before the law. Some of the nobles were in fact prepared to lighten the peasants' burdens, but the gist of their demands was for more power for themselves. Among other things, they asked for the election of judges by themselves and a say in local administration. For all its fame, the Commission led to nothing at all, and some think that Catherine's only real purpose was to strengthen her own position.

The demands of the nobles were in any case largely satisfied in the Charter of the Nobility of 1785. Under that, they no longer had compulsory service, were exempt from direct taxation, were declared immune from corporal punishment and could not have troops billeted on them, were free to dispose of their lands, could take part in any commercial or industrial enterprises, their position was made hereditary, and they had the right to be tried by their peers. They were also given a corporate organization, every province having its own corps of nobles which chose local officials from its own ranks, divided now into six classes. Their control over their serfs remained stronger than ever. The whole affair pleased the smaller nobles, but the richer ones took little notice and continued to look after their own interests in the capital. The whole thing amounts probably to a deal done by Catherine with the nobility at the expense of the peasants, or it could be regarded as a victory of Catherine over the nobles inasmuch as they were now once again being made to do something useful. In any event, it certainly had nothing whatever to do with enlightenment. For the peasants were more enslaved than ever, their talked-of Statute never saw the light of day, and the new criminal and civil codes remained a pleasant dream.

Catherine undertook also a considerable administrative reform; this was the great Ordinance of 1775. The chief need was for more units of local government because Peter's division of the country into eight 'Governments' proved too unwieldy. Catherine subdivided the country into far more manageable units by creating forty-two new 'Governments', each itself subdivided into districts. At the head of every 'Government' was an official, known variously as a Governor-General or as an Imperial Lieutenant, who was directly responsible to the monarch personally. Catherine also tried to make the administration more efficient, and justice more equitable, by establishing in each 'Government' four 'Colleges'; one a Government Council for administration, while the other three were a council for Finances, a Criminal Court, and a Civil Court; and besides those there was also held every year a 'Committee for Public Assistance', which was supposed to look after education and hygiene. Further, she also set up in every 'Government' a Court of Conscience, which had separate tribunals for hearing cases touching nobles, merchants, and free peasants as courts of equity (this reform was inspired by the English Court of Requests). The various classes had judges drawn from their own ranks. This whole scheme was reproduced on a small scale in the districts, with a chamber of finances and tribunals for the three classes. There is no denying the efficiency and the enlightenment of this huge body of reforms, although the legal reforms, if owing something to the spirit of the *philosophes*, owed something of their actual shape to English practice and Blackstone's writings.

Her work in reorganizing the machinery of central government was, on the other hand, simply a matter of efficiency—she ignored Diderot's earnest advice to recall the Commission of Deputies. Instead, the old Senate was allowed no real function, and Peter the Great's central ministerial 'colleges' were replaced by administrative departments. At the head of each department was a minister or chief, and all the ministers were under the Procurator-General of the Empire, the latter in turn being subject to the Empress's lover (for a long time that was Potemkin, who ruled as a sort of chief minister). So instead of the aristocratic monarchy of Peter there was now an autocrat and a subservient bureaucracy.

Catherine showed herself more truly enlightened in the sphere of education, and was fond of boasting about it in her correspondence with Diderot. She founded boarding-schools for the sons of the nobility, and in 1764 established the Smolny Institute for their daughters. This was followed two years later by a reform of the Military Academy, but the efforts until then hardly satisfied Diderot, who suggested that she should study the Austrian system. She took the advice, and Joseph II loaned her one of his experts (the Serb, Jancovitch). Out of this came the 'Statute of Popular Schools' in 1786. In every town there was to be established a 'little' (primary) school and for older children a 'principal' school; all classes were supposed to attend these. After that, abler children went to the high school or *Gymnasium*. This was a wonderful reform, though it applied to towns only, not to the countryside where dwelt the bulk of the population, so only 316 schools were actually in being by 1796. In practice, too, the nobles refused to send their children to them because they did not want them to associate with children of the lower classes.

Altogether, it is fair to describe Catherine as almost certainly enlightened in her wishes, but her work savoured far more of an efficient, rather than an enlightened, despotism. In any case she, with Peter, was one of the great architects of Russia as it was before the Revolution of 1917, and if she was not more enlightened in practice it was perhaps because of the difficulties of doing anything too sweeping in that direction in that vast and still backward country.

(b) *IN THE SCANDINAVIAN STATES*

The two Scandinavian States (Denmark, to which was joined Norway; and Sweden, which also ruled Finland) needed to restore the strength of their economy just as urgently after a great war as did the bigger Powers, but in their case the war was not the Seven Years War but the Great War of the North which ended in 1721. To hope to build anew the prosperity of their countries was a realistic ambition, but there could be no question at all of either of them trying to play a big part in international affairs as they had done in the seventeenth century. Henceforward they were very minor States, relying on diplomacy and alliances with bigger countries to give them a respectable European position. They set about their work of reconstruction in a similar fashion, encouraging agriculture, industry, commerce, and shipping, and showing great interest in scientific and technical research. Naturally, therefore, the ideas of the Physiocrats and the Enlightenment found a warm welcome in Scandinavia, especially after the middle of the century (before 1750 the Pietist Movement was strong there). But if the similarities between the two countries were marked, so were the differences, and they will have to be studied separately.

(i) *Denmark–Norway*

Denmark retained a firm belief in royal despotism after the royal *coup d'état* of 1660. Her first three monarchs in the eighteenth century all served the country well. Frederick IV (1699–1730) declared the peasants free of serfdom, or, more accurately, from *Vornedskab*, which tied them for life to the soil, which they worked not legally as serfs but as tenant-farmers subservient to landlords. (There was no need of such a reform in Norway, where the farmers all owned their own land.) His successor, Christian VI (1730–46), was obliged because of shortage of labour on the land to modify this reform somewhat by a compromise arrangement known as *Stavnsbaand*, by which the peasant was tied to his estate for as long as his liability to military service lasted, that is, from his fourteenth to his thirty-sixth year. Christian also tried to encourage agricultural improvements in Norway by offering prizes for the cultivation of root crops and for better cattle, but his efforts to do this in Denmark had less success because of the practice in that country of cultivating land in common. He called in experts from Germany to encourage the growing of potatoes and to begin land-reclamation on the Jutland heath. He also encouraged agriculture by prohibiting the entry of foreign corn into South Norway, and in return gave Norwegian manufactures of iron, glass, and other commodities a monopoly on the Danish market. The success of this rigid mercantilism was affected, however, by smuggling, and many new industries, which were helped by the Danish bank set up in 1736, found themselves murdered by foreign competition, such as the (smuggled) imports of English textiles. Companies were formed also for trade with Africa and the West Indies.

The Crown during this period also did well in foreign affairs, because the defeat of Sweden in the Great War of the North meant for Denmark the acquisition of the ducal parts of Schleswig and the end of the alliance, which had been so dangerous to Denmark, between Sweden and the Duke of Holstein-Gottorp. These gains were successfully defended against another threat from Sweden, backed by Russia, in 1723–7, and in 1742 the Danes came within the French orbit by a treaty with France which lasted until 1762. Real danger came in the reign of Frederick V (1746–66), a man without much personal energy who allowed sensible advisers to continue his predecessors' work for the improvement of the country's economy, but who found himself out of his depth when confronted with a threat from Russia. The Tsaritsa Elizabeth of Russia had declared the Duke of Holstein-Gottorp her heir, and the future Tsar had declared his intention of chasing the Royal House of Oldenburg from the throne of Denmark. He duly became Tsar in 1762 and promptly made peace with Frederick the Great in order to attack Denmark. France did not help, and the prospect, in spite of the determination of the Danes to fight to the end, seemed appalling. Fortunately the whole threat disappeared with the sudden deposition and death of the Tsar. Better still, in 1767 the Danish minister, Baron Johann von Bernstorff, negotiated a peaceful settlement and an alliance with Catherine the Great. It meant, however, the loss of any alliance with England or France and a promise to help the Russians to maintain the Constitution of Sweden, a Constitution which left the King of that country very weak. This was quite a heavy price for the Danes to pay in exchange for finally getting undisputed mastery over Schleswig and Holstein, and the international position of Denmark was still precarious. However, Denmark reorganized her armed forces, so she was not a country too easily trifled with.

Denmark thus far had endeavoured to strengthen herself, and her ways of doing so had certainly owed quite a lot to the Enlightenment.

The influence of that movement was still further felt in the next reign, that of Christian VII (1766–1808). Oddly enough, it was the fact that the King was mentally unbalanced that caused Reason to hold full sway in Denmark. This came about because power fell into the hands of first Struensee and then Count Andreas Bernstorff. (This Bernstorff was the nephew of the one already mentioned.) Bernstorff's reforms were more useful than those of Struensee, but have not always had the same attention, partly because the career of Struensee was much more dramatic. John Frederick Struensee (1737–72) was a doctor of German extraction who became all-powerful with the King because the ailing monarch relied on his medical help. He also became the lover of the Queen. This climb from obscurity was startling enough, but not more so than the reforms which Struensee, an ardent disciple of the Enlightenment, hastily enacted. Among them the most interesting were the abolition of the censorship and of judicial torture, a plan to help foundlings, the improvement of sanitation and hospitals, an economy-drive directed against too lavish spending at court, confiscation of some Church revenues, freedom of worship, some measures designed to limit the powers of the town corporations, and the exemption of private houses from moral supervision by the police. These reforms, together with many more, were not popular because they were introduced at a pace far too quick for people to absorb them. They also carried with them a danger to Denmark inasmuch as their total effect would have meant almost a loss of the national identity, for Struensee tried also to discourage Danish customs and the Danish language in favour of German. He made far too many enemies, and in 1772 some of the disgruntled aristocrats who resented his sole control of power hatched a successful plot against him and he was executed.

The chief author of the plot, Guldberg, soon undid all his work, and while that meant the end of Enlightenment in Denmark for the time being, it ended also the risk of the Germanization of the country. In 1784 the reaction under Guldberg came to an end, for Frederick, the King's nephew, pushed Guldberg aside and from then on he and Bernstorff dominated the King's counsels. They used their power to effect reforms that were more wisely carried out and therefore longer-lasting than those of Struensee. The censorship was once more abolished, education encouraged, but this time given a purely Danish character, and the rigours of the law once again softened by the abolition of torture, by less savage penalties, and by prison reform. They also came under the spell of Physiocratic doctrines and inaugurated economic freedom and crowned this noble work by first (1787) limiting feudal rights and second (1788) freeing the peasants from compulsory attachment to the land. Altogether this was a great and enduring work, which really did bring peace, prosperity, greater happiness, and the maintenance of national independence.

(ii) Sweden–Finland

Some enlightened reforms were also carried out in Sweden (with which was incorporated Finland). The nature of those reforms as well as the reasons for enacting them, while owing much to the *philosophes* and Physiocrats, cannot be properly appreciated without a brief look at the structure of Swedish politics in the eighteenth century. Of course that structure was in part a reflection of the social and economic structure of the country. Unfortunately, politics in eighteenth-century Sweden were unusually complicated.

The death of the warlike Charles XII, who, like his predecessor, had been able to rule as an almost complete despot, was followed by a strong revulsion against despotism. The result was that the Crown had to accept the Constitution of 1720, which stripped it of almost all its powers and invested them in the Diet (*Riksdag*). The long period of constitutional rule which then followed (it ended in 1772) is known as the 'period of freedom' (*Frihetstiden*). The King's Council remained, but it was now really the Council of the Estates, not of the Crown, and very soon it too was of little importance, most executive decisions being made by the most influential of the various committees of the Estates, the famous 'Secret Committee' (*Sekreta Utskottet*). Even this was not allowed entirely free scope because the Estates were still jealous of executive power.

Real power was held by the Diet alone. This consisted of four separate Estates—nobles, clergy, burghers, and peasants.

Of these the most important was the nobles' Estate. There were about 10,000 nobles in Sweden out of a population of between one and a half and two millions, and the head of every noble family, some thousand in number, had the right to sit in the noble Estate. They were not a very united body, for although they all enjoyed partial or complete exemption from most taxes and also dominated all the best official positions, both civil and military, they varied greatly in wealth and outlook. The largest group were the lesser nobility, who made their money from employment in government service, although they hastened to buy estates as soon as they could. The older and richer families, who frequently made money out of industrial enterprises such as the mining and manufacture of iron (their chief interest of this sort), viewed the lesser ones with scant favour. But the nobles were not a closed caste, and readily admitted new members to their ranks; these were not only successful business men but men distinguished in the arts and in science. From 1719 to 1792, 725 new nobles were made, but, as there was literally no room for them in their assembly room (*Riddarhus*), after 1762 new nobles were not allowed to take part in the proceedings. For a long time (until the mid-sixties of the century) the nobles contrived to be far more powerful than the other three Estates put together. They were helped in this by an Ordinance dating back to 1714 which held good until 1766; it divided society into forty classes according to occupation, and the first eleven classes of post, such as presidents of supreme courts, lords-lieutenant, admirals, etc., were reserved for nobles, although in practice this was not always strictly adhered to. Altogether, the position of the nobles was very strong in spite of their internal divisions: the greater nobles wanted voting to be by three classes, but after 1738 the more numerous lesser nobles defeated this, and so for the next quarter of a century it was really the lesser nobles who ruled Sweden.

The Second Estate was that of the clergy, consisting of the bishops and about fifty of the lower clergy. They were not very powerful, and were generally anti-noble.

The Third Estate was made up of some 120 burghers from the towns. Many of these were very rich manufacturers and traders, and as time went on their economic power grew greater. They could thus hope to challenge the power of the nobles, but for a long time tended to support that Estate.

The Fourth Estate consisted of about a hundred peasants chosen from the free landowning farmers. These mostly resented the power of their wealthier noble neighbours, and for protection from them favoured a strong monarchy.

It will be seen that the power of the nobles was precarious, because the clergy and peasants were hostile and because the Third Estate was growing richer. However, for a long time most of the Third Estate supported the nobles.

This is itself an oversimplified picture of the Estates and their members, and Swedish politics were complicated further by the fact that they tended to cut across the conflicting interests of Estate and class. Two parties emerged, based as much on differences over foreign policy as on economic and class differences. There were at first three, but one of them faded out soon after 1721, and the two-party alignment became clear in the elections of 1738, when the party in power led by Horn, Chairman of the Council, was defeated. Horn's opponents wanted a much more vigorous foreign policy so as to regain some of Sweden's lost territories, and, to deride their opponents, called them sleepy old men in nightcaps, and the name 'Caps' stuck to them. On the other hand, they emphasized their own martial ardour by calling themselves the 'Hats', in reference to military headgear. The 'Hats' won the election of 1738 and remained in power until 1765.

They favoured not only an energetic foreign policy but also a policy of mercantilism. Foreign adventures meant expanded armed forces and therefore more chance of employment and promotion for the nobility; while the merchant classes favoured, as they then did in most other countries, protectionism; and this probably accounts for the fact that most of the nobles were usually 'Hats' as well as most of the Third Estate. Hence the alliance between nobles and Third Estate.

Not that they disagreed with the 'Caps' in everything. Both parties realized the need to improve the country's resources, and as already pointed out, Sweden was a country that valued learning and the arts, so some reforms were made of an enlightened sort. The tenants of the Crown were allowed, on payment of a sum of money, to become free taxpaying farmers; in 1739 an Academy of Sciences was founded, chiefly to study new farming techniques; and, in 1757, farmers were allowed to cultivate their land separately instead of in common, in the hope that they would be encouraged to improve their methods. But a prime interest of the 'Hats' remained foreign affairs, and this was to be their downfall.

At the time of the War of the Austrian Succession the 'Hats' favoured France, and, encouraged by an alliance with that Power, launched in 1741 an attack on Russia. It went totally astray, and the upshot was a severe defeat. Russia overran Finland, and at the Peace of Abo in 1743 Sweden had to accept a Russian nominee, Adolphus Frederick of Holstein-Gottorp, as heir to the Swedish throne. For a time a large Russian force occupied Sweden and a Russian squadron was attached to the Swedish navy in support of Adolphus Frederick, but in 1744 the 'Hats' contrived to persuade the Russians to leave. It had been a very explosive situation for them, but they weathered the storm and soon the new heir forgot his attachment to Russia. Even more disastrous was the policy of the 'Hats' in the Seven Years War. They joined the coalition against Frederick of Prussia in order to win back Pomerania from him, but failed dismally to do so.

This lost them the last shreds of their prestige. The failure of the

'Hats' was roughly the same thing as the failure of the whole noble class. Many of the middle class, disillusioned, joined a coalition of the peasants and lower clergy against them. Their economic power was in any case growing relatively weaker, and their disastrous foreign policy touched off a mounting class resentment. The new coalition were called the 'Younger Caps'. They wanted an end not only of foreign adventures but also of the fiscal exemptions and privileged position of the nobles. In the election of 1765 they were completely victorious and there at once began a bitter party struggle. The 'Caps' favoured a relaxation of mercantilism, more agricultural reforms, freedom of the Press, the abolition of the privileged position of the nobility, and a peaceful foreign policy. The attack on the nobility was conducted with such venom that their whole position seemed on the point of tottering to a complete fall. There was perhaps nothing dangerous to the State in that but the foreign policy carried with it a threat to national independence. For the 'Caps' were closely linked to Russia, whose Ambassador distributed huge bribes among them (all parties in Sweden accepted bribes from foreign Powers), and Sweden was heading for virtual annexation by Russia. The collapse of the nobles' position and the loss of the independence of the country were both averted by the new King, Gustavus III.

Gustavus had no wish to be a helpless king in the style of Frederick I (1720–51) and Adolphus Frederick (1751–71). He had come very much under French influences, particularly those of the Physiocrats, and wanted to establish a 'legal despotism', such as they recommended, the better to carry out reforms. In August 1772 he decided to make himself supreme with the help of some loyal troops; the news leaked out and he was in danger of arrest, but on 21 August he surrounded the Diet with soldiers, and the Diet, with Gustavus's artillery pointing at it, voted a new Constitution. This did not make the King a despot, but a very strong head of the executive.

He used his power to push through various enlightened reforms. The liberty of the Press was restored and torture abolished. His finance minister, Liliencrantz, reformed the currency and balanced the budget. Internal customs duties were abolished (a Physiocratic idea). The law courts were reformed. Finally, the army and navy were reformed, so that Sweden would be able to offer a very tough resistance to Russia should the need arise. But the need did not arise, for the Russians, thwarted, preferred to go after easier prey. What Gustavus did not do was to permit any further encroachment on the privileged position of the nobility, and for a time he saved them from being swept away by the peasants and middle-class business and professional men. In fact, he favoured them, and as late as 1785 was thinking of excluding commoners from commissions in the army. Yet while he favoured their social privileges he had no intention of allowing them to dispute with him for political power. This soon led to discontent among them, and their attempts to regain political influence convinced the King that he had to break them. Therefore in 1789 he had passed an 'Act of Union and Security', and by this second *coup d'état* made himself a complete despot. In effect this meant a firm alliance of King and lower orders against the nobles, so the next instalment of 'enlightened' measures included reforms which ended their special position. He allowed non-manorial land to be acquired by non-nobles, and, biggest social change of all, flung open all posts to anyone with talent. The Physiocratic dream of equality of opportunity thus became a reality in Sweden.

In the Scandinavian countries, therefore, enlightened despotism had performed the double task of effecting reforms and of preserving the national independence.

(c) *IN PORTUGAL*

One of the most amazing successes of the Enlightenment happened in Portugal. For the first half of the eighteenth century this little State of some three million inhabitants seemed half asleep in the arms of the Catholic Church. Nobody did much work, the country did not keep itself in food, of industry there was hardly a trace; but the country was quite rich because of the trade in port wine with England and because of its imports of gold from its colony of Brazil. Portugal had more religious houses (about 900) than any country in Europe, the universities were ecclesiastical organizations, and the King allowed the Pope great influence. The government was a mild despotism, the *Cortes* (Parliament) not having been called since 1697, and the King ruled with the assistance of a Council of four men. Other bodies set up were a Council of War and a Council to deal with Brazil, while the number of financial advisers of the King was increased—this was all done just after 1640 when the country gained its independence from Spain. These bodies were advisory; for executive action there were Secretaries of State responsible to the King.

It was one of these secretaries, Joseph de Carvalho, created Marquis de Pombal, who reformed Portugal. A new king, Joseph I, came to the throne in 1750, and Pombal acquired a total ascendancy in the country until the death of the King in 1777.

His most spectacular work was his attack on the Church. That body controlled much of the wealth of the country as well as such mental activity as took place. Pombal first forbade the Inquisition to execute anyone without the consent of the government. He then went for higher game, and a brisk campaign against the Jesuits began. They were forbidden to come near the royal court, accused of misdoings in America, and in 1758 the Pope was persuaded to appoint Cardinal Saldanda to reform their Society. He forbade them to preach or to hear confessions, and in January 1759 Pombal accused them of a plot to kill the King, confiscated all their property, and expelled them all from Portugal. He then struck at the power of the nobles and broke their power by executing some who were accused of plotting against the King. That left the way clear for his programme of reforms.

Of these the most impressive were sweeping reforms in education. He opened 800 elementary schools, used Jesuit money to found a college at Lisbon, and modernized the universities by introducing the study of the sciences. Hardly less striking was a decree that declared all posts open to anyone with the necessary ability. He also reformed the administration by removing many useless officials. He simplified the judicial system. He also encouraged trade by the formation of new companies and by creating in 1756 an Oporto wine company. Last, he built up a useful army and improved the navy so that it comprised thirteen ships of the line and six frigates. Altogether, Pombal transformed Portugal from one of the most somnolent and obscurantist countries into one of the most outstanding examples of efficient and enlightened despotism.

(d) *IN SPAIN*

Spain, which in 1700 had appeared to be a pathetic cripple, regained a good deal of her former strength in the first half of the eighteenth century. The original impulse came from the advisers who were sent by Louis XIV to help his grandson on his accession to the Spanish throne. Thereafter in the reign of Philip V, who died in 1746, and of Ferdinand VI (1746–59) the work of regeneration was fairly constant and reasonably successful. True, it owed nothing to the kings themselves, and its motivation had nothing to do with enlightenment until the advent of Charles III in 1759. It came rather from the wife of Philip V, Elizabeth Farnese, and her advisers, Alberoni, Ripperda, and Patiño. They improved the finances by introducing honesty into their administration, established new industries, rebuilt the merchant and war fleets, improved the army, made commercial treaties, and encouraged commerce in every way they could. The results were impressive, for the King's income rose from 142 million *reals* to 211 million by 1737, and it was thanks to this that Spain was once more able to play a conspicuous, if not very successful, part in international affairs in the time of Elizabeth Farnese. This work was continued in the next reign by the great minister, Carvajal. However, it is usual to hail King Charles III, who ascended the throne in 1759 after many years of enlightened activities as ruler of Naples, as the greatest of the reforming kings of Spain in the eighteenth century.

Charles was thoroughly imbued with the spirit of the Enlightenment, and at first sight his tasks would appear to be made easier by the despotic position of the kings of Spain and by the fact that Spain seemed to be genuinely waking up after its long sleep in the second half of the seventeenth century. Signs of this were a considerable increase in population (which rose from about five millions in 1700 to about eight or nine millions by 1760) and by a slight but significant rise in industrial and commercial activity. Better still, there were clear indications of a more energetic and patriotic spirit and a more open-minded attitude to foreign ideas (for instance, the first Freemasons' lodge was set up in 1726, and some of the nobility were travelling abroad and returning with new ideas). But the obstacles to large-scale reform were tremendous. True, the nobles, in spite of their huge wealth, were not important politically. Far more serious would be opposition from the Church, which owned at least a quarter of the land and still had a thorough grasp of men's minds. It also had control over their bodies: the Inquisition had burnt thirty-four people to death for heresy in the previous reign, and not even Charles was ever able to stop this completely.

Charles, nevertheless, assisted by some enlightened ministers he had brought from Italy, such as Squillace, and by some native Spaniards of the same persuasion, such as Aranda and Florida Blanca, boldly launched an attack on the Church. A quarrel with the Inquisition ended in the discomfiture of that formidable body, and so Charles next turned against the still more influential Jesuits. In this he was helped by the hatred which most other clergy had for these 'warriors' of the Pope; indeed, the fall of the Jesuits in Spain, as everywhere else, while desired by the followers of the *philosophes*, came about as much because of the jealousy and hate of the other clergy as of the Enlightenment. The Jesuits in Spain were ill-advised enough to try to oppose the King in a project of his to get Bishop Palafox canonized, and still more foolish in attempting to attack his ministers. Their position seemed strong in 1765 with the publication of the Papal Bull *Apostolicum Pascendi*, which supported them, but in the next year they stirred up riots against the King, and he struck. On 31 March 1767 they were all suddenly bundled out of the country. All 2,746 of them thus had to take ship, and they sailed towards the Papal States, but were refused entry, partly because the King vindictively urged the Pope not to help them, and partly because they were too expensive to feed and pay. So, under the threat of Papal artillery, they steered away from the Papal States, and a long and wretched voyage around the Mediterranean then followed. Nobody would have them, and this must be one of the most pathetic incidents of the century. After all, whatever their faults, they had served their God with courage and faithfulness. In the end, some were allowed to take shelter in Corsica and the rest were admitted grudgingly into the Papal States.

Charles had thus won a supreme triumph for the Enlightenment against its most deadly enemies, but it can hardly be claimed that this did Spain very much good.

For the Jesuits were the backbone of what education there was in Spain—they had run seventy-two colleges in that country—and nothing much was put in their place except two colleges, one which the King founded, and the other which he merely reformed. Apart from that, there were attempts to reform the universities, which languidly provided a little out-of-date information, but these efforts made very little difference. For instance, the University of Salamanca, which had not taught mathematics for 150 years, finally stirred itself and appointed Diego de Torres Villarroel as its new professor for that study. But they did not pay him enough to live on, so, according to his own story, he supplemented his income by occasionally practising the varied skills of begging, smuggling, and bull-fighting. Perhaps it was fair to pay him a small salary, because he knew practically nothing about mathematics.

If the government did little by formal education to improve the condition of the nation, it did try to encourage a different outlook by other means. Here again it was helped by a spirit already present. In 1765 in the Basque country local enthusiasts formed the 'Basque Society of the Friends of the Country' (*Sociedad Vasgonada de los Amigos del Pais*) with the object of honouring trade and work (too many Spaniards had a contempt for work). The minister Campomanès in 1774 urged the formation of similar clubs everywhere else. The task of increasing the agricultural and industrial output of the country was, however, a big one, in spite of the fact that private enterprise had already made a start. Agriculture was hampered chiefly by the huge amounts of land owned by the Church and by the nobles. The peasants were mostly tenants without any security of tenure, and their work was hampered by the great *Mesta* (league of sheep-farmers) who drove sheep over their lands and prevented them from enclosing for improvements. Crushed also by dues and taxes, the peasants, except in the north, were miserable. Nothing could be done about the Church or the nobles, but the government whittled down the privileges of the *Mesta* and gave the peasants of Castile more security of tenure. In 1770 it mooted a project to share common lands among them, but nothing came of it. Rather more was done for industry. Physiocratic ideas of economic liberty were embraced, though these went hand in hand, out of sheer necessity, with State direction. The making of cottons and silks was allowed to escape largely from guild control. The results were fair—for example, by 1767 there were twenty factories at Barcelona making muslins, etc., and silk was thriving in five towns (Valencia, Murcia, Talavera, Seville, and Toledo). The government also tried to help trade by a project for a great road system radiating from Madrid.

There was therefore some, but not a huge, increase in production. The amount this yielded in taxable wealth did not help the government much because Church and nobles paid little and because the taxes were farmed. Nothing could be done about the first difficulty, but a start was made at taking the collection of taxes out of the hands of tax-farmers. The government remained poor (receiving a fifth of the revenues that the King of France had), and certainly too poor to be able to afford to play a big part in international politics or to help industry very much. This is the reason why it could do little to improve the armed forces, although the number of battleships possessed by the navy rose from forty-nine in 1761 to sixty-four in 1774. They were not made in Spain but bought from the English, and their crews lacked skill and spirit.

Spain under Charles III, therefore, was greatly influenced by the Enlightenment, but the reforms carried out, although impressive, could go no further because of the social structure of the country, a structure which the King could not tamper with to any serious extent.

(e) *IN ITALY*

Italy was not a single country politically. The Austrians ruled a good deal of the north, although in that area there were several small independent States, such as Piedmont-Savoy, the Republic of Venice, the Republic of Genoa, and Parma (ruled after 1748 by the son of Elizabeth Farnese), while across the centre of the country stretched the

Papal States, ruled by the Pope. Naples in the south was Austrian until 1748, after which it went to Don Carlos, elder son of Elizabeth Farnese, who also became King of Sicily (and of course afterwards became Charles III of Spain).

To outward appearance Italy, especially the north, seemed to be both charming and rich, but it was a land of violent contrasts, and terrible poverty existed in the south, although the Church, which did not pay taxes, was very wealthy (Naples had 50,000 monks, about the same number of priests, and 165 bishops and 21 archbishops; this in a population of five millions). Crime reached frightful proportions, and punishments were barbarous. Yet Italy saw a wonderful intellectual development in the eighteenth century. The country boasted Beccaria and the biologist Spallanzani, as well as the jurist Filangieri, to name only the most famous out of a large number who were keenly interested in the arts and sciences and who had been deeply influenced by the doctrines of the Enlightenment which entered the country from France.

The most astounding reform was the suppression of the Jesuits. This was clamoured for by advanced thinkers and by the princes all over the country—the latter were tired of their interference. The other clergy, who were jealous of the power of the Jesuits, joined in the movement. The Jesuits' bankruptcy in Paraguay, a country which they ruled, did them no good, and their position became perilous with the accession of Pope Clement XIV in 1769. He owed his position to the Italian Bourbons, to France, and to Spain, and the last two of these countries had already expelled the Jesuits. The Pope at first hesitated, but finally suppressed the entire Order in January 1773, and with them fell the strongest foe of the Enlightenment. The Jesuits fell partly because of the jealousy of other clergy, partly because of enlightened propaganda, and partly because even Catholic princes did not want the interference in their dominions of an Order peculiarly faithful to an outside Power —the Pope. Perhaps, too, they had become in a sense outdated, for their original purpose had been to fight the Protestant Reformation of the sixteenth century, and of that there was no longer any question.

As for other reforms, some rulers tried to improve the lot of the peasants. In Tuscany the Grand Duke Leopold abolished legal serfdom, though without decreasing the feudal dues payable by the peasants. In Piedmont, which had been in any case chiefly a land of free peasant-farmers, all traces of seigneurial rights were abolished, whereas in the Papal States there were no reforms of any description. As for Naples, a country enjoying the enlightened rule of Charles and his great minister Tanucci, the problem was hopeless because of the power of the nobles, who owned enormous estates, but some slight improvement was made by removing a few of the worst seigneurial abuses. As a general rule, the strength of benevolent governments in Italy was unequal to the task of dealing with the agrarian problem; the revolutionary force coming from France at the end of the century could do it, but no government of the Old Régime.

There were attempts made, however, within this creaking social framework to improve trade, industry, and agrarian production. Of these the most successful were in Naples, where Charles and Tanucci established a 'Junta of Commerce' on the advice of the French economist Vaucouleur, established industries with State subsidies, reformed the currency, and made treaties of commerce, although they failed to do anything much for agriculture. They improved the finances by better management and by taxing Church property (a very brave step), and so doubled the revenues between 1760 and 1789. They spent a great deal of the money on amusements. In Tuscany, land was reclaimed by drainage and the free circulation of corn permitted. Last, in Milan the enlightened Austrian government stopped all tax-farming and reduced tariffs, achieving marked improvements.

Italy, then, was no stranger to the Enlightenment.

(f) WEAKNESSES OF THE REFORMS

It is exceedingly difficult to make general statements about the activity of the Enlightened Despots throughout Europe as a whole. It is clear that one weakness was that it left no guarantee of permanence, because too much depended on the energy and personality of the princes and there was nothing to prevent reforms being neglected or reversed by their successors. Moreover, the reforms could generally only be carried out by an alliance between the monarch and privileged classes, such as the nobility, at the price of leaving the privileges of the latter untouched. But privilege based only on birth was not in keeping with the true spirit of the *philosophes*, who were trying to free Man from his shackles. To bring about the sort of society the *philosophes* really wanted, therefore, was not a political possibility for the enlightened despots. To achieve that, a far more revolutionary force was wanted. That force was to be found in France in 1789.

17 · 'Enlightened' Foreign Policy; the First Partition of Poland and the Russo-Turkish Wars of 1768–92

In their internal policies the Eastern Powers were influenced by the Enlightenment, even if their chief motive was simply to build up the strength of their States. Their foreign policy showed not the slightest trace of the influence of *la raison* but was entirely dominated by *raison d'État*; that is, by the need to protect or strengthen the country. 'Reasons of State', in the mind of Frederick the Great and Catherine the Great, was a sinister conception for which one can find a simple word: theft. Frederick had already displayed his notions of international morality by his unprovoked attack on Austria in 1740. After the Seven Years War he and Catherine looked around for more neighbours to plunder. Russia had designs on Turkey, and both Russia and Prussia had designs on Poland and Sweden; the prospective victims all shared an attractive inability to defend themselves.

The complete anarchy and weakness in Poland has already been described (in Chapter 5). Russia wanted all that country under her sole control, but Frederick the Great feared the further expansion of a country already dangerously powerful, and at first he preferred the continuation of a weak Poland in whose affairs he could continue to meddle. The question became acute with the death of King Augustus III of Poland in October 1763. Catherine decided to press the candidature for the throne of Poland of a Polish noble, Stanislaus Poniatowski, who had been her lover and through whom she counted on dominating Poland herself, to the exclusion of interference from other Powers. But she was nervous of the reaction of several European Powers, including France, a country which had for centuries taken an interest in Polish affairs. Frederick, on the other hand, decided that his own best interests would be served by an alliance with Russia, because he had a dread of having ever to fight a war on two fronts again and needed a Russian alliance to avoid this, all the more so because he could not trust England after her desertion of him in the Seven Years War. Moreover, if he were the ally of the Russians they could hardly exclude Prussian influence from Poland altogether. He was able to get his way because of the virtual isolation of Russia, and an alliance was signed between the two Eastern Powers in April 1764. They agreed to guarantee each other's territories (and thus Prussia got an invaluable ally for the defence of Silesia), to ensure the election of Stanislaus in Poland by force if necessary, and to maintain the Swedish as well as the Polish constitutions—that is to say, to keep both countries in a state of defencelessness. A secret clause undertook the support of the 'Dissidents' (Protestants and members of the Greek Orthodox faith) in Poland, and this would be certain to lead to serious disturbance in that strongly Catholic country.

In face of this alliance no other Power was able to do anything for the Poles, nor were the Poles able to do much for themselves. Some of them tried to secure the election of a general called Branicki, who would have tried to shake the country free of foreigners, but bribery and a show of force by the Russians frustrated this. As usual, the Poles were disunited, for the great 'Family', the Czartoryskis, to which Stanislaus Poniatowski belonged, hoped by co-operation with Russia to reform Poland. The result was the election of Stanislaus as King in September 1764. The hopes of the King and the 'Family' of achieving reforms were curtly dashed by the Russian Ambassador, but Stanislaus had to obey the Russians if only because he depended on them for money. The Russian interference soon included a claim for religious toleration for Polish members of the Greek Orthodox Church. This intensely irritated the King and the Polish gentry, but, in face of Russian troops around the Diet, they had to agree to this and in addition to perpetuate Polish anarchy by the retention of the *liberum veto* and to agree to a treaty placing the Polish Constitution under the guarantee of Russia (1768). This meant that Poland was under the single-handed control of Russia.

Russia had overstepped the mark too openly. Some of the Poles rose against them and formed a Confederation at Bar (in Podolia), and their example was followed elsewhere. The Russians forced Stanislaus to help Russian troops to fight them, and a miserable war began. There could be only one end to such a conflict, but the French were alarmed by Russian power in Poland, and they urged the Turks to declare war against Russia. This the Turks promptly did (October 1768). To fight a still great military Empire was no joke for Russia, but the worst difficulties were the vast distances the Russian troops had to march. Catherine did her best to fool her conscripts by telling them that they were engaged in a holy war against the infidel, and in spite of the terrible difficulties involved they made good progress and captured the provinces of Moldavia and Wallachia.

Once again, too much Russian success only brought fresh trouble for Catherine. Frederick, who had showered her with flattery at the time of the formation of the alliance of 1764 ('You speak, and the world is silent before you' was one of his remarks), was thoroughly alarmed by the Russian conquests. Furthermore, Russia was not allowing him any say in Poland. He now indulged in a brilliant diplomatic manœuvre. He knew quite well that since the Seven Years War Austrian relations with Russia had cooled, and that the Austrians were infuriated by the Russian conquest of Moldavia and Wallachia, provinces which the Austrians wanted for themselves. He therefore decided to obtain the co-operation of Austria to put pressure on Russia so that he could get part of Poland for himself. He met Joseph and Kaunitz at Neisse in August 1769, and did his best to charm both of them. He could be very charming when it suited him, and his flattery made a strong impression on Kaunitz, although Joseph said privately that he was a knave. However, Frederick got most of what he wanted, and he was able to offer Catherine the joint mediation of Prussia and Austria to end the Turkish War. The offer was not accepted, but another meeting between Frederick and Joseph at Neustadt in the summer of 1770 seemed ominous to Russia, the more so as Austria was clearly preparing to fight on the side of the Turks. Russia was already running into serious military difficulties, and the prospect now was of another and still bigger war to fight with Austria, and possibly with Prussia too. It was thus evident that Russia would have to pay Frederick his price to buy him off and if needs be to put pressure on Austria. That price was a share of Poland. Russia had of course always been opposed to any advance of Prussia in Poland, but it now seemed the lesser of two evils. Accordingly the Russians agreed to sign the First Partition Treaty of February 1772 with Frederick, and were glad to do it, for in the previous July the Austrians had signed a treaty of alliance with the Turks.

So far what had happened was that Frederick had taken advantage of Russian difficulties and the poor progress of the fighting in Poland and against the Turks, and of the Russian alarm that Austria might be added to their enemies, and that Prussia might help Austria as a result of Frederick's *rapprochement* with Joseph at their two meetings. The mainspring of the first partition of Poland was therefore Frederick the Great, for the Russians wanted it all for themselves and the Austrians did not want any sort of partition of Poland. The Austrians had, however, already put themselves into a false position by drifting into occupying the Polish territory of Zips in 1770. Then in 1771 the Russians had succeeded in capturing the Crimea, but were so exhausted that they offered the Turks an armistice and were ready to give back Moldavia and Wallachia to the Turks in exchange for the Crimea. Austria could not therefore in view of this, and of the Russian and Prussian agreement to partition Poland, do much to help the Turks, and could do nothing at all to prevent the first partition of Poland. Maria Theresa still hated the partition as a crime, but Joseph and Kaunitz, the realists, decided to get their share, and so Austria fell in with the plan of partition in August 1772. Maria Theresa said she was ashamed to show her face and called the partition 'a blot on my whole reign' which she only permitted because she was 'threatened with a war both with Russia and Prussia'.

Under the First Partition Treaty, Russia obtained the remainder of Livonia and the districts along the Rivers Dvina and Dnieper (i.e. White Russia), including the towns of Minsk and Vitebsk. This was not regarded as a very fertile area, but it included about 1,600,000 people. Austria got Little Poland, except for Cracow, and most of East Galicia, with about 2,600,000 people. Prussia got Ermeland, western Prussia, Posen, and land on the Lower Vistula except for Thorn and Danzig, with 900,000 people. The chief gainer was undoubtedly Prussia, because it now connected its territory from Königsberg to Magdeburg. As for Poland, it was reduced to a State of about seven million people, and was really governed by the Russian Ambassador. The Poles made valiant efforts to strengthen themselves by various reforms, but it was too late, and the Eastern Powers would certainly not permit Poland to recover its strength.

Sweden narrowly escaped the same fate as Poland, but Russian and Prussian hopes of partitioning that country were thwarted by the *coup*

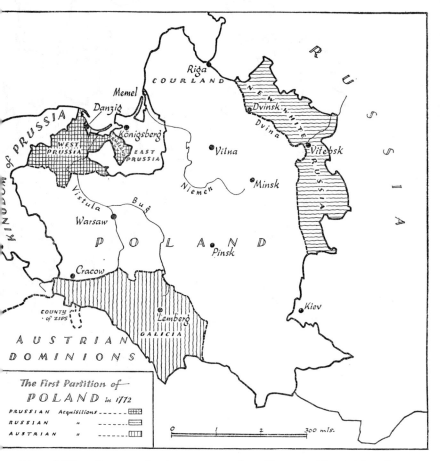

The First Partition of
POLAND in 1772

PRUSSIAN Acquisitions
RUSSIAN "
AUSTRIAN "

0   1   2   300 mls.

d'état of King Gustavus in August 1772 (see Chapter 16), and by the reforms which he at once carried out to strengthen his armed forces.

Russia was thus left with no hope of attacking Sweden, and had been obliged to fall in with Prussia's scheme to partition Poland. For consolation there was still the hope of important gains at the expense of the Turks, and after the First Partition Treaty of 1772 the Russians

EUROPE in 1789

0   3   600 mls.

Habsburg Territories.....

had their hands free to deal with them. In spite of that the campaign of 1773 went badly and both Russians and Turks were exhausted. The Russians did far better at the Treaty of Kutchuk-Kainardji (July 1774) than the military situation warranted. They were given Azov, Kertch, and the districts of Kuban and Terek. The independence of the Tartars of the Crimea was recognized by Turkey, and this would mean the whole area could be dominated by Russia. On the west side of the Black Sea, the Russians got the mouth of the Dnieper and the steppes between the Rivers Bug and Dnieper. They were also given the right to navigate the Black Sea and to pass the Straits. Last, and most ominous of all, they were given a vague right as protectors of the Greek Orthodox subjects of the Sultan (some twelve million), and so had unlimited excuses for interfering in Turkey. It was an immense triumph for Catherine; the Austrian statesman Thugut said that the Turkish Empire 'is from now on a sort of Russian province'.

Though these gains were so important, they did not satisfy Catherine. In 1782 she proposed a partition of Turkey to the Austrians. She offered them Bosnia, Herzegovina, and Serbia, while she was to take Moldavia, Wallachia, and Bessarabia. France showed itself so strongly opposed to this that the scheme was abandoned, and Catherine contented herself with annexing the Crimea. In 1787 she once more declared war on the Turks, and Austria joined the attack on them. In 1788 the Russians captured Ochakov, but the Austrian campaign was disastrous. In the next year the Austrians did better (but too late to save the collapse of many of Joseph's enlightened reforms) and in 1791 made gains on the Hungarian borders by the Peace of Sistowa. In 1792 by the Peace of Jassy the Russians got the lands between the Bug and the Dniester.

The foreign policy of the Eastern Powers, then, as the preceding sketch indicates, was the reverse of enlightened, since it raised the partitioning of weaker neighbours, without a shadow of excuse, almost to the level of a principle. The first partition of Poland was the crime of the century. As for the aggressions at the expense of Turkey, these opened in acute form the modern version of the 'Eastern Question'; that is, the fate of European Turkey, which was to plague Europe throughout the nineteenth century and to become a major cause of the Great War of 1914.

18 · The Influence of Science on Industry; the beginnings of the Industrial Revolution in England

England had no enlightened despot, or despot of any sort. The country was ruled by an oligarchy who manipulated most of the seats in the House of Commons, where ultimate authority resided. The country which had given birth to Newton and Locke therefore spent most of the eighteenth century quite satisfied with a system of government which, while far from being fully democratic, gave to all a surprising degree of liberty. Moreover, the country which emerged after a total victory in the Seven Years War felt no especial need to build up its power by the application of enlightened principles as understood on the continent of Europe. None the less in England science was taken up more eagerly than elsewhere. Sometimes enthusiasm for science was even expressed in poetic form, as in the long 'Hymn to Science' by Mark Akenside (1721–70). This poem calls science 'thou fair effusive ray', 'Queen of Manner, light of truth', and other nice names, and its last two verses run:

> Of wealth, pow'r, freedom, thou the cause;
> Foundress of order, cities, laws;
>   Of arts inventress, thou!

> Without thee what were humankind?
> How vast their wants, their thoughts how blind,
>   Their joys how mean, how few!
>
> Sun of the soul! thy beams unveil;
> Let others spread the daring sail
>   On Fortune's faithless sea,
> While undeluded, happier I
> From the vain tumult timely fly
>   And sit in peace with thee.

It is noticeable that, while the last verse addresses science with a religious fervour (there is a beautiful Christian hymn whose first line is similar: 'Sun of my soul, thou Saviour dear'), the writer is worshipping in the penultimate verse a Goddess who offers him wealth and power. However, it is the concern of the present chapter to deal not with such stuff, but to say something about the pursuit of wealth which it lauds, a pursuit involving a revolution in industry which the English were beginning in the second half of the eighteenth century, a revolution which science helped to bring about.

That revolution was to multiply English wealth a thousandfold and has made the material world as we know it; it continues to advance, changing the world with bewildering speed. The root of the matter is the use of machines to do much of the work previously attempted by human muscles, and to use power-driven machines to mass-produce goods for huge numbers of consumers. In the eighteenth century the power invented to drive the machines was steam; it has since been supplemented or replaced by gas, oil, electricity, and atomic energy. One single example will do for the moment to illustrate the results obtainable largely by using steam-driven machinery in place of human muscles and of such artifacts as water-mills; in just over a century (about 1760–1900) the production of cotton cloth in England rose by roughly 100,000 per cent. As the population in the same time rose to approximately eight times the number in about 1760, that means that, per head, the wealth of the inhabitants as far as that commodity is concerned multiplied over a hundred and twenty times. The process has since gone even further and faster in the U.S.A. It explains why industrialized countries are so very much wealthier than those that still use labourers carrying baskets or wielding shovels to build (for example) a new road, whereas the Americans race across the landscape with bulldozers.

However, this is to look at the twentieth century, not at the eighteenth, which is the concern of this book. It must also be admitted at once that in so far as this is meant as a history of continental Europe, rather than of England, it is hardly appropriate to say anything here about the Industrial Revolution because in the eighteenth century it did not affect the Continent at all, except that one or two beginnings might be found in France—if one looked for them with a powerful enough microscope. But because of those small beginnings in France, and because of the immense later importance of the Industrial Revolution, it seems justifiable to include the briefest of indications of some of the changes involved. Still less does it seem necessary to expatiate on whether it is appropriate to describe the changes as being quick enough to be called a 'revolution'. It seems anyway to be unprofitable to discuss the point, for nobody dreams of questioning the magnitude of the changes, but only whether it is right to describe as 'revolutionary' changes which have now been operating for two centuries. This is merely a matter of the time-scale one uses. Two hundred years sounds a long time if one is thinking of the life of butterflies, but for the greatest material changes in the entire half a million years of Man's history to be crammed into two hundred years appears to justify the use of the word 'revolution' as implying fast change.

Mass production by using power-driven machinery, then, began in England in the second half of the eighteenth century, and it is first of all instructive to have some sort of explanation as to why it should have begun there at that time. All the conditions necessary for this revolution were present in England.

In the first place, there is no sense in large-scale production unless there is a large number of potential customers. Britain in 1760 had only about five and a half million people, but the country, unlike most European ones, did not make it difficult for them to buy goods by erecting internal customs barriers; the whole country was one free trade area, and colonial as well as foreign markets were also available. (Internal free trade did exist elsewhere too—for example, in Russia after 1751—but most countries had a maze of internal customs barriers.) Second, communications had to be good, otherwise large quantities of raw materials and manufactured products cannot be moved to, and away from, factories. Apart from the fact that no part of England is more than about seventy miles from the sea, and that there was a great deal of coastal shipping, communications in England were extremely poor, but this weakness was quickly rectified. Third, large amounts of capital are required to set up factories with expensive machinery.

There was no lack of this. The seventeenth century had witnessed an expansion of trade so big as almost to justify one's referring to it as a commercial revolution. There was a lot of cash in England, and it tended to fall increasingly into the hands of those most likely to save and to invest, partly because the rise in the National Debt (it reached £861 million by 1815) meant that heavy taxes were levied on everyone so as to repay interest to the more moneyed people who had lent money to the government. The large amount of money available for borrowing led to a drop in the interest rates (the government paid about ten per cent in 1625 but only three per cent in 1756), and this made it possible to borrow cheaply for business purposes. That there was no reluctance to lend for such purposes is shown by the South Sea Bubble affair. Businesses expanded also because their owners showed a quite remarkable readiness to plough back profits into their business, unlike the French, who often preferred to buy a safe government job with their savings.

So much for customers, transport, and capital. It is obvious that other things are necessary as well. One of these is a large labour force. This was available from two sources: first, a natural rise in numbers because healthier living conditions and greater medical knowledge led to a fall in the death-rate (it fell from about 35·8 in 1740 to about 21·1 in 1821; briefly this means that fewer children died); secondly, changes in agricultural methods either drove people off the land or at least set them free to do other jobs. At first this labour was usually not skilled in the ways needed, but it was gradually trained by employers or inventors. Another essential is political stability, a thing which the English enjoyed after the storms of the seventeenth century had subsided and had left the country in the hands of an aristocracy which respected commerce instead of despising it, as many of the nobles on the Continent did. It would be wrong, however, to over-emphasize this point: many aristocrats on the Continent engaged in commerce, and in France, for example, the Duc de Croy was a rich industrialist; while as for Russia, the nobility there had among other things the monopoly of distilling spirits; and we have already noticed that the Swedish nobility often took to commerce. The English had further advantages; they included a well-organized banking system, immunity from the disturbance of foreign invasion, enormous quantities of coal, and, for good measure, a climate suited to the cotton industry.

If one adds up the conditions favouring mass production, what emerges is that while a good many countries had many of such conditions, England had them all, and in greater measure, than any other.

And finally England had, more than any other country, the last essential, which is simply the desire and the skill to carry out a revolution in industry.

It might seem a trifle odd to talk of the desire, but at least some very eminent economic historians have pointed out that all the ingredients necessary for an industrial revolution have been present elsewhere but nothing came of them. For instance, Imperial Rome had most of them, but technical skills were not used, if we are to take as typical the story of Suetonius who says (in his *Lives of the Caesars*, Book VIII) that the Emperor Vespasian once destroyed an invention because he thought it would cause unemployment, though he rewarded the inventor. The ancient Greeks also held mechanical skills in low esteem. One of them (Hero of Alexandria) invented a steam-engine, but it was used for faking miracles in the temple. Too much value should not be attached to this sort of explanation of why the ancient world did not become industrialized; at least, they may not have wanted such a development, but equally they could not have had it if they had wanted it, because they had no coal, and it is impossible to guess what other fuel they might have been able to use, for the area was not rich in wood either.

If there is room for argument about the desires of the ancient world, there is no doubt about the mental climate of eighteenth-century England. As Professor Ashton says: 'The industrial revolution was also a revolution of ideas . . . science had widened men's conception of the universe.' The inspiration of the changes was therefore science, and J. L. and Barbara Hammond say that 'it was natural for the disciples of Sir Isaac Newton to turn to industry', and 'science absorbed the interest and curiosity of the times'. Science, that is, as has been noticed in an earlier chapter, offered not only an understanding of Man's environment but also a chance to control it to enrich mankind. Naturally, some remained absorbed in the pursuit of knowledge for its own sake, but there was also a strong interest in more practical matters; and those with such an interest were quick to see the practical value of the great scientific revolution of the seventeenth century. Luckily for them, too, science at that time had not yet become so specialized as to be beyond the comprehension of intelligent men. This is shown by the large number of Fellows of the Royal Society who were engineers, ironmasters, industrial chemists, and instrument-makers, and as is equally shown by the large number of eminent scientists (among them were Franklin, Priestley, Black, Dalton, and Davy) who were in close contact with the chiefs of industry. Science provided the inspiration, but evidently it also provided the inventiveness without which the discoveries necessary to transform industry would not have seen the light of day. In some men, scientific and inventive ability were combined. And because they were combined in the central figure of the Industrial Revolution, we can begin a brief survey of some of the developments in some English industries with the steam-engine and the man who did most to develop it—James Watt (1736–1819).

Watt's name is linked more closely than that of anyone else with the invention of the steam-engine, and rightly so. But great inventive steps forward usually have their roots far back in the past, and this one had deeper roots than most. The honour of discovering the motive power of steam goes to Hero of Alexandria in the first century B.C., whose invention was never put to industrial use. His writings survived and were widely read at the time of the Renaissance and many people tried to use the force of steam, among them in the seventeenth century being the second Marquess of Worcester and a Frenchman, Papin. The first man to construct a steam-engine used in industry was an Englishman, Thomas Savery (1650–1715). His was appropriately called 'The Miners' Friend' because it was really a steam-driven pump for getting water out of mines. It was simply a boiler and a condenser with two pipes, the one running to the furnace and the other to the water to be pumped up. Steam went from the boiler to the condenser, was there cooled, and the vacuum thus created sucked up the water, fresh steam was let into the condenser, and the process repeated. Savery's invention, however, was not strong enough for such heavy work. A much improved version was invented by Thomas Newcomen (1663–1729). In this, the water was not sucked up directly into the condensing vessel but was drawn up by an ordinary pump connected to the engine. This had a piston in a cylinder, and the piston was connected to a lever-beam pivoting on a piece of masonry high above the ground. The pump-side of the beam pulled the piston up because the rods connecting it to the pump were heavier than the piston. Then the piston was forced down by the pressure of the atmosphere acting on a vacuum created by filling the cylinder with a jet of steam and then suddenly cooling it with a jet of water. Both jets were at first worked by turning cocks by hand, but they were afterwards geared to the lever-beam. So this is called an 'atmospheric' engine because it used the pressure of the atmosphere on a vacuum.

It was a magnificent achievement, but it suffered from the great disadvantage of being very wasteful with fuel. The alternate injection and condensation of steam meant that a monstrous quantity of fuel had to be used to reheat the cylinder after every stroke, for four-fifths of the steam produced was being used to heat up the cylinder again to a temperature at which the remaining fifth could do its work (otherwise the new injection of steam would all condense before the cylinder completed its upward stroke). In spite of this wastefulness, the engine was quite widely employed, and by 1765 there were about a hundred in use in the Tyne and Wear area.

The way to avoid this waste occurred to a Scottish instrument-maker, James Watt, while he was thinking about it in 1765 during a Sunday-afternoon stroll (a generation or so earlier, serious young men might have been thinking of less worldly matters on Sunday). The answer came in a flash: by means of a separate condenser which could be kept permanently cool while the cylinder was permanently hot. In the small-scale engine he then built, the steam, instead of being cooled and condensed in the cylinder itself, rushed into another vessel to fill a vacuum and was condensed there without lowering the temperature of the cylinder, which still had its vacuum to work with because of the exit of the steam. Many years of work were necessary before a satis-factory large engine could be constructed. Some of those difficulties were financial, but Watt also invented many supplementary devices to improve it, for instance, he put an air-tight cover on the cylinder and pushed the piston down by the pressure of steam instead of the pressure of air, thus making it truly a steam-engine. All this would have been enough to make his a great name, but he went on to convert the up and down motion to rotary motion and therefore he now had an engine capable of turning machinery (1781). Next he invented the double-action rotative engine, in which the expansive power of steam was applied to both ends of the piston (1782); in 1784 he invented the parallel motion, and further improvements followed soon after.

For the first time in the history of the world, therefore, steam-power could be used on a large scale to drive machinery, and it could be used, unlike, say, windmills dependent on the weather, or water-mills depen-dent on streams, in an unlimited way at any time or place. It soon transformed the lives of hundreds of thousands of workmen, and is the true originator of a revolution which was to transform the world, or important parts of it. For this reason one can agree that the Hammonds scarcely exaggerate when they say: 'If one man in the history of the world is to be taken as the author of modern civilization, it is this melancholy mechanic.'

After that verdict of the Hammonds, the remark of Professor Ashton, that 'the new form of power and the new transmitting mechanisms by which this was made to do work previously done by hand and muscle, were the pivot on which industry swung into the modern age', seems almost a meiosis. It is not possible here to give an adequate account of the ways in which industry did swing into the modern age and of the social and political effects of this great revolution. One or two brief examples might serve to indicate the nature and the scope of the transformation.

An almost magical difference was made to the iron industry, both by the steam-engine and by other inventions. The annual production of iron in Britain in 1700 was about 20,000 tons. The demand for iron was increasing, but British production was actually showing signs of a decline. This was because of lack of fuel. The fuel used in the main processes was charcoal, and the quantity of timber available was becoming exhausted. The need to get more, or a different, fuel was thus desperately urgent. Of course, there was unlimited coal in the country, but it could not be used. Iron was smelted in a blast-furnace fed by charcoal and raised to a high temperature by the blast from a large bellows driven by water-power. This took fourteen days, at the end of which time the molten iron was run off either into moulds, if cast-iron articles were wanted, or into sand furrows. The main furrow was called a 'sow' and smaller ones leading from it 'pigs'. When the iron cooled in the pigs it was hard and brittle, so for conversion into bar-iron malleable enough for use by smiths it was then taken to a great open-hearth forge called a 'finery' or a 'chaffery'. At the forge the iron was heated and hammered by a great hammer worked by a water-wheel. The heating and hammering was then repeated, by which time most of the impurities which had made the pig-iron so brittle were removed. More heating and hammering followed, and the iron was cut into bars; if smaller bars were needed it was taken to slitting and rolling mills. It was only in this very last process that coal could be used for heating because the sulphur in coal resulted in a product so brittle as to be unsuitable even for castings. That was the reason for dependence on the failing supply of charcoal, and it will be noticed also that the industry depended only a little less on water-power, and so on unreliable streams.

The first successful attempt to shake free of the need of charcoal was made in 1709 by Abraham Darby, of Coalbrookdale in Shropshire, who managed to produce good pig-iron smelted with coke. The local coal seems to have been fairly suited to this, but he also had very powerful blowing apparatus. Unfortunately, his iron was too impure for use by the forges, and his secrets were not generally known for a long time. His son about forty years later succeeded in making an improved pig-iron with coal, and the brothers Cranage nearly succeeded in making bar-iron from the coke-smelted pig by the use of coke. Total success, however, had to wait for the genius of Henry Cort (1740–1800). He put the pig-iron not straight into the forge but into an intermediate furnace called a 'reverberatory' or 'air' furnace which could be fed by coal since the sulphurous fumes did not affect it so badly because workmen prodded the iron through holes in the furnace with iron bars. This stirring, which was called 'puddling', caused the impurities to be burnt quickly away. The iron was then reheated and the remaining impurities removed by pressing it between iron rollers. This is one of the greatest events in the entire history of technology, for not only was production fifteen times faster than by the older methods, but, from first to last, coal could be used—and Britain had thousands of millions of tons of coal for the taking. The steam-engine completed the change, increasing production as well as freeing the industry from dependence on water-power. At first the engine was used to drive the bellows for the blast-furnace, but after Watt's discovery of a method of gearing it to rotary motion, it was also used to work the forge-hammers and for slitting and rolling.

The result can best be judged by simple figures. From 20,000 tons of iron produced in 1700, the figure rose to 68,000 tons in 1788 and to 250,000 tons in 1806. It was eagerly used for cannon, water-pipes, rails, and bridges, and somewhat later for ships and a host of other things.

Just as startling was the revolution in the cotton industry. Until the eighteenth century, cotton cloth was mostly made in India. England, however, imported and made up annually about two million pounds of raw cotton. There are very many processes involved in the business of making cloth out of raw cotton, but the two basic ones are spinning and weaving. Production on the weaving side was speeded up by John Kay in 1733. He improved the loom by his invention of the 'Flying Shuttle'; the shuttle was struck by hammers and so driven through the warp. This enabled one man to make cloth of a width that had previously taken two men. The consequent speeding up of weaving led to a demand for spinning to keep pace. For this, industry had to wait some time. In the late 1760s James Hargreaves invented a 'Spinning Jenny', which was a small hand-machine, by which a worker could spin eight threads at once, instead of only one, as on the old spinning-wheel. This device could be used in the workers' own homes; but this was not the case with the one invented by Richard Arkwright in 1769–75. He constructed a 'frame', worked by water-power. It was a roller-spinning frame which drew out the rovings before they passed to the spindle. A fresh advance was soon made (1779) with Samuel Crompton's 'Mule', so called because it had features of both the jenny and the water-frame. It produced a stronger and finer thread than Arkwright's frame. Of course it was not long before mules and spinning frames were being worked by steam-power, and spinning thus became a large-scale affair in factories instead of a slow one in people's homes.

Weaving followed spinning into the factories more slowly, but a power-loom was invented by Edmund Cartwright in 1784. It was at first useless, but it was improved by Radcliffe, who invented a dressing machine in 1803, and by Horrocks, who was a pioneer of its large-scale use. In 1813 there were 2,400 power-looms in Britain and twenty years later the number had jumped to 100,000. This vast increase in the use of machines was itself made possible by Eli Whitney's 'Gin' (1794), which immensely speeded up the cleaning of bolls of raw cotton.

A single set of figures will serve to illustrate the extent of the revolution in cotton. In 1764 Britain imported four million pounds of raw cotton; by 1833 more than 300 million pounds. This amazingly efficient industry was by then importing raw cotton from India, making it into cloth, and selling the cloth in India again at prices which the highly skilled Indian workers, still using hand-machines, could not rival.

These two industries were the most efficient, but others, notably pottery, made striking advances. But this is not the place to describe them, nor the growth of the coal industry which supplied the fuel, nor the improvements in transport brought about by work on roads, rivers, and canals, and, in the nineteenth century, by the invention of the railway locomotive. Nor should a history of Europe from 1660 to 1789 properly give indications of the social upheavals brought about in Britain by the revolution in industry, in particular by the change from a predominantly 'domestic' system of industry carried on in people's cottages to a factory system run by great capitalist chiefs. However, even such a brief sketch as this should not close without a bare mention of a book which was to have an enormous influence on the way in which the new industry was to function. The book was Adam Smith's *Enquiry into the Nature and Causes of the Wealth of Nations* (1776). In this the great Scottish economic thinker tore down the whole of mercantilist theory. Instead of the regulation of economic life by the State, he taught entire economic freedom. If, he said, regulations disappeared, and every man followed his personal self-interest, a natural balance and harmony would result; moreover, it would bring far greater efficiency.

He was the British exponent, therefore, of the Physiocratic doctrine of *laissez-faire*.

This chapter has only attempted to give the barest of indications of the beginning, in the second half of the eighteenth century in Britain, of a revolution which was already endlessly multiplying Britain's wealth and transforming the life of her citizens in ways that were followed later in other parts of Europe and in America. Such indications, it is hoped, serve to show something of one of the most tremendous ways in which the scientific revolution of the seventeenth century had, before the end of the eighteenth, begun to fashion the modern world. And since wealth so multiplied means a multiplication of military power, those countries which experienced an industrial revolution were to alter radically the 'balance of power' whose ups and downs in the period from 1660 to about 1790 we have been following in Europe.

Predominance in Europe in 1660 lay quite clearly in the West, and more particularly in France, England, and Holland, with Sweden hanging on to a precarious position of eminence in the North, and with Turkey still in appearance a menace in the South-east. By 1713 Holland had already dropped into insignificance, worn out by wars with France and England. By 1790 the power of Russia, Prussia, and Austria dominated Eastern Europe. England had won a great overseas empire by 1763, lost a great part of it by 1783, and had begun to grow again to a giant strength because of industrial change. The great strength of the Eastern Powers was based in part on the reforms they had carried out under the inspiration of the Enlightenment. By contrast the victorious France of Louis XIV seemed to have declined to the France of the Battle of Rossbach. The country which had done so much to spread enlightened ideas seemed to have grown weaker and weaker. France was none the less still a huge country of colossal potential strength, and, failing to tap those great reserves of strength by the agency of an enlightened despot, was to find them in an explosion which wrecked the Old Régime in France, wrecked it in most of Europe, and for a time wrecked the old balance of power as well.

19 · The Failure of the Monarchy to reform France, 1715–77

France provided the inspiration for the reforms of the enlightened despots, but provided it through her writers, not by her example. Yet in no country was the need for reform greater than in France. This was not so much due to any weakness in face of her neighbours, for France was even after 1763 a huge country and could not be defeated unless she were foolish enough to try fight most of Europe at once, as to the fact that, in the course of the eighteenth century, French institutions were growing ever more remote from the social and economic realities within the country, and unless the former were brought into line with the latter, an explosion was likely. But the kings of France who succeeded Louis XIV, namely Louis XV (1715–74) and Louis XVI (1774–92), utterly failed to make the necessary adjustments. As a result, the monarchy was destroyed, and the old France with it.

(a) ANALYSIS OF FRENCH SOCIETY IN THE EIGHTEENTH CENTURY

The system that Louis XIV had done so much to create rested on certain assumptions. The first of these was that the structure of French society was shaped like a pyramid, ever narrowing until it reached the solitary eminence, which was the King himself. At the base of it were the two poorest classes of the 'Third Estate', the *Tiers État*. These were the peasants—by far the more numerous—and the town workers, altogether totalling twenty million. The function of the peasants was to provide food and to pay most of the taxes, in return for which they received the King's protection in their traditional rights (which were not many, but, at least, very few of the peasants were serfs). Side by side with them were the workers of the towns, who produced goods and who were organized in guilds and given monopoly rights. Next above these workers, but also part of the *Tiers État*, were the *bourgeois*, the middle classes, who conducted the professions and trade. They too were privileged in one sense because they were protected from competition by the nobility. Above them again were three far more privileged groups. First were two sorts of nobles: the nobility of the robe, who superintended justice; and the nobility of the sword, who provided officers for the army and the personnel of the court. Both sorts of noble were immune from almost all taxation and had a virtual monopoly of the best positions in the State. The third privileged group was the Church, which looked after spiritual welfare, was very rich, drew a big income from tithes, and paid very little taxation.

Thus in theory everyone belonged to one of three 'Orders', each with its part to play in the life of the community—the Third Estate, comprising peasants, town workers, and *bourgeois*; and the two privileged groups of clergy and nobles who formed the other two Estates. At the head of all was the king, absolute and divine, father of all his people. The king was the head of the government in a very real sense in the time of Louis XIV, for the whole system of councils depended on him. There was no chief or prime minister; the various members were simply called to the council, of which the *Conseil d'en haut* was the leading one, by the king, and ceased to belong to it the moment he ceased to want them. They were entirely dependent on him, and the whole system, as Louis XIV had constructed it, turned on the existence of a king who would actively take decisions on advice, or without it, and be his own chief minister. Any decisions of the councils were his decisions, and his will was the law of the land. The most famous example of this was his personal *lettres de cachet*, which did not even go through the Chancellery, but which could by his order send anyone to jail or to exile, without trial, and without reason given. The whole administration and the whole of the law depended on him. What he gave the nation in return was internal peace (a very valuable thing after the *Frondes*), a great position in the world, and a marvellous show put on at Versailles. Nor was that show designed only for the gratification of important people. The kings of France were truly fathers of their people in the sense that anyone and everyone could gape around the gardens and palace at Versailles. When the king gave a ball, all Paris turned up without troubling about an invitation. French kings ate in public, died in public, and were even born in public. A king of France therefore needed to be a sort of superman to run Louis XIV's type of monarchy, taking all important decisions and living for his people.

The social and governmental order in France as outlined above (the latter of course is described in far more detail in Chapter 2) in so far as it ever existed at all, and naturally it did not exist in quite that simplified fashion, depended on the two assumptions that France consisted broadly of those three Estates and that the Estates would be ruled over by a very busy and very clever king. It depended also on a third assumption that everyone concerned would not be too discontented with his lot; and on a fourth assumption that the composition of society was stable.

The trouble was precisely that by the end of the reign of Louis XIV these assumptions were ceasing to correspond to realities; and by the middle of the eighteenth century they had ceased altogether to do so. This can be shown by a more detailed investigation into the real state of affairs.

The peasants for the most part had every reason to feel murderously discontented. Legally, the most unhappy were the serfs, but they are not of much importance because there were relatively few of them. The exact number is not known. Various expert estimates range from 300,000 to 1,500,000; a safe figure to accept would therefore be about a million. Serfdom was a status, and the word used for it was *mainmorte*; the serfs, whose status was something between that of a slave and a free man, were called *mainmortables*. *Mainmorte* was of two sorts, real and personal. The first meant that the serf could not bequeath goods or property to anyone not living in community with him, had to do unlimited work for his lord, and could be forced to pay to him as much as the lord could squeeze out. The second involved all that and also there were restrictions on their marriage rights, and a runaway serf could be pursued and brought back. Of the two sorts of *mainmorte*, real was in practice more burdensome, but personal more humiliating. The lot of both sorts of *mainmortables* was thus wretched, but their relatively small numbers eliminated them as a source of political upheaval.

Nevertheless, Louis XVI was enlightened enough to abolish *mainmorte* on his personal estates in 1779, in the hope that other landlords would follow suit, and he abolished the right to pursue runaway serfs (*droit de suite*) throughout France. The landlords viewed this with alarm, and there was no unanimous public opinion to support the King's action; indeed, the Academy of Besançon in 1778 gave a prize to an essay on *mainmorte*, by Grappin, which actually defended the system.

The King's enlightenment in regard to the land stopped abruptly at that limit. The huge majority of peasants were tenant-farmers, although a small number owned their land freehold. Practically all land in France fell into three classes: *mainmortable* land whose tenants were subject to real *mainmorte*, noble land owned directly by nobles, which was comparatively small in extent (certainly not more than thirty per cent, plus six per cent owned by the clergy), and non-noble land, by far the largest category. While the nobles did not own this last in the full sense of the word, its tenants had to pay feudal dues to the local nobles. Of course this means that nearly all peasants paid feudal dues, whether their tenancy was that of *métayage*, which meant a rent of half their produce in kind, or whether they were farmers paying money rents. The majority of French peasants were actually *métayers*. The feudal dues were numerous and very heavy, the most burdensome being the *lods et ventes*. As well as that, the peasants had to pay tithes to the Church and often had to use the *seigneur's* (lord's) mill, press, and bakery, where they were usually cheated, and on top of this they had to pay all the royal taxation as well—the *taille, gabelle, capitation,* and *vingtième*. The last two were supposed to be paid by the nobles also, but in practice they passed most of the burden on to the peasants. As if this were not already ridiculously heavy, they also had to do the *corvée royale* (unpaid forced labour on the roads) and had troops billeted on them. This makes a frightful picture, but it was still worse because many peasant holdings were ridiculously small, and also because of a rise in rents in the eighteenth century which was not matched by the rise in the price that the peasants got for their produce. They had to work for others in their spare time and often had to give up their land altogether. There arose a veritable rural proletariat, very much at the mercy of bad harvests or unemployment, hence the alarming amount of vagabondage in the country. Yet many peasants had risen superior to all this and managed to become quite prosperous.

The peasants varied tremendously throughout France in status and in wealth; so much so, that to lump them all together is misleading. They were not one class at all but several. It remains true, however, that the condition of the majority was so bad that revolts in the countryside were very frequent, although they were more serious in the seventeenth century than in the eighteenth. The agrarian problem nevertheless became increasingly urgent. Perhaps this was because on the whole the condition of the peasants had slightly improved since the days of Louis XIV, and they felt their plight more than can people who are totally crushed and dazed with misery; but it is more likely that they were increasingly resentful because of the decided attempts made by the nobility to extort more from them in the latter part of the eighteenth century. There was indeed at that time a 'feudal reaction', for rising prices were hitting the nobles, who sought a way out by digging up obsolete feudal rights and by getting more from existing ones. The situation was becoming more explosive all the time.

The King's contribution was, in spite of his enlightened attitude to *mainmorte*, to make matters worse. It is true that the government tried to encourage improved methods of cultivation. Under the influence of the Physiocrats, for example, an agicultural committee was set up by Bertin in 1761, attempts were made to have agricultural societies formed in each *généralité*, and in 1785 the government established a 'Committee for the Administration of Agriculture'. The government also employed the writer Toussaint to attack feudal dues in 1751 as part of its attempt at the time to force the clergy to pay taxes. On the other hand Louis XVI showed himself extraordinarily severe in enforcing his own feudal rights; for instance, an Edict of 26 July 1786 insisted on the payment of *lods et ventes* on land only doubtfully subject to that charge. What this adds up to is that in face of a worsening situation the Crown did not have a policy at all, and that what it did do was contradictory and harmful.

On the same social level as the peasants were the town industrial workers, who in theory were supposed to manufacture goods and were given monopoly rights. The real picture was far different. To begin with, at least half of French industrial production came from the workers in the countryside; that is, from peasants working for capitalists on a part- or full-time basis; and all of this was outside, and in competition with, the guilds of town workers. Ever since Colbert's day the government had tried to get all trades organized in *corporations* (guilds), subject to their *jurandes* (guild courts), within which trades were carried on by masters, tightly controlled apprentices, and employed craftsmen (the *compagnons*). The government's motive was mainly that it could extort various taxes under this system; but it failed, for large numbers of trades remained as 'free trades' (*métiers libres*), in which the apprentice system was much slacker. Inside the *corporations* there was terrible discontent because the masters generally treated the apprentices and *compagnons* very unfairly, and because it was becoming more and more difficult for the last two to become masters themselves. The industries of the country were therefore not performed by a single class, but were to a large extent managed, in the countryside, by capitalists employing a miserable lot of peasants, and, in the towns, by a privileged minority of masters lording it over the apprentices and *compagnons*. The whole system of the *corporations* and their *jurandes* was really concerned with maintaining an inefficient and privileged monopoly for masters, who exploited the public and their employees. The inefficiency and injustices of this system were abhorrent to the Physiocrats; and under their influence the government, after one last effort in 1767 to bring all trades within it, abandoned this policy and Turgot abolished the *corporations* in 1776, together with the associations (*compagnonages*) by means of which the *compagnons* had tried to improve their condition. This reform was abandoned on the fall of Turgot immediately after. But a lot of regulations hampering industry were cancelled in 1779 by Necker, and still more in 1780.

The lower ranks of the Third Estate, therefore, displayed huge disparities in status, ambition, and wealth, were seething with discontent, and riddled with jealousies and rivalries. The remaining portion of what was constitutionally the Third Estate, the *bourgeoisie*, or what can be loosely called the middle classes, was far less numerous than the peasants and craftsmen, but infinitely more powerful and diversified. These were the professional men (of whom the most influential were the lawyers), retired business men living on their *rentes*, and those engaged in commerce, who ranged from small shopkeepers to wealthy financiers, bankers, tax-farmers, industrialists, and great commercial chiefs. This class relatively was privileged too, for it was immune from the *taille*; but except for the very wealthy ones, who intermarried easily enough with the nobility and who mixed socially with the nobility on fairly equal terms, most of them were thoroughly discontented. They fiercely resented their social inferiority to the nobility, the humiliating snubs that were their constant portion, and the fact that the highest positions in the army and the Church were reserved for the nobility. The *bourgeois* were very conscious of their own ability and were frustrated by a privileged society which debarred them from the finest careers because of the accident of birth. The *bourgeois* therefore became thoroughly imbued with the doctrines of the *philosophes*; that is, with their belief in equality of opportunity and equality before the law.

They wanted an end to aristocratic privilege, and they were all the more dangerous to the existing régime because they were the natural leaders of the whole Third Estate and had the enormous mass of the peasants behind them. This was so because, to please the latter, they were prepared to demand also the end of the seigneurial régime, although not unanimously, for some of them owned feudal dues. The trouble was, then, that the *bourgeois* were often superior in wealth and brains to the nobles but were forced to accept a gallingly inferior social position. Here lies one of the chief parts played by the *philosophes* in causing the Revolution, for the *philosophes* provided the *bourgeois* with their aspirations and programme.

The *bourgeois* were becoming every day more important. The external commerce of France quadrupled in the course of the eighteenth century; this is a conservative estimate. The figures given by M. Henri Sée are: imports in 1715 worth 93 million *livres*, exports 122 million; imports in 1787, 611 million, and exports 542 million. Further indications of this mounting prosperity are given by the value of the trade done at the great fair at Beaucaire, which was 6 million in 1700, 14 million by 1750, and 41 million in 1788. Similarly the value of wine exports was 3,600,000 *livres* in 1745 and over 15 million by 1788. This upsurge of commerce, tantamount to a revolution in itself, meant that those handling it became richer and more numerous. There were even the beginnings of an industrial revolution in France as well. The *Académie des Sciences* encouraged interest in technical improvements, and the government established the *École des mines* in 1783. French inventions were chiefly in the chemical and textile industries. They were not numerous, but Bertholet discovered the use of chlorine as a bleaching agent, and there were inventions such as the first automatic loom for use in the silk industry in 1745 by Vaucason. Most of the inventions used by the French, however, came from England. They were brought in sometimes by English Jacobites, such as John Holker, who brought the spinning jennies to Rouen, or by men such as James Milne from Manchester, who set up the water-frame at Orleans, and Morgan, who used Crompton's mule in a velvet factory. Kay himself emigrated to France in 1747, but his flying shuttle was not very successful there. As for iron, the one really big works in France before 1789 was founded at Creusot by William Wilkinson[1] with the help of the French government, who gave him 3,000 *livres* a year and a free house. But these are only beginnings. The really important members of the *bourgeoisie* were the wealthy bankers and financiers.

---

[1] A brother of the famous ironmaster, John Wilkinson.

The Third Estate, therefore, was not a group of similarly placed people who were ready to go on occupying a lowly position, but an immensely variegated mass which in its lower elements was bitterly discontented with economic servitude, and which in its higher ranks was determined to obtain the place in society that it felt entitled to by its wealth, education, and brains. The *bourgeois* in particular were growing rapidly wealthier, and, under the influence of the *philosophes'* doctrines, were tending to regard themselves as the real 'nation' which should take the place of the privileged but rather useless upper Estates. Unless something were done about aristocratic privilege, an explosion might result.

The nobles themselves, if privileged, no more formed one homogeneous Estate than did the *Tiers État*. The number of people belonging to noble families was probably about 400,000. Their privileges were extensive. Most of them were enfeoffed; that is, they enjoyed seigneurial rights over land worked by peasants. They alone were entitled to carry coats of arms, and they had separate seats in the churches and separate burial-places. They did not pay the *taille*, and were not subject to the billeting of troops or the *corvée*. They could be tried for crimes only by the *parlements*, and if guilty of capital offences had the dubious honour of death by beheading instead of hanging. Last, they had a virtual monopoly of the best positions in the army, the Church, and the administration. Formerly, such positions could be entered by the *bourgeois*. But although in practice it was possible for a *bourgeois* with money to buy an army commission, the decree of 1781 restricted commissions to men who could show four quarterings of nobility; the higher ranks of the Church had become a noble monopoly by the eighteenth century; and as for the great legal and administrative offices which had originally been recruited from the *bourgeois*, these had become more and more of a closed shop for the 'nobility of the robe'.

Apart from this privileged position, the nobility had in common only the detestation of the Third Estate. Their ranks otherwise were split into fragments by differences of status, wealth, and ambition.

As to status and wealth: to begin with, there was a sharp difference between nobles who were presented at the royal court and those who were not. In 1760 a regulation laid it down that, unless noble descent could be proved to go back to the year 1400, a noble was ineligible for presentation. This was a serious matter for two reasons, in addition to the social value of presentation. One was that access to the royal court gave hope of generous pensions and offices—the King was in the habit of giving huge sums of money to court nobles; for instance, the Polignac family drew 700,000 *livres* a year this way without doing anything for it, the Duke of Chartres was given 150,000 *livres*, Madame de Pompadour distributed money to her friends and relations. If anything, this prodigality was worse in the reign of Louis XVI. Marie-Antoinette's friend the Princesse de Lamballe received a fortune, and the Counts of Artois and Provence got respectively 37 and 29 million *livres* to pay their debts. The other point about presentation was that without it an army officer could not rise above the rank of colonel, whatever his merits. Only about 4,000 noble families had been so presented, so the nobility contained a large and relatively unprivileged majority. This was a source of frightful bitterness, yet it was ceasing to have much real meaning in one sense, because a large number of the richest nobles did not bother with Versailles at all but mixed with the richest of the *bourgeoisie* in Paris society. Secondly the price rise of the eighteenth century, together with their fantastically extravagant way of living, forced all the nobles to look for more money. The usual trick was to extort more from the peasants in feudal dues. While this was the only source of income for the poorer nobles, some of the richer also went into business and industrial activity, which meant that French society was ceasing to be divided by birth; the true division was that of wealth. For instance, the Orleans family did not scruple to sublet part of their palace to vendors of various commodities, including lemonade, while the Comte de Rosen and others made fortunes out of ironworks and the West Indies commerce. On the other hand, many of the nobles were not wealthy and some were downright poor, ploughing their land sword at side. That was because there were in some cases as many as fifteen nobles trying to live off the dues of only one parish (as at Carentoir, in Brittany). This is rather exceptional, but it is true that large numbers of the nobles were in financial difficulties.

This vast difference of wealth within the nobility accounts largely for their differing aims and ambitions. The majority resented the way in which Richelieu, Mazarin, and Louis XIV had deprived them of all political influence, and grumbled at 'royal despotism'. The best-known exponent of this sort of discontent was the impoverished Comte de Boulainvilliers, whose two books, *Letters on the States-General* (1727) and *The old government of France* (1732), supported the political claims of the nobility by claiming that the nobles were descended from the conquering Franks and were somehow a superior race. Of course the nobles of this sort, although in 1787-9 often talking of liberty and reforms, stuck to their claim to political pre-eminence, while the majority insisted on feudal dues as well. On the other hand, there was a minority, mostly living in Paris, who mixed with the *bourgeois* and were ready to ask for a constitution, on the model of Montesquieu and of the English Constitution, for a different reason. Being wealthy, they were ready to throw in their lot altogether with the wealthy *bourgeois*, and to create a new society in which pre-eminence would go to wealth, not birth. This is their reason for demanding an English-style constitution, because they knew perfectly well that whatever liberty there was in England made no difference to the fact that that country was ruled by the wealthy. In other words, they were prepared to take the plunge and redraw society according to current realities, which amounted to the fact that differences of birth were ceasing to be of as much real importance as differences of wealth. Nor must we forget also the still smaller number of genuinely liberal nobles who wanted liberal reforms because they had become convinced by the *philosophes* of their justice and necessity.

The feudal nobility was thus divided by status, wealth, and purpose, and although prepared to help the nobility of the robe to attack the Crown, it did not see eye to eye with them either. The nobility of the robe had, as already observed, become almost entirely a closed caste. They, too, resented the encroachments of the royal power on what they regarded as their ancient rights, and they fought out through the *parlements*, which they dominated, a battle with the Crown which was to cause the downfall of the monarchy. The picture so far, then, is of the mass of the nation wanting to remove the privileges of the nobility, and growing ever more powerful in wealth and numbers; and of a nobility which was divided, but mostly anxious to keep its privileges *vis-à-vis* the *Tiers État*, and wanting for different reasons to increase their own power at the expense of the King. It only remains to consider the position of the other privileged Estate, that of the clergy, before seeing to what extent the monarchy was able or willing to satisfy the demands of the one, or to defend itself against the claims of the other.

The clergy were very wealthy collectively, and enjoyed virtual immunity from taxation; in fact, they taxed everyone else; for everybody, nobles included, had to pay tithes to them. Yet the clergy were hopelessly divided too. The highest positions in the Church had become a monopoly for the sons of the nobles, and the path to promotion for the ordinary priests was thus blocked. This was bad enough, but the bitterness thereby created was magnified a thousandfold by the fact that while the bishops and archbishops were generally paid huge stipends, the incomes of the parish priests were usually wretched. At the one end of the scale was a Bishop of Strasburg getting 800,000 *livres* a year and at the other were humble priests getting less than 1,000, while their assistants sometimes got as little as 200. The bishops usually rubbed salt into the wound by treating them haughtily—one of the kindest of the bishops complained that his *curés* (parish priests) stank of garlic, and the others did not approach their parish priests near enough to test the truth of this remark. The lower clergy therefore wanted the abolition of privileges, and favoured liberty, freedom of commerce, and equal political rights without distinction of Order. One of them remarked that 'the interest of the people and of the *curés* are inseparable', and it was this element in the clergy which was to ensure the triumph of the Third Estate in 1789. While the Church was thus divided by wealth, it was also split from top to bottom by the quarrel over Jansenism, and was disgraced by the behaviour of many of its members: many bishops enjoyed a gay and often immoral life in Paris, and neglected their duties, as did Louis de Bourbon-Condé, who drew 400,000 *livres* a year for being head of four abbeys, but whose nearest approach to abbatial activities was to build a marble tomb—for his pet monkey. Last of all, the spiritual authority of the Church was being quickly undermined by the ridicule of the *philosophes*. The Church was therefore rich but divided, and only the upper clergy, and not all of those, for there were some liberal bishops too, wished to retain a privileged position which the country at large was increasingly coming to think that they did not deserve.

Broadly speaking, therefore, the old system based on the three neat divisions of the country into Third Estate and the two privileged Orders of Nobles and Clergy, did not correspond to the facts; and the most important of those facts were the increasing power of the *bourgeoisie* and the extent to which the country was being transformed into a society in which wealth was becoming more important than birth. Yet while the newly wealthy, and the anciently oppressed, were becoming more and more restive at the continuation of a system which frustrated them, while giving to the nobles and clergy privilege without responsibility, most of the privileged groups were making an unusually strong attempt to keep and even extend their privileges. Therefore three of the tacit assumptions on which the Old Régime were based (listed earlier in this chapter), namely that France consisted broadly of three Estates with differing functions and status, that this state of affairs would be durable, and that most people would be content with it, had, by the middle of the eighteenth century, very largely ceased to be valid. Instead, there was every possibility of a head-on collision between the Third Estate and the other two.

The other, and most important, assumption was that the country would continue to have kings with the prestige, power, energy, and ability of a Louis XIV to make the governmental system work at all. In fact, as we have already seen, the *philosophes*, who were the mouthpieces of the aspirations of the *bourgeois*, pinned their hopes on a king who would use his position to introduce sweeping reforms by which all should be equal before the law in a free society allowing rewards to go to talent and with no privileges based on birth alone. The very important exception, of course, was Montesquieu, who wanted not an enlightened despot but a divided sovereignty, with his own class of aristocratic lawyers sharing power with the king. But instead of a sort of enlightened version of Louis XIV to end the old system and to lead them into the promised land, they got Louis XV and Louis XVI.

It would be incorrect to blame only those two Kings for the decline in the prestige of the French monarchy. Louis XIV had been very unpopular before the end of his reign. Besides, the monarchy was based on the religious theory of the Divine Right of Kings, a theory which had been defeated on the battlefields of the War of the Spanish Succession, with the result that the French King had been forced to recognize the legality of the English Revolution of 1688. Also, the very religion which supported the Divine Right theory was exposed to the merciless attacks of writers of genius from Bayle to Voltaire. It is true that the *philosophes* had no thought of attacking the prestige of the king, but to ridicule the Catholic religion was to undermine one of the most important props of his authority. Nor was the decline in the prestige of the Church entirely a matter of the *philosophes'* attacks, for Louis also had undermined the Church by his handling of the Huguenots and the Jansenists, particularly the latter (see Chapter 3), while the Church itself was partly to blame for its own internal divisions and the rift between upper and lower clergy, a rift which was yet another source of weakness. Yet when every allowance has been made, it remains true that Louis XIV's two successors gravely impaired the prestige of the monarchy.

One way in which they did that was purely political. Louis XV involved France in several wars, none of which brought any particular benefit to the country; rather did most of them appear to be mediocre attempts to pursue selfish dynastic aims, for instance the War of the

Polish Succession. As for the Seven Years War, it was not only a disaster but a disgrace. The mocking laughter at the humiliating defeat of Rossbach boded no good for the monarchy. It is true that Louis XVI's government was successful in the American War of Independence, but, as we shall see, at a frightful cost to the power as well as the prestige of the French monarchy; while the alliance with Austria, begun under Louis XV and continued under his successor, was heartily detested.

The other way in which these two Kings damaged their prestige arose chiefly from their own personality. Louis XV began, a charming and attractive boy, as the idol of the nation, and grew up to be 'Louis le bien aimé', Louis the well-beloved. When he died nobody offered up prayers for him, and his coffin was hurried to his resting-place amid the jeers of those who bothered to notice it. One of the cat-calls ('Voilà le plaisir des dames!') referred to the King's amatory pursuits, which did his reputation harm not so much because he had hundreds of mistresses but because of huge sums of money spent on them while people starved. The ladies concerned have been blamed, especially Madame de Pompadour, for exercising a bad influence on the King and for interfering disastrously in political matters. Madame de Pompadour did spend a lot of money, but it was not entirely wasted, for most of it went on beautiful works of art which would have been treasures for the country if they had been kept together after her death, and she greatly encouraged the factory at Sèvres which made French china world-famous. As for her bad influence on the King, that has been spitefully exaggerated, and in any case the responsibility is the King's, not hers, for any influence he allowed her. She did interfere in politics, but so did everybody else who could, and again that is the fault of the King, who was too lazy to run the country himself. She chose ministers for personal and prejudiced reasons, getting rid of Maurepas, for instance, and advancing Bernis and Choiseul, though it must be admitted that Choiseul was an excellent choice. It is tempting therefore to agree with the King's opinion of her (he called her 'the most delicious woman in France') and to blame him for allowing her to meddle, and for making it necessary for her to meddle, in political matters which she understood very imperfectly. As for the other famous mistress, Madame du Barry, who replaced Madame de Pompadour after the latter's death, she was gorgeous and expensive. She helped to cause the fall of Choiseul, but if she had grievous faults, grievously did she answer them, for the poor woman was beheaded under the Terror. Louis XV's unpopularity sprang from other causes as well, chiefly because people thought he was deliberately creating a famine in 1771. Nevertheless those who jeered at his death looked forward hopefully to the reign of his successor.

Unhappily, Louis XVI was politically incapable, and it was his political ineptitude that sank the monarchy. As for his personality, this dull and stodgy man, whose hobbies were over-eating and fiddling about with locks, did not have the personal presence to fill the Petit Trianon, much less the great palace at Versailles. On the credit side, he was well-behaved in private life. If he was not hated, his wife, the Austrian princess Marie-Antoinette, was loathed. Her chief vices were thoughtlessness and lack of tact. She was hated as much for the disasters that the Austrian alliance brought France as for any fault of her own; one of her nicknames was 'l'Autrichienne'. Her other nickname was 'Madame Déficit', but her extravagance was a drop in the ocean compared with the cost to France of the American War. And whatever her faults, her pitiful sufferings before her cruel execution more than paid for them.

The two successors of Louis XIV therefore failed completely to uphold the prestige of the monarchy. It is fair to point out three further causes of the weakness of the monarchy for which they cannot be blamed. The first was that Louis XIV had failed to use his great prestige and power to complete the task of making the kings of France truly despotic, although it is possible that he would not have succeeded even if he had tried. For while he had humbled the political power of the nobility, he had still left them, and particularly the nobility of the robe, enough influence to be able to thwart a weak king. In other words, he had not gone far enough. The second was the eternal weakness of all French kings—the financial system. The most vicious feature of this system was that those with most money paid practically no taxes while those with least had to carry the burden of the State. The government was not tapping the wealth of the country. It could manage with care in peacetime, but wars meant financial disaster. No king was ever strong enough to tax the privileged Orders properly, and it was the resistance of the nobility to tax reform that finally defeated the monarchy. As for the third weakness on the monarchy, one would be unjust to blame Louis XV and XVI for it altogether. For the trouble was that the system of royal councils demanded a king with the brains and energy of a Louis XIV to make it workable at all. Louis XIV had not created a united team of ministers with a prime minister at their head. At the top, to co-ordinate everything, his system could only work with a king. Louis had committed the crime of Frederick the Great and many another despot, namely, he had made no allowance for the possibility of having weak or incapable successors. For that it is a little hard to blame the successors.

France, then, in the eighteenth century, was a country in which a Third Estate demanding reform with an ever louder and more powerful voice was being thwarted by two privileged Orders who were on the whole trying both to keep the Third Estate down and to recover some of the authority they had previously lost to the monarchy. Over all, were two incapable Kings trying to run an unworkable constitution.

(b) NARRATIVE OF EVENTS

Trouble started at once with the death of Louis XIV and with the Regency of the Duke of Orleans. Louis's will allowed a considerable authority to the royal bastards and it had set up a Council of Regency with which Philip of Orleans was supposed to share power. Orleans made himself sole Regent by a sort of bloodless *coup d'état* and with the support of the *Parlement* of Paris. Louis's will was annulled, but the price paid was that Orleans gave back to the *parlements* the right of Remonstrance. It should perhaps be explained again at this point that the *parlements* were the thirteen great royal courts of law, of which that of Paris was the most important and whose (approximately) 1,100 members were the powerful nobility of the robe. In origin chiefly *bourgeois*, they had become an hereditary noble caste. The powers of the *parlements* had been threefold. First, they had strictly judicial functions as law courts. Second, they had a lot of police powers, in the exercise of which they frequently clashed with the royal *intendants*. Third, and most important, were the political powers that they claimed. The traditional way of promulgating royal decrees was to have them registered by the *parlements*. If the *parlements* did not like them, they drew up 'Remonstrances'. The king could reply by an order to obey him called *lettres de Jussion*, and, if the *parlements* still refused to obey, the king could see them personally and hold what was called a *lit de justice* (bed of justice, so called after a cushion he sat on). This was supposed to end the opposition, but if it did not, then the king could finish them by a *lettre de cachet* which ordered their imprisonment or exile to another town. This right of Remonstrance was a strong weapon only if a king lacked the force of personality necessary to overawe the *parlements*, and Louis XIV had been strong enough to keep them very much subordinate to him. The Regent had thus restored to them their most potent weapon, and this was the prologue to a long and bitter struggle between the King and the *parlements* which continued until 1789 and ended in the defeat of the King.

Perhaps one should not blame Orleans too much for this, because under any weak king the *parlements* would have reasserted their ancient rights. Besides, Orleans did what he could to correct the two weaknesses of the position of the monarchy. First, he saw that the system of Louis XIV could only be run by an exceptionally able and active king, so he tried to reform the structure of the government. He replaced the Secretaries of State by six councils, for war, navy, finance, commerce, home and foreign affairs, each with ten members. The members of each council were chosen from the nobles, including some who opposed the Regent, and from the royal officials. This can be regarded as an attempt to create a governmental machine and to give the nobles a chance to be genuinely useful. Second, Orleans tried to cure the Crown's chief weakness—finance. To do this he fell in with Law's schemes (see Chapter 9). Unhappily, the collapse of Law's schemes in 1720 meant not only the frustration of the Regent's financial hopes but also the collapse of his governmental reforms. The Regent himself died in 1723, leaving a weak and unreformed monarchy to face further trouble from the *parlements*, and the latter fought on the battlefields of religion and of finance.

The Regent's immediate successor, for the King himself was still too young, was the next in line among the princes of the royal blood, the Duke of Bourbon. Bourbon proved incapable, and the tutor of the King, Cardinal Fleury, ruled France from 1726 to 1743, the King allowing him to direct matters. Fleury tried to keep everything as peaceful as possible at home and abroad, and on the whole managed to do this, although control was gradually escaping him, especially in his last three years.

The most troublesome affair at home concerned Jansenism. The famous Bull, *Unigenitus* of 1713, had condemned Jansenism.[1] The *parlements* sided with the Jansenists, because they were furiously Gallican and anti-Jesuit, but they registered the Bull in 1729. Trouble broke out afresh in the 1730s, when Jansenist fervour was aroused by 'miracles' at the tomb of Deacon Pâris, but the *parlements* were not in favour of the wild enthusiasm produced by these, and Fleury managed to cool things down. In the field of foreign affairs, however, he was unable to prevent the senseless French participation in the War of the Austrian Succession.

---

[1] See Chapter 3.

After his death in 1743 Louis XV was determined not to have another chief minister with the powers that Fleury had held. The result soon showed the central weakness of the monarchy which Louis XIV had created, for while the King did not give support to any one minister, he was too lazy to fill the place of Louis XIV himself. The effect was chaos, with a succession of ministers not enjoying the consistent support of the King; his system of ruling by spying on them, and of having policies which often ran counter to theirs, meant erecting absence of government into a system. For about ten years after 1748, for instance, France really did not have a government, but saw vain attempts by Madame de Pompadour to find competent ministers. She did her best, but her chief concern was to allow nobody to bore the King. (She once turned Maurepas out of his presence because she read the signs of boredom on Louis's face.) In these circumstances it is therefore not surprising that France not only lost wars but that also the *parlements* were able to defeat the King over the questions of Jansenism and of finance, questions which soon came again to the fore. It will be convenient to deal with these separately, though they were interconnected.

The Archbishop of Paris, Beaumont, started the Jansenist controversy all over again by ordering the clergy to refuse the Sacraments to those unable to obtain a *billet de confession* signed by a priest who had accepted the Bull *Unigenitus*. The *parlements* supported the Jansenists (though the struggle was becoming equally a matter of resentment felt by the lower clergy against the bishops). About 1750 the Crown, or rather the minister Machault, was trying to get the clergy to pay more taxes, but the King took their side against the *parlements*, and, to reinforce his alliance with the Church against the *parlements*, the King had the taxes dropped. This did not stop the *Parlement* of Paris from issuing the *Grandes Remonstrances* of April 1753 in which was declared their right to defend the 'fundamental laws' of the kingdom. The uproar died down in 1756, when the Pope ordered the demand for *billets de confession* to be withdrawn. The triumphant *parlements* then turned on their old enemies, the Jesuits. The Seven Years War had ruined the Jesuits in the West Indies, and the *parlements* condemned the French Jesuits to pay the debts incurred. They then set up a commission to investigate the affairs of the Jesuits and it declared the rules of the Society incompatible with allegiance to the King. The King was reluctant to suppress the Jesuits, but he had lost the esteem of the whole nation to such an extent by the failures of the Seven Years War that he allowed the *Parlement* of Paris to abolish the Jesuit Order in France in 1762. Louis therefore had surrendered to the *parlements* over the whole question of Jansenists and Jesuits, and this was a mighty victory for the *parlements*. But this was to undermine one of the main supports at its very foundations, for the monarchy rested on the religious theory of Divine Right, and the Church was not only defeated by the *parlements* but discredited by the whole sordid business of the *billets de confession* (to the immense satisfaction of the *philosophes*, whose efforts to ridicule the Church were being made with the utmost boldness because the Church was divided).

The weakness of the Crown over religion was matched by its weakness over finance. The first big storm, of many, came in the period 1745–54 when Machault was Controller-General of the Finances. The War of the Austrian Succession had reduced the finances of the government to a state of desperation. Machault therefore proposed the levy of a new tax, the *vingtième*, to be imposed on all incomes and on all classes, including nobles and clergy. This was a great breach in the privileges of the latter, and it raised a storm from the *parlements*. The government ignored their opposition, but this time gave in to the clergy. In any case the tax proved impossible to collect in full from the nobles, who managed to force most of what they did pay out of the peasants.

The King had the good fortune in 1758 to obtain the services of a very able minister, the Duke of Choiseul. Choiseul's appointment came too late to avoid the catastrophic defeat of France in the Seven Years War, though he managed to give the English some anxious moments. But he was unable to do much about the finances, which after the war were naturally worse than ever. Another *vingtième* was imposed, but this aroused heated opposition from all quarters, even from the *philosophes*, for everyone said the tax was arbitrary. (It says something for the lack of political sense of the *philosophes*, at least on this occasion, for they were asking for a despotism to carry out reforms and then complaining when they got it.) Choiseul somewhat reluctantly attempted to soften the opposition of the *parlements* by sacrificing the Jesuits to their hatred. This only encouraged them to still stiffer opposition, and they began to aim at mastering the government and capturing legislative power. An occasion for fresh trouble soon arose. The military governor of Brittany, the Duke of Aiguillon, fell foul of the Estates of Brittany over a project to improve the roads. The *Parlement* of Rennes promptly supported the Estates, and a confused struggle arose between these two and the Duke, who was naturally supported by the royal *intendant*. Two features of this struggle, which dragged on from 1770 to 1775, were especially ominous. One was the alliance of the *parlements* with the feudal nobility—a somewhat uneasy alliance which thereafter gave the government terrible embarrassment. The other was really quite novel, for all the other *parlements* of the kingdom supported the *Parlement* of Rennes, and this meant postulating the corporative unity of all the *parlements*, a revolutionary attitude which cut across the tradition of the French Constitution. To make matters more difficult for the King, Choiseul himself almost certainly was secretly in sympathy with the *parlements*. If so, he was soon succeeded by ministers who certainly were not, and open war was to break out between government and *parlements*.

Choiseul's position in the government seemed strong because he had accumulated a large number of offices, but he was opposed by two ministers, Maupeou and the Abbé Terray. They had a great deal of influence because they were friends of Madame du Barry, the King's new mistress. To counteract her influence, therefore, Choiseul arranged a marriage between the Dauphin (the King's grandson) and Marie-Antoinette of Austria. This did not sweeten his relationship with Madame du Barry, Maupeou, and Terray; and to make matters worse, a furious argument broke out in the Council (*Conseil d'en haut*) over the question of giving support to France's ally, Spain, in a dispute with England about the Falkland Islands (December 1770). Choiseul wanted to help Spain, but the other two wanted to turn the energies of the government instead to an attack on the *parlements*. The King finally came down on the latter side, and Choiseul was dismissed. The new government was a triumvirate, with Maupeou as Chancellor and Keeper of the Seals (in effect the two titles usually went together, the former being honorific and real power resting with the *Garde des Sceaux*, or Keeper of the Seals), Terray as Controller-General of the Finances, and Aiguillon in charge of Foreign Affairs.

The crisis of the reign now arrived. The new men in the government were intelligent and tough, and decided to finish the resistance of the *parlements*. On 7 December 1770 a royal *lit de justice* forced the *Parlement* of Paris to register an Edict forbidding all concerted opposition by the *parlements* and the use of talk about their 'unity'. Nevertheless the *parlement* continued to protest, and suspended the administering of justice. This was open defiance, and the King decided that the time had come to end it once and for all. They were given one more chance to return to obedience, and they flatly refused. So in January 1771 the great step was taken, and the members of the *Parlement* of Paris were exiled. They were ordered to various uncomfortable parts of France. They did not cease their complaints, and some of the nobles and all the other *parlements* expressed their sympathy. But the King and his ministers stuck grimly to their decision. They decided on a drastic reform of the judicial system. In January 1772 Maupeou abolished the purchase of judicial posts, and thus at one blow wiped out the hereditary nobility of the robe, declared that justice should be free (that is, the numerous *épices*, fees, which made it so expensive were eliminated), and created a new *Parlement* of Paris, whose members were appointed by the King and whose powers were still further curtailed by giving some of its functions to six new high courts. This system was next extended to the provinces.

This was a tremendous reform, entailing as it did the obliteration of the most troublesome members of the privileged nobility. Its success could easily have meant further reforms, and a really great king might have brought in most of the *philosophe* programme. If he had, no doubt he would have saved the monarchy and averted a revolution by bringing French institutions into line with the true social and economic realities of the country, and at one bound he would have made France a truly modern State in which anomalies in the administration were swept away along with obsolete privileges; and instead would emerge a land in which careers were open to talent and in which all were equal before the law. However, the battle was by no means won. The government could count on the approval of the *philosophes* because they hated the *parlements*. Indeed, the latter had protested against *lettres de cachet* as an infringement of personal liberty, but only when they were the victims; in every other way the *parlementaires* were cruel obscurantists. They fought against the liberty of the Press, did their best to continue the persecution of the Huguenots, clung to judicial torture, and strongly defended all privilege, their own more particularly, but also those of the trade *corporations*. Small wonder that Diderot called them 'intolerant, bigoted, and stupid', while Voltaire, their most persistent foe, called them 'murderers'. Everything depended, then, on whether the government would stand firm against the uproar which the fallen magistrates were sure to create.

A virulent pamphlet war was at once waged against Maupeou. These used ominous words like 'liberty', 'natural rights', 'social contract', 'the rights of the nation', etc. It should be noticed that the *parlementaires* probably did just as much as the *philosophes* to popularize such notions, only for a very different reason. Their most telling propaganda was aimed at 'ministerial despotism'; they were able to bamboozle the public by saying that the King's actions were unconstitutional and despotic; and a good deal of this hypocritical nonsense was believed. It added greatly to Louis's unpopularity but, to his credit, he persisted in this great policy, for which he has never been sufficiently respected.

Nothing so happy was achieved for the eternal weakness of the finances. Possibly to tackle financial privilege, at that moment, would have been to risk too dangerous an opposition. At all events, Terray was faced in 1770 with a deficit of sixty-three millions, and he tried to meet this by minor reforms, such as one or two new indirect taxes, a reduction in the interest paid on the debt, better terms from the tax-farmers, and another *vingtième*. The extravagance of the court did not help matters, and popular resentment rose to frantic heights when the King's project to establish stores of grain (to prevent famine) were interpreted as designed to corner the market and drive up prices. At the time of his death in April 1774 the King was more unpopular than ever, and his action in destroying the *parlements* had made him less, and not more, liked.

Deplorably enough, even that was not to endure. The new King, Louis XVI, possessed not a half of the brains of any of the four preceding Bourbon kings. Almost his first deed was to recall the *parlements* and to bow to the clamour of the nobles of the robe and of the nobles of the sword by abolishing Maupeou's *parlement* and high courts (12 November 1774). He seemed timid in face of the agitation coming not only from them but from the Provincial Estates and even the towns as well. Moreover, the King was anxious to undo the work of the wicked Louis XV. The *parlements* on their return were greeted by the crowds with joyful acclamations—their propaganda, and the unpopularity of Louis XV, had thus saddled France again with the most selfish of the privileged classes—and although the King told the *parlements* that they would have to keep to their proper judicial functions, they were burning for revenge.

If the King seemed blindly to be destroying his own authority with one hand, he yet struck a great blow for reform with the other. He gave his confidence as head of the ministry to Maurepas, then an old man of seventy-three, and the key post of Controller-General of the Finances was given to Turgot. (Terray and Aiguillon were dismissed.) Though the reappearance of the *parlements* cast a gloom over the *philosophes*, the appointment of Turgot sent them wild with delight.

For Robert-Jacques Turgot (1727–81) was the most prominent of the Physiocrats, and the darling of the *philosophes*. He had contributed to the *Encyclopédie*, and had a distinguished record of enlightened rule in the *généralité* of Limoges, of which he had been the *intendant*. The work he now attempted as minister is of great importance, although it did not endure, because it possibly represented the last chance for the monarchy to reform France.[1]

The most pressing need was to reform the finances, but Turgot's aims went far beyond that. He wanted also to establish economic and religious liberty and social justice, and that is why he was described as having 'the heart of l'Hôpital[2] and the head of Lord Bacon'. He was also an administrator of great practical experience, and knew that reforms would have to be introduced gradually if they were not to arouse too much opposition.

He began by abolishing the grain stores of Louis XV, thereby gaining the confidence of the public, and then tackled the finances. The deficit in 1774 was forty-eight million *livres*. He made economies, of which the most surprising was a reduction of his own salary by nearly a half, which had a big moral, if a trivial financial, effect. He reduced the useless subsidies to France's allies and got more money out of the tax-farmers. All this was merely the time-honoured papering over the cracks that all finance ministers had tried when they had to, but much more significant were reductions on the customs duties on food entering Paris, so as to help the poor, and increased charges on carriages entering the city which everybody had to pay: nobles, clergy, and even the King. These measures reduced the deficit to eighteen millions.

He also allowed the free internal circulation of grain; that is, it could be sold in any part of France instead of only locally; this was an encouragement to production. The price of bread went up and riots broke out, but he stuck to his guns. He even tried to give full toleration to the Huguenots, but failed. His real purpose was to secure the 'collaboration of the monarchy with the nation', and to carry out a huge scheme for the reform of local government which should ensure equal and fair taxation and local handling of roads, canals, education, and charity. The plan was drawn up for him by Dupont de Nemours whose *Mémoire sur les municipalités* of 1775 enlarged ideas which Turgot had sketched in his article, 'Foundations', in the *Encyclopédie*. However, opposition to Turgot was mounting, and, realizing that his time was probably running out, he decided at the end of 1775 to bring in reforms with less caution than before. He issued six Edicts. One of them regularized the provisioning of Paris, but the others tore a great hole in the

---

[1] Not, strictly speaking, according to the concept of 'enlightened despotism', which was less controlled than the Physiocratic ideal of a 'legal despotism'. They meant, roughly, a despot who would respect 'natural law'.

[2] The tolerant minister of Catherine de Medici in the sixteenth century.

old fabric of French society. For he abolished the *corvée royale*, replacing it by a money payment. He also abolished the *corporations de métiers* (craft guilds) and their *jurandes*. The preamble to this Edict declared that there was a 'natural right to work' ('droit naturel de travailler'), and so Turgot had inaugurated total economic liberty. Anyone could freely engage in any occupation, and the antiquated monopolistic privileges of the guilds were swept away (with the exception of chemists, printers, and goldsmiths). The destruction of one set of privileges in accordance with the Physiocratic doctrines of liberty was meant to be the prelude to the destruction of all privileges.

It was not to be. Turgot was furiously opposed by the clergy, by the *parlements*, by the Farmers-General, by the masters of the guilds, by the Queen. Louis XVI took fright. Turgot spoke bravely to him of the fatal danger of yielding. He even dared to remind him of the fate of Charles I of England. Unhappily, Louis, no judge of a man or of a situation, thought that Turgot was impelled by vulgar personal ambition. Turgot then saw his next projects, for a ministry of education and for the redeeming of feudal dues, in jeopardy because one of the ministers, Vergennes, favoured a war with England, which would have wrecked any hope of reforming anything. He quarrelled with Vergennes, but the King supported the latter, and Turgot was dismissed on 12 May 1776. Voltaire accurately described this as 'a disaster'. With him fell all his reforms, and the last good chance to save the monarchy of the Old Régime.

The next Controller-General was Clugny, who failed to put the finances right, so in June 1777 the King called on the Swiss banker, Jacques Necker. Necker had a reputation for honesty and ability, but the situation called for more than that, for in 1778 the French decided to support the Americans in the War of Independence against the English. The French motive was a desire for revenge for the defeats of the Seven Years War. They got it, but it boomeranged back on themselves.

20 · The American War of Independence, 1775–83

(a) *EVENTS LEADING TO THE WAR*

Just twenty years after the triumph of the British in the Seven Years War the thirteen colonies in North America flung off their allegiance to the Crown and declared their independence, becoming the United States of America. This is clearly one of the most decisive happenings in the entire history of the world, but in a history of Europe from 1660 to 1789 we must confine ourselves to its significance for the Europe of that time.

The development of the colonies had been very rapid. This is most easily seen in the sheer size of their populations. Their population in 1714 was only about 400,000, but by 1763 it was about two million, and by 1783 nearly three million. This increase was in part natural, that is by births, but it owed much to immigration. Between 1700 and 1776 some 250,000 Ulster Scots, driven from home by the decay of their textile industry, by grasping landlords, and by religious grievances, poured into the colonies. Their Presbyterian religion disposed them to rebellion, or so it is often said, and actually many of them were to be found later in the ranks of the Continental Army. The other most important group were Germans, chiefly from the Palatinate.

The economic development of the colonies was even more impressive. In certain respects their industry rivalled and even surpassed that of Great Britain. For instance, in 1750 Parliament passed the Iron Act, which prohibited the setting up of any more slitting, plating, and steel mills in America—this was an attempt to protect the industry of the mother country from American competition. In spite of this, by 1775 there were more furnaces and forges in America than in Britain, and the American output of pig- and bar-iron was greater than the British. The American shipbuilding industry also seems to have been more efficient than the British. By the beginning of the eighteenth century Massachusetts Bay alone was building about 140 ships annually. By 1715 they were selling about 40 or 50 ships a year to English merchants, and by 1775 about thirty per cent of all the ships employed in the commerce of the mother country had been built in America—not surprisingly, since it cost almost twice as much to build a ship in England as in America. American ships also dominated the carrying trade in American waters; for example, of 496 ships clearing Boston (Massachusetts) in 1753 all but 64 had been built in Massachusetts Bay, and only 5 had a London registration. By 1775 seventy-five per cent of the commerce of the continental colonies was carried in American ships. In addition, the Americans had a huge trade in naval stores produced by them—pitch, turpentine, anchors, chains, sails, and so on. Nor was that all, for their pottery, stoneware, and glassware industries were highly competitive, and American rum had pushed English gin out of the American market.

The American fishing industry was no less prosperous. It had virtually a monopoly in the Gulf of Maine and dominated the cod fisheries off Nova Scotia. The products of the American soil were no less successful. American milling and meat-packing competed successfully with English; for instance, by 1775 Pennsylvania alone was exporting 350,000 barrels of flour per annum; there were huge exports of rice and enormous exports of tobacco; and furs and timber were also important.

The English authorities had for many years tried to place all commerce involving English overseas possessions under regulation. The broad principle was to make England the *entrepôt* of the trade of the colonies. For instance, goods from Europe and the Far East intended for America had to come to England first. Also, 'enumerated' articles produced in America had to come first to England; they were at first chiefly tobacco, sugar, cotton, indigo, and ginger, but the list became longer and longer with the years: in 1704 rice, molasses, and rum were added to it; in 1705 tar, pitch, resin, turpentine, hemp, and masts; in 1721 copper and certain furs, and so it went on. Various Acts completely prohibited certain American exports: raw wool in 1699, beaver hats in 1732, and so on.

This system of control has been much criticized as unfairly restricting American trade in the interests of the mother country. In fairness to the English authorities it should be said that the enumerated articles had a monopoly on the English market and in some cases exporters were given bounties for exporting to England; that a big trade was done in articles not on the list; that many exemptions were granted; that in the case of tobacco the English industry was deliberately ruined for the benefit of the Americans; and that American shipping had grown up under the shelter of the Navigation Acts. Indeed, if the English regulations had been harmful to America its impressive economic growth would not have taken place, and an American historian (Mr Lawrence H. Gipson) says of the whole system of control that the Americans 'were among its chief beneficiaries'. Perhaps one of the most important points about it was that the English were lax in enforcing the laws, so that English control was not in practice burdensome to the Americans.

However, it is obvious that by 1763 the Americans were very rapidly coming to complete economic maturity and that anything looking like an unfair extension of controls in the interests of England might cause trouble. But such trouble would be unlikely to come from a unanimous opposition. The chief influence in the colonies was in the hands of the wealthy merchants and industrialists, who formed an aristocracy of wealth along the coast, and who indulged also in land speculation, with the result that land tended to become concentrated into great estates. This caused many of the poorer colonists to push westward in search of land, although even the frontier land was often bought up by rich speculators along the coast. It is roughly true, therefore, that a wide split developed between the merchant aristocracy on the coast and the tenant-farmers and frontiersmen inland. The aristocracy also had political control, for the various colonial legislatures were elected by property-owners; in Massachusetts and Connecticut, for example, only sixteen per cent of the population had the vote. This added to the grievances of the back-country farmers, who were often heavily in debt to the merchant aristocrats, who were taxed to support the administration and often to support an established Church not to their liking, and who claimed that they were not given enough defence against the Indians. To their complaints were often added those of the artisans of the towns. The poorer farmers sometimes rebelled, but they were always defeated.

In these internal quarrels the British government had surprisingly little say. The colonies had been founded separately, most often by grants to proprietors, but by 1752 eight of the thirteen were royal provinces, three were subject to proprietors (Maryland, Pennsylvania, and Delaware), and two (Rhode Island and Connecticut) were ruled by assemblies of voters who elected their own governor. All had a 'popular' assembly elected by the voters, and there was also a council selected from the powerful and wealthy families of each colony and chosen by various methods, but usually by the royal governor, though in Massachusetts by the 'Lower House'; and certain of the others had different arrangements. The powers possessed by the colonial legislatures were very extensive. They could make laws for the general and local affairs of the colony and levy certain taxes. They were limited only by the provision that their acts could not run contrary to the laws of England or to the terms of their charter. Their chief strength lay in the fact that they paid the salaries of the governors and of the administrative officials. Whatever the theory, or whatever the local differences in the government of the colonies, therefore, it is certain that by 1750 the colonies were virtually self-governing. The wretched governors had very little real authority and had to dance to the tune of their legislative assemblies and of the British government; in practice if there was any contradiction between the wishes of the two sets of masters they usually fell in with the desires of the locals. On the other hand, the aristocracy which dominated the assemblies were themselves fighting a battle on two fronts; that is, against agrarian discontent and increasing demands for more self-government from the poorer farmers and frontiersmen, and against increasing attempts at greater control on the part of the British government.

It was that policy by the British government which was to do much to cause the war for independence. That policy took the form chiefly of increases in taxes. Yet it would be grotesque to suppose that the ties with England were severed because of money only. Britain was after all the 'mother country', and to it the colonists were attached by very strong and very natural ties of affection as well as of interest. As late as 1764, few Americans would have described themselves as 'American'. They would have called themselves 'Englishmen'. Many writers have made the point that, sooner or later, the interests of the vast land, very different from England, and separated from it by 3,000 miles of water, would have resulted in a political separation. It is even suggested that the Americans would be certain to go their own way the moment that danger from the French was removed, as it was, or seemed to be, by 1763. Possibly this is so, but it is certain that for a very long time the majority of the colonists did not think so. The truth is that, for many of the colonists to reject the title of British subject and to think of themselves as Americans, there had to take place an alienation of the mind of the colonists from the mother country. Professor Arthur M. Schlesinger, the distinguished American historian, has shown in a recent (1959) and very brilliant book, *Prelude to Independence*, how such an alienation was effected. A word or two about the 'American mind' is therefore appropriate at this point.

Education in the colonies had reached standards that are truly astonishing, when allowance is made for the initial need to ensure the necessities of life. From the first, a great and widespread interest was shown in it. The foundation of Harvard College in Boston took place as early as 1635, and the Massachusetts legislature tried, without much success at first, to provide free elementary education also. The various Churches were also active in founding schools. A remarkable number of famous colleges were founded in the eighteenth century, after that of William and Mary College in 1693 in Virginia. They included Yale (1716, Connecticut), Brown (1764, Rhode Island), the College of New Jersey (started in 1747 and moved in 1756 to Princeton), Dartmouth College (1767), the Medical College at Philadelphia (1765), King's (Columbia) (1754), and others. By 1775 hundreds of students were graduating annually from these. Some also went overseas to study at Oxford and Cambridge, and far larger numbers went to Edinburgh, to the Middle Temple, and to the Universities of Paris and Leyden. Nor was instruction at lower levels neglected. Quite apart from the schools run by most of the religious bodies, most of the New England communities had public elementary education, there were large numbers of schools run by the private enterprise of their teachers, and in many of the larger towns there were grammar schools as well. There was also a good deal of self-education; it is amazing and delightful to learn that there were back-country farmers who could read Latin, and one of the shrewdest men in America, Benjamin Franklin, although he founded a college, never graduated from one.

Education among the colonists was therefore very widespread, and it was far from being shallow. Naturally, the students learnt what was necessary for their careers such as medicine or law, but other subjects were widely studied. Professor Charles A. Beard names four books as being supremely important. They were: *Coke upon Littleton*, the classic treatise on English common law, which defended the legal rights of the subject; Adam Ferguson's *Essay on the History of Civil Society*; Locke's two *Treatises of Civil Government*: and Montesquieu's *L'Esprit des Lois*. All the doctrines of the *philosophes* were circulating in America, prominent among them being the notion of natural rights to life, liberty, and the pursuit of happiness. One of the men steeped in these ideas was Thomas Jefferson. It would be a dangerous state of affairs if the numerous holders of these ideas were ever to fall foul of the British government.

It would be more dangerous still if the most potent weapon for influencing opinion, the Press, took up a hostile attitude. The first American newspaper was the Boston *News-Letter*, which first appeared in April 1704. The further growth of newspapers was facilitated by the rise of the postal service. A local post office was started in Massachusetts in 1639. This example was followed in other colonies, and in 1692, under a royal patent of that year, an intercolonial postal service was established as a private enterprise. Fifteen years later it was taken over by the British government and greatly developed under successive postmasters, of whom the most famous was Benjamin Franklin, who took up the appointment in 1753. The result was not only greatly to help correspondence between individuals but also to facilitate the wide circulation of newspapers. These accordingly grew in number; Professor Schlesinger puts the number at thirty-eight by 1775. As it turned out, very many of them conducted a fierce propaganda war against the government. Men like John Adams and his kinsman Samuel Adams fought with courage, tenacity, and often with complete lack of scruple, to keep alive a strong sense of grievance against the mother country in face of the comparative indifference of most of the colonists, an indifference which indeed at times almost brought the handful of radicals to the point of despair. But the work was done; as Professor Schlesinger says, 'The Revolution was effected before the war commenced. The Revolution was in the hearts and minds of the people. This radical change in the principles, opinions, sentiments, and affections of the people was the real American Revolution.'

If the ideas of Locke and of the *philosophes* found a ready reception in America, and if a number of able propagandists for that and other reasons soon took up an attitude of inveterate hostility towards the British government, it was still necessary, in order that enough of the colonists should want to join a movement for independence, to give them enough grievances for the propagandists to work on. These, in the years after 1763, the British government did not fail to provide.

The policy of the British government after 1763 was not a clear-cut affair. Its aims, and the energy with which they were pursued, varied greatly with successive ministries, with the need to devote attention to other matters, and with the pressures which different groups of merchants and other interested parties were able to exert. Broadly, however, two policies were pursued with a certain amount of consistency. They were to extend the political and the economic control of the mother country over the colonies. It is not surprising that they met with political and economic opposition.

There was of course nothing new about either aim. The point is that such attempts as had hitherto been made to implement them had on the whole been failures. The self-government of the colonies had gone on increasing, and the attempts to control their economic life had been largely ignored. The colonists had been helped for a long time by the indifference of the head of the British government, Sir Robert Walpole, who during his long period of office (1721-42) had let them do much as they pleased because he preferred not to arouse opposition anywhere.

Things changed very soon after his time. For one thing, it had been seen clearly enough during the Seven Years War that the different colonies were reluctant to pursue a common defence policy. After the war, the rapid expansion of the frontier would obviously entail trouble with the Indians. So the decision was taken to keep a standing army in America. This was itself a new idea. A Quartering Act of 1765 ordered the colonial legislatures to pay for some of the needs of the British troops. The second policy aimed at controlling relations with the Indians and at controlling frontier expansion; this found expression in the Royal Proclamation of 1763. Both these policies were strongly resented, but it was the third that produced a real storm. The Seven Years War had sent the British National Debt up to an immense figure. On the other hand, previous British attempts to regulate American commercial life, in the interests of British merchants, by a series of mercantilist regulations and prohibitions on American trade, had not been much obeyed. More important, there was an immense amount of smuggling and of trading with, for example, the French West Indies, which made nonsense of British attempts to restrict the Americans to the dual role of supplying primary products for England only, and of acting as a closed market for English merchants and manufacturers. The government now decided on several measures to make the Americans pay a part of the costs of defence, and also to enforce and extend the trade regulations.

In 1763 an Act of Parliament authorized the use of naval vessels to stop smuggling, and an Order in Council planned reforms in the customs service, which were duly effected in the next year by the 'Sugar Act'. This Act also reaffirmed the Molasses Act of 1733, which had been a dead letter. The new duty on sugar was to be threepence instead of sixpence a gallon, and the merchants were alarmed because its enforcement would ruin the rum industry. But the storm broke with the passing of the Stamp Act of 1765.

The English minister, Grenville, decided that about £60,000 per annum could be raised if the Americans were made to use stamps on newspapers, legal documents, and business transactions. The amount was really trifling, but the great importance of the Act was that it implied the right of the British Parliament to levy internal taxes in America. It did not seem at first sight an unfair or an unwise measure. In view of the very heavy taxation imposed on the English themselves for Imperial defence, it seemed not unreasonable to ask the Americans for a mere £60,000 to help in the support of a garrison for their own protection, especially as there was considerable popular distress in England at the time. The London agents of the American colonies told Grenville that the Act was fair, and many important Americans accepted appointments as Stamp Distributors in the colonies.

All the more unexpected, therefore, was the violence of the American reaction to the Stamp Act. By its very nature it was likely to meet with objections from the most vocal and influential of the colonists—the journalists, lawyers, and merchants—but opposition was by no means confined to them. When the first protests proved unavailing, there was serious and widespread rioting. The Stamp Distributors went in fear of their lives, and no member of the public dared to use the stamps even had he wished to.

Serious as was the rioting, the verbal protests were graver still. It has already been seen that the colonists had grown to economic and intellectual maturity. With that was now fast developing political maturity. Not for nothing was Locke's *Treatise of Civil Government* as familiar to them as the Bible, as we are told by a famous American historian (Mr Edmund S. Morgan). The Americans were heirs to the Revolution of 1688 just as much as were their brothers in England. They were beginning to wonder by what right Parliament could tax them without their consent. As early as 1760 the fiery young lawyer, James Otis, in the famous Writs of Assistance case, declared that parliamentary legislation was invalid in the colonies. A year later the Connecticut Assembly, while admitting that Parliament had the right to regulate trade, denied its authority to levy internal taxes in America. This attitude was now adopted by nine of the colonial legislatures, who sent representatives to a 'Stamp Act Congress', which for good measure talked of 'natural rights' and 'laws of nature'. Even this Congress, however, had no sort of desire for independence from the mother country, and admitted in a general sense the subordination of the colonies to the British Parliament. To that extent the colonists were not entirely out of sympathy with Grenville, for, to do Grenville justice, he seems to have had some sort of vision of the Empire with a supreme centre and the outer parts helping each other.

The government was handicapped also by the attitude of many prominent English statesmen. Chief of these was no less a person than William Pitt. He said that Parliament had the right to legislate for, but not to tax, the colonies. His meaning is far from clear, but he might have intended giving the colonies very great autonomous rights within possibly some sort of federalized empire and attached to it by various emotional and other ties symbolized by common affection for the Crown. Unhappily, such a notion was too far ahead of circumstances, if only because vital to it was a king above party politics—a phenomenon not then existing.

What ruined the Stamp Act, however, more than the above considerations was an American boycott of English goods and a refusal by Americans to pay their debts to English merchants. Such was the clamour raised by the latter at the prospect of ruin that Grenville's government fell, to be replaced by that of Lord Rockingham, and the Stamp Act was repealed in 1766. The government also reduced the duty on sugar to one penny. This surrender was accompanied by a face-saving Declaratory Act, which reaffirmed the government's right to legislate for the colonies. The Americans ignored this and rejoiced at their practical victory, drinking the health of William Pitt and even of George III. For a time the colonies were fairly quiet, although there was still some opposition to the Quartering Act.

This was all very well, but for the British government it meant that the colonists were still not contributing to the heavy cost (about £400,000 a year) of defence. Nor did it appear that the English taxpayers either could or would pay any more. There were bread riots in England, and the government sustained a defeat in the House of Commons over the land tax, which was running at what was thought to be the scarcely endurable figure of four shillings in the pound. Furthermore, the opinion was growing in England that it was most unfair for the English to be crushed by taxes while the Americans paid nothing.

In spite of these difficulties it seemed likely that the English government would adopt a conciliatory policy, for the Rockingham government fell and was replaced by that of Grafton and Pitt, who were well disposed towards the colonists. But Grafton did little; Pitt, who was ill, soon resigned; and the direction of colonial matters fell into the hands of Hillsborough and others, who determined to take a firmer line. Townshend, in charge of the Treasury, declared that he knew how to extract taxes from the Americans without offending them.

Townshend appears to have mistaken the nature of the American objections to the Stamp Act. He may have been innocently misled by some of the Americans themselves, most notably Benjamin Franklin. Franklin testified before the House of Commons, 13 February 1766, about the American attitude, and gave the impression that the Americans only objected to internal taxes, not to taxes on imports and exports for the purpose of regulating trade. His analysis of the situation was wholly mistaken, and may have influenced Townshend. The latter, at all events, was now to embark on a policy that instead of getting money out of the Americans was to force many of them to realize that logically an objection to taxes really meant a demand for independence, for though the colonists talked of 'no taxation without representation' (i.e. in Parliament) few of them wanted to send representatives to Westminster. Townshend's measures were to bring the Americans to political maturity.

On 26 July 1767, Parliament accordingly passed his Revenue Act, which revealed his famous scheme for painless extraction. This consisted of extra duties to be placed on the importation of glass, paper, paint, and tea. In the case of tea the duty paid on import to England was, however, given back on re-export to America, which meant that the price of tea to the colonial consumers was reduced. It was expected to raise £40,000 a year from these measures. At the same time the government took further steps to prevent smuggling by setting up a separate American customs service and new Admiralty Courts to enforce the laws. Here again the amount of money involved was not large. But the money to be obtained from the new duties was to be used to pay the salaries of the colonial governors and officials, and this clearly meant an intention to make them independent of the colonial legislatures, thus greatly strengthening the position of the government's subordinates in relation to the colonists.

Inevitably, there was once again violent opposition in the colonies. This time it was by no means as unanimous as at the time of the Stamp Act. Ever since 1763 there had been a growth in every colony of 'popular' parties. These were revolutionary extremists. Their leaders were drawn from all classes of society; some were merchant or planter aristocrats, but more of them were lawyers and middle-class men. The most important of them were Richard Henry Lee, Thomas Jefferson, Samuel Adams, John Adams, Christopher Gadsden, and James Otis (the last was the leading inspiration of the Stamp Act Congress). They were united in their ardent support of American liberties, and drew considerable support from the mechanics and artisans, especially in times of depression. They received little support, however, from the governing oligarchies who controlled the colonial legislatures, and were viewed with increasing alarm by the wealthier merchants generally. Large numbers of back-country farmers also opposed them because the 'popular' leaders were indifferent or hostile to the political and econo-mic claims of the tenant-farmers. By 1767 the merchants too were becoming alarmed by the popular parties, fearing not only loss of trade because of clashes with the British government, but also the loss of their own dominant political position to the popular leaders. Consequently some of the merchants could only be brought to agree to fresh boycotts of British goods because they were frightened of the popular leaders and of the mobs they controlled. The merchants of Boston, for instance, at first refused to stop importing British goods, and those of Philadelphia were even longer in agreeing to this measure.

There was, however, enough of a boycott and enough violence to make the new taxes a complete failure. In 1769 only £5,561 was collected, and the figure for 1770 was £2,727. The result was therefore another British defeat, and in December 1770 Lord North's govern-ment repealed Townshend's Revenue Act, greatly to the relief of the American merchants, who hoped to regain their trading losses and also the political control which was being wrested from them by the popular leaders. Once again, however, the British government attempted to save its face by retaining the duty on tea, which seemed a matter of small importance because the Americans went on smuggling it.

If the British government's retreat came as a welcome relief to the colonial aristocracy and particularly to the merchant aristocrats, it infuriated the popular leaders. They tried to force the merchants to keep up the anti-British boycott, but failed. They were also not very happy at a trade revival which then occurred and which removed economic discontent, and with it much ammunition for propaganda. Nevertheless, the popular leaders kept up their agitation, and in this they were able to use the 'Boston massacre' of 5 March 1770. The newspapers of that town, which had a British garrison and was the headquarters of the hated Customs Service, kept up abuse of the British, and a mob stoned and snowballed a party of soldiers. They fired, although the commanding officer, according to his own statement, had ordered them not to, and four or five men were killed and several wounded.

The popular leaders made the most of it, but the soldiers were then moved out of the town, some of them tried and two punished, and most of the merchants of the town refused to stop importing British goods and were glad to be quiet for a year or two. Undismayed, the popular leaders, James Otis, Samuel Adams, and others, kept up agitation through their control of the Boston town meeting. In 1772 as a result of the *Gaspée* affair, when a revenue cutter was destroyed by the inhabitants of Rhode Island, assisted by Jefferson, Patrick Henry, and Richard Henry Lee of Virginia, they persuaded first the Virginia legislature and then the others to set up standing committees to keep in touch with each other and to concert measures of resistance against the British whenever necessary. They thus had, by the middle of 1773, an organization which covered the thirteen colonies for resisting the British. All they then needed was something to inflame public opinion, and once more the British government obligingly gave it them.

This was the Tea Act of 1773. There was still a duty of threepence on every pound of tea imported into America; the Act allowed the East India Company to import its tea directly into America instead of bringing it first to Britain, and to appoint its own agents to market it. The agents were of course American merchants, but the smugglers were badly hit because, as a result of the direct selling to America, the tea could be sold more cheaply than before, and smuggling ceased to be profitable. There was also complaint from some of the more honest merchants, but the real importance of the Act was that it gave the popular leaders a chance. They held a meeting in Philadelphia which passed resolutions once more saying that the British had no right to tax the Americans because the latter were not represented in Parliament, thus repeating an argument that had by then become time-honoured in America, and which was indeed a difficult one for the beneficiaries of the revolt against the Stuart kings to answer. They demanded that the tea be sent back. Similar action was taken at other places, and the secret revolutionary organization, the Sons of Liberty, called for a boycott. The most definite action came in Boston, where the Boston Committee of Correspondence, under the leadership of Samuel Adams, incited the mob, with the result that a cargo of tea was dumped in the harbour on 16 December 1773.

This deed infuriated the British government and Parliament. It was resolved to take stern action in reply to what was regarded as a deliberate provocation. Four Acts were quickly passed, known from that day to this as the 'Intolerable Acts'. The Boston Port Act closed that port until the tea was paid for. The Massachusetts Government Act greatly reduced the powers of the Massachusetts legislature and increased those of the royal governor. The other two provided for the billeting of British soldiers and for the trial out of the colony of British officials administering the colony (in case of their being accused of crimes in carrying out their duties). At the same time the Quebec Act, not connected with the others, aroused bitterness because it gave toleration to the Catholics in Canada and transferred the region north-west of the Ohio River to Canada.

The Boston Committee of Correspondence at once sent messages to all the other colonies urging a boycott of British goods. At first they were not very successful for although the other popular leaders gave their warm support, the merchants generally were lukewarm; indeed, they only joined in demonstrations in the hope of being able to control a movement which alarmed them. The Boston merchants not only refused to join a boycott but even offered the Governor to pay for the tea, although they had had no hand in its destruction, if he would reopen the port. They made a desperate attempt to capture control of the town meeting, but in any case the whole question was already transferred to a wider stage, for meetings elsewhere had agreed to call a Continental Congress, and the attempts of the Boston merchants to abolish the Boston Committee of Correspondence were too late.

There was still a chance that the conservative merchants would capture control of the First Continental Congress, which met on 5 September 1774 in Philadelphia. The conservatives were hopelessly outmanoeuvred by Samuel Adams, and the policy of the popular leaders was adopted. It was resolved to stop all trade with Britain and to draw up a Declaration of Rights. This set out all their grievances. Finally, it was agreed to meet again on 10 May 1775 unless the demands were met: the Congress virtually said that they were ready to fight, and an envenomed stream of newspaper articles and pamphlets supported them, frankly stating, in at least one instance, that they were aiming at independence. Very few newspapers supported the British government, and one of those that did was run from the safety of a British warship. The 'alienation of the mind of the American people from the mother country' was indeed nearly complete, although there were large numbers who still remained loyal. The popular leaders and the Press had been at work, as had Locke and Montesquieu, in helping to inspire them; but there was still work to do.

Given the rigid attitude which the British Cabinet had taken up, because it and the King thought that surrender was out of the question, the war was inevitable. The Americans prepared stocks of arms and began forming regiments of soldiers. The first clash occurred when the new Governor of Massachusetts, General Gage, sent troops to seize arms known to be at Concord. The troops were attacked by American militia at Lexington on 19 April 1775, and the war had begun.

The British troops were outnumbered and driven back to Boston, where Gage found himself virtually besieged. The Americans controlled the heights near it, so he attacked them on 17 June at Bunker Hill. The British drove them off the hill but suffered such heavy losses in doing so that it was better for the Americans than a victory, for it showed they could do well against regular troops, and enormously stimulated their enthusiasm.

In the meantime the Second Continental Congress had met on 10 May and appointed George Washington as commander-in-chief in New England. Even at that late hour there were still plenty of American conservatives who wished to remain loyal, or at least to patch up the quarrel. But they got no help from the British government, which had all along underestimated and misunderstood the Americans. The popular leaders were not simply selfish rabble-rousers, as the British government thought, but patriots imbued with ideas of liberty and convinced that American legislatures ought to have the same rights within America as the British Parliament had in Great Britain. British ineptitude turned what had first been a desire for self-government within the Empire to a determination to fight for independence outside it, and ended by convincing many of the more conservative Americans of all classes that that was the only solution. So when the American conservatives managed to persuade the Congress to address one more petition to the King as late as 8 July 1775, a month after the Battle of Bunker Hill, all they got in return was the American Prohibitory Act, which the British Parliament passed in December 1775, virtually declaring all Americans to be outlaws. Soon after, the Americans were debating their Declaration of Independence. Many among the aristocracy were still against independence, for the sentimental ties with the mother country were still strong. Many of them also feared that independence would lead to social and political revolution at home and that the poorer classes would seize power. Some merchants, too, feared loss of trade with the British. Unhappily, the British certainly gave those loyal to them little encouragement; the revolutionary leaders gained the ascendancy, and on 4 July 1776 Congress adopted the document.

The Declaration of Independence was drawn up by Thomas Jefferson, Benjamin Franklin, Roger Sherman, John Adams, and Robert R. Livingston. It gave a long list of the various ways in which George III had oppressed and wronged the colonists. But the opening words form the most famous part of the Declaration. 'We hold these truths to be self-evident, that all men are created equal, that they are endowed by their Creator with certain unalienable Rights, that among these are Life, Liberty, and the pursuit of Happiness. That to secure these rights, Governments are instituted among Men, deriving their just powers from the consent of the governed, That whenever any Form of Government becomes destructive of these ends, it is the Right of the People to alter or to abolish it. . . .'

These words faithfully echo Locke and the *philosophes*, who had thus won a triumph far greater than that reflected by the work of any 'Enlightened Despot'. A new and great country was born, bearing the doctrines of the *philosophes* on its banners.

(b) THE WAR

The new country had proclaimed its independence, but still had to fight for it. At first sight its chances of success did not appear to be good. The American forces were poorly equipped, and, since Congress had no right to levy taxes, they had to depend on grants from the separate States. Nor was there complete unity in their ranks, and large numbers were either indifferent to the war or loyal to the British government. The British on the other hand were a Great Power, with comparatively limitless resources and complete command of the sea. Yet the Americans were victorious. The chief reasons for this were: the British direction of the war, which was quite amazingly inept; the dauntless courage of such American leaders as George Washington; and the intervention of the French, followed by that of the Spaniards and Dutch.

As might be expected, the war went badly for the Americans at first. Washington's troops were defeated on Long Island in August 1776, and had to retreat. Two small victories, at Trenton in December 1776 and at Princeton in January 1777, were followed by another disaster to Washington at the Battle of Brandywine, and he was forced to spend a dismal winter at Valley Forge, almost at the end of his tether.

Then came a dramatic American success in the north, a success that

was to be the major turning-point of the war. The English government
had worked out a plan to split the country into two parts, and then deal

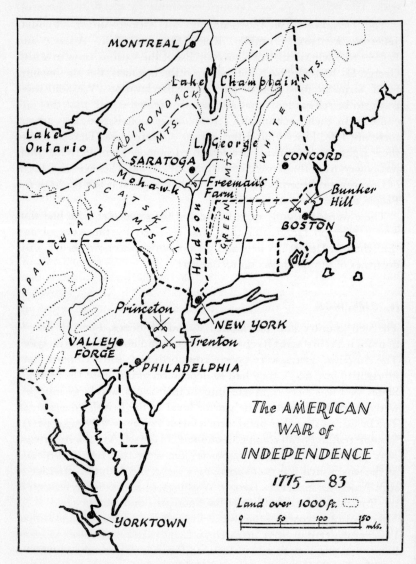

easily with each, by holding the line of the Hudson Valley. To effect
this, General Burgoyne, a competent officer in charge of a very good
army, was to advance from Canada (he had already invaded northern

New York) and to join an army under General Lord Howe, which was supposed to advance up the Hudson Valley from the town of New York. The whole plan was bungled hopelessly by the British government, who failed to give Howe precise orders. The result was that, after a good start, Burgoyne's army was attacked by greatly superior numbers of Americans, while the troops under Clinton, sent by Howe, did not arrive; two battles at Freeman's Farm were followed by the surrender of Burgoyne and his entire army to General Gates at Saratoga on 17 October 1777.

This was a tremendous encouragement to the Americans. But its effects went far beyond America. The French felt considerable sympathy for the American cause, and some volunteers such as La Fayette, Noailles, and Ségur had joined the Americans. French society was also deeply impressed by the simplicity of the dress and manners of Benjamin Franklin, whom Congress had dispatched as envoy to Paris in December 1776. The French foreign minister, Vergennes, had been in favour of helping the colonies from the start, but the policy was deemed too risky. Saratoga settled the matter, for it now seemed certain that France and the Americans could defeat the British. Exactly one day after hearing the news of Saratoga, the French King approved a treaty of alliance with the Americans (6 December); it was signed on 6 February 1778. The French aim was to get revenge for the defeat of the Seven Years War and to recover some of the losses in the West Indies. The Spaniards described the French behaviour as 'acting like Don Quixote', but on 16 June 1779 Spain too declared war on Britain, chiefly in the hope of recovering Gibraltar and Florida. On 20 December 1780 quarrels between the English and Dutch over the right of search at sea, and the Dutch help to the American commerce raider, Paul Jones, led the British to declare war on the Dutch. These events made an enormous difference to the American cause, for they received money and troops from the French, while the English found themselves engaged in a world war involving fighting in the West Indies and Gibraltar, and the enemy fleets outnumbered the British. In fact, it is likely that Britain herself could have been invaded had not the Spaniards dissipated their energies in an unsuccessful attempt to take Gibraltar. Worse still for the British, arguments over the right of search led to the formation of the 'Armed Neutrality of the North' in 1780, an association between Russia, Sweden, and Denmark, and although this did not result in war with Britain, it placed further strain on her naval resources.

The effects of loss of control of the sea were soon felt. In October 1779 the French Admiral d'Estaing co-operated with the Americans in an attempt to recapture Savannah. The English had captured that town late in the previous year and had gone on to overrun Georgia and the two Carolinas. The allied attack failed, and the English General Lord Cornwallis won more victories against the Americans and headed for Virginia. His troops were tired and he decided to rest them in Yorktown on the coast of Virginia, where he hoped to get reinforcements by sea. The British Navy failed to get them to him; instead, a French and American army under La Fayette and Washington penned him in there while a French fleet under De Grasse landed French troops and prevented aid from the British navy. This led to the surrender of Cornwallis and all his army on 19 October 1781.

This proved to be virtually the end of the war in America. The English had scarcely the resources, and certainly lacked the spirit, to make another big effort against the Americans. Further fighting took place in the West Indies and at Gibraltar, in which the British on the whole more than held their own. But the British quietly negotiated for a peace with the Americans, who for their part had no desire to go on fighting to get conquests for the French and Spaniards, and who found Rockingham's new government in Britain ready to be friendly. The negotiations were conducted without the knowledge of the French, but when they realized the American intentions, and when they could see that the British resistance continued to be stronger than they had bargained for, they too were prepared to make peace.

The Treaty of Versailles, signed on 3 September 1783, acknowledged the independence of the United States of America. The British also gave to the U.S.A. the right to fish off Newfoundland and recognized the Mississippi as the western boundary of the United States. Spain got back Minorca and Florida. France got Tobago, St Pierre and Miquelon, and recovered St Lucia, her settlements in India, and Goree and Senegal, as well as the Newfoundland fishing rights.

Those are the bare facts. The war had also provided France and the world with an example of successful rebellion in the cause of liberty. This caused rejoicings in Europe, and not least in France. As a triumph for the French monarchy it was short-lived and expensive.

21 · The Collapse of the Old Régime in France, 1778–87; the Aristocratic Revolution of 1787–8; and the victory of the Third Estate, 1789

(a) THE COLLAPSE OF THE OLD RÉGIME

The American Revolution, it is usually agreed, helped to cause one in France. Arthur Young said in 1788 that 'the American Revolution has laid the foundations of another in France'. Lord Acton was later to write that 'the Americans provided France with a finished model of revolution both in thought and action'. There certainly was an influence, but its precise nature is difficult to determine.

One can only accept Lord Acton's verdict regarding the influence of the Americans on French revolutionary thought with some reservations. The Americans contributed practically nothing to French political theory; rather did they in their Declaration of Rights and in the Constitution draw their inspiration from Montesquieu and others. The chief mental effect in France was of a different sort. The French imagined the Americans to be a people close to nature, of a primitive simplicity yet carrying out the ideas of Locke and Turgot. This illusion of American simplicity (the Americans in the towns were actually as sophisticated as anyone in Europe) was fostered by writers such as Crèvecœur, a French emigrant to America, who wrote *Letters from an American Farmer*, in which he speaks of the Americans as people who 'combine the enlightenment of civilization with the simplicity of ancient times'; and such as Brissot, who praised the Quakers. More influential, by far, was Benjamin Franklin. He was himself a philosopher and an associate of Voltaire, besides being a distinguished scientist. The French associated the American Revolution with his name, for they knew and cared little about Washington, Jefferson, John Adams, and the other great American leaders. They were charmed and astonished that a man of humble origins should rise to be a great statesman, and he seemed to personify, as the *Mercure de France* said, 'the innate love of liberty which is inseparable from the sky and the lakes and the forests of the New World'; to the French he was the Man of Nature himself. At the time Rousseau had an immense vogue in France for his advocacy of the simple, natural life, and Franklin seemed a living proof of Rousseau's idea of the nobility of the simple man. Franklin himself fostered this reputation. On his first visit to Paris he had dressed like any other man of position, but on taking up his post as representative of Congress in Paris in 1776 he did not wear a wig and dressed like a Quaker. He became all the rage; Madame Vigée-Lebrun said 'no man in Paris was more *à la mode* than Dr Franklin'. Franklin therefore had a twofold influence: he helped to cause admiration for the Americans in France, and to create a general tendency to admire liberty and simplicity. Also, by being the scientific friend of Voltaire and the propagator of Rousseauesque simplicity, he provided a synthesis of the two aspects of the *philosophes*' teachings.

The Americans therefore contributed more in France to the creation of an attitude of mind favourable to liberty than to specific political thought. That attitude was revolutionary and republican; Condorcet said that republican ideas became openly admired. In addition, the Americans certainly provided the French with certain constitutional precedents: for instance, the Civil Constitution of the Clergy in France under the Constituent Assembly owed much to the American separation of Church and State; the Declaration of the Rights of Man followed the American Declaration of Rights, and some of the constitutions of the separate American States were greatly admired, particularly that of Pennsylvania because of its unicameralism. But unicameralism had long been advocated by Turgot before its adoption in Pennsylvania, and the American Federal Constitution of 1787 was not admired in

France because of its bicameralism and because of the great powers it gave the President.

The influence of America on French political thought and practice is difficult to measure; but there is no doubt at all about the effects of the

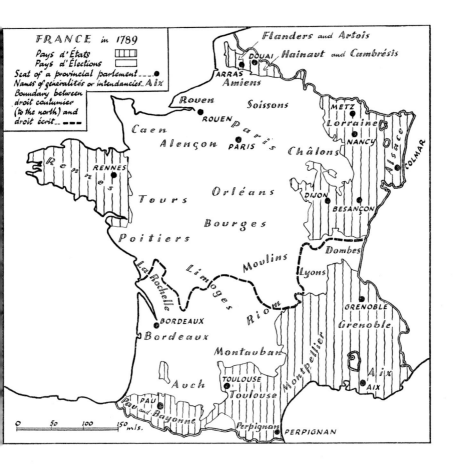

War of American Independence on the French finances. Turgot warned the King that a war would reduce the State to bankruptcy, and he was right. The war cost the French about 1,500 million *livres*. With this problem Necker wrestled as best he could. He tried the usual nibbling at the tax-farmers' profits, but this gave little relief. So he fell back on extravagant borrowing at an interest rate of ten per cent. Maurepas, jealous of Necker's popularity, attacked him late in 1780. Necker's reply was to publish his famous *Compte Rendu*. This was a sort of revolution in itself, as it claimed to be a sort of Budget statement, an unheard-of thing in France, where the finances had always been a State secret. People rushed to buy copies, of which 100,000 were immediately sold. The *Compte Rendu* was not wholly honest, for it painted the state of the finances in brighter colours than the sad facts warranted, but it made Necker's reputation as a financial genius and enabled him to borrow more. Necker took further advantage of this popularity to demand almost dictatorial powers from the King; he was in fact thinking of sweeping administrative reforms. In this ambition he failed, for Maurepas persuaded the King that Necker would arouse too violent an opposition, especially from the *parlements*. The result was that Necker was dismissed in May 1781.

His successor was Charles-Alexandre de Calonne, a cultivated and able man, who had been an *intendant* at Metz and at Lille. His first idea was to restore public confidence in the financial situation by an honest administration, but in the meantime that situation was so desperate that he had to keep on borrowing. This he did with feverish reckless-ness; in a few years he had raised 800 millions, partly by selling offices and such expedients, but mostly by borrowing. This meant swift descent into bankruptcy, and it caused anxiety among the bankers and speculators, because a bankruptcy would involve them in heavy losses. They therefore tended to side with those who wanted an end of privilege in France, for unless the privileged classes were made to pay taxes a crash was certain. The financiers loudly demanded economies, and, the deficit being no longer possible of concealment, Calonne had to satisfy them. He produced a big programme of reform. This included the calling of provincial assemblies chosen from all landowners, great and small; freedom for the sale of grain; the substitution of a money payment for the *corvée*; and, most revolutionary step of all, the creation of a new land tax payable by everyone without exception. That would mean hitting the privileged Orders where it most hurt, and Calonne knew perfectly well that his proposals, which were embodied in six edicts, would get a very rough reception from the *parlements*, who would have to register them before they could become law. He therefore proposed to the King that the government should first seek the support of as many nobles as possible by calling a meeting of notables. This gathering of a selected number of nobles was an old device of the French Constitution, but, needless to say, it was very rarely used by a strong king. To call the notables together to get support for specific measures in these circumstances was tantamount to a self-condemnation and a surrender by an 'absolute' monarchy.

(b) THE ARISTOCRATIC REVOLUTION OF 1787–8

The First Meeting of Notables met early in 1787. Its members were in no hurry to agree to new taxes, and demanded details of the financial reforms, which Calonne had left pleasantly vague. In addition to the new land tax, he demanded among other things the suppression of internal customs barriers and a reform of the *gabelle*. The nobles accepted his idea of provincial assemblies, but flatly refused to agree to his land tax, and Calonne was attacked so bitterly, not only by all the privileged Orders but also by the Queen and the other ministers, that the King gave way before the storm and dismissed him (April 1787).

To remove Calonne did nothing to solve the financial problem, and Calonne's proposals alone could do that. So his successor, Loménie de Brienne, the young and clever Archbishop of Toulouse, though ignorant of financial matters, once more demanded approval of them from the notables. As the situation was deteriorating every day, he added to them a new stamp tax. Most of the nobles again refused, but the *parlementaires* among them said that they merited further consideration. By this they meant that the proposals should be put direct to the *parlements*; it was a move to get power for themselves alone. The notables were dismissed on 25 May 1787, leaving the government with no alternative but to fall in with the suggestion. At once there was tumultuous opposition in Paris to which the King replied by holding a *lit de justice*. The *Parlement* of Paris talked about 'reason and justice' and of the 'rights of the nation'. The King answered by exiling its members to Troyes. But the propaganda of the *parlements* had done its work only too well. They had so cleverly represented the financial reforms as arbitrary taxation imposed by a despotic government that the bulk of the population thought the *parlements* to be defenders of liberty. In reality, all they were doing was to defend the privileges of their own class. As soon as the members of the Paris *Parlement* arrived at Troyes, they demanded the calling of the States-General, the ancient deliberative body, consisting of representatives of all three Estates, namely, Clergy, Nobles, and *Tiers État* (Third Estate). This implied a demand for a constitutional monarchy, for the States-General would evidently share power with the Crown, which was one reason why the kings had not called the States-General since 1614. The clamour of the

Parlement of Paris was supported by that of all the provincial *parlements* and, worse still, by rioting mobs.

In face of this violence, the King once more yielded. Brienne cancelled the land tax and proposed instead two *vingtièmes*, which would as usual be paid largely by the peasants. This meant the total collapse of the Calonne-Brienne reforms. It also meant one more proof of the inability of the monarchy to effect fundamental changes in the system of privilege. More than that, in order to get even the *vingtièmes* accepted, the government agreed to call the States-General for the year 1792, and did this before putting the necessary edicts before the *Parlement* of Paris, which was recalled from its exile. The King held a royal session of the *Parlement* at Paris on 19 November 1787, only to find that his surrenders had merely served to arouse the *Parlement* to fresh boldness. Its members declared his edicts illegal (the word used by the Duke of Orleans, no friend of the King). The King, with one of the fits of firmness occasionally displayed by weak men, thereupon, in reply to their continued protests, to which they now added the demand for the calling of the States-General in 1789, instead of in 1792, as he had promised, forced them to register his edicts. That did not stop them from persisting in disobedient talk, at which the King arrested two of them and exiled the Duke of Orleans. The *Parlement* of Paris declared the *lettres de cachet* under which the arrests were made to be illegal, but the King held firm and even forced them to register an Edict giving religious toleration to the Huguenots. The winter passed more quietly, but the *Parlement* of Paris was planning another counter-attack for April 1788.

This came in the shape of fresh Remonstrances. The King's speech replying to them, most significantly said that the powers they claimed were harmful to the 'nation'; in other words, both parties to the dispute were appealing to the mass of French people, to the millions who hitherto had had no political claims of their own. The King then tried to arrest two of the *parlementaires* and went on to institute a reform to cripple the authority of the *parlements*. He swept away most of their judicial functions, creating instead a *Cour plénière* (Plenary Court) with the sole right to register edicts, and forty-seven new courts throughout France. This reduced the number of the magistrates of the Paris *Parlement* to sixty-seven, and as even these were left with little work, the King kindly gave them an indefinite 'holiday'. These measures failed, for the nation supported the *parlements*, not the King. Riots occurred all over France; the other *parlements* refused to register the King's reforms; some of the clergy supported the *parlements*. The troops, who were not particularly enthusiastic, were stoned by the populace. It was no longer just a number of riots, but a revolution. The propaganda of the *parlements* persuaded the nation that they were defending the country from a despotism, and as bad luck would have it, people were all the more ready to riot because of hunger. There was considerable urban unemployment because the trade treaty with England, signed in 1786, had exposed French industry to a competition with English machinery which it could not meet on equal terms, and, to make matters worse, there was great distress because of a couple of bad harvests. The great mass of the French nation at last had leaders, and rose against the despotism that was trying to rescue them from their real enemies—the privileged Orders. The first really revolutionary step was taken by the Provincial Estates of Dauphiné, who convoked themselves without royal permission. Under their leaders, Mounier and Barnave, they demanded Estates-General for all the kingdom, with power to vote taxes, and the abolition of the *lettres de cachet*. Nobody troubled to take action against these rebellious Estates of Dauphiné.

In face of this revolt of the privileged Orders, supported by the mass of the nation, who imagined the former to be their champions, the government could no longer govern; it no longer commanded obedience. So on 8 August 1788 the government capitulated. It abolished the Plenary Court, and agreed to call the States-General on the date demanded by the *Parlement*: that is, 1 May 1789. Eight days later the State suspended payments; it was a partial bankruptcy.

That was the first French Revolution. The King had surrendered to the privileged Orders. However, this Revolution of the Aristocrats had only succeeded because it was supported by the physical force of the mass of the nation. The triumph of the aristocrats was complete, but it would therefore last just as long as they could continue to receive the support of that mass by the pose of being champions of liberty and of the 'rights of the nation' to which they had been fond of referring. If the pose were to be seen for what it was, and if new leaders could win the support of the mass of the people, then the power of the numerically insignificant aristocrats would melt rapidly away.

The privileged Orders soon betrayed their real intentions. The King had recalled Necker, who was highly popular and so was able to stave off a total financial collapse by fresh borrowing. He also abolished the *Cour plénière*, thus returning to the *parlements* the right to register edicts. He made it possible for the financial crisis to be shelved for the moment, but also made it possible for the *parlements* to turn their attention to their purely political ambitions, all the more easily because Necker abandoned all his earlier plans for reform and sacrificed the capable Lamoignon, the *Garde des Sceaux*, replacing him by the much weaker Barentin. He even, in a final act of folly, promised to call the States-General for January 1789, although there was no hope of making all the necessary arrangements by that date. In fact, the government maintained a nervous silence about how they were to be convoked at all. This silence was broken on 25 September 1788 by the *Parlement* of Paris. It demanded that the States-General should be called according to the forms observed at their last meeting in 1614. But the Third Estate wanted the whole of the States-General to meet as one body and with a doubling of their own membership, so that in a single body the representatives of the Third would be as numerous as those of the combined nobles and clergy. The demand of the *Parlement* meant instead that the States-General should meet and deliberate as three separate Orders and vote, not by the majority of all the deputies, but as complete Orders, that is to say that the Third Estate would be outnumbered two to one by the privileged Orders. This would be to frustrate all hope of liberal reform and to hand over the direction of the country to the aristocracy. Fearing popular commotion, the government hastily decided to consult the notables on this absolutely vital issue, so the Second Meeting of Notables took place (144 in number) on 5 October. The government hoped that these would prove more reasonable. The hope was vain. The notables insisted on the separation of the three Orders. They even insisted on giving the vote for the elections to the Third Estate to servants, so as to drown the more enlightened members of the Third Estate in a flood of popular ignorance.

(c) THE VICTORY OF THE THIRD ESTATE, 1789

Parlement and notables had thus clearly revealed their intentions, intentions which, so far, they had concealed behind a smoke-screen of hypocritical verbiage about the 'rights of the nation', 'liberty', the evils of 'royal despotism', and so on. All the fine talk had meant nothing but a means to win popular support, to force the King to call the States-General. Once called, the States would be dominated by the privileged classes. They had played their hand cleverly up to that moment, but to insist on the vote 'by Order' was too haughtily and carelessly to reveal their aims. There was an outburst of indignation from the disillusioned Third Estate, and a very violent reaction of public opinion against the Paris *Parlement* and the notables. Mallet du Pan said in January 1789 that it was no longer primarily a question of royal despotism, but of a war between the Third Estate and the other two Orders. The war was fought on paper. The King had, somewhat rashly, made a general appeal to cultivated men to give their opinions about reforms, and in answer to this appeared a torrent of pamphlets. The writers who had until 25 September been supporting the cause of the *parlements* now turned their pens against them. The chief theme was the demand by the Third Estate for the doubling of their number and for the vote 'by head' instead of 'by Order'. This was the gist of the most famous of the pamphlets, written by the Abbé Sieyès and called *Qu'est-ce que le Tiers État?* His answer was that until then it had been 'nothing', and that it ought to be 'everything'. The nobles, he said, 'are strangers in our midst'. Another famous pamphlet by the Comte de Mirabeau asked if it was just that 'two Orders who are not the nation should prevail over the nation' ('si les deux ordres qui ne sont pas la nation l'emportent sur la nation'). Others demanded that the States-General should have control over taxation and legislation. The Marquis de Casaux demanded liberty of the Press, and he was supported in this by Mirabeau.

Sieyès, Mirabeau, Casaux; the first was a priest and the other two were nobles. It might well be asked why these members of the two privileged Orders were fighting for the Third Estate. The answer is, as has already been explained (in Chapter 19), that the lower clergy had many among them who identified themselves with the mass of the nation rather than with the upper clergy; while many nobles sided with the Third Estate because they were quite prepared to sweep away the Old Régime based on birth and create a State run by the wealthy, which would give them far more power than did empty titles, and they therefore allied with the richer *bourgeoisie*. Others genuinely believed in liberal reforms after reading the works of the *philosophes*, and one or two impoverished nobles could see more scope for their talents in a reformed society (Mirabeau was one of these). So in addition to the pamphlets, there also appeared the formation of the 'national' or 'patriot' party. This was in the main an alliance of the richer *bourgeois* with some of the richer nobles, but the group included clergy and poorer nobles also. Some of the most prominent members were the Duke of Orleans, the Duke of La Rochefoucauld-Liancourt, the Marquis de La Fayette, the Marquis de Condorcet, Talleyrand (who was Bishop of Autun), Sieyès, and Mirabeau. In addition to this group political clubs in large numbers were formed in Paris and in the provinces, and the popular agitation was such that the *intendant* of Franche-Comté wrote to Necker and said that, unless a decision about the construction of the States-General were made by the government in their favour, then there would be a general insurrection of 600,000 men in the province.

Necker therefore bowed to the inevitable and granted the doubling of the membership of the Third Estate, but still said nothing about the vote by head or by Order. The ultimate victory of the Third seemed none the less assured because of popular pressure. Unhappily, there was terrible economic distress among the masses. The industrial workers were flung out of work in thousands, partly because of English competition following the trade treaty of 1786. For instance, there were as many as 20,000 unemployed, out of a labour force of 48,000, in Lyons alone. The condition of the peasantry was worse. For half a dozen years before 1787 agricultural prices had been low, which hit all the peasants. In 1785 a drought killed off a lot of cattle. Thus with no sort of reserves they were left to face the disastrously bad harvests of 1787 and 1788. At once the price of bread shot up, causing great wretchedness and hunger. As a result there were widespread riots and pillage. Thousands of famished vagabonds roamed the country. The troops were helpless or sympathetic. The masses blamed the privileged classes for their sufferings. On the other hand they hoped that the States-General would bring in happier times, and were prepared to support the middle-class programme by force.

Soon everyone had a chance to produce his notions of a programme. The elections for the States-General were held early in 1789. The total number of deputies elected was 1,165, of whom rather less than 600 belonged to the Third Estate, the other two having roughly equal numbers. The Third were normally chosen by indirect universal male suffrage (the voters had to be aged twenty-five or over): that is, the electors chose committees who then chose the deputy. Because of their superior education, this resulted in a predominant number of deputies drawn from the professions (chiefly lawyers) and business men. The clergy elected a majority of lower clergy, the remainder being bishops. All the deputies of all three Estates brought with them *Cahiers des doléances* (a list of grievances and of desired reforms). These *Cahiers* are naturally of very great interest, though they do not mirror the wishes of the nation with perfect fidelity because, for instance, the peasants in many cases had no hand in drawing them up, and sometimes the *bourgeois* suppressed the primary *Cahiers* when these ran counter to their own ideas. The range of demands was so great that an accurate summary is impossible. However, there was no demand for the abolition of the monarchy. The peasants hoped that the King would cure all their troubles, and demanded the abolition of feudal dues. Most of the *Cahiers* of the Third Estate asked for a new constitution; the rights of man; the abolition of judicial torture, of *lettres de cachet*, and of fiscal privileges. They asked also for liberty of the Press, the admission of all Frenchmen to any career, frequent meetings of the States-General, and provincial assemblies instead of ministerial despotism and *intendants* (that is, they wanted a vast decentralization). The *Cahiers* of the clergy were mixed, because of the split within their ranks, as were also those of the nobles, but a fair number of the actual deputies were in favour of liberal reforms—probably about two hundred priests and about ninety nobles.

The first meeting of the States-General took place on 5 May 1789. The Third Estate were first bored by a speech from the King, and by one from Barentin which was quite inaudible. They were then infuriated by a harangue from Necker, which lasted three hours and which made no mention of constitutional reform. Necker also adhered to the vote by Order. This attitude was maintained by the privileged Orders on the following day, whereupon the Third, who were meeting in a separate room, refused to begin any business, and the States as such were promptly paralysed. For some days the members of the Third refused to conduct the preliminary business of verifying their powers. On 10 June they invited the other two Orders to join them so as to form an undivided body. A few clergy did so, and on 17 June the Third declared that they formed a 'National Assembly'. Two days later the majority of the clergy voted for union with them, and on 20 June when the deputies went to their chamber they found it locked. Louis XVI had decided to try to insist on the separation of the Orders, and announced there would be a royal session on 23 June; but the deputies were not to be fobbed off in this manner, so they went to an adjoining tennis court and swore a solemn oath that they would not separate until they had given France a constitution. Louis then made a few concessions, but not the ones chiefly wanted. The Third remained disobedient and the majority of the clergy and forty-seven nobles joined them; on 27 June the King caved in and invited the remainder of the privileged to follow their example. The *bourgeois* victory over the King and the other two Orders appeared complete, and in the early days of July they prepared to debate a constitution. Henceforward, therefore, we can call their Assembly by the name by which it has always been known: the Constituent Assembly.

As yet the victory was by no means complete. It was thought that the King regarded the Assembly as rebels, and he gave menacing indications that he would so treat them as soon as he was able. An increasing number of troops were called into the area of Paris and Versailles, and on 11 July Necker was dismissed, being replaced by the Baron de Breteuil, who appeared to favour a firmer line. Worse still, many of the aristocrats started to recruit armed followers, and it was thought that the government was appealing for help from foreign Powers. A 'Great Fear' swept the country, caused by these suspicions and by the activities of bands of half-starved vagabonds.

From these fears the *bourgeois* were delivered by the masses. There had already occurred many bread riots; the food situation in 1789 was worse than ever. The only hope for the masses lay in the Assembly, and when the dismissal of Necker seemed to herald worse things to come from the King, the Paris mob rose, and more to attack the government than to save the Assembly, seized 32,000 muskets at the Invalides, and on 14 July went in irresistible numbers to get more from the famous prison-fortress, the Bastille. They were helped by some of the troops, because the junior officers despaired of promotion and the rank and file were hard hit by rising prices (they had to buy some of their own food out of their pay). The place was taken and destroyed; the garrison was massacred. This cruelty, which persisted throughout the Revolution until it was obviously safe from plots by the King and the aristocrats, and safe from the threat against it from foreign Powers, was caused by the fear engendered by such plots and threats. Some of the aristocrats fled abroad, the Comte d'Artois being among the first of what was to become a wholesale exodus. Suspected persons were massacred, and this spread to the countryside, where the peasants burned châteaux, destroyed enclosing fences, tore up archives and records of seigneurial rights, and murdered nobles. The whole of the urban and rural workers were in wild revolt.

This suited the *bourgeois*, because it paralysed the King and any hope of a counter-revolution, but it also frightened them. Order was only restored with great difficulty, and then only to a limited extent; the collection of taxes, for instance, became practically impossible. The Assembly was gradually able to regain some sort of authority in the towns, but it was evident that only radical reforms would calm the peasants. The Assembly was preparing to vote on the Declaration of Rights with which it was proposed to preface the Constitution. The Declaration ceased to be as urgent as the agrarian question, so it was decided to satisfy the peasants; order had to be restored somehow and to appeal to royal troops was unthinkable; besides, the Assembly owed

the peasants and the town workers an immense debt for its own existence. In a sort of frenzy of enthusiasm, the Assembly, on the famous
night of 4 August, voted one reforming measure after another. Equality
of taxation was decreed, then all feudal rights were abolished. The
Assembly said that 'the feudal régime is entirely destroyed', but in fact
some of the dues had to be redeemed by the peasants, and payment for
the redemption would cost them considerable sums for years. Then
came equality of judicial punishments; and equality of opportunity,
which meant that at last all careers depended on talent, not birth. The
sale of government posts was abolished. Other decrees abolished certain
unpopular Church customs, such as plurality and the payment of
annates to the Pope.

Taken together, the reforms most nobly (whatever the immediate
motives underlying them) established the end of feudalism and of the
rural dominance of the nobles, and established the judicial equality of
all Frenchmen as well as their equality of opportunity. The Old Régime
in France was dead; that demanded by the *philosophes* was born.

Epilogue · The making of the Liberal Constitution, 1789–91

The reforms of the night of 4 August were only the first moves towards building a new France. Unhappily, before the complete task could be done, it proved necessary to overcome more opposition from the King. Not that there was much resistance left in him. He had already tried to make his peace with Paris, where the municipal government had been pushed aside by the populace, who had set up their own government, supported by a civic guard. He had visited the town on 17 July and accepted a badge in the new revolutionary colours (the tricolour, of red, white, and blue). He had also recalled Necker, though that states-man had little influence thereafter. A fresh attempt by Louis to overawe Paris a little later led to the march to Versailles of a mob of hungry women, surveyed at a discreet distance by La Fayette and a section of the newly formed *bourgeois* National Guard. The King and his family were obliged to go back to Paris and to live in the Tuileries Palace (the residence of the French kings before the building of Versailles). The King was virtually a prisoner from then (6 October 1789) onwards. He was thus obliged to agree, with as good a grace as he could muster, to all the measures of the Assembly. In fact, his only real hope of salvation now lay in accepting the confidential advice given him by Mirabeau, the most formidable orator in the Assembly, which was to accept the situation and play the part of a constitutional monarch. Had the King done so he still had a chance to keep his throne as a loved and respected monarch.

It was not to be. The King did not trust Mirabeau. Mirabeau was certainly a great statesman, but he had a dissolute private life and his financial probity was more than doubtful. The King therefore paid this somewhat moth-eaten lion for his advice, but did not follow it. Finally, for a number of reasons, one of which was that he was disgusted by the reforms which the Constituent Assembly had effected in the Church, by the Civil Constitution of the Clergy, the King and his family fled in disguise towards the eastern frontier in order to get the help of Austrian troops to put down the Revolution (20 June 1791). Even this was mismanaged. The King was recognized at Varennes, when only a few hundred yards from friendly troops, and brought back to Paris. This did not lead to the deposition of the King, because some of the deputies, including La Fayette, realized that his position had been made intolerable, but he was suspended from his functions on 25 June until he signed the new Constitution on 14 September 1791. But this flight to Varennes, while producing a more moderate party of deputies who tried to give the King more power under the new Constitution, also produced a republican group wishing to abolish the monarchy. (It also produced a disorderly mob which met to sign a petition for his dethronement. The mob refused to disperse when ordered to by Bailly, the Mayor of Paris, and was fired on, at the Champ de Mars, by the National Guard commanded by La Fayette, 17 July 1791.) However, the King could do no more to hinder the Assembly in its work of reforming and reconstructing France.

The Constituent Assembly had the gigantic task of providing France with a new constitution and a new administrative and judicial system. It also had to regulate the country's economic life and to solve the financial problem. Not least, it had to deal with foreign Powers. It began with a 'Declaration of the Rights of man and of the citizen', which was inspired partly by the American example. It stated that 'men are born and remain free and equal in rights'. 'These rights are liberty, property, security, and resistance to oppression.' This has more than an echo of Locke and the *philosophes*, but the deputies were thinking of concrete injustices under the Old Régime, not merely theorizing. The Declaration also said that man had a duty to defend those rights and that the State is nothing else than the community of citizens expressing their general will (*volonté générale*) in the laws that embody their rights. The Declaration, then, which was the preamble to the new Constitution, was also the death-knell of the Old Régime, and, because the Assembly destroyed class privilege, was also a statement of the principles on which the new France was based and which the Revolution translated into fact. Liberty and equality before the law, and equality of opportunity, in short, the dream of the *philosophes*, became realities. This proved an immense source of inspiration to the French, drawing forth the hidden energies of masses of people who had never before had the chance to use their abilities.

The Constitution was a thoroughly middle-class affair, but the work of a middle class which had come to distrust the King. Voting for the legislative body was based on a property qualification, with the result that about four and a half million 'active' citizens had the vote, while three million 'passive' citizens had no say in elections. Here again is an echo of Locke, although the Constituent Assembly was not thinking directly of him. The Constitution was also based on the principle of securing liberty by the separation of the powers of the executive, legislature, and judiciary. In practice, the King, although he was declared to be the head of the executive, appointed ministers and ambassadors, had diplomatic initiative, and a suspensive veto (of four years' duration) over legislation, had little power. He could issue no order without the signature of a minister, and ministers were answerable to the Assembly. All real power lay with the Assembly, which could not be dissolved and had no Second Chamber to check it. Hence what appeared to be a constitutional monarchy was in reality a *bourgeois* republic.

The Assembly, on the other hand, gave itself hardly any control over local administration. The reaction against the 'ministerial despotism' and the *intendants* of the Bourbon kings resulted in a vast decentralization of the administration of the kingdom. France was divided into eighty-three *départements*, which were in turn subdivided into districts, and these into cantons. The officials were all elected, and there was no central authority over them: a fact which led to chaos. Similarly, the *parlements* were all suppressed, their place being taken by *juges de paix* in the cantons, by a court of five judges in the districts, and by a court of four judges in the *départements*, with appeal to a Court of Cassation in Paris. All judges were elected by active citizens, and the Court of Cassation by the *départements*; the King and the Legislature had no say at all in the administration of justice.

The Assembly's economic policy was almost wholly Physiocratic. This inspiration explains the distinction made between active and passive citizens. It explains also the enthusiasm with which feudalism was abolished on the night of 4 August, the permission given to enclose land (in spite of the opposition of most peasants), and the restoration of free trade in grain within France. It explains no less the abolition of the guilds and of any right of association for trade purposes, by the Le Chapelier Law of 1791. This free-for-all meant, of course, liberty for the richer *bourgeois* to do as they wished with the workers, the liberty of the strong to oppress the weak. It also explains the Assembly's determination to try a single land tax, which failed totally, and to confiscate the lands of the Church.

The creation of a *bourgeois* State based on legal and economic liberty did nothing to solve the financial problem. On the contrary, it made it worse. The old (and admittedly bad) system of taxation was swept away, but the new taxes imposed by the Constituent Assembly failed to bring in enough money with enough speed, and the liquidation of the Old Régime proved enormously costly; the Debt had actually risen by over 1,000 million *livres*. The Assembly first tried a 'patriotic contribution', fresh borrowing, and other paltry measures, but without success. As Mirabeau told them, in one of his most powerful speeches, which made the deputies go pale with fright, 'hideous bankruptcy' stared them in the face. The solution adopted was to confiscate the lands of the Church, on the assumption that they belonged to the nation. (The Assembly contained some Jansenists and Protestants, the former predominating in its Ecclesiastical Committee.) Four hundred million *livres* worth of land were taken to begin with, as security for interest-bearing *assignats* for that amount. The *assignats* were next made into legal tender. In other words, the Assembly had created paper-money backed by Church land as security. Unfortunately nobody knew what those lands were worth, and in any case they were not at once free from ecclesiastical control and from private debts and so forth. Naturally, therefore, the *assignats* depreciated in terms of the metal coinage; in fact, the government itself bought metal coinage for *assignats* at a steadily increasing loss, this practice being legalized by the Decree of 17 May 1791. The mass of paper was soon multiplied and led to a sharp inflation and in turn to popular distress, a distress that was one cause of the counter-revolutionary war in La Vendée.

The spoliation of the Church did not please many of the clergy. The confiscation of Church property on 10 November 1789 was followed by the dissolution of most of the monastic houses in February 1790, but provision was made for the payment of priests. Not many clergy were

THE LIBERAL CONSTITUTION, 1789-91

ready to echo the violent objections raised against this by the Bishop of Tréguier, who anathematized the whole Revolution. It was otherwise with the Civil Constitution of the Clergy, which the Constituent Assembly made law on 12 July 1790. This suppressed all cathedral chapters and decreed that all bishops were to be elected by the electors of the *départements*, and priests by the electors of districts; every *département* was made into a bishopric; and the clergy were to be paid fixed salaries. The authority of the Pope was not asked for. Gallican in sympathy, the French bishops tacitly agreed to these changes, but asked for a national council of clergy to take the canonical measures deemed necessary to effect the reforms. The Constituent Assembly refused, so the bishops turned for permission to the Pope. His reply was slow in coming, and the Constituent Assembly imposed an oath of loyalty to the Civil Constitution on the clergy. With no canonical authority of any sort, they would not take the oath. Out of one hundred and thirty-five bishops, only four took it, and when at length the Pope condemned the Civil Constitution about 50,000 priests likewise refused —more than half the total number. Instead of creating a reformed and national Church which would consolidate the new régime, as they had intended, the deputies of the Constituent Assembly had thus made fifty-five per cent of the priests, who were sacked, into enemies. This reacted violently on French society, and was a godsend to the aristo-crats, whose efforts at making a civil war, which did break out in La Vendée and elsewhere, were now supported by peasants who had no love for aristocrats but who still loved their Church. One of the refrac-tory priests in La Vendée said that 'such was the popular fury that it was enough to have been to the Mass said by the intruding priests [i.e. those taking the oath to obey the Civil Constitution] to be first imprisoned and then knocked on the head or shot'. Another enemy which the Constituent Assembly made for itself by the Church reform was of course Louis XVI. He had to accept it (on 26 December 1790), but what remained of any desire of his to side with the Revolution vanished. This was the cause of his having sought the help of the Emperor.

The Constituent Assembly did not show itself any more tactful in its dealings with foreign nations. It weakened its alliance with Spain by refusing to help in a dispute then taking place between that Power and Britain over the Nootka Sound affair. It also seized Avignon from the Pope in September 1791, and annoyed some of its German neighbours by its abolition of feudal privileges, which they still held under the Treaty of Westphalia, in Alsace.

Its task finished, the Constituent Assembly ended on 30 September 1791, to make way for the new legislative body to be elected under the Constitution. The *bourgeois* had made many enemies of their Revolution, both at home and abroad, enemies who were to put their work in peril. Despite the cost in blood to be paid by Frenchmen and foreigners, they had also made France into a land of liberty, a land which most gloriously affirmed the dignity and the worth of men. Above all, they had made France a land of hope, a hope which was soon to spread beyond her borders. It was most beautifully expressed in Wordsworth's *Prelude*, but it is more fitting to quote a great Frenchman, even though he was probably speaking not without irony; Mirabeau said: 'Il n'est pas loin de nous, peut-être, ce moment où la liberté réalisera le vœu de la philosophie, absoudra l'espèce humaine du crime de la guerre et proclamera la paix universelle; alors le bonheur des peuples sera le seul but des législateurs, la seule force des lois, la seule gloire des nations. . . .' ('Perhaps the moment is not far from us when Liberty will bring about the desire of Philosophy, will absolve mankind from the crime of war and will proclaim universal peace; then the happiness of peoples will be the only aim of lawmakers, the only sanction for laws, and the only glory of nations. . . .')

That hope still lives.

CHRONOLOGICAL TABLE

1543 Copernicus, *De Revolutionibus Orbium Coelestium*. Vesalius, *De Humani Corporis Fabrica*.

1598 Edict of Nantes (toleration granted to Huguenots in France).

1617 Peace of Stolbova (Russia and Sweden).

1618 Thirty Years War begins with revolt in Bohemia.

1625 Grotius, *De Jure Belli et Pacis*.

1628 Harvey, *De Motu Cordis*.

1637 Descartes, *Discourse on Method*. Arnauld, *De la fréquente communion*.

1642–6 First English Civil War.

1645 Treaty of Bromsebro (Sweden and Denmark make peace).

1648–52 The *Frondes* (French Civil Wars).

1648 Second English Civil War. Treaties of Münster and Osnabrück (Peace of Westphalia) end Thirty Years War. Formal independence of Swiss Cantons and of United Provinces (Holland) recognized.

1649 King Charles I executed (England).

1651 English Navigation Act (directed against Dutch). Hobbes, *Leviathan*.

1657 Pascal, *Lettres provinciales*.

1659 Treaty of the Pyrenees ends war between France and Spain.

1660 Return of Charles II to England. Treaties of Oliva and Copenhagen end Northern War. Royal *coup d'état* in Denmark.

1661 Beginning of personal rule of Louis XIV. Treaty of Kardis (Sweden and Russia end hostilities). Boyle, *Sceptical Chymist*.

1662 Declaration of Indulgence (toleration) issued, withdrawn after opposition from Parliament (England).

1664 French increase tariffs (aimed against Dutch). French West Indies Company founded. Battle of St Gotthard (Turks defeated by Austrians) and Truce of Vasvar.

1665–7 Second Anglo-Dutch War (Peace of Breda, 1667).

1666 Tokoli leads revolt of Hungarians against Austria.

1667 Treaty of Andrusova (Poland and Russia make peace). *Ordonnance civile* (French legal reforms). Eternal Edict in Holland (aimed against Orange family). War of Devolution (Louis XIV attacks Spanish Netherlands) begins.

1668 Triple Alliance (England, Holland, Sweden, against France). Peace of Aix-la-Chapelle ends War of Devolution.

1669 *Ordonnance des eaux et forêts* and *Ordonnance criminelle* (French legal reforms).

1670 First Secret Treaty of Dover (French and Charles II of England plan attack against Dutch).

1671 Second Secret Treaty of Dover.

1672 Dutch War (France and England against Dutch) begins. Second Declaration of Indulgence, granting religious toleration, issued in England. French invasion of Holland, murder of John and Cornelius de Witt at The Hague. William of Orange comes to power in Holland. Battle of Sole Bay (Dutch defeat English and French fleets). Treaty of Buczacs (Turks and Poles make peace).

1673 *Ordonnance du commerce* (France). Test Act (English Parliament nullifies the Declaration of Indulgence and excludes Catholics from all public office). Battle of Khoczim (John Sobieski of Poland defeats Turks). Alliance of Holland and Emperor against France.

1674 England withdraws from Dutch War. Grand Alliance of The Hague against France. Another revolt of Hungarians led by Tokoli against Austrians. Sweden declares war on Emperor and Brandenburg.

1675 Battle of Lemburg (Poles defeat Turks).

1675-9 War of Scania (Sweden against Denmark).

1675 Battle of Fehrbellin (Brandenburg defeats Swedes).

1676 Treaty of Zurawno (Poland makes peace with Turks).

1678 Treaty of Nymegen (France ends war with Dutch and Emperor). Locke, two *Treatises of Civil Government* (published 1689).

1679 Treaty of Saint-Germain-en-Laye ends Swedish-Brandenburg War. Treaty of Fontainebleau ends War of Scania (Sweden-Denmark).

1680 *Ordonnance de la Marine* (France). Royal *coup d'état* in Sweden.

1681 Louis XIV begins fresh aggressions (The 'Reunions').

1682 Alliance of Denmark and Brandenburg (against Sweden). 'Four Gallican Articles' (France). Brandenburg African Company founded.

1683 Siege of Vienna by Turks and their defeat by Sobieski.

1684 Truce of Ratisbon. Holy League (Poland, Emperor, Venice, Malta, against Turks). Emperor captures Pest.

1685 Revocation of the Edict of Nantes. Edict of Potsdam (Great Elector welcomes Huguenots to Brandenburg).

1686 Russia joins Holy League. Emperor captures Buda. League of Augsburg (Emperor, Brandenburg, Holland, Sweden, Spain, etc., against France).

1687 Venetians capture the Morea. Battle of Mohacs (Emperor defeats Turks). Newton, *Principia*.

1688 Revolution in England; flight of James II.

1689 French devastate the Palatinate; William of Orange becomes King of England; Bill of Rights. France declares war on Spain; War of League of Augsburg against France begins; England joins the League. Locke, *First Letter concerning Toleration*.

1690 Battle of Beachy Head (French defeat English fleet). Battle of the Boyne (English victory in Ireland). Battle of Fleurus (French defeat Austrians). Locke, *Essay concerning Human Understanding*.

1692 Battle of La Hogue (English defeat French fleet).

1693 Battle of Neerwinden (French defeat Dutch). Battle of Marsaglia (French defeat Savoy).

1694 Bank of England founded.

1695 Bayle, *Dictionnaire*.

1697 Peace of Ryswick ends War of League of Augsburg. Battle of Zenta (Emperor defeats Turks). Peter the Great begins his travels in the West.

1698 First Partition Treaty; King of Spain's first Will.

1699 Peace of Karlowitz ends war against the Turks.

1700 Second Partition Treaty; King of Spain's second Will. Great War of the North begins (Russia, Denmark, Poland, against Sweden). Sweden defeats Denmark; Denmark ends participation in the war at Peace of Traventhal. Charles XII of Sweden defeats Russians at Battle of Narva.

1701 Grand Alliance against France (England, Holland, Emperor).

1702 War of the Spanish Succession begins.

1703 Portugal allies with England.

1704 English capture Gibraltar. Marlborough defeats Bavarians at the Battle of the Schellenberg and defeats French at Battle of Blenheim. Peter the Great begins building of St Petersburg.

1705 Capture of Barcelona by Peterborough. Papal Bull *Vineam Domini* condemning Jansenists.

1706 Battle of Ramillies (Marlborough defeats French). Defeat of Poland by Charles XII; Treaty of Altranstädt.

1708 Battle of Oudenarde (Marlborough defeats French).

1709 Battle of Malplaquet (Marlborough defeats French). Battle of Poltava (complete defeat of Charles XII by Peter the Great). Destruction of Jansenist centre at Port-Royal.

1711 Turks declare war on Russia. Founding of South Seas Company (England).

1713 Russo-Turkish War ends with Treaty of Adrianople. Papal Bull *Unigenitus*.

1713 Treaty of Utrecht.

1714 Treaties of Rastatt and Baden.

1715 Death of Louis XIV.

1716 Anglo-French alliance.

1717 Triple Alliance (England, France, Holland).

1718 Spain attacks Sicily. English alliance with Emperor. Battle of Cape Passaro (Spanish fleet sunk by English).

1719 Treaty of Stockholm ends war between Sweden and Hanover.

1720 Second Treaty of Stockholm ends Swedish-Prussian War. Spain joins Quadruple Alliance. Failure of Law's schemes in France and of English South Seas Company. Danish liberal constitution.

1721 Treaty of Nystad (Sweden, Russia) ends Great War of the North. Peter the Great assumes title of 'Emperor of all the Russias'. Montesquieu, *Lettres persanes*.

1722 Ostend Company founded.

1725 Treaty between Spain and the Emperor, countered by the Herrenhausen alliance (England, France).

1726 Alliance between the Emperor and Russia. Voltaire visits England. Swift, *Gulliver's Travels*.

1727 Russo-English Commercial Treaty.

1728 Congress of Soissons. Gay, *Beggar's Opera*.

1729 Treaty of Seville (England, Spain).

1731 Second Treaty of Vienna (England, Emperor, Spain, Holland).

1732 France allies with Bavaria and Poland. Treaty of Loewenwolde (Emperor, Russia).

1733 Treaty of the Escorial ('Bourbon Family Compact') between France and Spain. Beginning of War of the Polish Succession. Molasses Act (America).

1734 Voltaire, *Lettres philosophiques*. Dubos, *Histoire critique de l'établissement de la monarchie française*.

1735 Linnaeus, *Systema Naturae*. Russo-Turkish War.

1737 Austro-Turkish War.

1738 Treaty of Vienna ends War of the Polish Succession. Alliance between France and Sweden.

1739 Two Treaties of Belgrade end hostilities between Russia and Turks, and Emperor and Turks. Anglo-Spanish War ('War of Jenkins's Ear') begins.

1740 Frederick the Great of Prussia invades Silesia. Start of War of the Austrian Succession and First Silesian War.

1741 Battle of Mollwitz (Prussians beat Austrians). Prussian-Austrian armistice at Klein-Schnellendorf. Sweden attacks Russia.

1742 Charles-Albert of Bavaria elected Emperor. Treaty of Berlin (Prussia-Austria) ends First Silesian War.

1743 Peace of Abo after Swedish defeat by Russia. Battle of Dettingen (English defeat French). Treaty of Hanau (England-Bavaria). Treaty of Worms (England-Sardinia). Treaty of Fontainebleau (France-Spain).

1744 Second Silesian War begins. First Carnatic War (in India) begins.

1745 Battle of Fontenoy (French defeat English). Capture of Louisburg by New Englanders. Treaty of Dresden, ending Second Silesian War.

1746 French capture Madras.

1748 Treaty of Aix-la-Chapelle ends War of the Austrian Succession. Montesquieu, *L'Esprit des Lois*. Toussaint, *Les Mœurs*.

1751 Clive captures and defends Arcot. Beginning of publication of the *Encyclopédie*.

1754 Defeat of Washington at Fort Necessity. Rousseau, *Discourse on Inequality*. Condillac, *Traité des Sensations*.

1755 Defeat of Braddock's attempt to capture Fort Duquesne. *Grandes Remonstrances* of the *Parlement* of Paris. Cantillon, *Essai du Commerce*.

1756 English ally with Prussia by Convention of Westminster. First Treaty of Versailles (France allies with Austria). Austro-Russian treaty of alliance. Frederick the Great begins Seven Years War by invasion of Saxony. 'Black Hole' of Calcutta. French capture Minorca and Forts Oswego and George.

1757 Second Treaty of Versailles (France, Austria). 18 June, Battle of Kolin (Frederick the Great defeated by Austrians). 26 July, English defeated by French at Hastenbeck. 5 November, Battle of Rossbach (French and Imperialists defeated by Frederick the Great). 8 September, Convention of Klosterzeven (English, French). 5 December, Battle of Leuthen (Frederick the Great defeats Austrians). 22 June, Battle of Plassey (English defeat Nawab of Bengal). 9 August, French capture Fort William Henry.

1758 English capture Goree. English capture Louisburg and Fort Duquesne. English defeated at Fort Ticonderoga. 25 August, Battle of Zorndorf (Russians and Swedes defeated by Frederick the Great). 14 October, Battle of Hochkirch (Frederick defeated by Austrians). Helvétius, *De l'Esprit*.

1759 English capture Quebec, Ticonderoga, Crown Point, and Niagara. English fleets defeat French at Battles of Lagos and Quiberon Bay. 1 August, Battle of Minden (Ferdinand of Brunswick defeats French). 12 August, Battle of Kunersdorf (Russians and Austrians defeat Frederick the Great). Jesuits expelled from Portugal.

1760 Frederick the Great defeats Austrians and Russians at Battle of Liegnitz and Austrians at Battle of Torgau. English capture Montreal. Battle of Wandewash (India) (English defeat French). Rousseau, *La Nouvelle Héloïse*.

1761 Frederick the Great defeats French at Battle of Villinghausen. English capture Pondicherry.

1762 Russians and Swedes make peace with Prussia. Frederick defeats Austrians at Battle of Burkersdorf. Danish alliance with France. England declares war on Spain. Jesuits expelled from France. Rousseau, *Émile* and *Du contrat social*.

1763 Peace of Paris and of Hubertusburg end Seven Years War. Compulsory elementary education in Prussia. Catherine the Great of Russia holds a 'Commission' to discuss reforms. Death of Augustus III of Poland. Royal Proclamation restricting westward movement of American colonists.

1764 Prussia East India Company founded. Beccaria, *Dei delitti e delle pene*. Sugar Act (America). Alliance of Prussia and Russia. Stanislaus Poniatowski elected King of Poland.

1765 'Cap' victory in Swedish elections. James Watt's steam-engine. Quartering Act, Stamp Act, Stamp Act Congress, and boycott of English goods in America.

1766 Repeal of Stamp Act, enactment of Declaratory Act (America).

1767 Townshend's Revenue Act and Admiralty Courts (America). Commission of Reforms in Russia. Danes ally with Russia. Jesuits expelled from Spain.

1768 Confederation of Bar (Poland). Turks declare war on Russia.

1769 Frederick the Great interviews Joseph II of Austria.

1770 Second interview of Frederick and Joseph. Choiseul dismissed (France). Repeal of Revenue Act; 'Boston Massacre' (America). D'Holbach, *Le vrai sens du système de la Nature*. Paris *Parlement* exiled.

1772 Partition Treaty (Russia, Prussia, followed by Austria, partition Poland). *Gaspée* Affair (America). Royal *coup d'état* in Sweden. Fall of Struensee (Denmark). Maupeou's reforms (France).

1773 Pope abolishes Jesuit Order. Tea Act and Boston Tea Party. Bromberg Canal connecting Vistula and Oder built. Peasants' and Cossacks' Revolt (Russia).

1774 'Intolerable Acts' and Quebec Act, First Continental Congress (America). Death of Louis XV; accession of Louis XVI and abolition of Maupeou's reforms; appointment of Turgot (France). Treaty of Kutchuk-Kainardji ends Russo-Turkish War. Goethe, *The Sorrows of Young Werther*.

1775 Battle of Lexington and Battle of Bunker Hill; American Prohibitory Act. Turgot's Six Edicts (France). Reform of Administration in Russia.

1776 American Declaration of Independence; start of formal war. Fall of Turgot (France). Adam Smith, *Wealth of Nations*. Washington defeated on Long Island, victorious at Trenton Bridge.

1777 Washington wins Battle of Princeton. Washington defeated at Battle of Brandywine. English General Burgoyne defeated by General Gates at two Battles of Freeman's Farm. Burgoyne surrenders at Saratoga.

1778 France allies with Americans.

1779 Spain allies with Americans. Crompton's 'Mule' invented.

1780 England declares war on the Dutch. Armed Neutrality (Russia, Sweden, Denmark) formed with England as its likely opponent.

1781 Necker's *Compte Rendu*. Surrender of English General Cornwallis at Yorktown. Freeing of serfs in Austrian dominions, Toleration Edict (Austrian dominions). Dismissal of Necker, appointment of Calonne, Calonne's reforms (France).

1782 Ending of monopoly of the guilds (Austrian dominions).

1783 Treaty of Versailles ends American War of Independence; American colonies become independent U.S.A.

1784 Joseph II (Austria) makes trade treaty with Russia. Cartwright's power loom invented.

1785 'Charter of the Nobility' (Russia).

1786 Anglo-French trade treaty. 'Popular Schools' decreed (Russia).

1787 Legal reforms (Austrian dominions). Russia and Austria declare war on the Turks. First Meeting of the Notables; dismissal of Calonne; appointment of Brienne; exile of the Paris *Parlement*; collapse of Brienne's reforms; government agrees to call the States-General for 1792 (France).

1788 Revolt in Austrian 'hereditary dominions'. Serfs freed in Denmark. French *parlements* largely replaced by new *Cour plénière*; *Cour plénière* abolished and government agrees to call States-General in 1789; Necker recalled, Paris *Parlement* demands vote in States-General to be by Order; Second Meeting of the Notables.

1789 Revolt in Netherlands against Joseph II's reforms. 5 May, meeting of States-General; 20 June, Tennis Court Oath; 27 June, King orders noble and clerical Estates to join Third (National Assembly); 11 July, Necker dismissed; 14 July, fall of Bastille; 4 August, feudal system abolished. Lavoisier, *Traité élémentaire de chimie.* 'Act of Union and Security' (Sweden).

1791 Peace of Sistowa (Austria-Turkey). 20 June, Flight to Varennes; 17 July, Civil Constitution of the Clergy; 14 September, French Constitution; 30 September, end of Constituent Assembly.

1792 Peace of Jassy (Russia and Turks).

BIBLIOGRAPHICAL NOTE

No attempt can be made here to give anything approaching a full bibliography. The following list is merely intended to indicate some of the most important and interesting works.

A. GENERAL WORKS

1 The following books in the series *Peuples et Civilisations*, eds. L. Halphen and P. Sagnac are all very good and contain full bibliographies:

H. Hauser. *La Prépondérance espagnole, 1559–1660.*

P. Sagnac and A. de St Léger. *La Prépondérance française, 1661–1715.*

A. Muret. *La Prépondérance anglaise, 1715–1763.*

P. Sagnac. *La Fin de l'Ancien régime et la révolution américaine, 1763–1789.*

G. Lefèbvre. *La Révolution française.* (New edition, 1951.)

2 The following works in the American series *The Rise of Modern Europe*, ed. William L. Langer, can be consulted with pleasure and profit:

C. J. Friedrich. *The Age of the Baroque, 1610–1660.*

F. L. Nussbaum. *The Triumph of Science and Reason, 1660–1685.*

J. B. Wolf. *The Emergence of the Great Powers, 1685–1715.*

P. Roberts. *The Quest for Security, 1715–1740.*

W. L. Dorn. *Competition for Empire, 1740–63.*

L. Gershoy. *From Despotism to Revolution, 1763–89.*

3 Teachers will find the following invaluable (in the series *Clio: Introduction aux Études historiques*):

E. Préclin and V. Tapié. *Le xviie siècle* and *Le xviiie siècle*.

4 *The Cambridge Modern History*. This is now regarded as out of date, although large parts of it are still useful. However, the *New Cambridge Modern History* is in process of production, and in this the only volumes yet published on our period, viz.: *Vol. V, The Ascendancy of France, 1648–88* and *Vol. VII, The Old Régime, 1713–63*, may be strongly recommended.

5 C. J. H. Hayes. *A Political and Cultural History of Modern Europe*.

6 R. Mousnier and E. Labrousse. *Le xviiie siècle*. (In the new series, *Histoire générale des Civilisations*.)

7 Students should consult the following collections of documents:

(a) The very important series, *English Historical Documents* (general editor, David C. Douglas), which is now being produced. The volumes as yet available for our period are both magnificent, viz. *Vol. VIII, 1660–1714* (ed. A. Browning); *Vol. IX, American Colonial Documents to 1776* (ed. Merrill Jensen).

(b) W. F. Reddaway. *Select Documents of European History, Vol. II, 1492–1715*.

(c) H. Butterfield. *Select Documents of European History, Vol. III, 1715–1920*.

(d) M. Stephens (ed.). *Orators of the French Revolution* (2 vols.).

B. WORKS DEALING WITH PARTICULAR TOPICS AND COUNTRIES

1 THE SCIENTIFIC REVOLUTION (Chapters 1 and 14).

H. Butterfield. *The Origins of Modern Science*. (A good elementary introduction.)

A. R. Hall. *The Scientific Revolution, 1500–1800*. (A more detailed, and an excellent book.) Strongly recommended also is C. Singer, *A Short History of Science to the nineteenth century*.

For a huge and authoritative survey, profusely illustrated, the student should consult R. Taton (ed.), *Histoire générale des sciences, Tome 2, 1450–1800*.

A most interesting book, not so much a history as a source-book compiled from the literature relating to technology, is F. Klemm, *A History of Western Technology* (trans. D. W. Singer).

For the earlier history of science, see (a) B. Farrington, *Greek Science* (2 vols.) and (b) C. H. Haskins, *Studies in the History of Medieval Science*.

To understand the thought of the ancient Greeks, the student should at least read (a) Aristotle's *Ethics* (trans. W. D. Ross) and (b) Plato's *Republic* (trans. F. M. Cornford). A clear and authoritative (and eminently readable) summary of the whole of European philosophy is provided by Bertrand Russell, *A History of Western Philosophy*; his views on science may be supplemented by reading A. N. Whitehead, *Science and the Modern World*.

The following individual studies are all very interesting:

A. Armitage. *Copernicus, the founder of Modern Astronomy*.

E. N. da C. Andrade. *Sir Isaac Newton*. (Most clear and charmingly written. It may be supplemented by the larger *Life* by L. T. More.)

F. Sherwood Taylor. *Galileo and the Freedom of Thought*.

H. P. Bayon. *William Harvey, Physician and Biologist*.

See also the essay by M. Boas, 'The Establishment of the Mechanical Philosophy' (*Isis*, Vol. X, 1952).

2 THE EUROPEAN MENTAL REVOLUTION AND THE *PHILOSOPHE* MOVEMENT (Chapters 6 and 14).

Most students will hardly have time to read all the works referred to in the text, but it is suggested that as a minimum they should read (a) Locke's second *Treatise of Civil Government* (ed. P. Laslett, 1959); his *Essay concerning the Human Understanding*; and his *Letter Concerning Toleration*; (b) as much of Voltaire as possible, say, his *Lettres philosophiques*, and for sheer enjoyment, his *Candide*; (c) Rousseau's *Du contrat social* (a good edition is by C. E. Vaughan; it is also translated by G. D. H. Cole) and *Émile*; (d) Hobbes's *Leviathan*; and (e) the *Discours Préliminaire de l'Encyclopédie* of D'Alembert (ed. F. Picavet).

It should hardly be necessary to point out that Christian apologists and their opponents in the seventeenth and eighteenth centuries (as well as the public at large) were thoroughly steeped in the Holy Bible, so that anyone wishing to enter the minds of Europeans of former days should read it carefully for that reason, as well as for its sacred character.

A valuable general book on the seventeenth century is G. N. Clark, *The Seventeenth Century*.

The following are all indispensable:

(a) P. Hazard. *La crise de la conscience européenne, 1680–1715.* (There is a good translation published under the title, *The European Mind*.)

(b) P. Hazard. *La Pensée européenne au XVIIIième Siècle.* (This is also available in translation.)

(c) D. Mornet. *Les Origines intellectuelles de la Révolution française.*

(d) B. H. Kingsley Martin. *French Liberal Thought in the Eighteenth Century.* (2nd edition, 1954.)

(e) G. Weulersse. *Les Physiocrates.*

Others worth consulting are (a) H. Sée, *L'Évolution de la pensée politique en France au 18e siècle*, and (b) R. B. Mowat, *The Age of Reason*.

There are plenty of good works about the various writers, e.g. A. Cobban, *Rousseau and the Modern State*, and the works by H. N. Brailsford, C. E. Vulliamy, and W. H. Wickwar respectively on Voltaire, Rousseau, and Baron d'Holbach.

3 FRANCE

E. Lavisse (ed.). *Histoire de France.* (The great classic.)

G. Pagès. *La Monarchie d'Ancien Régime en France.* (A very neat account.)

E. C. Lodge. *Sully, Colbert, Turgot.* (A useful sketch.)

C. Federn. *Mazarin.* (Excellent.)

Memoirs of the Cardinal de Retz (2 vols. in the Everyman series, with an introduction by D. Ogg).

P. Gaxotte. *La France de Louis XIV.* (Very readable.)

Louis XIV. *Mémoires pour l'instruction du Dauphin* (ed. Lognon, Paris, 1927).

Two interesting short accounts of Louis XIV are (a) M. Ashley, *Louis XIV and the Greatness of France* and (b) D. Ogg, *Louis XIV*.

H. Sée. *La France économique et sociale au XVIIIe siècle.* (A brilliant short account.)

F. C. Green. *The Ancien Régime.*

A. Cobban. *History of France, 1715–1799.*

Very useful on the statesmen concerned are:

(a) D. Dakin. *Turgot and the Ancien Régime in France.*

(b) E. Chapuisat. *Necker.*

394

(c) A. Goodwin. 'Calonne, the Assembly of French Notables of 1787' (*English Historical Review*, Vol. 61, 1946).

The best account of the last years of the Old Régime is provided by the following works of G. Lefèbvre, all obtainable at the Centre de Documentation Universitaire, Paris:

(a) *La Révolution aristocratique.*

(b) *La Révolution de 1789.*

(c) *La Fuite du Roi.*

For the beginnings of the French Revolution see also the first few chapters of A. Mathiez, *La Révolution Française*, and for thorough accounts in English, J. M. Thompson, *The French Revolution*, and G. Lefèbvre, *The Coming of the French Revolution* (tr. Palmer).

No reading of this period is complete without De Tocqueville, *L'Ancien Régime*, and Arthur Young's *Travels in France*.

Worth consulting also is S. Herbert, *The Fall of Feudalism in France*.

4 THE LOW COUNTRIES

G. J. Renier. *The Dutch Nation*. A splendid survey.

More detailed works on our period are:

A. Renaudet. *Les Pays-Bas espagnoles et les Provinces Unies de 1598 à 1714.* (Excellent.)

G. N. Clark. *The Dutch Alliance and the War against French Trade (1688–97).* (Very good, as is also: G. J. Renier, *William of Orange.*)

The classic work on all periods of Belgian history is the huge *Histoire de la Belgique* by H. Pirenne.

5 GERMANY

S. H. Steinberg. *A Short History of Germany*. (A good survey, as is also A. J. P. Taylor's pungent *The Course of German History.*)

Bryce. *The Holy Roman Empire*. (See also G. Barraclough, *The Medieval Empire: Idea and Reality*—Historical Association pamphlet.)

W. H. Bruford. *Germany in the Eighteenth Century.*

L. Bruhl. *L'Allemagne depuis Leibniz.*

6 PRUSSIA

A. Waddington. *Histoire de Prusse*. (Excellent, but stops at 1740.)

S. B. Fay. *The Rise of Brandenburg-Prussia to 1786*. (Very good.)

F. Schevill. *The Great Elector*. (Probably the best account in English.)

R. Ergang. *The Potsdam Führer: Frederick William I, Father of Prussian Militarism.* (Outstandingly good, and most readable.)

P. Gaxotte. *Frédéric II*. (Very readable, and probably Gaxotte's best work.)

G. P. Gooch. *Frederick the Great*. (A fine work by a great authority.) Another interesting life is by W. F. Reddaway.

R. Koser. *Geschichte Friedrichs des Grossen*. (The best work for those able to read German.)

G. A. Craig. *The Politics of the Prussian Army, 1640–1945*. (The first chapter offers an excellent summary up to 1806.)

Marriot and Robertson. *The Evolution of Prussia.*

7 THE HABSBURGS

A. J. P. Taylor. *The Habsburg Monarchy*. (Brilliant, as usual.)

G. P. Gooch. *Maria Theresa, and other studies*. (Excellent.)

S. K. Padover. *The Revolutionary Emperor: Joseph II*. (An important work.)

R. W. Seton-Watson. *A History of the Czechs and Slovaks*. (A work by a famous expert.)

C. A. Macartney. *Hungary: A Short History*. (Probably the best history of Hungary in the English language.)

8 POLAND

The best of a rather scanty supply of books in English is *The Cambridge History of Poland*. Two volumes cover the periods to 1696 and 1697–1933. Also see R. Nisbet Bain, *The Last King of Poland and his contemporaries*.

9 SPAIN AND PORTUGAL

R. Trevor Davies. *The Golden Century of Spain*.

J. B. Trend. *The Civilisation of Spain*. (A very good introduction.)

R. Altamira. (*a*) *A History of Spain* and (*b*) *History of Spanish Civilization*. (Two books by a famous historian.)

F. Rousseau. *Le Règne de Charles III*.

H. V. Livermore. *A History of Portugal*.

10 SCANDINAVIA

Very useful introductions are by R. Nisbet Bain, *Scandinavia* and *Charles XII*. Nearly all the best works on Sweden are in the Swedish language, but the student will find the article on the Swedish nobility by M. Roberts in the collected *The European Nobility in the Eighteenth Century* (ed. A. Goodwin) most helpful and stimulating. Nisbet Bain's chapters in *The Cambridge Modern History* are also very sound, as are the sections in the relevant volumes of the *Peuples et Civilisations* series. See also K. Svanstrom and C. F. Palmstierna, *History of Sweden*.

For Denmark a useful introduction is J. H. S. Birch, *Denmark in History* and the General Works already cited.

11 ITALY

See General Works.

12 RUSSIA

Good introductions are: B. Pares, *A History of Russia*, and especially B. H. Sumner, *Survey of Russian History*: the latter gives a first-rate bibliography, to which the reader is referred.

13 THE OTTOMAN TURKS

The best introduction is W. S. Davis, *A Short History of the Near East*. Otherwise see General Works.

14 ENGLAND

It is scarcely appropriate here to attempt a satisfactory selection out of the huge number of good available books. However, the best one-volume history of England is that by K. Feiling. (See also his two books on the Tory Party, which cover our period.) The volumes in the Oxford History of England covering the period are all useful (by G. N. Clark, B. Williams, and S. Watson; Sir George Clark's volume on *The Later Stuarts*—2nd edition, 1955—being especially enjoyable). A very neat introduction to the seventeenth-century political problems is provided by J. R. Tanner's work, *English Constitutional Conflicts of the Seventeenth Century*, but the best thing to do is consult the various learned periodicals. The various works of H. R. Trevor-Roper and of Christopher Hill will be found especially stimulating, and it would be absurd to miss Mr Hill's *The Century of Revolution, 1603–1715* (1961). For the eighteenth century, many students might find Namier's works too detailed; if so, they are urged to consult V. H. H. Green, *The Hanoverians*, which contains a detailed bibliography and which is itself a good introduction to the period.

15 THE AMERICAN WAR OF INDEPENDENCE

The number of good books is so large that it seems invidious to select a few. A sound plan is to consult M. Jensen's volume in the series *English Historical Documents*. The book has a very good bibliography, and Professor Jensen himself gives a wonderful survey of American history up to 1776. But it would be a pity to miss two books by Arthur M. Schlesinger, *The Colonial Merchants and the American Revolution* and *Prelude to Independence*. Valuable also are Edmund S. Morgan, *The Birth of the Republic*; Lawrence H. Gipson, *The Coming of the Revolution 1763–75*; and Charles R. Ritcheson, *British Politics and the American Revolution*.

16 MILITARY HISTORY

The great classic of A. T. Mahan, *The Influence of Sea Power on History, 1660–1783*, should certainly be read. Two fascinating works by modern experts are B. H. Liddell Hart, *The Decisive Wars of History*, and J. F. C. Fuller, *The Decisive Battles of the Western World* (Vol. II). (General Fuller's accounts of battles are fascinating, but his summaries of events leading to the wars must be taken with more reserve.)

17 ECONOMIC HISTORY

For Mercantilism, see E. Heckscher's famous *Mercantilism*; J. F. Rees's article on 'Mercantilism' in *History* (Vol. 24, 1939); Heckscher's article in *Economic History Review* (Vol. 7, 1946–7); and C. Wilson's *Mercantilism* (Historical Association pamphlet, 1958).

For good economic surveys see:

(a) H. Heaton. *Economic History of Europe* (revised edition, 1948).

(b) A. Birnie. *An Economic History of Europe, 1760–1939*.

(c) H. Sée. *Histoire économique de France, Le Moyen Age et l'Ancien Régime*.

(d) S. B. Fay. *From Adam Smith to the Present Day*.

(e) W. H. B. Court. *Concise Economic History of Britain from 1750 to Recent Times*.

(f) H. Sée. *Les origines du Capitalisme Moderne*.

See also R. H. Tawney. *Religion and the Rise of Capitalism*.

The best introductions to the Industrial Revolution are:

(a) P. Mantoux. *The Industrial Revolution in the Eighteenth Century*.

(b) T. S. Ashton. *The Industrial Revolution*. (Brief, but a delightfully written masterpiece.)

Very stimulating also is J. L. and Barbara Hammond's *The Rise of Modern Industry*.

18 THE ENLIGHTENED DESPOTS

Easily the best summary, except that it does not deal with Russia, is P. Vaucher, *Le Despotisme Éclairé, 1740–89*, which has useful bibliographical notes. Apart from that, the reader should consult the works already listed dealing with the countries concerned, and the General Works cited at the beginning of this note.

Index

INDEX

INDEX

Saxony—*contd.*
  and Seven Years War, 228, 230, 231, 237, 244; reaction against the Enlightenment, 287
Scania, 89; War of, 92
Sceptical Chymist, The, 46
Scheldt, River, closed to navigation, 11, 165
Schellenberg, Battle of, 156–7
Schleswig, 173, 294
Scientific Societies, 268
'Secret', 212
Secretaries of State (France), 51, 52, 341
Sekreta Utskottet, 296
Senegal, 366
Sejm, 102
Serbia, 194, 314
Serfs, in Hungary, 279; in the Habsburg German States, 281; in Russia, 289–92; in Denmark, 293; in Tuscany 305; in Prussia, 207; in France, *see Mainmorte*
Seville, 143, 304; Treaty of, 188
Shaftesbury, 1st Lord, 133; 2nd Lord, 130
Shirley, William, 219
Sicily, 80, 147, 161, 175, 192; transferred to Savoy, 164; attacked by Spain, 179; given to Charles of Spain, 194
Sieyès, Abbé, 257, 375
Silesia, 10, 108, 170, 171, 278; invaded by Frederick the Great, 198–9, 209; ceded to Prussia, 211, 214, 215; and England, 212, 225; and Maria Theresa, 224; in Seven Years War, 230, 236, 237, 238; in reign of Frederick the Great, 272–3; and Prusso-Russian alliance of 1764, 308
Simon, Richard, 129
Siraj-ud-daulah, 242
Sistowa, Peace of, 314
Six Nations, Confederation of, 219
Slavonia, 112
Smith, Adam, 20, 324–5
Smolensk, 95, 102
Smolny Institute, 292
Sobieski, *see* John Sobieski
Social Contract, 345; views of Hobbes on, 138; views of Locke on, 139–40. *See also Du contrat social*
Sociedad Vasgonada de los Amigos del Pais, 303
Soissons, Congress of, 188
Sole Bay, Battle of, 78
Sonderhausen, Battle of, 236
Sonnenfels, Joseph von, 282
Sons of Liberty, 360
Sophia, Tsarevna of Russia, 95, 96
Sorrows of Young Werther, The, 269
Soubise, Marshal, 231, 234
South Sea Company, 182, 197, 216–17
Spain, 3, 8; weakness of, 11, 18, 143–5; and Portugal, 73–4, 75, 164; and War of Devolution, 72–6; and Louis XIV's Dutch War, 79, 81; and the Reunions,

82; and War of the League of Augsburg, 83, 85, 87; and the Partition Treaties, 75, 145–9; and Spanish Succession War, 152, 153, 154, 160, 161, 162; losses at Utrecht, 163–4; attempts to recover Italian possessions, 175, 176, 178–80, 183–4, 186–9; and Triple Alliance, 177; and Austrian Succession War, 210, 211, 213–15; and War of Jenkins's Ear, 196–8, 216–17; joins Seven Years War, 239–40; losses at Peace of Paris, 244; and the Enlightenment, 301–4; dispute with England in 1770 over Falkland Islands, 344; dispute over Nootka Sound, 384; and American War of Independence, 363–6
Spallanzani, 248, 305
Sparr, Freiherr von, 116
Spinoza, 24, 129
Stahl, 248
Stamp Act, 356–7, 358
'Stamp Act Congress', 357, 359
Stanhope, 177, 178, 179, 183
Stanislaus Leszczynski, King of Poland, 170, 191, 192, 193, 194
Stanislaus Poniatowski, King of Poland, 308, 309
Starhemberg, 226, 227
States-General (French), 23, 334, 371, 372, 373; elections for, 376; meeting of 1789, 377
Statute of Popular Schools, 292
Stavnsbaand, 293
Steam Engine, 319, 320–2, 323, 324
Stettin, 13, 92, 119, 275
Stockholm, Treaties of, 174; Scientific Society, 268
Straits, 314
Stralsund, 92, 173
Strasburg, 82, 83, 87, 154, 164, 213
Streltsi, 95, 97, 98
Struensee, 295
Styria, Duchy of, 10, 280, 286
Styrum, Marshal, 153
Subdélégués, 52
'Sugar Act', 356
Suliman the Magnificent, 105, 106
Superior, Lake, 55
Supreme Economic Council, 285
Surintendant des Finances, 50, 51
Sweden, in Thirty Years War, 3, 10; rise of, 13, 89; strategic weakness of, 14, 89; and Triple Alliance, 75; alliance with Louis XIV, 79, 80, 81, 89–91; and League of Augsburg, 84; and the Danes, 89; and Peace of Westphalia, 89; 'reduction' of 1680, 92; reforms of Charles XI, 92–3; and Great War of the North, Chap. 8, 294; and Alberoni, 179; and Elizabeth Farnese, 186, 187; and French alliance of 1738, 194; and War

INDEX

Verden, 89, 173, 174, 177
Verdun, 82
Vergennes, 244, 348, 365
Versailles, 69–70, 148, 252, 327, 328, 334, 378, 380
Versailles, Treaty of: (1756) 227, (1757) 228, (1759) 237, (1783) 366
Vesalius, 41
Vespasian, Emperor, 319
Viborg, 174
Victor Amadeus of Savoy, 164
Vienna, 10, 280, 282, 283, 285; siege of, 109–11
Vienna, First Treaty of, 186; Second Treaty of, 187; Third Treaty of, 189, 193; Treaty of 1738, 192–3
Vigo, 153
Villars, Marshal, 61, 150, 152, 153, 162, 163
Villaviciosa, Battle of, 162
Villeneuve, 194
Villeroi, Marshal, 150, 156, 157, 160
Villinghausen, Battle of, 237
Vineam Domini, 65
Vincennes, Fort, 218
Vingtième, 329, 343, 346, 372
Virginia, 220, 221, 353, 360, 366
Vitebsk, 310
Voivodes, 100
Voltaire (François-Marie Arouet), 48, 128, 268, 269; visit to England, 250–1; his writings, 251–3; attitude to Rousseau, 260; and the *Encyclopédie*, 266; and Frederick the Great, 268, 272–3; and the *parlements*, 252, 345; and the Church, 251–2, 337; and Turgot, 348; and Franklin, 368
Vonck, 285
Vornedskab, 293
Vossem, Treaty of, 118

Wabash, River, 218
Wager, Admiral, 187
Wallachia, 108, 112, 194, 309, 310, 314
Walpole, Sir Robert, attitude to France, 177; and the 'Whig Schism', 178; and the Emperor, 183, 185; handling of the alliance of Spain and the Emperor, 187–9; and the Polish Succession War, 191, 193; and preponderance of England, 189, 196; and dispute with Spain, 197–8, 211; and Parliament, 255; and the American Colonies, 355
Wandewash, Battle of, 243
Warburg, Battle of, 237

Warsaw, 118, 170
Washington, George, and struggle against France, 220; and War of Independence, 362, 363, 366
Watt, James, 320–2, 323
Wealth of Nations, 20, 324
Wedel, General, 235, 236
Weimar, 287
West Indies, 334, 355; struggle between British and French to 1748, 216–18, 219; and Seven Years War, 238–40, 244; and Denmark, 294; and American War of Independence, 365, 366
West Indies Company (French), 55
Westminster, Treaty of, 79; Convention of, 212, 226, 227, 228
Westphalia, 211, 237
Westphalia, Peace of, 2, 3, 6, 7, 9, 12, 89, 384
Whigs, 24, 149, 161, 163, 178
White Russia, 310
Whitney, Eli, 324
Wiener Neustadt, 224
Wilkinson, William, 332
William III, King of England (William of Orange), 142, 150; and Revolution of 1688, 24–5; rise to power in Holland, 77–8; and French invasion, 78–80; and War of the League of Augsburg, 85, 86; and Divine Right, 122; and Partition Treaties, 147–9
William IV of Orange, 215
William and Mary College, 353
William Henry, Fort, 240
Wismar, 89, 174
Witt, John de, 15, 77–8
Witt, Cornelius de, 78
Wittelsbach, 145. See also Bavaria
Wolfe, General, 241
Wolff, Christian, 268
Wollin, Island of, 89
Worms, Treaty of, 212
Wusterhausen, Treaty of, 200

Yale, 353
Yorktown, 366

Zenta, Battle of, 112
Zinzendorf, 269
Zips, 310
Zorndorf, Battle of, 236
Züllichau, Battle of, 236
Zurawno, Treaty of, 108
Zweibrücken, 82